The Cross-Cultural
Challenge to
Social Psychology

The Cross-Cultural Challenge to Social Psychology

Editor
Michael Harris Bond

CROSS-CULTURAL RESEARCH AND METHODOLOGY SERIES
VOLUME 11

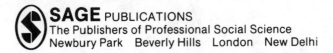
SAGE PUBLICATIONS
The Publishers of Professional Social Science
Newbury Park   Beverly Hills   London   New Delhi

For information address:

SAGE Publications, Inc.
2111 West Hillcrest Drive
Newbury Park, California 91320

SAGE Publications Inc.
275 South Beverly Drive
Beverly Hills
California 90212

SAGE Publications Ltd.
28 Banner Street
London EC1Y 8QE
England

SAGE PUBLICATIONS India Pvt. Ltd.
M-32 Market
Greater Kailash I
New Delhi 110 048 India

Printed in the United States of America

Library of Congress Cataloging-in-Publication Data

Main entry under title:

The Cross-cultural challenge to social psychology.

   (Cross-cultural research and methodology series ;
v. 11)
    Bibliography: p.
    Includes index.
    1. Social psychology—Cross-cultural studies.
I. Bond, Michael Harris, 1944-   II. Series.
HM251.C935   1988   302   88-11350
ISBN 0-8039-3042-9

FIRST PRINTING 1988

Contents

Foreword   7

Introduction

     Michael Harris Bond   9

PART I. SOME MAINSTREAM CHALLENGES TO CROSS-CULTURAL PSYCHOLOGY

1. How Does One Describe a Platypus? An Outsider's Questions for Cross-Cultural Psychology
   James T. Tedeschi   14

2. Why Not Cross-Cultural Psychology? A Characterization of Some Mainstream Views
   Roy S. Malpass   29

3. On Titles, Citations, and Outlets: What Do Mainstreamers Want?
   Ladd Wheeler and Harry Reis   36

4. On the Limitations of Cross-Cultural Research in Social Psychology
   David M. Messick   41

PART II. STATEMENTS OF SOME GENERAL CROSS-CULTURAL RESEARCH IN SOCIAL PSYCHOLOGY

5. Social Science and Social Psychology: The Cross-Cultural Link
   William K. Gabrenya, Jr.   48

6. Will Societal Modernization Eventually Eliminate Cross-Cultural Psychological Differences?
   Kuo-shu Yang   67

7. J'Accuse
   Gustav Jahoda   86

8. Cross-Cultural Replications: A Prerequisite for the Validation of Social Psychological Laws
   Irit Sharon and Yehuda Amir   96

9. Putting the Etic to Work: Applying Social Psychological Principles in Cross-Cultural Settings
   Joseph E. Trimble   109

10. Cross-Cultural Contributions to
    Theory in Social Psychology
    Harry C. Triandis   122

11. Cross-Cultural Psychology in
    a Post-Empiricist Era
    André Kukla   141

**PART III. INSTRUCTIVE CONTENT AREAS IN
            CROSS-CULTURAL SOCIAL PSYCHOLOGY**

12. Organizational Structure and Processes
    Peter B. Smith and Monir Tayeb   153

13. Culture and Intergroup Processes
    William B. Gudykunst   165

14. Cultural Influences on Group Processes
    Leon Mann   182

15. Interpersonal Behavior: Cross-Cultural
    and Historical Perspectives
    John Adamopoulos   196

16. Cultural Roots of Aggressive Behavior
    Marshall H. Segall   208

17. Theoretical Advances in Justice Behavior:
    Some Cross-Cultural Inputs
    Kwok Leung   218

18. Attribution Theory and Processes:
    A Cross-Cultural Perspective
    Garth J.O. Fletcher and Colleen Ward   230

19. Person Perception in
    Cross-Cultural Perspective
    Leslie Zebrowitz-McArthur   245

20. Bridging the Content-Structure
    Dichotomy: Culture and the Self
    Joan G. Miller   266

PART IV. SOME MAINSTREAMERS' REAPPRAISALS

21. A Second Look at the Platypus: A Reprise
    James T. Tedeschi   282

22. Coda
    David M. Messick   286

References   290

Index   329

About the Authors   333

Foreword

The Sage Series on Cross-Cultural Research and Methodology was created to present comparative studies on cross-cultural topics and interdisciplinary research. Inaugurated in 1975, the Series is designed to satisfy a growing need to integrate research method and theory and to dissect issues from a comparative perspective; a truly international approach to the study of behavioral, social, and cultural variables can be done only within such a methodological framework.

Each volume in the series presents substantive cross-cultural studies and considerations of the strengths, interrelationships, and weaknesses of its various methodologies, drawing upon work done in anthropology, political science, psychology, and sociology. Both individual researchers knowledgeable in more than one discipline and teams of specialists with differing disciplinary backgrounds have contributed to the Series. While each individual volume may represent the integration of only a few disciplines, *the cumulative totality of the Series reflects an effort to bridge gaps of methodology and conceptualization across the various disciplines and many cultures.*

This volume attempts to help answer one of the most important questions that may be asked in any branch of Psychology, but in this case Social Psychology: To what extent can laws and theories in Social Psychology be generalized across cultures? As the title of the book suggests, cross-cultural research in social psychology challenges so-called "mainstream" Psychology (with mainstream essentially construed as Euro-American domination of this branch of Psychology) to accommodate its findings from various cultures, and to broaden its vistas beyond its traditionally rather narrow data base. The issues are many and complex in this matter of generalizeability, however; surely there are many ways to look at the whole set of problems. Michael Bond has been deeply involved for several years with this concern about generalizeability. This concern was converted into action, which in part resulted in this volume. Bond enlisted the cooperation of a very impressive slate of authors, all of whom were asked to write papers especially prepared for this important volume. A conference was organized in which these issues could be discussed; held in June, 1987, at the Nag's Head Conference Center in North Carolina, most of the chapter authors attended and as a result were able to improve their papers by reflecting on what others had to say.

The result of all of this prior work and preparation is a book that we believe should be read by anyone in Psychology who has ever pondered the matter of the cultural generalizeability of social psychological principles. We are very pleased that Michael Bond was able to sustain his enthusiasm and energy for the nearly three years it took to coordinate all aspects of this project. Most important, we join Bond in expressing the hope that all who read this book will feel more informed about all of the issues involved, and moved to do something about them.

—Walter J. Lonner
Western Washington University

—John W. Berry
Queen's University

Acknowledgment

That this book appeared so promptly is due in large measure to the selfless stewardship of Walter J. Lonner. He set, and continues to set, an inspiring example of professionalism and colleagueship. Thanks, Walt!

—Michael H. Bond
Chinese University of
Hong Kong

Introduction

MICHAEL HARRIS BOND

Hoist sail, my dear boy, and steer clear of culture.

—Epicurus

I began my academic journey as a cross-cultural psychologist by happenstance rather than forethought. My wife and I were eager to spend some time living overseas before giving ourselves to more received careers. As a teacher of English for second-language learners, she commanded a more exportable skill than did I as a social psychologist. So, in 1971, graduate educations completed, we arrived in Japan and I embarked on a professional odyssey without any training in Japanese, anthropology, or the methodological base of cross-cultural psychology.

Undaunted by the innocence of my preparation, I began collecting data. Not surprisingly, my first empirical exploration of these perilous seas was summarily rejected by the *Journal of Cross-Cultural Psychology* for reasons that would now lead me to the same editorial decision. As an introduction to the many ironies that abound in doing cross-cultural psychology, I subsequently received more reprint requests for this hasty foray than I have for any subsequent travels narrated in that same journal.

Almost all the requests came from the United States. I now believe that the reason for the interest was that my collaborator and I had compared Japanese responses on Rotter's I-E scale with those of Americans (Bond & Tornatsky, 1973). Locus of control is a psychological construct that parcels the causes for events into internal and external forces, a division consistent with a Western philosophical tradition focused by Descartes (Russell, 1945). This happy marriage of the psychological and philosophical realms has generated an avalanche of American research aimed at establishing the validity of this construct (see, e.g., Phares, 1978). A bridge to Japan could therefore carry considerable traffic and American colleagues were consequently interested in such ready extensions of the known into the perplexing.

Research conducted in the United States informs us that we humans seek out information that holds promise of confirming our established constructions of reality (Swann & Read, 1981a, 1981b). It is perhaps for this reason that cross-cultural studies using American personality tests and their implicit constructions of human nature are so attractive to

9

American researchers despite their many flaws (Brislin, Lonner, & Thorndike, 1973). In this vein, Kuhn (1962) had described research "as a strenuous and devoted attempt to force nature into the conceptual boxes supplied by professional education" (p. 5). I considered this a cynical statement when I first read it in graduate school, but alternative glosses on life were beginning to make themselves felt overseas.

For at this same time an article based on my dissertation was published (Bond, 1972). Being separated from the mainstream by a large ocean, I followed the reactions to my first solo voyage with intense concern. It fell into the well of the *Citation Index* without a sound. This fate surprised me, since the article had been published in an APA journal and concerned the self-fulfilling prophecy, a fascinating topic with a respectable pedigree (Merton, 1948). The problem, I later realized, was that the results of that 1972 research had demonstrated not the fulfilling of a prophecy but its *reversal*. I could well have taken heed from my earlier reading of Kuhn (1962), who had asserted that "in science . . . novelty emerges only with difficulty, manifested by resistance, against a background provided by expectation" (p. 64). To be fair, subsequent developments in this topic area have resulted in greater attention to the disconfirmation of prophecies (Ickes, Paterson, Rajecki, & Tanford, 1982), but this early surprise of mine was a sobering preparation for the doing of cross-cultural psychology. For later experience as a practitioner in these less-charted waters has confirmed my earlier discovery that departures from expectation are typically ignored.

This fact of life was forcefully revealed to me when I was selecting a textbook for my social psychology course in Hong Kong, my next port of call. Of those available in English (or indeed in Chinese!), none had a cross-cultural supplement, and only a few made the occasional reference to this or that cross-cultural study. I was acutely embarrassed about teaching a discipline that aspired to claims of scientific universality when I knew much of the information to be limited in its applicability to my Chinese students. Fortunately, they were less concerned, as many were really seeking an introduction to American culture by taking my course!

I say "American" throughout this introduction because it is a fact of our disciplinary life in social psychology that its professional center of gravity is there. Most social psychologists were born and practice there, most theorizing and data collection are undertaken there, most prestigious journals and texts are published there, most students are trained and socialized there, most institutional and financial support is available there, etc., etc. The consequences of channeling our discipline into American culture confines are less obvious, but widely lamented (Gergen, 1973, 1978; Pepitone, 1976, 1981; Sampson, 1977, 1981, 1985).

There are of course other areas where social psychology is "done" at levels numerically worthy of attention. Canada, West Germany, and England spring to mind. The available cross-cultural research, however, suggests that persons in these nation-states perceive the interpersonal world through much the same prism of values as do Americans (Chinese Culture Connection, 1987; Hofstede, 1980). Indeed, some scholars have been so bold as to assert that the science of psychology is practiced in these countries precisely because their citizenries share certain key values (Sampson, 1981). It seems less than likely, then, that psychological productions will emerge from these satellites at serious variance with those produced in the United States of America. Thus most social psychology continues to chart the same worldview.

This state of affairs is most personally vexing for those of us who practice social psychology outside these centers and frequently find patterns of results different from those discovered in this "mainstream." Loving what we have suffered, perhaps more than most, to unearth, we frequently wonder why such promising landfalls are not mapped more often by mainstream cartographers. After all, no person is an island, and professional recognition is one form of confirmation that our scientific voyages on this earth are not in vain.

At this point, I usually pause. My travels, having taken me this far, have also alerted me to the Chinese proverb that "a suspicious mind casts its own shadows." Obviously, I do not approach the productions of cross-cultural psychology, especially my own, with dispassion. It has occurred to me in reflective moments that I may have freighted the convoy with more cargo than it can carry in order to commandeer for myself and my traveling companions an outpost on the scientific map. On the other hand, of course, there is a host of plausible reasons why the discipline of social psychology continues to ignore cross-cultural findings. These reasons, if I present them, are typically unflattering and suggest dire consequences for our discipline, if the present state continues.

In the early 1980s, I decided to cut short this game of one-handed bridge and put cross-cultural, social psychology to a test in the scientific House of Commons. What would happen, I wondered, if a group of fair-minded mainstreamers and cross-culturalists were to confront one another? How might our positions change and develop?

In the back of my mind, perhaps, was another shard from Kuhn's (1962) seminal work, *The Structure of Scientific Revolutions*:

Finally, at a still higher level, there is another set of commitments without which no man is a scientist. The scientist must, for example, be concerned to understand the world and to extend the precision and scope with which it has been ordered. That commitment must, in turn, lead him to scrutinize, either for himself or through colleagues, some aspect of nature in great empirical detail. And, if that scrutiny displays pockets of apparent disorder, then these must challenge him to a new refinement of his observational techniques or to a further articulation of his theories. (p. 42)

Kuhn had, of course, warned that dramatic conversions were extremely unlikely in any form of scientific confrontation over paradigms. I took heart, however, from the belief that cross-cultural psychology did not constitute a paradigm shift of major proportions, but rather an extension of the familiar into the unknown. Indeed, a reanalysis of my dissertation data had shown that people *do* change their first impressions (Bond, 1987); perhaps also psychologists their positions!

In my view it was essential to engage mainstreamers in this confrontation. After all, the putative isolation of cross-culturalists would not be affected by more preaching to the converted. An interactive format would set the stage for some mutual learning, but would entail my finding courageous mainstreamers to enter the eye of this typhoon. It was also necessary to select representatives who had sufficient interest in a cross-cultural approach to spend their time in such a pursuit. This interest immediately biases the sample, of course, so a further requirement was that all mainstream representatives had established reputations enabling them to speak with some credibility for their constituencies.

My fantasy was to have the various mainstreamers throw down their respective gauntlets to focus the audience's attention. These challenges would detail what each wanted from the cross-cultural field to broaden his or her own understanding. They might also take the opportunity to point out where the cross-cultural yield had fallen short of the quotas required.

Cross-culturalists would then present their case. The first group would offer a broader view of the context from which cross-cultural work is now brought forth and consider its capacity to enrich the mainstream. A second group was to tackle a range of content areas where in my opinion cross-cultural research had already demonstrated its ability to undercut or cement mainstream presumptions to universality. Writers in both groups of cross-culturalists were to be selective, tendentious, and, within the bounds of scientific decorum, provocative. Their corporate goal was to draw the attention, and perhaps fire, of the mainstreamers with arguments that could not be reasonably ignored.

I envisaged the third act of this drama to constitute its linchpin. The mainstreamers would be invited to reflect on these cross-cultural offerings in light of their initial challenges. Had their concerns been addressed? If so, had they been satisfied or merely strengthened? Perhaps new irritations had arisen, so that other or deeper considerations now seemed necessary.

Such was my fantasy. As with most fantasies, it spoke to whispering fears. Was my own commitment to cross-cultural psychology ill-founded? Was I yet another rebel merely seeking support for my peculiar vision? Was it time to return home?

In 1985 I decided to test my fantasy in the crucible of our discipline—the response of colleagues to the above proposal. I made a short list of the best persons I knew for each side of the House and wrote letters of inquiry. To my amazement everyone replied and over 90% accepted my invitation to participate. Their eventual papers went through a number of editorial iterations and many were then presented to members of "Operations Mainstream" at a Nag's Head conference in June 1987. The revisions that emerged after this encounter were gathered together into the book you now hold.

Marx once observed that "philosophers never analyzed the world differently, but the problem is to change it." My hope is that we may have been able to change the world in the course of analyzing it. This change will be personal in its first flowerings and focused on a rather small corner of the scientific arena. My intuition, however, is that its present size does not reflect its future importance for me or for you.

Consider the flowering of a garden, though differing in kind, color, form, and shape, yet, inasmuch as they are refreshed by the waters of one spring, revived by the breath of one wind, invigorated by the rays of one sun, this diversity increaseth their charm, and addeth unto their beauty. How unpleasing to the eye if all the flowers and the plants, the leaves and the blossoms, the fruits, the branches and the trees of that garden were all of the same shape and color! Diversity of hues, form, and shape enricheth and adorneth the garden, and heighteneth the effect thereof.

—Abdu'l-Baha

1

HOW DOES ONE
DESCRIBE A PLATYPUS?
An Outsider's Questions
for Cross-Cultural Psychology

JAMES T. TEDESCHI

One wonders whether cross-cultural psychology originated in Australia. There one can find such exotic fauna as the kangaroo, the duck-billed platypus, and the ostrich. Strange, improbable combinations of biological characteristics that appear to be borrowed from across the various phyla are found in these fascinating creatures. Cross-cultural psychology seems to be classifiable with these exotic, hard-to-classify, and improbable organisms (well, on reflection all organisms are improbable). In any case, cross-cultural psychology appears to be neither fish nor fowl. I am in the position of the visitor who asks the zookeeper to explain to me what these creatures really are, where they come from, and whether they are dangerous or have endearing anthropomorphic characteristics, and whether they perform any important ecological functions.

Most readers expect to learn something from a writer, but in this chapter they learn only what a neophyte's impressions are about cross-cultural psychology after only a brief glimpse at the literature bearing that label. The author is a mainstream, laboratory-oriented social psychologist, trained as a rat psychologist at the University of Michigan many years ago. The editor asked me to contribute to this book because I have coauthored introductory and advanced textbooks in social psychology. Neither of these books had very much in them that could be identified as cross-cultural psychology. They are not unique in their disregard of cross-cultural psychology. No textbook in social psychology (to my knowledge) has a chapter with that title, nor does any discuss at any length an area of research or science having such an identity.

A review by a Polish psychologist of our advanced textbook in social

AUTHOR'S NOTE: The comments by Mike Bond and Erich Kirschler on a draft of this chapter are much appreciated.

psychology (Tedeschi & Lindskold, 1976) remarked that it was a virtual encyclopedia of North American laboratory social psychology. I am still wondering whether that was a positive evaluation. It is clear in any case that the limits of the book were clearly perceived. In 1976, when the book was published, it probably was a rather good representation of psychological social psychology, which was primarily a North American laboratory science. Ten years later there are many critical voices pointing to the limitations of a social science that does not consider indigenous psychologies, cultural context, and methodological pluralism.

Given the current, rather long-enduring crisis in social psychology and the evident desire to strike out in new directions, it may well be asked why cross-cultural psychology continues to be ignored by mainstream social psychologists. There may of course be many reasons textbook writers in social psychology ignore cross-cultural psychology. Among these reasons are lack of knowledge about cross-cultural psychology, skepticism about its methodology, and the failure of cross-cultural psychology to devise theories or carry out research that captures the imagination of mainstreamers. There is not at present a visible body of knowledge identified with such a separate discipline, knowledge that is perceived as vital or critical for extending our understanding of human social behavior.

The present chapter will be devoted to raising questions for cross-cultural psychologists, primarily inspired by a desire to learn whatever they have to teach me.

CLASSIFICATION: WHAT IS CROSS-CULTURAL PSYCHOLOGY?

Interdisciplinary Sciences

The number of social sciences has been growing rapidly since World War II. Clearly, the complexity of human social behavior generates a series of problems to be solved beyond the range of any one level of analysis or any delimited set of allied methodologies. There appears to be a core to each social science around which most activity centers, although there are always a number of people on the periphery or at the interface of other sciences. In social psychology the core appears to be a concern for how a person perceives, cognizes, and reacts to social reality in achieving interpersonal goals, typically, but not always, in short-term interaction sequences.

Of course, one can find social psychologists on an interface with other disciplines, such as biology, individual psychology, sociology, economics, history, anthropology, and political science. They begin to place adjectives in their titles and call themselves political psychologists, economic psychologists, psychohistorians, and so on. While I would be the last to discourage such pioneering spirit and the fruitful ideas that may be imported across intellectual barriers, skepticism that each and every group that finds an interesting intellectual niche deserves legitimate status as a separate science does not seem out of place. A little of that Missouri spirit, which says "show me," may be invoked as a challenge rather than as an attempt to discourage.

Psychology differentiated into subdisciplines because the various problems of interest required different levels of analysis in terms of theory and, as a consequence, different methodologies. Do cross-cultural psychologists expect to spread themselves over all the subdisciplines of psychology as well as the whole range of the social sciences? The courage of such aspirations may not be matched by the wisdom to achieve them.

One sign that a new science is emerging on the intellectual scene is the appearance of a textbook with the name of the science in its title. For example, the inception of social psychology is often viewed as coincident with the textbooks written by Cooley (1902) and McDougall (1908). The books with the title "cross-cultural psychology" that I leafed through before sitting down in front of the word processor were in most cases edited books, and were in all cases addressed to other scholars. I found a reference to a textbook on cross-cultural psychology but did not have an opportunity to look at it. It is useful for someone like myself, who knows little about the theories or research current in cross-cultural psychology, to be able to obtain an overview of the field by reading a textbook.[1]

Distinctive Aspects of a Science

It could be argued that if it looks like a duck, walks like a duck, and quacks like a duck, it is not a platypus. Applied to cross-cultural psychology, the argument reduces to the question of whether the subject matter (or the types of problems studied), the level of analysis of important theoretical concepts, and the methods used are sufficiently distinct to justify an identity as a separate discipline. It would not seem reasonable to consider a German social psychologist as working in a different discipline than a North American colleague merely because they carry out research in different cultures. If they use essentially the same basic theories and methods, there would seem to be little reason to consider them as working in different social sciences. This observation raises the question: "Are cross-cultural psychologists simply social psychologists working in different cultures?" If not, what distinct factors serve to differentiate them from mainstream social psychologists, who also believe they are seeking universal laws of behavior and do not believe they need confirmation of this from cross-cultural research.

An undergraduate professor once taught that psychology is what psychologists do—a behavioristic definition! The relevant answer to my question about cross-cultural psychology might include descriptions of the theories, methods, and beliefs developed by, used by, or held by cross-cultural psychologists. Of course, the paradigms (in any of the Kuhnian senses) of cross-cultural psychology should be different in some significant way from those of other social science disciplines to justify viewing it as a separate science. For example, it may be asked, "If cross-cultural theories have been formulated, do they explain different phenomena than the theories developed by North American social psychologists, or are they competing or alternative theories?"

If cross-cultural theories only apply existing social psychological theories to explain variations in behavior across cultures, they might be of little interest to social psychologists. That is, an extension of the mainstream theory of social psychology developed primarily in North America to explain the behavior of individuals in other cultures would not automatically add substantially to the explanation of behavior, although it might give us more confidence in its universality. Of course, one function of a social psychology writ large would be to legitimate and hence make more universally acceptable North American theories about social behavior. My hunch, however, is that cross-cultural psychologists tend to be skeptical about the generalizability of social psychological theories developed by American practitioners.

Social Psychology and Cross-Cultural Psychology

The question about how cross-cultural psychology might be defined could be turned back on me in the form of asking how I would define social psychology. Defining a science, after all, will not lead to the same concise and unambiguous meanings or denotations that might be achieved in devising theoretical or empirical terms used within the science. There have been a number of papers defining the two, three, or four social psychologies that can be discerned (House, 1977; Liska,

1977). For example, House has differentiated psychological and sociological social psychologies in terms of the different methodologies. It seems clear that sociologists tend to focus more on institutional, demographic, and group effects on rates of various kinds of behaviors that occur in a society, whereas psychologists tend to focus on relatively unstructured short-term interactions of persons (typically strangers) who have limited goals. There are also associated preferences for special methodologies. Sociologists prefer field research, survey techniques, and correlational methods, while psychologists maintain a preference for laboratory experiments. Despite these differences of emphasis, the phenomena of interest for both orientations are persons who are interdependent in terms of reinforcements, and the predominant concern is with social influences and social control.

Are there divisions in cross-cultural psychology that mirror those found in social psychology? That is, are there sociological and psychological cross-culturalists? Perhaps cross-cultural psychology is concerned with a wider range of topics than is social psychology (however defined). My obsession with the platypus was brought on by pursuing the table of contents of the *Handbook of Cross-Cultural Psychology*. An impressive array of topics was covered in this multi-volume work, including language, emotions, cognitions, developmental issues, personality, social psychology, and psychopathology. Deep respect must be given to anyone who can develop a cross-cultural theory to explain all of those phenomena! Well, that is an unreasonable expectation. Instead, we would expect a number of medium-range theories to explain some subset of these phenomena, just as occurs in mainstream social psychology. It might be premature to expect such development in an aspiring young discipline. Nevertheless, I would like to have a clearer grasp of the special set of problems these phenomena pose for the cross-cultural psychologist, which is different in some fundamental way from the set of problems perceived by mainstream psychologists. Then I would have a clear conception about the nature of cross-cultural psychology.

Focus on Scope
of Psychological Theories

One stereotype that I have held of a cross-cultural psychologist is of someone who merely replicates in a different society experiments originally carried out in a North American laboratory. The rationale for such research is believed to be a concern for examining external validity, or, in the widest sense, the universality of social psychological principles or processes. To the extent that the stereotype is true I would expect to find that cross-cultural psychologists adopt existing theory from social psychology and add a dimension or two to account for variations in behavior in "foreign" cultures. Indeed, much of the research in cross-cultural psychology appears to support my stereotype. Consider a current argument about the nature of inferred processes that are assumed to be universal. One would hope that cross-cultural psychology would be able to provide special evidence to help us evaluate disputed theoretical concepts and processes. For example, Gergen (1982) claims that the self is a reconstruction of experience that is useful in discourse with others, but self is not an internal agent guiding or controlling behavior. A very different view proffered by Epstein (1973) is that the person's theory of self is the most important determinant of both cognitions and behavior. Thus Gergen views self as a product of historical and societal circumstances that serves a function in social interactions. Epstein's theory provides a deeper cognitive analysis of self that focuses on intrapsychic processes that result in social behavior. The difference between these two theorists is over the function of self. Is it a useful social construction or is it a vital cognitive core of the individual? Perhaps neither of these theories is adequate to explain the relevant facts. This is a vital issue and one to which someone with knowledge of a wide range of cultures might very well contribute. There are many other such issues that might be tackled by cross-cultural psychology: related questions about the causes of aggression (why so many homicides in the United States, as compared to Japan?), a need in individuals to maintain consistent cognitions (is there an internal need or are there wide variations across societies in concern for being consistent?), and an enormous number of other questions that are fundamental issues for psychological science.

Social anthropologists have provided information shedding some light on some of these questions. Examination of indigenous psychologies has shown that there are wide variations in what counts as self. According to Heelas (1981), indigenous psychologies differ with respect to distinctions made between internal and external control, public and private, subjective and objective, reason and emotion, inner and outer, and conscious and unconscious. Historians have also informed us about the evolution of the self over time. It is clear that the self-theories of serfs in Medieval Europe were quite different from those of most middle-class college students in our contemporary universities (Lyons, 1978).

What have cross-cultural psychologists contributed to the study of the self? How does a cross-cultural approach to studying this problem differ from either anthropolitical, historical, or social psychological approaches? A very different function for a cross-cultural psychologist would be to evaluate the universality of postulated psychological processes or entities, such as romantic love and other emotional states, the relation of anger to aggression, the function of self in society, and so forth.

Cultural Anthropology
and Cross-Cultural Psychology

An anthropologist colleague suggested to me that behavior that is universal is the concern of the psychologist, but indigenous psychology is the province of the anthropologist. Where between these two points, the particular and the general, does the cross-cultural psychologist stand? The expected answer is that cross-cultural psychology straddles the gap between these polar extremes. But without a body of knowledge to support such aspirations, this answer would be unconvincing. However one defines "culture," there appears to be some difficulty in treating it as an environmental factor in any stimulus-response relationship within explanatory systems of human social behavior. What does the concept of "culture" mean for cross-cultural psychologists?

In perusing the *Journal of Cross-Cultural Psychology,* I found articles critical of the concept of "culture" and even an article by Jahoda (1984) that argued that a concept of culture is not critical for a cross-cultural psychologist. Is there general agreement about this? Directing a similar question to myself, I would argue (paraphrasing Allport) that "social" for social psychologists has a shared definition: the impact on the thought, feelings, or behavior of a person of the actual, implied, or imagined presence of others. Is there a shared working definition for cross-cultural psychology?

A levels-of-analysis problem seems apparent in the very name "cross-cultural psychology." I take "culture" to be a central construct in anthropology. There is no consensus, however, about what culture means (precisely). One of the fundamental issues concerning the cultural (or social) anthropologist is how to conceptualize culture in basic theories of human thought and behavior. Malinowski, Boas, Morgan, Levi-Strauss, and Steward have proposed very different theories of culture and human behavior (see Sahlins, 1976a). Whatever culture is, it is different from the kind of reality described by natural scientists.

Culture is the product of human thought and behavior and is handed down from generation to generation (Linton, 1956). Clearly, culture refers to myriad complex processes and much content. Just as one would argue that "physical reality" would be too broad to describe any state of affairs and that it would be better to break it down into decibels, millimicrons, centigrade, degrees, and so on, so the term *culture* appears equally breathtaking in its scope of reference. For the most part, social scientists refer to institutions, groups, roles, and norms (among other concepts) as discriminable aspects of a culture. Thus (the devil's advocate argues) culture is less important as a theoretical concept than as a generic term.

Are cross-cultural psychologists familiar with the history of this kind of scholarship in anthropology? Do they borrow from this intellectual tradition, or is there a tendency to try to reduce anthropology to psychology? As a knee-jerk antireductionist, I would have grave doubts that anthropology can be reduced to psychology, or vice versa. If a theoretical system is to be developed linking culture to behavior, is it necessary to trace the action of systems through subsystems to groups and individuals? Some attempts have been made by biologically-oriented scientists to develop systems theories. These attempts have not met with very much success. Are the prospects for tying together different levels-of-analysis any better in cross-cultural psychology than in biopsychology or sociobiology?

The basic problems of cross-cultural psychology seem clearly different from either anthropology or psychology. One way to conceptualize the difference is to think of cross-cultural psychology as the obverse of the study of personality in psychology. The main issue in the area of personality is the alleged consistency of an individual's behaviors across a wide range of dissimilar situations. Furthermore, some individuals adopt one pattern of behavior for those different situations and other individuals display different patterns of behavior over the same range of situations.

Cross-cultural psychology tackles an even more difficult problem. In social psychology the task of defining social situations has remained largely intractable even within cultures. The examination and isolation of components of cultures for research purposes appear to be even more formidable problems. Some progress in solving these theoretical and methodological tasks might inform us about how to account for behaviors or processes that appear to vary across cultures? But it is difficult even to establish the fact of such cultural differences. Even within cultures the reliability and/or replicability of social psychological research is not impressive, and frequently equal and opposite results are found in the same research paradigm as a function of a wide range of variables.[2] The failure to replicate results is seldom accepted as a disconfirmation of a theory in mainstream social psychology. Methodological differences or failure to control for some extraneous variables are the favorite rationalizations provided to preserve existing theories in the face of contradictory findings. If these responses to replication failure exist between Harvard and Yale, they should be all the more strident when the contradictory findings occur between (say) Hong Kong and Kuwait. It is a problem to determine if differences obtained across cultures are due to real cultural differences that affect individual behaviors or whether there are other uncontrolled factors that would account for such differences.

WHAT ARE THE
METHODOLOGIES USED IN
CROSS-CULTURAL RESEARCH?

It has been generally accepted by philosophers of science that theoretical perspectives (or "paradigms") shape the way scientists perceive the world (Feyerabend, 1970; Kuhn, 1962; Lakatos, 1970). Furthermore, theories tend to dictate methods. While biopsychologists, learning theorists, psychophysicists, and social psychologists all belong to the same basic discipline, the methods used by each specialty area tend to be preconfigured to their special sets of problems. It would hardly be considered adequate by a psychologist interested in brain function to give subjects attitude scales, neither would a social psychologist be especially interested in brain scans, EEGs, or potassium pumps. All this is by way of asking if cross-cultural psychologists have developed methodologies specially tailored to help answer the questions that are unique to their discipline.

The tendency of social psychologists to depend upon laboratory experiments carried out with undergraduate college students raises questions about context, experimental artifacts, artificiality, and ecological validity. But what are the alternatives? The laboratory-oriented social psychologist is concerned with maintaining control over extraneous variables in order to establish functional relationships between variables. Widespread skepticism has been expressed by critics of laboratory experiments. It has been argued that laboratory experiments do not include contextual factors and hence are inadequate for isolating "laws" of human behavior. The answer is to flee the laboratory to the "real world" in search of "relevance." But what about the lack of controls in field experiments, natural observations, surveys, interviews, or longitudinal studies? Must we choose between strict reliability and sloppy validity? Have cross-cultural psychologists invented new methods for research and are they more apt to use multiple methods in studying a given phenomenon than the average North American social psychologist?

A concern for factors that transcend the individual might render the laboratory experiment an inadequate tool for studying many problems that might interest a cross-cultural psychologist. Anthropologists, sociologists, economists, and political scientists seldom perform laboratory experiments because their theories (and problems) cannot be tested by observing individual or interpersonal behaviors under such highly controlled circumstances. To the extent that cross-cultural psychology is undefined and searching for an identity, it could be expected that eclecticism would prevail with regard to methodological choice. This expectation is confirmed by scanning Volume 2 of the *Handbook of Cross-Cultural Psychology*, which looks quite a bit like Volume 2 of the *Handbook of Social Psychology*.

There are social psychologists (notably, McGuire, 1967, 1983) who advocate methodological pluralism and especially opt for methods that are not confined to laboratory experiments. Typically, nonlaboratory methods for establishing cause-effect relationships, such as Liseral, time series analyses, and multiple regression technique, require the a priori articulation of a specific model.

This way of proceeding is characteristic of microeconomics. A model is articulated, and then data are gathered to evaluate the model through powerful statistical methods. This strategy for discovery is impressive when a complex a priori model is found to be consistent with a pattern of data. It is also a strategy that often develops when a set of very complex processes operates in interaction with one another, especially when there are temporal intervals involved that preclude the use of laboratory experiments. Given these considerations, I expected model building and testing to be an important strategy among cross-cultural psychologists. However, my superficial perusal of the literature did not indicate that this was an important mode of inquiry in cross-cultural psychology.

While there may be unsolved methodological problems in cross-cultural psychology, their clear recognition is the first step in their resolution. Technological innovation has played an important role in the history of science. There is no reason to be pessimistic about the inventiveness of cross-cultural psychologists. But until such methods are developed and are widely used, it is difficult to have much confidence about straightforward cross-cultural comparisons of measurements on dependent variables.

IS CROSS-CULTURAL PSYCHOLOGY POSSIBLE?

Science Versus History

The number of people who call themselves cross-cultural psychologists is relatively small, and many of them have been trained as social psychologists. It might be assumed, then, that they are experiencing the same intellectual schisms as their social psychologist peers. One schism is between those who argue that social psychology is a science, like any natural science, and those who view social psychology as more akin to history (Gergen, 1974). We are familiar enough with the positivistic or logical empiricist philosophies that have justified behavioristic and neobehavioristic schools of psychology (e.g., Skinner, 1938; Tolman, 1952). At the other philosophical pole, Harre (1981) has argued against a scientistic view of social psychology, which is essentially the view that it is much like the natural sciences. In the scientific view social psychologists seek out the causes and natural laws of behavior. Harre believes that there are no universal laws of behavior; instead, behavior is a form of dramatization that occurs within a structure of rules. The combination of dramatism and praxis is probably unique within each culture. If Harre is correct, then the methods typically used by psychologists, which are geared to find differences between experimental conditions rather than functions that occur within certain definable contexts, are inappropriate to the study of social behavior. What impact has this kind of argument had on the practices of cross-cultural psychology? Are the methods used more like those of anthropologists who live within a culture and keep careful journals recording their observations, or is the predominant method one of laboratory experiment? If one is to distinguish practice from exhortation, it seems clear that most cross-cultural psychology utilizes the laboratory, and the methods tend to be identical to those used by psychologists in the subdiscipline akin to the problem approached by the cross-cultural psychologist.

The Influence of Constructionism

An important metatheoretical development has been the rise of constructionism in social psychological theory (McGuire, 1983). It has developed from a series of influences, including hermeneutics, the Whorfian hypothesis that reality is constructed through language, the philosophy of Ernst Cassirer, and symbolic interactionism. Cassirer (1944) argued that humans construct a symbolic net through which all experience is filtered and interpreted. Symbolic interactionists believe that the individual constructs a unique view of reality, including notions of self, which serves as the basis for behavior. The individual's construction of reality is based on other people's constructions and his or her own experiences. Symbols have become only remotely attached to any external reality. Hence, understanding and explaining human behavior requires examination of their symbolic networks. Attempts to connect behavior to the environment as described in any objective way are doomed to failure. The current focus on cognitions in social psychology is not inconsistent with a constructionist viewpoint. Yet the focus on environmental factors ("culture") might be expected to give cross-cultural psychologists a different perspective. Thus it might be expected that there would be a tendency to be less oriented to cognitive psychology and more to social interactions (i.e., behavior) among cross-cultural psychologists than among mainstream social psychologists. Is such an expectation justified?

Cultural Relativism

Cultural anthropology has sometimes seemed to adopt a position of cultural relativism. It is difficult to learn to live in an alien culture and often culture shock is experienced. Small details that serve as cues for responses between people may be missed or misinterpreted, or nuances in concepts may be so different from any prior experience as to be completely misunderstood. The ideological backgrounds people carry around in their heads serve as frames of reference for construing the meanings of events and actions, provide rules guiding behavior, and promote some values over others. The problems of understanding an alien culture are sufficiently great as to have apparently misled a great anthropologist, Margaret Mead (1935), in her studies of New Guinea tribes.

The diversity of behaviors across cultures recorded by anthropologists is sufficient to raise the question of whether there are any universal patterns of behavior. Even in the case of the norm of reciprocity, which Gouldner (1960) and Mauss (1967) claim is universal, the factors that affect obligation to repay favors or gifts appear to be so different across societies as to require a different set of conditions for predicting behavior for people in each culture studied. There seems to be a real question here about whether there is some overarching "cross-cultural" theory that can explain all the similarities and the differences that occur.

Disagreements have been emerging over the last decade about the status of theories, methods, and appropriate levels of analysis in social psychology. Triandis (1975), among others, has lamented the low level of abstraction involved in most social psychological theories. Often what is considered "theory" is no more than a one-shot intuitive hypothesis (see Tedeschi, Gaes, Riordan, & Quigley-Fernandez, 1981). In response to this kind of criticism it could be asked if the concern for cultural context has led to more complex and sophisticated theories by cross-cultural psychologists. It is one thing to exhort others to construct more complex (and "true") theories, and another to do it oneself. Mainstream social psychologists, who are located primarily in North America and Europe, are not likely to be attentive to cross-cultural theories unless their own theories are challenged in their "domain," which of course consists of people in developed industrial societies. If cross-cultural psychologists simply modify or extend the theories of mainstream psychology to explain the differences they obtain in other societies, no real modification is needed to explain behavior that was used for comparison, since that has already been explained by the unmodified versions of the relevant theories. To gain attention, the cross-cultural psychologist will need to render problematic phenomena that mainstream social psychologists believe they already understand.

There may also be the danger that "grand theories" are simply too far removed from any observations that can be made with present methods. Instead of biting off more than one can chew, patience requires the development of a basis for advances in a science. Thomas Kuhn (1962) has argued that natural scientists have made progress because they have concerned themselves with solvable problems. Kuhn laments that social scientists tend to tackle huge, unmanageable, and unsolvable problems, and hence it should not be surprising if little progress is made. A focus on a problem, such as what factors contribute to conformity, may lead investigators over time to some interesting theories and experimental findings. It can be expected that cross-cultural psychology will add to the information about problems already under investigation by other psychologists. However, I would also like to know if there are unique problems that have been developed or that can be considered the special province of the cross-cultural psychologists.

Ideology and Cross-Cultural Psychology

Bergmann (1951), in a classic paper, argued that the social sciences must be ideological in their early stages. The values and ways of thinking in a society engulf the social scientist just as they do everyone else. Hence, the behavior that attracts attention, the explanations that are offered as theories, and the means utilized to test the theories are necessarily culture-bound. Applied to the present state of psychological theories, one would hardly expect a challenge to the assertion that psychology is imbued with the ideologies associated with North American culture. Some discussion of how some ideological factors have become incorporated into psychological theories has occurred in some of our major journals (e.g., Sampson, 1977).

In my view any cross-cultural psychologist would have to be anti-mainstream social psychology in the sense that intellectual challenges would be posed to ideologies indigenous to contemporary social psychology. Of course, the challengers would themselves carry an ideological lens through which they also view the world. Out of the multiplicity of viewpoints an enrichment of theories and of research problems should occur. The fact that ideas originate in an ideological context is not an impediment to science. The scientist wants to examine empirically the merits of the theories in terms of their explanatory power, and should be unconcerned about the personal factors associated with the scientists who develop the theories.

At the risk of sounding much less nationalistic than I really am, let the slogan ring out, "May anti-Americanism prevail among cross-cultural psychologists!" An important current philosopher of science (Feyerabend, 1970) has argued that one way to encourage more rapid development in science is to deliberately proliferate the variety of theories available to test. Certainly, there is a poverty of good theory in the so-called "soft" areas of psychology, including social, personality, and developmental psychology. Cross-cultural psychology may in the future be a rich source of ideas for bringing about a proliferation of theories.

CONCLUSION

This chapter began as an inquiry into the nature and functions of a cross-cultural psychology. When I started writing this chapter I had genuine doubts about the nature and functions of cross-cultural psychology. Of course, I have raised many questions, some of which have probably received solid responses in the literature (but have eluded me), while others are controversial, or have yet to be considered. But some of the questions tended to answer themselves. For example, however else cross-cultural psychology may be defined, the scientific examination of variations in psychological processes across cultures is certainly an important function. Pursuit of this objective promises an enrichment of our understanding of human behavior by adding more dimensions to our descriptions of the environment and by challenging the ideologically based theories of North American psychologists. If cross-cultural psychology offered no more than this promise, it would richly deserve to flourish. I have convinced myself that a platypus may look a little peculiar to North Americans, but they enrich our view of nature and increase our understanding of the animal kingdom. Now I am ready to listen to the answers to my questions, and to include them if I ever write another textbook in psychology.

NOTES

1. I have been informed by the editor that there is one textbook that presents a limited perspective for the field of cross-cultural psychology written by Marshall Segall in 1980. Segall and several collaborators are currently at work on a more ambitious textbook on the topic.

2. A good example of a phenomenon that is very sensitive to independent variables manipulations is the polarization effect. Risky shifts and conservative shifts have been found, and, in the case of nonhypothetical events, no shift at all (see Tedeschi, Lindskold, & Rosenfeld, 1986).

2

WHY NOT CROSS-CULTURAL PSYCHOLOGY?
A Characterization of Some Mainstream Views

ROY S. MALPASS

> Fields of academic inquiry are defined by groups of scholars who agree in
> advance not to ask certain fundamental questions.[1]

Our task is twofold. First, it is to understand how it is that a field of
scholarship the research findings of which are bounded by the population from which its subject samples are drawn can virtually ignore the
majority of the world's population and nearly all of its obvious and rich
variations in living and thinking. Second, it is to demonstrate that
theoretical and empirical knowledge derived from and encompassing
the world's cultural diversity is indispensable to the maturity of
psychological science. While the volume as a whole addresses the second
task, the present discussion will attempt only to bring the first into focus,
and to sharpen the challenge to cross-cultural psychology. To this end
there are some positions that should be stated and examined.

LOCAL SAMPLES
ARE ADEQUATE SAMPLES

Individuals in Western nations adequately represent human populations everywhere. This is because we share certain life processes and
environmental demands with human populations everywhere. Humans
the world over, in common with many other animals, share a broad
range of life necessities. All are members of a kinship system of some
kind and have to recognize kin and nonkin. They have to remember
individuals, objects, and events of many kinds, draw connections among
them, and act on the basis of some integration of this information. While
the contexts in which these activities take place may vary widely around
the world, and while the concrete appearance of the contexts will appear
to be extremely discrepant, the portions of the process that are of
interest to psychologists are precisely the commonalities. While the

specific criteria that enter into decision processes may well be extremely discrepant when hunting and gathering groups are compared with Chicago commodities traders, the decision processes themselves must be highly similar. If they are not, they very likely cannot be studied by nonnatives, or by the extremely powerful methods of Western psychological science. This approach has many components.

Theory is the thing. The scientific study of human behavior is an abstract, theoretical enterprise that is oriented to understanding psychological processes. It is not very important whether or not, for example, we can predict social decision making with individualistic criteria imported from North American into collectivist societies. However, it would be very important to find that once we have gotten over our ethnocentrism and fit the appropriate collectivist values and sources of influence into the prediction model, we could not predict, because collectivists work differently than individualists at the level of process!

So long as one is theory-oriented one will also be process-oriented, and incommensurabilities due to concrete and highly "local" content (as opposed to process) will not be particularly interesting. The object of study, for example, might be how retrieval mnemonics work to enhance the availability of otherwise inaccessible "memories." The specific memories don't matter much, and the fact that people in different societies find different things frightening, humorous, or distinctive is beside the point. To attempt to do interpretable and comparable studies against the background of such uncontrollable (and maybe even unknowable) variations is an invitation to disaster. Besides, everybody knows that the Bahumphs[2] have to have memory processes to get along, and no one can imagine any other kind of memory structure apart from some sort of associative structure.

Concrete cultural differences get in the way. If investigators are to spend time and energy trying to figure out how to incorporate Bahumphian memory phenomenon into their theories, they should first have some reason to believe that these phenomena are matters of process, and not content-category epiphenomena. This is because the major reason that the specific structure of these categories in memory is of any interest is that one has to know about it to get beyond it to the problem of memory process. There is little of interest about the specifics of these categories in their own right. So why should we master the object categorizations of the Bahumphs when it is very likely that when we do we will be dealing once more with a common form of associative memory? We know the one back home so much better that we can be much more effective studying memory processes in that already familiar context.

Because of the very great amount of effort needed to master the culturally specific forms and materials that must be understood before studies of process can become interpretable, studying the Bahumphs is simply a waste of time. And in the end, we would probably do it badly because we lack the implicit knowledge needed to make the explicit scientific enterprise work.

In contrast, if one is interested in the possibility that, for example, the importance rankings of various social entities ("values") differs greatly in different kinds of cultural systems, that this has implications for whom one can consult when one has certain problems, and that this in turn has ramifications for gender egalitarianism and outgroup stereotyping, that's fine, and maybe is interesting. But it will be most interesting to those whose theoretical sentences refer to content-level categories rather than to process categories.

Concrete cultural differences are not important. Cultural differences are trivial because they are at the wrong level of abstraction, and stand as "medium" rather than "thing" in relation to the objects of study. The readily observable differences among cultural groups are probably superficial, and represent little if any differences at the level of psychological process. One finds support for this proposition in one of the classic studies of cross-cultural research, the work of Segall, Campbell, and Herskovits (1966) on cultural influences on perception. The idea is, of course, that the documented cultural differences in susceptibility to different classes of visual illusions result from exposing people with the same perceptual learning system to very different perceptual inputs. Humans reared in carpentered living environments will develop susceptibility to illusions like the Mueller-Lyer figure, and humans reared in environments containing vast visual vistas will develop susceptibility to perspective illusions, such as the horizontal-vertical illusion.

A matter of preference. Perhaps an important difference between cross-culturalists and mainstreamers who are resolutely ignorant of the cross-cultural literature is their prior belief about whether we have to demonstrate empirically that the obvious differences are trivial, or whether we have to demonstrate that the obvious differences are important. Cross-culturalists are likely to believe that the obvious differences may represent fundamental differences, and that they can't be ignored until proven unimportant. Others appear to hold the contrasting belief.

Of course the real challenge is this: Is there any evidence of real differences in cognitive or other psychological processes across cultures? The implied position is that any social phenomena, based on contrasting cultural conventions (like social values) that are processed by common processes to achieve contrasting results, are in fact epiphenomenal: intriguing, but not very important; to be explained away, but not to be explained in their own right.

Placed in this context, the problem becomes one of preference for the level of phenomena at which one wants to work. At some levels everything is different, and the question is how to achieve some sense of the "psychological unity of mankind." At another level, everything is the same, and the different cultural forms just make one smile.

SCIENTIFIC PSYCHOLOGY
IS A LOCAL CULTURAL FORM

The sociology of the profession provides another set of views of cross-cultural psychology. Scientific psychology is a Euro-American enterprise, and it is reflexive—it refers to its own cultural environment as the central subject matter. This is not bad, nor is it a hypocrisy. It simply means that we are the object of our study. If others want to study their psychological processes, in their social/psychological environments, and can do so in ways that contribute to a common development of knowledge, they are welcome to do so. Then we will have something to talk about. The reflexive state is the default state of the scholarly "program." Theory is developed in this default state, and the prestigious people are in the default state.

Professional individuation. Professionals seek to carve out specialized niches for themselves. Scientific thinking and thinking about one's personal professional development take place in the same head, organized around the same activities. The use of various phenomena as "challenges" to the dominant core theory can be thought of in association with the individuation process. The challenge is often from outside the theoretical domain proper, and may take the form ". . . if theory X is correct, we should be able to understand how [fill in your professionally individuating phenomenon] works." The choice of phenomena for study is determined by many factors. One of these is an interest in differences among human societies, so one sort of challenge is to ask whether core theory can explain exotic cultural phenomena. The question becomes, "If the dominant mainstream thinking is valid, how can one account for the fact that the Bahumphians . . . !"

"Speciation" of subfields. A corner of the scientific social system develops in this process. It may even become a "field," to which new

participants are recruited and in which new professional organizations are formed. The participants in this field may wonder why their work is ignored by the mainstream. The answer is clear. It is ignored because they and their favorite problems are professionally and scientifically peripheral. The problems never were a matter of central theoretical importance, having come from outside the theoretical domain in the first place, and they continue not to be. Increasingly more participants in the developing subfield receive their professional socialization from older participants. But they still look to the central areas of their discipline for identity and guidance. These peripherals, as in any social system, may want recognition from the mainstream, or they may become alienated, establish ties elsewhere, or become anomic.

The development of disciplines. The development of disciplines is not entirely rational, and it is not highly responsive to logical argument. At one time I believed that there was an elegant design to the structure of our discipline. Knowledge unfolded over time in waves of viewpoints made necessary by earlier attempts to penetrate more deeply into truth, and by the ultimately revealed weaknesses of earlier positions. I attribute this naive belief to the revisionist byproducts of carefully organized lectures by a series of very capable undergraduate and graduate professors. This belief had begun to crack even before reading about paradigms, and scientific revolutions.

The content of our field contains much that is of great interest. But is the knowledge we have attained available because it is more important than the knowledge we did not get, or is it present simply because a few people worked on these rather than other problems? According to this view, the latter is more nearly the case. And according to this view, cross-cultural psychology will dominate if people central to the discipline communicate its importance, and its feasibility as a career development vehicle. In this connection, the relative difficulty of getting data in the first place, and interpretable data in the second place, is not to be overlooked.

Cultural membership constrains theorizing. You have to be *of* a culture to generate new theory that has relevance for a culture. This view seems to me to be a more thoughtful extension of some of the views outlined above. It has its roots in an awareness of the importance of phenomenological analysis in the developments of large chunks of psychology's scholarly program—from the Gestalt psychologists in perception to Asch and Heider in social psychology.

If the scientific intellectual strategy aids our determining the basis or validity of interesting ideas, it does not help much in generating new ones. We have lots of courses in research methods, and none that I know of on how to have new ideas and to think well. The source of new and interesting ideas is in the thoughts, reading, and life experiences of people working in the field. In contrast to the explicated and public conceptualizations that are the material of scientific analysis, these are implicit aspects of intellectual life that may evolve into grist for the scientific mill. We have enough difficulty thinking incisively in our own culture. Is it really reasonable to expect those of us socialized in one cultural milieu to achieve a working grasp of another? From this perspective it seems presumptuous even to try.

A LOOSE RELATIONSHIP
BETWEEN THEORY AND DATA

A major problem with cross-cultural research—whether or not it is ultimately published in the more prestigious journals—is that in extremely few cases are there explicit falsifiable theories under investigation and development. I have already complained of the prevalent use of the weak, confirmatory strategy in cross-cultural research (Malpass, 1977a, 1977b), so I don't have to go over that ground here. While methodological treatises abound (see, for example, Lonner & Berry, 1986; Triandis & Berry, 1980; and any recent volume of the *Journal of Cross-Cultural Psychology*), so do studies with weak conceptual development and uncertain interpretation. But certainly this is not unique to cross-cultural research.

I do not mean to endorse the "spineless wretch" theory of cross-cultural scholarship. Cultural differences on most psychological measures are either not clearly interpretable, or are interpretable only with heroic levels of theoretical and empirical rigor. To move from the control and clarity of the experimental laboratory into the inherently uncertain difficulties of cross-cultural research is to have one's tolerance for ambiguity challenged and one's standards of rigor threatened. Established scholars entering cross-cultural research experiences for the first time take great risks with their reputations. From this perspective, mainstreamers may avoid the cultural domain because they know when to leave well enough alone!

It is not clear from the above remarks whether cross-culturalists have to do better, do less, do different, or do anything to bring about some greater sense of integration with the discipline's mainstream. Clearly, investigations of theoretical problems emanating from the mainstream using paradigmatic empirical approaches can sometimes find enthusiastic acceptance. But it seems to me that this is not really the question posed in this volume. From the cross-cultural point of view, what is needed is a higher level of sophistication in the mainstream about the constraints of culture on behavior—not to mention the constraints of culture on generalizations from data. From this perspective to accept the mainstream definition of the problem is often to lose sight of the phenomenon. But people cannot be expected to accept another way of constructing their intellectual lives without clear evidence of its utility. Communicating the utility of the cross-cultural strategy is the task of this volume.

NOTES

1. I do not know the source of this gem of academic wisdom. Allan Wicker told it to me, but he denies authorship.

2. The Bahumphs are a fictitious and universally exotic tribe.

3

ON TITLES, CITATIONS, AND OUTLETS
What Do Mainstreamers Want?

LADD WHEELER
HARRY REIS

A typical title in the *Journal of Cross-Cultural Psychology* might be "A Cross-Cultural Study of Resource-Allocation Behavior: Bahumphia[1] and Xoma."[2] We can read articles about Ibo communities in Nigeria, about rural and urban New Guineans, about the Inupiat Eskimo and Tlingit and Haida villages, about two Cree communities in Manitoba, about the Rosebud Sioux, about Afrikaners and South African Indians, about South India and Malaysia, and so forth.

Perhaps many of these articles are theoretically interesting and methodologically sophisticated, but they don't create the slightest bit of interest for us mainstreamers, and we will not read them. Because such comparisons are so common in the *Journal of Cross-Cultural Psychology*, we will not subscribe to that journal. We have never been to these places and know nothing about them. To make good sense of these studies, we would need in-depth knowledge of the cultures, and we simply don't have it and don't have the time or inclination to acquire it.

We believe, as Euro-American social psychologists, that our primary job is to understand our culture. That is, of course, a very controversial statement, one that would make some other mainstreamers squirm and scratch. Some would foam at the mouth and try to bite us. Is our science, they would ask, to be confined to a particular culture during a particular historical period? We don't really want to take a strong position on that question, having neither the evangelical fervor of some of our colleagues nor the philosophical sophistication of others. What we would say is that it takes more intellectual resources than we have just to understand our own current culture (while teaching classes, publishing and reviewing articles, serving on committees, maintaining friendships, and keeping the lawn mowed). We just don't have time to read about the Xomanians.

You may argue that we cannot understand one culture in isolation—that it is a single-case design. That is correct, but it seems to us dreadfully important to know, for example, that beautiful people are perceived differently and treated differently than ugly people in Euro-American culture, from birth to death. What would be gained from investigating the same phenomenon in Xoma? If we found the "what is beautiful is good" stereotype to also hold in Xoma, we certainly could not claim universality, because there still might be a nonblack crow somewhere else. If we found that the stereotype did not hold in Xoma, that would not lessen its practical importance in Western culture. True, it would raise interesting theoretical questions, but not knowing Xoma, we would have no way to deal with them.

Does all this mean that we see no value in cross-cultural research? Certainly not! If, instead of investigating resource allocation in Bahumphia and Xoma, one did it in North America and China, or even more specifically in Rochester and Hong Kong, we would be far more interested. One culture we know, and the other can be drawn through reading books such as Michael Bond's *The Psychology of the Chinese People* and numerous articles, or through talking to some of the 900,000 Chinese in this country. We are suggesting that mainstreamers are likely to be interested in comparisons of Euro-American groups and other major known or knowable cultures. It is likely that particular mainstreamers will become interested in and knowledgeable about one other major culture that differs from Euro-American culture on some important dimension, collectivism-individualism, for example, or power distance. Through the work of Hofstede, Triandis, Bond, and others, we know something about the dimensions and the relative placement of various cultures on them. Through the work of a number of cross-cultural psychologists, we know a good deal about how differences on these dimensions affect various social psychological processes. These cross-culturalists have laid a firm foundation on which others (mainstreamers) can join them in a cooperative house-raising. We might even suggest that mainstreamers and the cross-culturalists form a covenant. The mainstreamers need the cross-culturalists to lead them out of their provincial and often uninspired wilderness; the cross-culturalists need the mainstreamers to bear witness to their work.

To determine whether mainstreamers ignore cross-cultural work, we conducted a small study, comparing the citation frequency of two groups of articles appearing in the *Journal of Personality and Social Psychology* in 1974-1976. Group 1 (n = 8) consisted of the cross-cultural articles and Group 2 (n = 16) consisted of the mainstream articles immediately preceding and following the cross-cultural paper. We counted the citations through 1986 of these articles in the *Science Citation Index*.[3] One mainstream article was a clear outlier with a very large number of citations, and we peremptorily discarded it. The remaining articles showed no significant difference in citation frequency between the cross-cultural and comparison groups (13.8 and 16.1 mean citations, respectively). We also looked at where the cross-cultural articles had been cited and found that the vast majority of citations were not in cross-cultural journals. It appears, then, that cross-cultural articles published in mainstream journals are not ignored.

We also looked at the number of cross-cultural articles in *JPSP* in the 1984-1986 period, although it is too early to tell anything about citation frequency. The number of cross-cultural articles increased 10%, to 16, in the 10-year period, while the number of other articles increased only 8.9%, to 786. Extrapolating from a doubling every 10 years of the number of cross-cultural articles and an increase of 9% in other types of articles, cross-cultural articles will achieve parity and then supremacy sometime after the middle of the twenty-first century. During the period 2064-2066, there will be 2,367 articles per year, or 197 for each of the 12 issues. At an average weight of .75 ounces per article, determined by weighing a sample of recent issues, each issue of *JPSP* will weigh 9.2 pounds. This is silly, of course, because everything will be on tiny little chips that we'll never be able to find.

So what *does* the mainstream want? It seems to us that the mainstream is not interested in studies of culture, that is, in studies that describe the peculiarities of Bahumphia and Xoma. Rather, we are interested in studies that utilize known differences between two (or more) cultures to demonstrate the impact of those known differences on social behavior. Findings derived from the former kind of research are limited; they tell me only about Bahumphia and Xoma. The latter kind of research is more broadly generalizable; it tells one about the process by which cultural practices and characteristics influence behavior. Within the constraints of randomization, third-variable causality, and so forth, these principles ought to be applicable to understanding behavior in any culture, once its standing on the underlying variable is assessed.

Let us be a bit more specific for a moment. Consider a recent study by Hewstone and Ward (1985), which we consider exemplary of the sort of cross-cultural research to which the mainstream does attend. Their study was designed to test hypotheses about group context and ethnocentric attribution (the tendency to attribute positive behaviors internally and negative behaviors externally within one's own group, and to reverse this pattern for out-group members). Pettigrew (1979) called this "the ultimate attribution error." Hewstone and Ward first studied this phenomenon in Malaysia with students of Chinese and Malay extraction. Malays attributed causality as expected, but the

Chinese *favored* the out-group. This difference might be due to either of two general factors: a tendency of Chinese persons to be generous and self-effacing in their judgments of causality, or a tendency of Chinese in Malaysia to have adopted the Malaysian culture's generally anti-Chinese stereotypes. To distinguish these possibilities, Hewstone and Ward replicated their study in Singapore, where Chinese persons are not considered to be of lower status than Malays. The same pattern was found among Malays, whereas Chinese students did not favor either group. Thus, they concluded, the out-group favoritism shown by Chinese students in Malaysia was likely due to their own lower status in Malaysia, whereas the differences shown in Singapore were likely due to socialization practices within the two cultures.

One reason we know about this study is that it was published in the *Journal of Personality and Social Psychology*, required reading for any mainstreamer. It is dreadful that cross-culturalists tend to isolate their work in the *Journal of Cross-Cultural Psychology* and far more esoteric outlets. Some of you believe that you can't publish in mainstream journals because editors and reviewers aren't sympathetic. Nothing could be further from the truth! All other things being equal, a cross-cultural article will be judged more leniently than a mainstream article because (a) it is harder to do methodologically pure cross-cultural work, and (b) mainstreamers know that their journals are too provincial. Of course, the rejection rate in the *Journal of Personality and Social Psychology* is in the low eighties, and even with some leniency the odds are against acceptance, but it is better to try than simply to address your manuscript to the *Journal of Social Psychology*. We would even suggest that you ask an editor of the *Journal of Personality and Social Psychology* or the *Personality and Social Psychology Bulletin* to publish a special issue of cross-cultural papers, much like the one planned on the integration of personality and social psychology. So Hewstone and Ward (and others, of course) are to be commended for their choice of publication outlet. Because we are supposed to be critical, we will make one criticism. Instead of the title "Ethnocentrism and Causal Attribution in Southeast Asia," how about "Is the Ultimate Attribution Error Also Universal?" That data were collected in Southeast Asia is of scant importance and may present an initial barrier to readership.

Although Hewstone and Ward's is not the only paradigm we believe mainstreamers would find appealing, it has several desirable features, the most important of which is the systematic attempt to control "third" variables confounded with cultural group (here, status within the local culture). Another paradigm that we believe would attract considerable attention involves contrasting groups known to vary along a single dimension. A recent study by the Chinese Culture Connection (1987) lays the groundwork for such an approach. Using a survey of Chinese values, they were able to characterize 22 cultures along the dimension of "integration." (An added benefit of this study is its careful attention to equating methodological and sampling procedures, thereby eliminating potential artifacts.) West Germany and the Netherlands were ranked highest, and Pakistan, India, and Bangladesh were lowest (the United States was in the middle). These scores might be used to select cultures for research on the impact of collectivism on social behavior. In fact, many theoreticians have speculated that this characteristic is an important component of such phenomena as reward allocation practices, in-group-out-group polarization, and intimacy (e.g., Dion & Dion, in press; Sampson, 1986). If so, one might examine these phenomena in representatively selected cultures to see whether they covary with collectivism as hypothesized.

We are mainstreamers who have recently, by dint of a sabbatical to one of us, and with help from Michael Bond, dipped our toes into the cross-cultural waters (Wheeler, in press). We are still in the process of analyzing and understanding most of our data, and we are impressed with the intellectual challenge. In the first chapter of the *Handbook of Cross-Cultural Psychology*, Harry Triandis emphatically suggests that the current generation of cross-culturalists should concentrate on demonstrating cultural similarities rather than differences. We found that admonition puzzling because you can't dictate what you will find when you do research. Larry McMurtry (1968) quoted a cowboy aphorism: "Love is like the dew. It's as likely to fall on a turd as on a rose." Cross-cultural research is as likely to fall on differences as on similarities. Our purpose as psychologists is to understand principles from one culture to another. That is the great intellectual challenge for all of us.

NOTES

1. A mythical country brought to our attention by Roy Malpass.
2. A small biotech company we would buy on further weakness.
3. We thank Erica Colwell for collecting these data.

4

ON THE LIMITATIONS
OF CROSS-CULTURAL RESEARCH
IN SOCIAL PSYCHOLOGY

DAVID M. MESSICK

As one of those social psychologists whose goal is to pose a challenge from the "mainstream," I have elected to argue a position that will not be popular with my cross-cultural colleagues—namely, that cross-cultural research has only a limited role in social psychology. I will argue that cross-cultural replications of social psychological experiments are probably unwise, and that there are sound reasons why cross-culturally inspired theoretical studies are scarce. By advancing this position, I hope to elicit from my cross-cultural colleagues the assumptions and presuppositions that they make regarding the proper conduct of social psychological research. If mainstream and cross-cultural social psychologists differ with regard to their goals or schemas about why we do research, then the position I will defend should highlight these differences and expose them to scrutiny. If our goals and assumptions about the proper conduct of research agree, then this position will provide a starting point for a dialogue about the ways in which cross-cultural research might influence social psychological research and vice versa.

Let me immediately deny that my position in this essay reflects xenophobia or hostility toward other cultures. I have lived and done experiments in different countries and I have found these experiences deeply rewarding. The question that I will deal with concerns the scientific status and value of cross-cultural research and not the benefits (and costs) of cross-cultural experiences.

THE GOAL OF SOCIAL PSYCHOLOGY

At the risk of being simplistic, let me propose that the goal of social psychology is to try to explain the regularities that we observe in social behavior. By regularities, I mean systematic observations, often obtained in experimental contexts, that constitute the empirical phenomena at issue. By explain, I mean we try to construct theories that go beyond our observations and that make the observations necessary consequences of the theory. I assume that the theories that we construct will be complicated and that it will be difficult to make specific predictions from them in real world settings. It is one thing to claim, for instance, that we are attracted to similar others (although even that apparently uncontroversial generalization is being questioned; Rosenbaum, 1986), but it is something completely different to predict how much attraction will be measured in a specific situation when a person of a particular description is exposed in some context to another person who is similar to some degree and in some particular way. Our theory tells us that the attraction will depend on a variety of factors and that we should be prepared to say, "It depends," with annoying frequency. This is not the fault, but rather the virtue of the theory.

THE ROLES OF
CROSS-CULTURAL RESEARCH

If one accepts this account of why it is that we do social psychological research, and in particular the assumption that we do it to build theories and not to construct catalogues of social psychological factlets, then we have a basis for thinking about how cross-cultural research fits into this process. I will suggest that there are two distinct roles that cross-cultural research can play. The first of these roles involves the assessment of the generality of empirical phenomena and the second involves the use of culture as a theoretical variable. With regard to the latter issue I will offer three suggestions as to why there seems to be so little cross-cultural research in mainstream social psychology.

Empirical generality. An obvious role for cross-cultural research is to assess the generalizability of the empirical phenomena that constitute the fundamental facts of a theory. Do people like similar others more than dissimilar others in Mombasa, Minsk, and Montevideo, as well as in Madison and Manhattan? Does social loafing occur in Tokyo, Tripoli, and Timbuctu? Does one find self-serving biases among peasants in Laos or El Salvador? In answering questions of this type, cross-cultural research can help to bracket the generality of the empirical foundations of our science.

The central question that we must keep before us is this: What is the value of such knowledge with regard to understanding the causes of the phenomenon? What is the social psychologist who is interested in egocentric biases, for instance, to make of the hypothetical fact that

Loatian farmers do not display the false consensus effect that seems as easy as baby fat to find among college students in the United States? Presumably, our social psychologist knows a number of factors that influence the strength of the effect, and she or he can probably specify conditions under which the effect will disappear. So what is the conceptual significance of the failure to find the effect among Laotian farmers? The answer to this question is likely to remain obscure for one simple reason—there are so many differences between U.S. undergraduates and Laotian farmers that it will be virtually impossible to attribute the difference in their responses to a specific factor or combination of factors.

This leads to my first conclusion. Using cross-cultural research to delimit the generality of an empirical relationship in a theoretically informative way is an unadvisable research strategy. (I must quickly confess that I have often ignored this conclusion; see, for instance, Samuelson, Messick, Rutte, and Wilke, 1984, or Liebrand, Messick, and Wolters, 1986.) If the phenomenon occurs in a different culture, one may be pleased at the robustness of the effect, but one must also conclude, at least with regard to the phenomenon at hand, that culture is unimportant. If the result does not replicate, on the other hand, the negative results could have a variety of possible causes. Thus the outcome of a cross-cultural replication is likely either to show that culture is unimportant for the phenomenon or to produce an uninterpretable result.

This first conclusion is based on an assumption that I want to make explicit. The assumption is that we do research to try to understand, to construct theories of the phenomena that we observe, not just to collect data. Documenting the ways in which people behave differently in different cultures is interesting and often very useful. It is important to know that what we call a house in English others call *casa* or *maison* or *huis,* and so on. In fact, foreign-language texts and dictionaries are among the most useful books that exist for helping a person from one culture understand the behavior of people in a different culture. However, I have never thought of my foreign-language dictionaries as a body of data that requires a social psychological theory. Likewise, while it is interesting and often useful to know that different cultures have different norms regarding promptness, honesty, nudity, or which side of the road on which to drive, these differences are not necessarily any more relevant to social psychological theory than the house-*maison* difference. Studies like the well-known paper by Feldman (1968) seem more like intercultural dictionaries of honesty and helpfulness than probes of social psychological theory.

Culture as theory. Cross-cultural research can also be used to evaluate hypotheses in which culture is a theoretical variable. I quickly confess that I am unfamiliar with much research of this type. On the other hand, I am familiar with the broad outlines, at least, of much of the research that has been done in mainstream social psychology in the past decade or so. From these two observations, I infer that research employing culture as a theoretical variable has not made conspicuous channels in the mainstream. If this inference is correct, one may ask why it is that cross-cultural work has not had a larger impact. One hypothesis that I will dismiss out of hand is that traditional social psychologists are hopelessly parochial and reject cross-cultural research because of provincial myopia. Most social psychologists with whom I am acquainted, both American and non-American, are sophisticated individuals with ecumenical interests. We need a better explanation. Maybe there are important reasons why the mainstream is not clogged with deep and revealing insights that derive from cross-cultural studies. Let me suggest three.

(1) Whatever the purpose of the research, whether it is for replication or to test cultural theories, cross-cultural research is more costly than research in a single location. The costs involve not only obvious factors like postage, increased number of subjects, standardization of procedures, translations, back-translations, and so on, but also more subtle difficulties entailed in maintaining coordination and timing with other research groups, resolving disputes about procedures, interpretations, and writing responsibilities, and providing support in terms of ideas and funding. The cost of cross-cultural research is certainly not a profound characteristic and it would be easy to underestimate its importance. Recall, however, that we all make cost-benefit tradeoffs in the way we allocate our time, and the real question is, what are the *incremental* benefits that we gain by doing cross-cultural research that justify the increased costs?

A similar point pertains to doing experiments with subject populations other than college students in the United States. For most experimenters, it is cheaper and more convenient to use college sophomores in their research than it is to employ factory workers, sales clerks, or pensioners. We can all share Sears's (1986) concern with the potential bias that may result from the nearly exclusive reliance on this narrow segment of the population, but few of us are likely to *do* anything about this concern until we have a good reason to.

(2) Not only are the costs of cross-cultural research greater than those of research in a single location, but cross-cultural findings are also more vulnerable to alternative interpretations than home-grown findings.

There are more ways to go wrong and to make mistakes. Good experimental design dictates the comparison of like with like and relies heavily on randomization. With most cross-cultural studies, subjects cannot be randomly assigned to cultures, and, as I noted earlier, it is nearly impossible to ensure that one and only one factor differs between cultures—to ensure, in other words, that like is being compared with like.

A recent controversy regarding the Sapir-Whorf hypothesis provides an excellent illustration of these problems. Bloom (1981) has argued that because the English language contains markers for counterfactual statements—the subjective—whereas Chinese does not, it would follow from the Sapir-Whorf hypothesis, the proposition that different languages cause people to think about and perceive their worlds differently, that English-speaking people would be better able to comprehend counterfactual stories than Chinese-speaking individuals. Consistent with this hypothesis, Bloom (1981) found that Chinese speakers were less likely to give counterfactual interpretations to a counterfactual story that they had read than were English speakers.

Au (1983, 1984), however, has called Bloom's conclusions into question. Au (1983) was critical of Bloom's work for a number of reasons, the most important of which were that Bloom did not use random assignment of subjects to linguistic conditions and that the story that the subjects read had been originally written in English and had then been translated, rather unidiomatically, according to Au, into Chinese. In Au's efforts to replicate Bloom's results, she used bilingual students in Hong Kong and randomly assigned students to read either an English or a Chinese version of the counterfactual story. She tried to ensure in addition that the two versions of the story were equally idiomatic. Under these conditions, Au found extremely high rates of correct interpretations of the story for both Chinese and English stories, and she found no differences at all between the two languages. In an interesting twist, Au had the idiomatic Chinese version of the story translated back into English by Chinese students whose translations were unidiomatic, and had those stories read by a sample of American high school students. The rate of correct interpretations dropped from nearly perfect in Chinese to slightly better than 50% with one of the English versions. Au's work suggests that it is the quality of the prose and perhaps the educational level of the reader that determine whether people will interpret a counterfactual story correctly, not the language in which the story is told.

The point of this is simply that it is probably easier to find intercultural differences than it is to prove that they have something important to do with cultural, or, in this instance, linguistic differences.

(3) The third issue concerns how culture is to be treated in social psychological theory. If culture is to be thought of as a psychological variable, what kind of variable is it? Cross-cultural experiments typically operationalize culture as an individual difference variable simply by using samples of subjects from different cultural categories or different countries. Such samples will generally differ from each other in a variety of ways, as I mentioned before. Even if subjects are students at universities in their respective countries, that very status signifies different things in different nations. In some countries, being a university student requires not only academic talent, but also political connectedness or conventionality. In other countries, university status indicates that a student is in the upper 2 or 3% of the academic distribution. In yet other places, university status implies a certain level of economic security. Like is not being compared with like and the interpretation of behavioral differences becomes a matter of conjecture. When cultural variables are implemented as individual difference variables, research outcomes are subject to all the ambiguities that plague research on individual differences within a culture (e.g., gender differences), plus a host of new ones.

One interesting recent experiment suggests a way around this problem. A study by Hoffman, Lau, and Johnson (1986) demonstrated how cross-cultural, or, specifically, cross-linguistic, hypotheses could be tested using random assignment of subjects (in part) to experimental conditions. As in the experiments of Au (1983), students who were bilingual in English and Chinese were randomly assigned to read personality descriptions of stimulus persons for which there was a label and, hence, presumably a schema or easily accessible concept either in Chinese (and not English) or in English (and not in Chinese). Hoffman et al. (1986) reported data that the schematic processing of the information was dependent on the language used. There was a greater tendency, for instance, for subjects to judge erroneously that they had seen information consistent with the personality descriptions when the language in which the subjects read the descriptions matched the language having the simple label for the personality. What this study did not demonstrate, however, is that the processing of person information is different in English and Chinese. What differed between cultures was the content of the easily coded personality types. The processing of information about the schemas seemed the same.

While most cross-cultural research views culture as an individual difference, it does not seem necessary to do so. To the extent that different norms or expectations for behavior characterize different cultures, one can presumably study the impact of cultures, that is, norms and expectations, on behavior within a single laboratory. Was it not Milgram's (1974) goal in his famous obedience studies to teach us something about the "culture" of the Third Reich? Sherif's (1936) early research on the autokinetic effect presumably told us something about how we are influenced by the norms implied by the behavior of others.

I am suggesting that it may be misleading to view cultural differences exclusively as differences between people rather than differences between the institutions, norms, or expectations that elicit different behavior patterns. The question of why different cultures have different norms and institutions is an interesting question, but it is a question that falls more into the domain of history and anthropology than social psychology. The fact that it is a legal norm for people to drive on the left side of the road in Great Britain creates many differences between the behavior of the British and other people. The opportunities for fatal confusions are great enough that many crosswalks in London warn visitors of the correct direction in which to look to spot oncoming traffic. For the sake of safety, it is important to appreciate this cultural difference, but it is unlikely that the difference manifests important social psychological qualities that differentiate the British from others.

This then leads to my second and final conclusion, which shall take the form of a prognosis. Cross-cultural research will have an impact in mainstream social psychology when the conceptual significance of cultural differences is understood well enough to allow hypotheses about psychological processes to be phrased in cultural terms, and when the hypotheses cannot be evaluated more easily and precisely intraculturally. Until that time, cultural differences are likely to remain of the "we say house, they say *maison*; we drive on the right, they drive on the left" variety, and such differences are unlikely to alter the current of the mainstream.

5

SOCIAL SCIENCE AND SOCIAL PSYCHOLOGY
The Cross-Cultural Link

WILLIAM K. GABRENYA, Jr.

DOONESBURY. © 1986 G. B. Trudeau. Reprinted with permission of Universal Press Syndicate. All rights reserved.

AUTHOR'S NOTE: I would like to thank Bruce J. Biddle, Michael H. Bond, and Samuel Karson for reviewing earlier versions of this chapter. Errors, outrageous statements, and deficiencies that remain are my own.

North American social psychology and Michael Doonesbury have much in common: They are white, middle class, educated, idealistic (but practical), likable, interesting. They are also naive, culturally pristine, politically ineffectual, and out of touch with social processes that are bigger than themselves. They seem to inhabit a charmed world that only occasionally intersects with the many other worlds on this planet. Their responses to these intersections, rare as they may be, are predictably disconcerting.

In this chapter I will attempt to demonstrate how social psychology can break its sociocultural insularity and come into a viable interaction with other cultural and intellectual worlds. My dual thesis is that this liberation can be accomplished by establishing a close and continuing relationship with the social sciences, and that one way such a relationship can be developed is through an intermediary, a "culture broker" as it were: cross-cultural psychology. (See Jahoda, 1986, for a discussion of other ways that cross-cultural psychology can aid in straightening out social psychology.) I will discuss some existing social psychological theorizing that can contribute to this relationship, and I will attempt to dismiss a few of the misgivings that social psychologists might have in coming into contact with the uncertainties of other worlds. Finally, I will offer an antithesis to the second part of my thesis: that social psychology (and Mike Doonesbury) are the products of material forces on which this chapter, indeed this book, can have little impact.

THESIS: SOCIAL PSYCHOLOGY
NEEDS THE SOCIAL SCIENCES

Two Insularities

A growing number of psychologists have railed against psychology's and social psychology's cultural insularity and isolation from the social sciences. Early charges of this sort came during the "Crisis" years, most often from individuals I respectfully refer to as the "deviants" of our discipline: Gergen (1973), Moscovici (1972), Pepitone (1976), and others. Despite the waning of the Crisis, criticism along the same lines continues:

Social psychologists seem to be deliberately insulating themselves from clinical, sociological, anthropological, and a variety of other sources of knowledge about human behavior.... The administrative functions of a department serve to preserve what may be outmoded disciplinary identities and inappropriately compartmentalized research. (R. Jones, 1986, p. 537)

Concerns such as these have become increasingly widespread, and seem to have penetrated the inner circle of establishment psychology (e.g., Kennedy, Scheirer, & Rogers, 1984; Spence, 1985).

Effects of Insularity

Many psychologists have commented on the nature and effects of this broad charge of insularity. I will briefly summarize these earlier comments and point out how these problems are at least in part a result of social psychology's isolation from the social sciences.

A value laden science. One point of view is that social psychology is too wrapped up in what it is doing to consider the relationship between its enterprise and the social milieu in which it exists (Hogan & Elmer, 1978; R. Jones, 1986; Pepitone, 1981; Sampson, 1977, 1981; Spence, 1985). The effect of American individualism on American psychology has received the most attention. "American psychology, invented in and by American society, went on to invent its subject matter: the self-contained individual" (Sarason, 1981, pp. 835-836). Pepitone (1981) notes how the values of psychology as a whole—empiricism, objectivism, behaviorism, operationalism, reductionism, materialism, mechanism, universalism, and individualism—have in turn shaped social psychology, particularly its individuocentric treatment of group dynamics. The charge that psychology is value-laden has led to the development of a literature on the issue of values in psychological science, and has encouraged many psychologists to take positions on the issue (see Fiske & Shweder, 1986). Spence (1985) and others have noted that a better understanding of our own cultural values might alert us to our biases and help us overcome them. I see this concern as a very healthy sign that psychology is less naive about its relationship to society and more aware of the relevance of the philosophy of science to what it is doing. I believe that additional contact with the social sciences in which these issues are continually debated, especially sociology, will encourage more such debate within psychology. Psychology may be one of the few social or behavioral sciences that does not emphasize philosophy of science in its graduate training (Hogan & Elmer, 1978), pointing to a traditional lack of disagreement among psychologists on such basic issues.

Incomplete, imbalanced range of phenomena. Several critics have pointed out that social psychology has failed to study some important areas of social life, such as religion, social class, and political economy, but has expended considerable energy in other areas, particularly those involving "cool" cognition such as consistency theory, attribution theory, person perception, and much of what falls under the general category "social cognition" (e.g., Latane, 1986; Sarason, 1981; Sears, 1986). Along somewhat the same lines as Carlson (1984), Sarason (1981) charges that social psychology is insufficiently social: "Social psychology had never come to grips with the history, culture, and organization of American society" (p. 832). He blames this problem on psychology's individualistic bias. I would extend this explanation to include the deep rift between psychology and the social sciences that work with issues such as religion, social class, culture, and organizations at a higher level of analysis and with different methods than those in psychology.

Sarason's (1981) point about an "asocial psychology" is made in the context of charges that clinical psychology's imitation of post-World War II psychiatry is misdirected. He blames this misdirection in part on social psychology. He claims that if social psychology had been more social it would have been the basis for a clinical psychology that might have taken a nonpsychiatric course, emphasizing primary prevention (Albee, 1986) and the social determinants of maladjustment, and possessing the capacity to work effectively within the political environment to formulate public policies to aid this effort. Since clinical psychology may be the major area of application of social psychological concepts (see Weary & Mirels, 1982), social psychology's insularity, asocial nature, or incompleteness can have broad implications outside of the laboratory (R. Jones, 1986).

Generalizability. A third effect of insularity is to reduce the external validity or generalizability of social psychological findings and theories. Sears (1986) and Findley and Cooper (1981) have demonstrated the extent to which social psychologists study college student "subjects" in laboratory settings. Few social psychology studies systematically explore the generalizability of theories to other populations within this society, despite evidence that the theories do not necessarily generalize (e.g., Biddle, Warneke, & Petty, in press). This issue has given cross-cultural psychologists a sense of mission, and they have made a ministry of pointing out how the cross-cultural method can aid in enhancing external validity within and across cultures (e.g., Brislin, 1980). The problem runs deeper than merely performing replications in exotic places, however. Psychological *theories* lack external validity in the sense that they fail to include "hooks" to variables that are usually outside of social psychology's individual-oriented "family" of variables

(Pepitone, 1976). Pepitone suggests that increased interaction with social science would provide social psychology access to the families of variables with which they customarily work, including ecological, economic, and sociopolitical conceptions.

Crippled research programs. Spence (1985) and others have pointed out that psychologists tend to bury themselves in their data and lose track of the larger issues to which their research speaks. On the one hand, this tendency may be a result of the individualistic value-bias that has received considerable attention over the past decade. However, I suspect that it is also due to a great extent to the proclivity of social psychologists to be oblivious to the relationship of their research to that of the social sciences. Sometimes this naivete leads to seriously crippled research programs, such as the gaming research that was popular during the Vietnam War. As E. Jones (1985) points out, this (voluminous) research has been severely criticized for trying to apply laboratory bargaining studies performed with individuals to real-world conflict among nation-states (e.g., see Pepitone, 1976, 1981). Social psychology wanted to help out, to change the world, but did not have the tools to do so.

Triviality of effects. A recurring criticism of social psychology from the Crisis era to the present has been that its research effects account for little variance, can be obtained only by "running" unacquainted subjects in sterile laboratory settings, and are often merely demonstrations of already-accepted hypotheses (e.g., Chapanis, 1967; Jahoda, 1979; McGuire, 1973; Triandis, 1975). Dissonance theory has been a favorite target. These and other critics (e.g., Hogan & Elmer, 1978; Pepitone, 1981; Secord, 1986) have suggested that a more complex array of variables must be considered if behavior is to be understood and predicted, including social structure, social roles, situations, normative systems, historical change, and so on. These are not variables that can be used without learning something about their century-long development in sociology, anthropology, and other social sciences. Proper consideration of such variables should also have an appropriate humbling effect: Much of social psychology may be viewed as working with more "residual variability," observable only after the large effects of these other variables have been hidden through experimental controls.

The psychology of the American people. Some social psychologists have noted that social psychology is essentially a very odd way of doing anthropological, ethnographic research (e.g., Laundauer, in D'Andrade, 1986), that it is implicitly a psychology of the American people (Bond, 1986). Bond points out that research on the Chinese is explicitly or implicitly comparative with the West or the United States, but that U.S.

research is "innocent of historical or cultural overlay" (p. 217). U.S. psychology seems unaware of the anthropological nature of its work. I suggest that an ongoing, interactive relationship with anthropology would help remedy this situation.

Getting Worse?

Two decades after the beginning of social psychology's Crisis, there are indications that the field is becoming more insular rather than less so. One unfortunate development is the infusion of personality concepts into social psychology (Carlson, 1984). Despite the work of the interactionists in the personality area, personality is still viewed as a dispositional, internal construct that resides in individuals, not collectivities (Sampson, 1981), and its growing presence in social psychology leads to a more individuocentric focus that promotes insularity. A second problematic development is the social cognition movement, which might be viewed as an heir to the Crisis. In its attempt to develop a rigorous, universalistic social psychology, the social cognition group has brought to social psychology an even lower unit of analysis deep inside the organism, and has promoted cultural and disciplinary insularity to a greater extent than any other single development. The Crisis also seems to have encouraged an interest in applied social psychology and "relevance." Whereas this is a good sign, it is disturbing to note that social psychology seems to "spin off" these areas (e.g., Proshansky, 1976), maintaining a core that is relatively narrow.

THESIS: CULTURE BROKERING

The second part of this chapter's dual thesis is that cross-cultural psychology can act as a culture broker to help bring social psychology in contact with social science and the psychologies of other societies.

Geography Lessons

A culture broker must share many of the characteristics of the cultures it seeks to broker. Cross-cultural psychology's position between social psychology, social science, and the psychologies of other societies enables it to perform this culture broker rule. One way that this intermediate position of cross-cultural psychology can be assessed is to examine the citation practices of individuals publishing in psychology, social science, and cross-cultural journals. Citation patterns may indicate several interesting things about journal article authors, including what journals they read or at least scan for relevant papers, the extent to which their research interests are similar to those of members of the scientific subdisciplines the cited journals serve, and the extent to which various subdisciplines offer theoretical or methodological approaches deemed useful or appropriate.

A content analysis of 3,305 journal references in 177 papers recently appearing in the *Journal of Personality and Social Psychology* (JPSP), the *Journal of Cross-Cultural Psychology* (JCCP), *Ethos,* the *American Anthropologist,* and the *American Sociological Review* was performed for this chapter. The cultural insularity of mainstream social psychology was illustrated in the lower percentage of foreign journals cited by *JPSP* (3%) than by *JCCP* (10%) or the three social science journals (6, 10, and 4%). Its isolation from the social sciences is evident in the percentage of social science journals cited by *JPSP* (10%), in contrast to *JCCP* (21%) and the social science journals (47, 65, and 68%).

Theory and Practice

One means by which cross-cultural psychology can perform a culture broker function is through the diffusion of its theoretical and methodological practices into mainstream social psychology. At the theoretical level, cross-cultural psychologists must, due to the phenomena they study, be sensitive to variables normally in the purview of social science. They find it important to tie social and personality variables to social structural variables and often to the ecological and economic variables that in turn underlie social structure. The outstanding example of this research approach is Berry's (1976) study of the relationships among ecology, social structure, acculturation to the West, psychological differentiation, and conformity in 17 culture groups. Cross-cultural psychologists must also be sensitive to subcultural variations, since these differences are often as important as differences between nation-states. A well-known example of this kind of research is the Lambert, Hamers, and Fraser-Smith (1979) study. These investigators found that parental child-rearing values are nearly as often a function of social class as of nationality in a study of 10 ethnic groups around the world. Consideration of these cultural, subcultural, and structural variables leads cross-cultural psychologists to be more explicit about the "scope conditions" (Jahoda, 1979; Sell & Martin, 1983; Walker & Cohen, 1985) of their hypotheses—their degree of external and construct validity—than are social psychologists. Cross-cultural psychology, almost by definition, must consider the variables—at any level of analysis—that constrain the generality of its findings. Put more strongly, cross-cultural psychologists cannot afford to be naive about the limiting conditions of their theoretical statements.

Cross-cultural psychology may be an ideal broker in reducing social psychology's cultural insularity through its concern with particular cultures. Cross-cultural psychology is necessarily tied to specific cultures in two ways. First, since most cross-cultural psychologists are working in part in cultures other than their own, they must reconcile their scientific, possibly ethnocentric or value-biased interpretations of the causes and meanings of the behaviors they observe with those of the people they are studying. Traditional social psychologists, however, working as they do almost exclusively with their own children (i.e., white, middle-class college sophomores), need not grapple with this problem and can safely make assumptions about the phenomenological experiences of their subjects (ultimately producing culturally bound theories). Cross-culturalists are forced to think in a more culturally "decentered" or nonethnocentric manner, and can in turn pass the insights gained through this exercise, if not the decenteredness itself, on to their colleagues. Second, cross-cultural psychologists must be aware of—or, better yet, *expert in*—the local conditions of all the people they are studying, approximating anthropologists' "area" specializations (but see Doob, 1980, and the "sin of opportunism"). (Social psychologists are of course true experts in the local conditions of their own research.) Cross-culturalists, by being forced to be aware of the local conditions in which they work, must have a far broader understanding of both their own and other cultures. The diffusion of this cultural sensitivity to social psychology, although good in its own right, imbues social psychology with content normally found only in the social sciences.

The challenge to social psychology is to develop the right hooks to social and cultural variables, many of which are outside of the individual level of analysis. Theory development, I feel, should "get grander" than it has been for many years, and the new theories should explicitly include the places where culture has an effect and where individual volitional behavior interfaces with social structure. A good example of an attempt to insert cultural hooks in attribution theory can be found in Bond (1983), in which he lists five ways in which cultural variables can affect attributional processes. Triandis (Chap. 10, this volume) performs a similar analysis at a somewhat higher level.

Course Work

The act of teaching or taking a course in cross-cultural psychology inevitably brings both instructor and students into closer contact with the social sciences.

Something for the teacher. From the instructor's point of view, the preparation of a comprehensive cross-cultural psychology course can be a minitour of social science. The beauty of cross-cultural psychology is that it has no real boundaries. Ideally, the instructor should have a passable understanding of elementary cultural anthropology and a better knowledge of psychological anthropology, including culture and personality studies, cognitive anthropology, cross-cultural anthropology (i.e., hologeisic research), and transcultural psychiatry. On the psychology side, teaching such a course encourages generalism because the research covers a wide range of subdisciplinary areas, such as perception, cognition, child development, social psychology, personality and values, group interaction, and clinical psychology. An indeterminable number of specific topics ranging throughout the social sciences can be included in such a course, including ethnicity and ethnic groups, social class, intercultural communication, sojourner adjustment, psychological assessment, poverty, immigration, bilingualism, and so on. Psychological and anthropological principles must be integrated, and theoretical approaches must be identified to perform these integrations.

Teaching such a course, more so perhaps than performing cross-cultural research in any particular area, forces the instructor to think like a social scientist rather than a psychologist, and to view psychology in a much broader manner. Taken-for-granted value biases within psychology are readily apparent when psychology is placed in context with the social sciences, and the (comparatively small) degree to which psychological processes contribute to the course of history becomes clear.

Something for the student. Much of what I have said about the instructor's experience also holds true for students taking a course in cross-cultural psychology. However, whereas the typical cross-cultural psychology course instructor is already among "the Chosen," the students probably are not. By taking such a course, students gain the broader perspective that the instructor has already discovered in preparing the course, and an eye-opening bonus—a sensitivity to culture and an understanding of the place of psychology in relation to the social sciences. My experience is that many students come out of such a course seeing "culture" everywhere they look, highly sensitized to certain features of their own society, and more understanding of others. What in psychology seemed reasonable, necessary, and obvious is a little less so, and they take some basic or hidden assumptions in psychology a little less for granted.

Clinical psychology is somewhat ahead of other areas of psychology in this regard. The Vail Conference in which the Doctor of Psychology (Psy.D.) clinical-practitioner model of professional training was developed recognized the unmet mental health service needs of ethnic U.S. populations and called for training in these areas. A small but growing number of clinical programs, including my own, offer or require courses related to cross-cultural psychology (Bernal & Padilla, 1982). A cross-cultural instructor in a Psy.D. program has a unique opportunity to circumvent the social research → clinical research → clinical application process by directly impressing upon clinical students the importance of structural, cultural, and subcultural variables to their profession. I believe such an instructor has a responsibility to "demystify" students concerning clinical psychology's relationship to the society in which it operates, perhaps in so doing supplying clinical psychology the tools it needs to move in some of the directions Sarason (1981) favors.

Brokering by Doing

Cross-cultural psychology may have an integrating effect through the kinds of behaviors that cross-cultural psychologists naturally perform if they are active in the area.

Brokering people. Since cross-cultural research is exceedingly difficult and must normally be performed collaboratively, cross-cultural psychologists must maintain contacts with psychologists in other parts of the world. A recent example of such collaboration is the work of the Chinese Culture Connection (1987), 23 psychologists who worked together to perform a 22-nation study of Michael Bond's Chinese Values Survey. Collaboration of this sort on the part of cross-cultural psychologists in psychology departments reduces psychology's cultural insularity and leads to a cross-fertilization of ideas that aids all involved. Cross-cultural psychologists become, in a sense, transnational brokers of personal contacts and ideas; conduits, if you will.

License to deviate. Cross-cultural psychologists are deviants within their discipline, or, as Cole (1984, p. 1000) puts it, cross-cultural psychology is a "slightly miscreant stepchild" of psychology. Many cross-cultural psychologists have found niches within establishment psychology, and as such psychology has given a deviant subgroup license to work in-between, in the areas that fall outside of psychology or on the boundaries of several disciplines. Cross-cultural psychologists in such situations have the freedom and perhaps the responsibility to read and be otherwise active throughout the social sciences, acting as intellectual culture brokers, bringing to each something of the other.

SOME STRATEGIES FOR INTEGRATION

I have argued that social psychology needs increased integration with the social sciences and that cross-cultural psychology can aid in performing this integration. It would be difficult and possibly inappropriate to map out precisely what an "integrated social psychology" would look like. However, some general features can be discussed. An integrated social psychology would not be cross-cultural psychology, at least as the latter area currently exists. I see cross-cultural psychology as a go-between, not a goal, for social psychology. An integrated social psychology would develop theories of broad scope with explicitly formulated hooks to society and culture (e.g., Triandis, Chap. 10, this volume). Whereas it might investigate many of the current social and interpersonal phenomena, it would do so in a manner that recognizes and assesses the broadest possible set of variables that determine these phenomena historically and contemporaneously. Pepitone (1976, 1981) has suggested three families of variables, in addition to individual-oriented psychology, that social psychology should incorporate in its theorizing: sociocultural, ecological, and biological.

Structural Symbolic Interactionism

By "structural symbolic interactionism" I refer to Sheldon Stryker's (1980, 1985) social structural version of symbolic interactionism. In this theoretical synthesis he attempts to combine what he views as the best of classic symbolic interactionism (Blumer, 1969) and of role theory (Biddle, 1979). As I interpret Stryker's theory, he seeks to account for both the "improvisational" and the "impositional" natures of human social behavior. Symbolic interactionism emphasizes the improvisational aspect of behavior—spontaneous, volitional, and undetermined—and recognizes the constraints society places on this behavior through the mechanisms of the socially constructed self. Although symbolic interactionism and psychological social psychology differ in the former's emphasis on free will, social interaction, and societal influences, the approaches are not too far apart in their attention to individual actors as the immediate and interesting source of behavior.

Role theory presents the impositional view of human behavior. A variety of flavors of role theory have been developed in the last century (see Biddle, 1986), all of which have in common an attempt to describe and understand behavior from a "top-down" point of view. Persons are located within a matrix of social positions that are created, for the most part, by the social system, and behavior is regulated by the expectations society (i.e., individuals in other social positions) places on people in positions. House (1977) locates role theory within the "psychological sociology" version of social psychology, thereby emphasizing role theory's intermittent interest in the relationship between social positions and personality.

I suspect psychological social psychology's aversion to role theory is due in part to its seemingly static nature. By viewing people as virtual automatons in an incredibly complex machinery of interacting social positions, little is left for a social psychology of the individual. Of course, behavior may indeed be best explained by structural considerations (Pepitone, 1976, 1981; Triandis, 1975), and psychological social psychology may be working with only residual variation. On the other hand, this picture of role theory is incomplete since it is the cognitive and affective processes of individuals that link social structural role positions with people's actual behavior, and these processes are subject to traditional social psychological analysis. Biddle (1979) presents such an analysis, attempting to demonstrate how the existing theory and research of both the sociological and the psychological social psychologies contribute to an understanding of role theory.

The strength of Stryker's theory is in attempting to account for both the regularity and the diversity of social behavior, or what the psychological anthropologist Wallace (1970) terms the "replication of uniformity" and "organization of diversity" approaches to understanding personality and culture. Pepitone's (1976) call for a more normative social psychology—one that takes account of the stable norms and social constraints on social behavior—echoes Stryker's position. An integrated social psychology might adopt Stryker's general approach to incorporating individual and sociocultural variables, possibly substituting its own motivational conceptualizations for those of symbolic interactionism.

Ecological Approaches

As I interpret them, ecological or materialist approaches to behavior share four emphases or principles: (1) objects and events exist and affect behavior and culture both independently and in conjunction with their subjective or phenomenological representations; (2) humans are essentially rational; (3) the objective environment presents rational humans with contingencies to which (4) their behaviors and cultural institutions are more-or-less rational adaptions (Harris, 1979; LeVine, 1973; McArthur & Baron, 1983). An integrated social psychology must look beyond the relationship between individual behavior and sociocultural variables to the ecological or material conditions underlying society and culture on the one hand, and social settings or situations on the other. Pointing again to its broader function, ecological approaches are not new to cross-cultural psychology. Many cross-cultural psychologists have explicitly adopted models developed from Whiting (Whiting & Whiting, 1975) that follow a materialist logic yet deemphasize the Whiting/Kardiner "projective system" (e.g., Berry, 1976; Yang, 1981). The strongest ecological statements at present comes from anthropology, although social psychology has begun to show some interest in the approach.

Cultural materialism. The Whiting and cross-cultural ecological models have much in common with the theorizing of the brilliant and controversial anthropologist Marvin Harris. Harris's (1968, 1979) theory of cultural materialism is a positivist, nondialectical materialism derived for the most part from the sociologist Marx and the anthropologist Leslie White (White, 1959). More a strategy or approach than a formal theory, Harris seeks to demystify cultural practices by demonstrating their origin in structural or infrastructural conditions. It is through demystification that an approach such as Harris's can aid social psychology. Social psychology's location of the source of behavior within the individual and its inattention to the normative or social structures within which behavior occurs contributes to what Harris labels "cognitive idealism" and LeVine (1973) terms the "psychological reductionist" school of culture-and-personality. In misplacing the ultimate source of behavior, cognitive idealism has serious implications for applied psychology, particularly clinical, as it encourages holding people rather than social, cultural, political, and economic conditions responsible for their problems. Likewise, Sampson (1981), taking more a materialist than a dialectical approach, points out how American cognitive psychology has adopted a cognitive idealist position and, to the extent that it is accepted as scientific truth within the discipline and by the lay public, can be viewed as a form of ideology through its rationalization of the status quo.

Ecology in social psychology. McArthur and Baron's (1983) ecological theory of social perception may stand as a landmark in bringing ecological thinking (back) into social psychology. Their concern is with the ecological basis of the behavior of individuals, in contrast to Harris's emphasis on the development of social institutions. Of particular interest is their analysis of perceptual error, in which they point out the inherent rationality and adaptability of seemingly erroneous judgments. It is too soon to determine, however, whether their pioneering work will have an impact on mainstream social psychology.

Dialectics, Values, and Alternatives

An objection to psychological social psychology's "getting involved" with social science might be that sociological social psychology is antipositivistic or that the social sciences are bogged down in irreconcilable epistemological conflicts originating in value biases rather than scientific methods. However, as many social psychologists have recently pointed out, these same issues have now come social psychology's way. A fairly comprehensive discussion of these problems can be found in Fiske and Shweder's (1986) *Metatheory in Social Science*, an excellent volume that illustrates the variety of positions that can be taken. I believe that the only alternative for an integrated social psychology is the moderate position taken by Harris (1979), Spence (1985), Jahoda (1986), and others that recognizes the problem of value biases but rejects radical relativism and dialectics. Harris (1979) takes a "strongly moderate" position, pointing out the superiority of Western science, the advantage of etic analysis, and the deleterious effects dialectical philosophy has had on materialism (i.e., Marxists-Leninism).

> We must recognize that there are many ways of knowing, but we must also recognize that it is not mere ethnocentric puffery to assert that science is a way of knowing that has a unique transcendent value for all human beings. (p. 27)

ANTITHESIS: LITTLE WILL CHANGE

I would like to point out several reasons why I believe that journal articles, chapters, and books such as this one will have little impact on social psychology. I will discuss several somewhat complementary reasons for expecting this lack of efficacy on our part: material, disciplinary, and cognitive.

Reward Structure

An integrated social psychology, were it to flourish, would require more careful theoretical work on the one hand, and research in a variety of settings with many types of participants on the other. The present reward contingencies, particularly publication pressures, at both the predoctoral and pretenure career phases both impede theory development (Carlson, 1984; Wachtel, 1980) and constrain the kinds of phenomena we can study (Hogan & Elmer, 1978; Sears, 1986). The effects of these contingencies on the development of cross-cultural psychology, where research is difficult to perform, are easy to see. Levine (1984) vividly, and with a sense of humor often associated with hindsight, describes some of the difficulties he experienced in his pace-of-life research (Levine & Bartlett, 1984). Cross-cultural studies take years to set up and perform, and a variety of pitfalls not encountered in social psychology must be avoided. Untenured assistant professors cannot afford the slow pace of cross-cultural research when they must compete with faculty who publish several refereed papers each year.

Pioneers in a changing social psychology would also encounter the funding problem faced by cross-cultural psychologists. Although cross-cultural research is expensive, neither social science nor behavioral science agencies are likely to fund projects that fall in-between, outside of the mainstreams of each area.

Disciplinary Considerations

An integrated social psychology would be much broader than present psychological social psychology in two ways: It would take into account the work of other disciplines, and it would work with a wider range of social phenomena. The informational overload that interdisciplinary awareness might produce is considerable.

Psychological social psychology is already a large subdiscipline in which few social psychologists read outside their own interest areas. Informal or semiformal networks (sometimes termed "mutual admiration societies") are common, and may be viewed as incipient subdisciplines. I suspect social psychology has reached the limits of its growth as a single subdiscipline of psychology, and that it would fly apart if more breadth were asked of it.

The fractionation of social psychology runs counter to what I hope to see, and may be avoided in two ways. First, the kind of theorizing that would be performed might help reduce the amount of information to be handled by placing it within encompassing theoretical interpretations.

Phenomena and lines of research might be found to be similar and interchangeable. For example, at a midrange level of theorizing within social psychology, Fishbein and Ajzen's (1975) analysis of attitudes provided an overarching conceptualization that reduced the complexity and disorganization of the area. At a higher level of analysis, Harris (1979) has attempted to apply his cultural materialist approach to making sense of a variety of otherwise disparate and irreconcilable social and psychological phenomena. The challenge to grand theory, of course, is to keep all levels of analysis, from individual to sociocultural, in equal focus.

A technological fix to the fractionation problem might be available in the form of computer technology that allows researchers to access easily a large amount of information throughout the social and behavioral sciences from their desktops. The CD-ROM (a laser disk storage medium), with its immense capacity, is a current example of such a technology, and is currently being used to store the *Psychological Abstracts* database (12 years of abstracts on two disks; American Psychological Association, 1986). The CD-ROM type of technology may be for social science theory what mainframe computers and statistical packages were for empirical research. While it is true that desktop access to hundreds of journals in dozens of languages would in itself produce a massive overload, analogous to the mound of computer printouts that every data analysis seems to build, I expect that we will learn to sift through this information as efficiently as we have learned to excavate our mounds of printouts. Grand theory and careful synthesis would also help. The imbalance of "*activity* at the expense of *thought*" (Wachtel, 1980, p. 399) brought on in part, I suspect, by the trivially simple analysis of complex data made possible by the technological innovations of the 1960s may be redressed by trivially simple access to a world of ideas made possible by the technological innovations of the 1980s.

Problems of communication among social scientists who speak different languages would also stand between social psychology and integration, particularly the incorporation of ideas from other culturally indigenous psychologies (Berry, 1978). Smith (1978) has noted the decline of language requirements in graduate schools; this trend has yet to reverse. The experience of cross-cultural psychology is instructive here, in that the best research is collaborative and requires the interaction of individuals with a bewildering variety of linguistic backgrounds (e.g., the Chinese Culture Connection, 1987). However, psychologists who do not speak the universal language of cross-cultural psychology—English—rarely come to the attention of the discipline.

Materialism and Disciplinary Development

The materialist or economic approach (e.g., Harris) can be used to understand changes in interests, methods, and theoretical approaches in scientific disciplines and their subdisciplines. Some analyses of psychology are consistent with a materialist approach. House (1977) pointed out the relationships between the theoretical approaches of sociology, sociological social psychology, and psychological social psychology, and their competing positions within academia during the late nineteenth and early twentieth centuries. Sarason (1981) outlined how events following World War II shaped modern clinical psychology, and E. Jones (1985) traced modern social psychology to events associated with the war. Finison (1986) argued that the Society for the Psychological Study of Social Issues was born of the Depression. Likewise, greater tolerance of intermarriage, easier travel, changes in immigration laws, historical events, and communication technology are influences bearing on cross-cultural psychology from the outside that are not under our control.

This analysis suggests that the major change in social psychology advocated here will not occur without appropriate societal or personal events. For example, Cole (1984) suggested that little change will occur in psychology's cultural insularity "until events force even more attention to be paid to the international sphere as a source of important social knowledge" (p. 1001). These events seem to be shaping and energizing cross-cultural psychology; the extent to which they and unforeseen others contribute to an integrated social psychology is yet to be seen.

Cognitive Ecology

As material conditions affect the development of scientific disciplines, the "cognitive ecology" of scientists may influence their overall perspectives on their craft. By "cognitive ecology" I mean the day-to-day intellectual work environment in which scientists develop hypotheses and plan and implement and interpret their research. The reward structure, both material and social, experienced by social psychologists promotes narrowly defined research programs that produce short-term studies employing readily available respondents. This situation in turn presents social psychologists with a cognitive ecology that includes intense attention to the fine details of laboratory manipulations and to the phenomenological experience of American middle-class college sophomores.

There are two ways that this ecology may affect psychologists' perspectives. The rational, adaptive social psychologist must immerse him- or herself in the narrow variability of lab and subject. Such allocation of finite cognitive resources to the minutiae of a research program precludes an active and ongoing consideration of larger sociocultural questions, leading the social psychologist to feel that these questions are the concern of a different discipline. The less empirical, sociological social psychologists may have an advantage in being less concerned with the details of empirical research, and more at leisure to consider these broader issues.

The second effect of social psychologists' cognitive ecology is on what they find interesting, important, and personally relevant in their research. The scientist who focuses on human variation within a highly restricted range may come to find this variation interesting and relevant to daily life, even if it had not been so at the outset. This attitude change may occur because (1) the researched variation is a subset of the restricted but personally relevant natural variation within which the scientist lives as a member of his or her society, (2) it becomes highly familiar, or (3) the scientist faces a difficult and stimulating challenge in trying to control and understand it. Although this effect of ecology on preferences is functional and adaptive in reconciling affect with required behavior (connoting a dissonance process or a value-socialization process; Parsons, 1951), and certainly motivates the scientist to work hard, it is dysfunctional in that it severely limits the scope of the theories he or she develops. Spence (1985) recognized the tendency of psychologists to get lost in their research:

> Psychologists have been overly prone to bury themselves in the data from laboratory and other contrived, constricted situations and to lose track of the broader questions that initially sent them there. The result may be bodies of data and theories spun around them that are relevant only to arcane laboratory paradigms and are ultimately sterile or trivial. (p. 1286)

RECONCILIATION

Reconciling a deterministic view of the development of social psychology with the seemingly volitional attempt of a growing number of people to change the discipline is difficult, unless these attempts are themselves viewed, certainly unsatisfactorily, within the same determined system. Such a synthesis will not be attempted here. Harris's (1979) solution to this dilemma is to back away from absolute infrastructural or structural determinism, and suggest that superstructural elements such as ideology have effects on infrastructure and structure that serve to maintain the cultural system. He goes somewhat further in distinguishing between "system-maintaining" and "system-transforming" values, the former serving the status quo, the latter contributing to its alteration. System-transforming values originate in the contradictions of the system. For example, concerning U.S. poverty, "Material pauperization and exploitation breed not only apathy but also anger and revolutionary zeal" (p. 303).

Social psychology and social science have developed considerable contradictions since the brighter era of the 1950s and 1960s (Converse, 1986; Shweder & Fiske, 1986). My hope is that an awareness of the limitations of social psychology, along with an understanding of the powerful forces that have shaped it and that maintain its present state, will generate appropriate system-transforming values in response to these contradictions. Cross-cultural psychology may strengthen these values through its behavior as a culture broker and through direct agitation in volumes such as this one. Perhaps through these efforts an integrated social psychology will develop, and social psychology/Mike Doonesbury will reach out to the other worlds with which it has heretofore had little knowledge and contact.

6

WILL SOCIETAL MODERNIZATION EVENTUALLY ELIMINATE CROSS-CULTURAL PSYCHOLOGICAL DIFFERENCES?

KUO-SHU YANG

Modernization at the societal level is the process involved in a particular kind of basic institutional transformation. It represents an unprecedented development of social institutions or systems, a change that will lead to a fundamental transformation in our way of life. Modernization, while overlapping with industrial revolution, is distinguishable from industrialization, a process relating economic development to manufacturing and the technical skills required (Apter, 1965). It is by no means justifiable, however, to analyze modernization exclusively in economic terms. Economic modernization, as defined by Ward and Rustow (1964), includes intense application of scientific technology and inanimate sources of energy, high specialization of labor and interdependence of impersonal markets, large-scale financing and concentration of economic decision making, and rising levels of material well-being. Modernization encompasses, but is far more than, economic development, including many changes that fall outside the strictly economic domain (Morse, 1969).

It is also impossible to understand modernization fully in terms of political development, although the latter is an essential facet of the former. According to Huntington (1966), political modernization is composed of three major processes: the replacement of a large number of traditional authorities by a single national political authority, the emergence of new political functions that must be managed by new administrative hierarchies chosen on the basis of achievement rather than ascription, and increased participation in politics by social groups throughout society, along with the development of new institutions such as political parties and interest groups to organize this participation. All these processes constitute important elements of overall modernization, but they are not equivalent to this pervasive societal change.

While societal modernization includes both economic and political development, it also has some other important features, especially those pertaining to the sociocultural domain. Particularly relevant are those aspects that are mainly related to changes in education, occupation, religion, urbanization, and communication. Sociocultural changes are reflected in such processes as the expansion of education, the diversification of occupations, the secularization of religion, the intensification of urbanization, and the development of mass communications. All these significant changes, which are neither economic nor political, define what may be called sociocultural modernization.

Societal modernization may thus be defined as a complex syndrome of interrelated economic, political, and sociocultural changes in a society. Or it may be said to be composed of economic modernization, political modernization, and sociocultural modernization. Societal modernization in this sense is a global phenomenon in the contemporary world, originating in Western Europe centuries ago. Since then, it has spread to the rest of the world—first to the other areas of Europe, then to America and Oceania, and finally to Asia and Africa. By now, modernization has induced social change even in small, peripheral societies (for example, see Chirot, 1976).

While Western societies began to be modernized at an earlier date than did non-Western societies, societal modernization represents a revolutionary change in the institutional pattern for all the peoples of the world. All societies are being transformed in the same general direction, for modernization is the latest stage in the history of humankind aiming at a better life in a better society. It is *new* to all societies, Western and non-Western. The major modern features created by such a new process cannot be found in traditional Western societies any more than they can in traditional non-Western ones. It is in this sense that modernization is not Westernization in its strict and narrow sense—the acceptance of traditionally Western things by a non-Western society.

THE HYPOTHESIS OF
PSYCHOLOGICAL CONVERGENCE

Is societal modernization a universal solvent that will dissolve the residues of premodern characteristics in every changing society? Or, putting the question in a simpler way, are modernizing societies becoming alike? As a crucial question of central theoretical interest in the social and behavioral sciences, it has been extensively debated by theorists and researchers for various academic camps (for comprehensive reviews of the pros and cons, the reader is referred to Meyer, 1970; and Weinberg, 1969). One of the major proponents giving an affirmative answer to the above question is Levy (1966), who has argued that all societies are becoming "alike" in their central features as a result of modernization. He claims that as the level of modernization increases, the degree of structural uniformity among relatively modernized societies continually increases, regardless of how diverse these societies may originally have been. While Levy fully accepts differences in historical developments, they are of no moment in the modern development of societies—the future, not the past, is the relevant issue.

Many other social scientists, such as Apter (1965), Black (1966), Kerr, Dunlop, Herbison, and Myers (1960), Karsh and Cole (1968), and Feldman and Moore (1962), have suggested or advanced basically the same idea. The thesis of emerging similarity in this form may be called the hypothesis of societal convergence. It must be hastily pointed out that such a convergence hypothesis has been criticized by some scholars as groundless and without sound empirical evidence. Discussions of these skeptical criticisms may be found in Myer's (1970) and Weinberg's (1969) reviews of the relevant literature.

Value change has long been regarded by social scientists as an important aspect of social change induced by the process of modernization. For this and other reasons, proponents of societal convergence tend to take the view that the hypothesis is equally applicable to the change of values. They tend to emphasize or imply a universal pattern of modernity not only in institutions but also in values. Some scholars, especially those with a social psychological perspective, go even further to consider the convergence of modern values along with other modern psychological characteristics to result from the worldwide diffusion of modern institutions. In other words, they prefer to view psychological transformation as a consequence of societal transformation and psychological convergence as a consequence of societal transformation and psychological convergence as a consequence of societal convergence during the course of modernization. For example, Inkeles and Smith (1974), after defining the modern institutional pattern in terms of large-scale industry, intensive urbanization, effective transportation, mass communication, rational bureaucratic organizations, and mass education, express their conviction that societies with such an institutional pattern encourage the development of a particular type of human being who functions in those societies effectively.

Kahl (1968), like Inkeles and Smith, also posits that values and attitudes tend to converge in industrializing societies. He has pointed out that his research findings support the position of Inkeles that societal structures tend to change toward convergence in modernizing societies regardless of previously different national traditions. Inkeles and Smith and Kahl are not alone in venturing the notion of psychological convergence as an outcome of societal convergence. Other behavioral scientists like Cantril (1965), Hofstede (1980), 1977), McClelland (1961), and Pye (1966) also have proposed similar ideas based upon research findings of different types in different psychological domains.

For the sake of clarity and simplicity, ideas of psychological convergence as set forth by previous theorists may be reformulated to form the following hypothesis:

Hypothesis of psychological convergence: The peoples of all modernizing societies are becoming similar to each other in their psychological characteristics.

The hypothesis so stated is in its relatively strong form. Several corollaries may be derived from it. For the purpose of illustration, five will be specified here:

Corollary A: The degree of similarity in psychological characteristics between highly modernized societies will be significantly higher than that between traditional societies.

Corollary B: The degree of similarity in psychological characteristics between highly modernized societies will be significantly higher than that between any of them and any traditional society.

Corollary C: As a developing society acquires more modern institutions, its population will come to include more and more members with modern psychological characteristics.

Corollary D: As a developing society acquires more modern institutions, its members will have a larger number of modern psychological characteristics or a higher level of each of them.

Corollary E: As a developing society acquires more modern institutions, its members' modern psychological characteristics will gradually replace their traditional psychological characteristics.

Relevant empirical work directly or indirectly addressed to the hypothesis of psychological convergence will be reviewed in the next two sections.

THE EVIDENCE FOR THE HYPOTHESIS

A comprehensive review of the relevant literature reveals that results more or less supporting the hypothesis of psychological convergence may be found in quite a number of previous studies. These empirical investigations can be roughly classified into two groups: those adopting an individual-modernity paradigm and those adopting some other paradigm. Since studies in the first group are more systematic and relevant to the validity of the hypothesis, their findings will be reviewed first.

Studies with an Individual-Modernity Paradigm

Individual modernity has been defined by Inkeles (1966) and Inkeles and Smith (1974) as a set of attitudes, values, and ways of feeling and thinking, presumably of the sort either generated by or required for effective participation in a modern society. Under the influence of this and similar definitions, a research paradigm has been formed, the essential feature of which is to construct a standardized sociopsychological measure of individual modernity and then to identify its determinants and consequences. The most ambitious empirical endeavor with such a paradigm has been undertaken by Inkeles (1966) and Inkeles and Smith (1974), in which comprehensive, standardized scales are used to collect data on modernity for examples of adults from six different developing countries—Argentina, Chile, India, Pakistan, Israel, and Nigeria. They find a syndrome of common psychological characteristics across all national samples, a constellation that defines a model of the modern person.

The modern person's personality, as it emerges from their study, is characterized by the following major elements: (a) receptivity to new experiences; (b) openness to innovation and change; (c) tendency to form or hold opinions over problems and issues that arise not only in the immediate environment but also outside it; (d) being energetic in acquiring information and facts; (e) orientation to the present or future, rather than to the past; (f) planning and organizing beliefs as a way of handling life; (g) mastery of the environment in order to advance individual purposes and goals, rather than complete domination by environmental needs; (h) confidence that the world is calculable and that other people and institutions can be relied upon to fulfill obligations and responsibilities; (i) awareness of the dignity of others and a disposition to show respect for them; (j) faith in science and technology; (k) possession of educational and occupational aspirations; (l) belief in distributive justice, in rewards based upon social contribution and not according to either whim or special properties of the person not related to such a contribution (Inkeles, 1966; Inkeles & Smith, 1974). Among these characteristics, they especially emphasize that the modern individual is an informed participant citizen with a marked sense of personal efficacy. The modern person is highly independent and autonomous in relations to traditional sources of influence, and ready for new experiences and ideas, that is, relatively open-minded and cognitively flexible (Inkeles & Smith, 1974).

The next influential study with an individual-modernity paradigm was conducted by Kahl (1968). He administered his standardized modernism scales to samples of adults in Brazil, Mexico, and the United

States, finding that values tended to converge into the same core syndrome of modernism in all three countries. This complex consists of seven closely interrelated components: (a) activism, (b) low integration with relatives, (c) preference for urban life, (d) individualism, (e) low urban stratification subcommunity stratification, (f) mass-media participation, and (g) rigid stratification of life chances. Additional values associated with modernism are trust in people, propensity to take risks in career, favorable attitudes toward manual work, distaste for traditional institutions and agencies of coercion, and an attitude in favor of modern roles within the nuclear family.

There have been other investigations in which data on individual modernity or modernism were collected for respondents from only one country. Some of these studies have also provided data showing the existence of the intranational coherence of modern psychological characteristics. Moreover, their findings, when put together, suggest important cross-national overlap in certain characteristics. Empirical studies of this sort are many, but only those that are more relevant to the present purpose will be briefly reviewed.

One of these single-nation studies was done by Guthrie (1970, 1977) in the Philippines. He administered his Traditional-Modern Interview Schedule to Filipino men and women from four communities at various distances from Manila to assess the psychological effects of modernization. The obtained results revealed that the more modern Filipinos, in comparison with the traditional, generally tended to have a greater sense of individual responsibility and individual control, a higher personal independence from politics in contrast to family-based political control, and a greater sense of efficacy—the idea that an individual's decisions and activities significantly determine his or her success. Apparently, what is stressed in this new behavior pattern is self-reliance.

Some modernity scales have been constructed in the context of studying family or fertility behavior (e.g., Bagozzi & Loo, 1978; Goldberg, 1974, 1975; Portes, 1973). Two of them, created by Schnaiberg (1970a, 1970b) and Armer and Youtz (1971), have been used to collect data that are relevant in evaluating the hypothesis of psychological convergence. Schnaiberg used data from the well-known Ankara Family Study, in which a large number of married women living in Ankara City and four selected villages in Ankara Province, Turkey, were interviewed. He developed a modernity scale and used it to study the impact of the amount and timing of urban residential experience on attitudes and behavior. He defined modernism in terms of six dimensions: (a) involvement in a broad information network through the use of mass media, (b) freedom from extended family ties, (c) involvement in an egalitarian conjugal union (preference for a nuclear family role structure), (d) freedom from intensive religious involvement, (e) involvement in an adaptive relation to an environment that extends beyond the local community and local norms (or, simply, an extralocal orientation), and (f) involvement in a suprafamilial economic system through the purchase of manufactured goods, rather than depending upon home production alone. Although the correlation matrix among these six dimensions of modernism did not reveal anything like a perfect linear association among them, they did all correlate with one another positively and their correlation matrix was dominated by one major factor: the "emancipation" of women with urban residential experience and higher education. These findings seem to indicate that there is a considerable level of coherence of attitudinal and behavioral characteristics among individuals who have been exposed to modernizing influences, such as urban residence and education.

Armer and Youtz's (1971) modernity scale was developed in the Islamic communities of Kano City, which is part of the larger Kano metropolitan area in northern Nigeria. Using a factor-analytic procedure, these investigators extracted a common principal factor of individual modernity composed of six main value orientations found in data collected from a sample of young Nigerian men. These psychological orientations may be briefly described as mastery (efficacy and activism), tolerance of other groups, belief in empirical causality, orientation to the future, independence from family ties, and receptivity to change. All of these dimensions were found to correlate positively with formal education as a modernizing factor.

In addition to the modernity or modernism studies of Guthrie, Schnaiberg, and Armen, there is another relevant program of rather large-scale research in which data were collected from only one society. This is the series of studies conducted by Yang (for a review, see Yang, 1981, 1985, 1986a, 1986b; Yang & Hchu, 1974). Adopting an indigenous approach, Yang and his associates have developed three successive scales of individual modernity specifically applicable to Chinese residents in Taiwan and related these modernism measures to various kinds of psychological and behavioral variables in a series of correlational and experimental studies. Empirical results have indicated that the more modernized Chinese in Taiwan tend to be stronger in their needs for exhibition, autonomy, intraception, heterosexuality, and individual-oriented achievement; higher in their preferences for activity, self-indulgence, and individualistic relationship and their beliefs in egalitarianism, internal control, and sex equality; and greater in such temperamental traits as sociability, extraversion, dominance, flexibility, tolerance, and masculinity. Combined, these psychological and behavioral characteristics form a partial portrait of the modern Chinese in the rapidly industrializing Chinese society.

It should be pointed out that Yang's indigenous modernity measures and their psychological and behavioral correlates have implications beyond their local meanings. They may well be related to important features of pancultural modernism. This plausibility has been demonstrated in a study by Singh and Inkeles (1968), in which a correlation of .56 was found between an indigenous Indian Scale of modernity and the long form of Inkeles's modernity scale. The two scales are quite different in their rationale and content, but they appear to measure similar characteristics of psychological modernity. Inkeles's scales were originally constructed on the basis of data collected in six different societies, of which India was one. Singh and Inkeles's finding thus attests to the fact that modern characteristics of people in a society tapped by an *emic* measure relate highly with modern characteristics of the same group assessed by an *etic* measure. Given this finding, one would expect that different emic measures of individual modernity constructed on the basis of data from one or more countries will converge with each other. Evidence supporting this expectation has been provided by Armer and Schnaiberg (1972), in which the four modernity scales constructed by Smith and Inkeles (1966), Kahl (1968), Schnaiberg (1970a, 1970b), and Armer (1970) are found to correlate substantially with each other (intercorrelations ranged from .40 to .64). The modernity measures were also found to be associated with scores on anomie and alienation, which may be regarded as negative aspects of the modern psychological syndrome (see also Suzman, 1973). However, inconsistent relationships across countries between anomie and modernity measures have been reported in Almond and Verba's (1963) and Inkeles's (1969) studies.

Studies with Other Paradigms

So much for the relevant results from studies with an individual-modernity paradigm. In fact, there are many other less relevant studies on individual modernity or modernism that, for one reason or another, have not been reviewed here. Among them are those by Cunningham (1972), Dawson (1967), Grasmick (1973), Holsinger (1973), Klineberg (1973), Sack (1973), Stephenson (1968), Suzman (1973), and Williamson (1970). In addition, there also are cross-cultural investigations without an individual modernity paradigm that have reported data potentially supporting the hypothesis of psychological convergence.

Hofstede's (1980, 1982, 1983) comparative study of work-related values covers an unusually large number of more than 40 national cultures. Through a factor analysis of country averages for his value measures, he was able to identify four dimensions of culture, respectively labeled as power distance (the extent to which the less powerful member of institutions and organizations accept that power is distributed unequally), uncertainty avoidance (the extent to which people feel threatened by ambiguous situations), individualism (a situation in which people are supposed to look after themselves and their immediate families only), and masculinity (a situation in which the dominant values in society are success, money, and things). His international data reveal that GNP correlates negatively with power distance and uncertainty avoidance, positively with individualism, and has no statistically significant relation with masculinity. The results suggest that as a nation is becoming industrialized during the process of economic development, its people will acquire this value pattern.

Inglehart (1977, 1982) has gone even further to assume that, independent of their cultural background, highly industrialized societies should develop postmaterialist (postbourgeois) values. He factor analyzed cross-cultural data collected from such countries as Belgium, Denmark, France, Germany, Italy, Ireland, Luxembourg, the Netherlands, Switzerland, and the United States and identified two major factors. First was the materialist-postmaterialist value factor. Additional analysis indicated that wealthier countries such as Belgium, the Netherlands, the United States, Switzerland, Luxembourg, and France have relatively high proportions of postmaterialists. Based upon these and other relevant findings, Inglehart argued that, as a society becomes highly industrialized, its members' materialist values will be gradually replaced by postmaterialist values that reflect the functioning of social needs (belongingness, participation, and esteem) and self-actualization needs (aesthetic and intellectual) in the Maslovian sense.

The third relevant multinational research was carried out by Lerner (1958), who made a comprehensive and penetrating analysis of modernization in six countries (Turkey, Lebanon, Egypt, Syria, Jordan, and Iran) and their peoples in the Middle East. The central cross-cultural finding of the study was that high empathy characterizes a modern society, with its urbanism, industrialism, literacy, and participation. In a modern society, more individuals exhibit higher empathic capacity (to conceive of, and take, the role of the other) than in any previous society. A similar conclusion has been reached in later studies by Rogers (1969) and other investigators.

As for McClelland's (1961) multinational study, well known to most psychologists, a much larger sample of countries was drawn to include all the nations in the world outside the tropics in which usable storybooks for children either existed or could be obtained. McClelland related the achievement motive levels of more than twenty countries, assessed through the thematic apperceptive analysis of children's stories, to estimates of economic development for the same countries, obtaining significant positive correlations. These findings, and those obtained by his disciples (e.g., Bradburn & Berlew, 1961; Rosen, 1964, 1971), have been considered as evidence for achievement motivation as a determinant of economic development. On the other hand, the same findings may also be interpreted as indicating that an achievement orientation or syndrome is one of the results of economic growth, an essential facet of societal modernization.

The last set of cross-culturally oriented studies to be mentioned here is the resarch on Witkin's well-known variable of psychological differentiation. Previous studies, conducted by different investigators in different societies (for reviews, see Berry, 1976; Witkin & Berry, 1975), in general support the conclusion that scores on differentiation tasks show an increase in psychological differentiation as a function of acculturation influences. This means that greater psychological differentiation is a characteristic associated with further adaptation during culture contact and social change.

Core Modern Psychological Characteristics

So far, we have made a brief review of the major empirical research that provides supportive evidence for the hypothesis of psychological onvergence. The modern psychological characteristics found in these studies show a considerable degree of overlap. While some later investigators are influenced by their precursors in defining individual modernity or modernism, the overlap of the personal qualities defined as modern in different studies may be interpreted as further confirming the existence of the cross-cultural convergence in certain psychological characteristics under the impact of societal modernization. In order to have a clearer idea about the overlapping qualities, a list of 20 characteristics is extracted to represent the core components of modern man's psychological syndrome. Each of the modern qualities listed below has been empirically identified in at least two studies reviewed above. These characteristics, more or less related to each other, are arranged with respect to the number of their identifying studies, as indicated in the parentheses:

(1) sense of personal efficacy (antifatalism) (Armer, Guthrie, Inkeles, Kahl, Yang)
(2) low integration with relatives (Armer, Guthrie, Inkeles, Kahl, Schnaiberg)
(3) egalitarian attitudes (Hofstede, Inglehart, Yang)
(4) openness to innovation and change (Armer, Doob, Inglehart, Inkeles)
(5) belief in sex equality (Doob, Inkeles, Schnaiberg, Yang)
(6) achievement motivation (Bradburn, McClelland, Rosen, Yang)
(7) individualistic orientation (Hofstede, Kahl, Yang)
(8) independence or self-reliance (Guthrie, Yang)
(9) active participation (Inglehart, Kahl, Yang)
(10) tolerance of and respect for others (Armer, Inkeles, Yang)
(11) cognitive and behavioral flexibility (Inkeles, Kahl, Yang)
(12) future orientation (Armer, Inkeles)
(13) psychological differentiation (Berry, Witkin)
(14) empathetic capacity (Lerner, Rogers)
(15) need for information (Inkeles, Schnaiberg)
(16) propensity to take risks in life (Kahl, Hofstede)
(17) extralegal orientation (nonlocalism) (Doob, Schnaiberg)
(18) secularization in religious belief (Schnaiberg)
(19) preference for urban life (Kahl)
(20) educational and occupational aspirations (Inkeles)

It should be pointed out that the results of the studies reviewed in this section support the hypothesis of psychological convergence only at a very general level. No empirical data have been collected particularly for the testing of the specific corollaries derived from the central hypothesis in the last section. Effort is needed in the future by social and behavioral scientists to design better-conceived investigations specifically devoted to evaluating the validity of these and other corollaries.

Before concluding this section, one more comment must be made. Facing the above list of core modern psychological characteristics, one would feel unable to resist the temptation to ask the question: Is this modern constellation the same as Hofstede's (1980) and Waterman's (1984) individualism on the left pole of the individualism-collectivism construct, as conceptualized by Hui and Triandis (1984) and Triandis (1985)? A check of the 20 traits against the various definitions of individualism given by these theorists reveals that 12 (1-9, 14, 16-17) of them (about two-thirds) rather clearly reflect, in one way or another, some different aspects of this complex, comprehensive concept, whereas the other 8 (10-13, 15, 18-20) fail to have any obvious connection with it. It should be noted that the first nine traits, most agreed upon by previous investigators as modern, are all individualistic-oriented in nature. The above facts indicate that, while individualism is the most important constituent of individual modernity or modernism, as defined by the 20 characteristics, the latter apparently includes significant components of other kinds. This means psychological modernity is a much broader concept than individualism.

Moreover, if individualism is regarded as an antithesis of collectivism, as Hui and Triandis (1984) and Triandis (1985) claimed, the cross-cultural convergence into that pattern of modernism of which the former is the major constituent will result in a replacement of the latter by the former. One implication of this inference is that collectivism will eventually be a useless concept for cross-cultural research when societies in the world have all become sufficiently industrialized. Nevertheless, the possibility may exist that individualism and collectivism are neither antitheses to each other nor the two poles of the same continuum. Instead, they might be two separate syndromes only partially related to each other, just as individual modernity and traditionality are (Yang, 1986). If this is the case, the cross-cultural emergence of the modernity syndrome will not necessarily lead to the decline of collectivism under the impact of societal modernization. As a matter of fact, Yang's (1986) empirical research has already demonstrated that some individualistic components (e.g., social isolation/self-reliance and optimism/assertiveness) of individual modernity failed to have a substantial correlation with certain collectivistic components (e.g., submission to authority and filial piety/ancestral worship) of individual traditionality (see also below).

THE EVIDENCE AGAINST THE HYPOTHESIS
OF PSYCHOLOGICAL CONVERGENCE

Evidence alleged to be against the hypothesis has been put forward in terms of three criticisms. The most direct criticism is simply that the peoples of different modernizing societies do not *all* converge toward the same psychological syndrome. The second criticism challenges the intracultural coherence of modern psychological characteristics to form a well-integrated syndrome. The third criticism emphasizes that traditional and modern psychological characteristics are able to coexist without conflict and that the old are not necessarily replaced by the new.

The core meaning of psychological convergence is that the same basic modern psychological qualities are found among people in *all* modernizing societies. There exist in the literature empirical results that seem to be in contradiction to this universality aspect of the convergence hypothesis. Some of these results are from studies by Sack (1973), Chiu (1979), Flanagan (1979, 1980), and Ike (1973). In Sack's study, one of Kahl's modernism scales was applied to respondents in Tunisia and data were then factor analyzed to explore whether the factorial structure of the scale was cross-culturally invariant. Almost half of the items were found to have a low factor loading on the principal axis, suggesting that the factorial composition of the attitudinal syndrome as measured by the scale is quite different in Tunisia.

Another study giving results somewhat inconsistent with the universality of psychological convergence is that by Chiu (1979), who administered a newly constructed scale of modernism to 10 Chinese communities in Taiwan, some rural and the others urban. The obtained data were analyzed by the method of simultaneous confirmatory factor analysis for multiple populations. The number of factors identified was quite different across communities as subcultures. Even for those communities that had the same number of factors, the factor patterns were not the same. These findings were interpreted as indicating that the cross-community (or cross-subculture) convergence of the modernity syndrome is questionable.

As may be recalled, Inglehart (1977) provided data suggesting a trend for the most industrially advanced European and North American countries to develop postmaterialist values. According to the convergence hypothesis, one would expect that all highly industrialized societies would show a similar trend. However, Flanagan (1979, 1980) and Ike (1973) have failed to find a linear change from materialist to postmaterialist values in Japan, which has been considered one of the most industrialized countries in the world.

Empirical investigations such as the ones mentioned above have not been numerous. Generally, the evidence against a universal convergence of psychological syndrome provided by those studies has been fragmentary and unsystematic. In most cases, the obtained data can at best demonstrate that the structural composition of the psychological syndrome in question is more or less different in different societies or communities. As a matter of degree, this variation in cross-cultural composition may just be a reflection of the fact that the societies compared are at different stages of societal modernization. As two societies are compared for their people's psychological convergence the difference in the psychological syndrome would be a function of their distance apart on the road of social change induced by modernization. Thus an ideal condition for testing the universality of psychological convergence is to study societies of comparable degrees of societal modernization. Previous investigators, however, have never made their comparisons under such a condition.

The next criticism against the convergence hypothesis focuses on the thesis of intracultural coherence of modern psychological characteristics to form a well-organized syndrome. Negative evidence may be found in studies by Armer and Youtz (1971), Klineberg (1974), and Yang, 1986). In their study with a probability-area sample of male youth in Kano, Nigeria, Armer and Youtz factor analyzed scores on ten modern value orientations and found that only six had high factor loadings on the principal axis. The remaining items seemed not to be associated with this major factor. There thus was insufficient unity among the ten value indices to consider modernism a unitary concept. This implication is further confirmed in a study by Klineberg (1974), who applied Inkeles's scale in Tunisia. Only slightly more than 10% of the total variance was found to be accounted for by the first unrotated factor for Tunisian parents and adolescents. Klineberg considered this finding as evidence pointing to the multidimensional character of psychological modernity. In consequence, he performed a varimax factor analysis and extracted four factors as the multiple components of modernity (i.e., Family Independence, Personal Efficacy, New Socialization, and Economic Optimism).

Data contradictory to the intracultural coherence of modern psychological characteristics can also be found in Yang's (1986b) recent construction of new multidimensional scales measuring individual traditionality and modernity for use with Chinese people in Taiwan. Two initial scales of about 300 items each, one for traditionality and one for modernity, were created and administered to large samples of Chinese adults and college students. Separate factor analyses identified five oblique factors of Chinese modernity (Egalitarianism/Open-Mindedness, Social Isolation/Self-Reliance, Optimism/Assertiveness, Affective Hedonism, and Sex Equality). The intercorrelations between the traditionality components revealed that, while all the factors tended to be positively correlated and statistically significant, the sizes of the coefficients were by no means even and uniform. As for the five modernity components, their intercorrelations indicated that Egalitarianism/Open-Mindedness had a relatively closer positive relationship with Affective Hedonism and Sex Equality. Social Isolation/Self-Reliance had no statistically significant relationships with Optimism/Assertiveness and Sex Equality. The remaining correlations, all positive in sign, fell in between. These results make it necessary to treat psychological modernity as a multifaceted phenomenon.

The evidence given in the above and other relevant studies unequivocally points to the fact that modern psychological characteristics simply do not cohere to form a well-unified syndrome. Individual modernism may be composed of separate components with or without substantial correlations. Actually, most, if not all, proponents of the hypothesis of psychological convergence have realized this fact and somehow incorporated the idea of multidimensionality into the construction of their measuring instruments. Few of them have strongly claimed that the cross-cultural convergence of modern psychological characteristics presupposes the intracultural coherence of the same characteristics. There is no a priori theoretical basis from which to infer a logical connection between psychological convergence and coherence. Any assumption of such a connection may be regarded as a fallacy in which a concept or phenomenon at the aggregate level is inappropriately related to a concept or phenomenon at the individual level. This macro-micro fallacy makes the issue of intracultural coherence a completely groundless criticism of the cross-cultural convergence of modern psychological characteristics.

Finally, we come to the third criticism against the convergence hypothesis. Bendix (1967) and Gusfield (1967) have succinctly pointed out that tradition and modernity do not necessarily involve conflicting values and behavior and that traditional characteristics need not be replaced by modern ones. Levine (1968) has emphasized the flexibility of traditional cultures to the effect that the contents of premodern culture do not persist completely unchanged and, instead, the innovative capacity of the culture is usually able to synthesize at least some of these contents with some of the modern characteristics. Bendix's, Gusfield's, and Levine's arguments have been supported by findings in later studies, in addition to those presented in their own papers (e.g., Graves & Graves, 1978; Nishihira, 1974; Trommsdorff, 1983; Yang, 1986b).

In order to investigate the effects of societal modernization on behavior in an island community, Graves and Graves (1978) collected experimental data in Aitutaki, one island of the Cook Islands (a New Zealand protectorate until 1965) and reported that both generous, cooperative (traditional) and rivalrous, competitive ("modern") predispositions coexist among people who seem to be retaining a strong identification with their traditional values.

Nishihira (1974) analyzed longitudinal data collected in Japan from first successive nationwide surveys spanning a twenty-year period and found that certain questions always produced stable results, demonstrating constant national traits. For instance, about 80% of the respondents across surveys indicated a preference for work superiors who forced them to work hard, even to the extent of sometimes bending work rules, but who showed an active concern for their welfare in private matters outside the job. Also working with Japanese survey data, Trommsdorff (1983) has presented findings indicating that strong traditional values such as group solidarity, interpersonal harmony, paternalism, and familism are coexisting with quite modern values such as achievement and competition, and that along with democratic values exist beliefs in hierarchical social structures and in authority, obedience, and inequality of men and women.

Additional evidence comes from Yang's (1986b) Taiwan study with separate scales for the measurement of individual modernity and traditionality. While a negative correlation of about $-.50$ was found between the total scores on the two overall scales, the five modernity components did not correlate uniformly with the five traditionality components. Egalitarianism/Open-Mindedness, Affective Hedonism, and Sex Equality tended to have substantially higher negative correlations with Submission to Authority, Passivity/Conservativeness, Fatalism/Defensiveness, and Male Dominance than they did with Filial Piety/Ancestral Worship. The other two modernity factors, Social Isolation/Self-Reliance and Optimism/Assertiveness, had a zero or a low negative or a low positive correlation with the five traditionality factors. These results strongly suggest that filial piety, a revered traditional value for the Chinese, can coexist with all the five major sets of modern attitudes. The other four components of traditionality are able to stand side-by-side with at least two components of modernity, namely, social isolation/self-reliance and optimism-assertiveness. This result means that some important traditional attitudes and beliefs cannot be as easily displaced by modern ones as some would expect.

However, proponents of the hypothesis of psychological convergence may contend that the perpetuation of some traditional values, beliefs, or behavior in some modernizing societies may be due to the combination of two factors: the unusual importance and rigidity of these cultural elements in the traditional stages of those societies, and the insufficiency in strength and duration of the accumulated influences of societal modernization. Jacobs and Campbell's (1961) well-known experiment has dramatically demonstrated that even an arbitrary, simple tradition or norm temporarily created in a laboratory microculture can perpetuate for quite a number of "generations." In the case of a functionally important and rigid tradition or norm with a history of long standing in a natural, complex society, it must be able to transmit for a much greater number of generations and to persist even against the emergence of some new and modern characteristics, especially in a developing country where societal modernization has not been strong and long enough.

SYNTHESIS: A FINAL WORD

While the supporting results do suggest that there is a kernel of truth in the convergence hypothesis, the inconsistent findings make it necessary that the strong version of the central hypothesis and its corollaries (especially Corollary E), as formulated earlier in this chapter, be somehow revised. To accomplish this, conceptual distinctions between the various kinds of psychological characteristics commonly shared by individuals in the same society must first be made. One sensible approach is to classify those characteristics into two rather broad categories: functional and nonfunctional. A functional psychological characteristic may be defined as an attitude, value, or behavior that is helpful or instrumental in the adjustment of most (if not all) individuals in a society to some aspects or features of the social life in that society. A nonfunctional psychological characteristic is an attitude, value, or behavior that does not have such a function for adjustment and is purely stylistic, expressive, or terminal in nature. Functional characteristics may be further divided into three subcategories: (a) General-functional characteristics are those attitudes, values, or behaviors that are helpful or instrumental in the adjustment of most (if not all) individuals in a society to some aspects or features of social life that are common to all human societies; (b) specific-functional characteristics are those attitudes, values, or behavior that are helpful or instrumental in the adjustment of most (if not all) individuals in a society to some aspects or features of social life that are specific to societies of the same type (there are four major types of traditional societies—agrarian, gathering, pastoral, and hunting, and one major type of modern society—industrial); (c) unique-functional characteristics are those attitudes, values, or behavior that are helpful or instrumental in the adjustment of most (if not all) individuals in a society to some aspects or features of social life that are unique to that particular society. As for nonfunctional characteristics, most of them would be unique in the sense that they can be found only among individuals in one society. Nevertheless, since all human beings have many basic morphological, physiological, and psychological qualities in common, the possibility of the existence of general nonfunctional characteristics cannot be completely ruled out.

In the course of societal modernization, different kinds of psychological characteristics may be differentially affected. For obvious reasons, societal transformation will mainly affect some of the functional psychological characteristics. As agrarian, gathering, pastoral, or hunting societies are changing into industrial societies, its members' old specific-functional characteristics will gradually lose their instrumentality and eventually disappear. Meanwhile, new specific-functional characteristics (specific to all societies of the industrial type) will be formed to make adjustment to the new aspects or features of social life in an industrial society much easier. Traditional societies widely differ in their types of social life as constrained by different economic systems (agrarian, gathering, pastoral, and hunting). In order to adjust smoothly to these enormously distinct types of social-economical imperatives, peoples in different, traditional societies will have to develop different sets of specific-functional characteristics. All these traditional characteristics will be replaced by the same set of modern specific-functional ones as a result of the social transformation into some form of industrial society. It is mainly in this rather limited sense that we can say there has been a trend toward cross-cultural convergence of certain psychological characteristics.

On the other hand, societal modernization will have no significant influences on the general-functional, unique-functional, and nonfunctional characteristics, although for different reasons. Individuals in a traditional society and those in a modern one will have the same general-functional characteristics simply because these qualities are possessed by all human beings. Unique-functional characteristics of individuals in a traditional society are related only to the unique aspects or features of that particular society. So far as these unique aspects or features remain unaffected by the societal modernization, these characteristics will continue without change. Nonfunctional characteristics are stylistic, expressive, or terminal without substantial functions for adjustment in life and will therefore remain insensitive to social change. It is of course also possible that new, unique nonfunctional characteristics are formed during the process for the society to advance to its modern phase.

According to this analysis, there exists the possibility that the confirming and the disconfirming evidence for the convergence hypothesis mainly concern different kinds of psychological characteristics. An inspection of the twenty core components of the modern psychological syndrome reveals that most, if not all, may be regarded as specific-functional characteristics helpful or instrumental, in one way or another, in one's adjustment to the social life of a modern society. On the other hand, among the traditional psychological characteristics that still coexist with the modern ones, many would be classified as general-functional (filial piety is an example), unique-functional (using chopsticks by the Chinese is another example), and nonfunctional characteristics. The remaining traditional characteristics may be cases of the specific-functional kind with unusual rigidity and they will hence need a much longer time, or a much higher degree of societal modernization, to be weakened or abolished.

The above discussion has demonstrated that the evidence for the hypothesis of psychological convergence may be reasonably reconciled (hence synthesized) with the evidence against the hypothesis. Based upon this discussion, our original central hypothesis may be revised into the following form:

> *Revised Hypothesis of Psychological Convergence:* The peoples of all modernizing societies are becoming similar to each other in psychological characteristics of the *specific-functional* kind.

With this truncated and weaker version of the hypothesis, all the six original corollaries may be revised accordingly. It should be pointed out that this revised hypothesis serves two functions at the same time: to reflect the achievement of previous empirical studies and to derive testable working hypotheses for future research in this area.

Now we are in a better position to answer the question raised in the beginning of this paper: Will societal modernization eventually eliminate cross-cultural psychological differences? This general question should not be answered simplistically. According to the revised hypothesis and the discussion in the above, only those different sets of traditional psychological characteristics that are specific-functional will be gradually replaced by the same set of modern psychological characteristics during societal modernization. All the other kinds of traditional characteristics will remain unchanged and co-exist with the modern ones. In other words, societal modernization can weaken or eliminate cross-cultural differences only across specific-functional characteristics, but not across the characteristics of the other kinds.

7

J'ACCUSE
GUSTAV JAHODA

". . . the facts of culture are absent from research and theory in social psychology." (Pepitone, 1986)

The targets of my polemic are in the main those experimental social psychologists who are responsible for the contents of textbooks and the major journals in the field. It should be made clear at the outset that the critiques are directed at psychologists holding certain views, but it so happens that these are mostly to be found in the United States. With few exceptions, they display minimal concern for cross-cultural psychology, often on the grounds that it has little to offer them. The complacent assumptions underlying this view will be examined and mainline experimental social psychologists challenged either to justify or to abandon their pretensions.

THE MARKETING OF
AMERICAN SOCIAL PSYCHOLOGY

While this heading may sound offensive, it only reflects the fact of American dominance in this field and furthermore that American textbook writers seldom take any notice of what is being done in the rest of the world. In order to document what text authors say about their subject, a dozen textbooks published during the 1980s were scrutinized and some fairly typical extracts are reproduced below[1]:

(A) More than any other field of inquiry, social psychology concerns itself with the study of fundamental human endeavors. The unique mission of social psychology is to understand how and why people behave as they do when they are with others, and the effect that such social experiences have on the way they will later think, feel and subsequently act.

(B) (Starts with an Allen cartoon series.) For many of us, as for Allen, love relationships seem irrational and absurd. Our experience provides us with little understanding of love. And that is where SOCIAL PSYCHOLOGY comes in. The goal of social psychology is to understand social and socially caused phenomena—such as love—and by understanding them, to gain some control over them.

(C) Welcome to social psychology. If you are meeting social psychology for the first time, you are about to begin a journey into a new way of looking at yourself and other people. On this journey you will explore the social side of human existence: the way your thoughts, feelings, and actions are influenced by other people.... I want you not only to learn its principles and findings and to recognize its tremendous practical value, but also to have fun in the process.

In addition to such mawkish phraseology, reminiscent of Madison Avenue hype, the texts are also sprinkled with petty pictures often serving no real purpose at all. Yet the texts also invariably pontificate about social psychology's being science, usually with a simplistic exposition of what is supposed to be scientific method. It is enough to make me, at least, cringe with embarrassment.

Leaving all that aside, consider what claims are being made for social psychology. Essentially, these boil down to two:

(1) social psychology deals with universal human processes
(2) social psychology studies the psychological processes of the individual as affected by the direct or indirect presence of others (generally based on Allport's 1968 definition)

Neither of these claims will stand up to closer scrutiny, and some preliminary remarks will be made about the first, concerning alleged universality. It is not merely unsupported by evidence but inherently implausible. Recently, Sears (1986) has once again pointed out the narrow data base of American social psychology, suggesting that it be extended to the general population. But why stop there? Surely the logic of the argument would demand extensive cross-cultural studies, since Americans are hardly a representative sample of our species and its varied cultural patterns.

The second claim has been lucidly discussed in relation to its historical background by Pepitone (1981), who described it as the "individuocentric bias," attributing it chiefly to the aspiration of aligning oneself with the natural sciences. Among European scholars, Tajfel (1972) in particular has subjected this bias to a devastating critique, while Doise (1982) epitomized the major weakness of experimental social psychology in the following sentence:

The experimenter manipulating independent variables aims at complete control of the processes studied and tends to forget their insertion into a social context very much wider than that of the experimental situation. (pp. 25-26, my translation)

If these two points are granted, the importance of cultural factors becomes immediately evident. However, it may be objected that a critique based on the necessarily oversimplified content of introductory textbooks is hardly fair. Hence a brief look at what is supposed to be the more serious research literature will be indicated.

THE JOURNALS: MORE AND MORE
ABOUT LESS AND LESS

Scanning recent volumes of the major journals was, for me, a depressing experience. There were of course some exciting and important articles, but the bulk of the contributions consisted of what I would regard as rather futile exercises conducted almost invariably with college students. There tends to be a stark contrast between lofty declarations of aims and the often pedestrian and sometimes bizarre studies carried out with admirable methodological sophistication.

The theories or models referred to in such articles practically never mention anything about range of applicability, thereby tacitly implying universality. There was a time when this kind of issue seems to have concerned some editors. Thus until 1980 the instructions to authors in the *Journal of Personality and Social Psychology* were as follows:

> Submitted manuscripts should delineate an important question and provide a clear answer to it. In the case of research reports, this will often require demonstration that the reported results are generalizable beyond a single research setting.

Subsequently, this requirement was dropped, perhaps because it was honored more in the breach than in the observance.

In order to substantiate my allegations fully, it would have been necessary to undertake an extensive content analysis, for which I have neither the time nor the inclination. Instead, I shall offer three arbitrarily selected examples on a theme that is remarkably salient in the literature, namely, relationships between the sexes. They are drawn from the *Journal of Personality and Social Psychology* and the *Journal of Experimental Social Psychology*, premier journals in the field. In summarizing them, I have stripped their pretentious jargon down to essentials, thereby exposing the poverty of the core.

(D) Choosing a situation in which to begin a relationship: Ss were asked if they preferred to interact in a romantic or nonromantic type of situation and this was related to a personality trait.

(E) The role of expertise in processing social interaction scripts: It was found that those who had been on more dates were able to arrange bits of "dating scripts" in proper order more quickly.

(F) Male and female undergraduates were exposed to a horror movie. Men enjoyed the movie most in the company of a distressed woman, while women enjoyed it least in the company of a distressed man.

In considering the possible range of generality of the theoretical claims that are nearly always made, however trivial the study, some questions must be asked:

(1) Are the theories or models relevant outside American culture? Do they address themselves to problems that are meaningful within a radically different cultural setting?
(2) Could the experiments, or conceptually equivalent ones, be carried out in such a setting?

I submit that in a very large proportion of the articles in the literature, the answers to both questions would have to be negative. In the present instance it is immediately evident in case D that a hypothesis based on the notion of "romantic" is culture-bound. Similarly, the rating-and-dating complex of E is a typically North American phenomenon that has not even a close counterpart in Europe. It is discussed in the context of a cognitive theory of social skills, though the connection appears tenuous. The last of the illustrations, F, is rather more interesting since its theory is more ambitious, suggesting an evolutionary basis (man the hunter versus woman needing his protection) for the differential development of effect. The chain of inference is lengthy and its links are weak, but it probably would be possible to formulate derivations of the theory that could be tested cross-culturally without recourse to horror movies. Since the so-called "gender-role socialization model of affect" is regarded as an evolutionary product and thus very general, such an attempt ought to be made if one wishes to go beyond mere speculation. If suitable replications in different cultural settings demand too many resources, one could at the very least draw on the ethnographic literature in search of support. None of this was done, or apparently even intended, and so one is left with an elaborate theoretical edifice resting upon an absurdly narrow support.

This brings me to the fact that experimental social psychologists, and regrettably even some cross-cultural ones, are apt to take little notice of the work of anthropologists. When it comes to questions about generality of social-psychological findings, comparative ethnographic material can be most helpful and failure to use it rather wasteful. An example is a recent study by Leung and Lind (1986) dealing with procedural justice. They surveyed several investigations that had found a preference for adversary procedures of dispute resolution, noting that none of these had been done in a non-Western country. Then they reviewed various cross-cultural studies and even cited some anthropological writings throwing doubt on the generality of these findings. They then carried out a replication in Hong Kong, where no such preference was found. The question I am raising is whether it is really worth devoting a great deal of time and energy to demonstrate with statistical elegance something that has long been a commonplace for anthropologists. For instance, in her introductory anthropology text, Mair (1972) wrote that in traditional countries "the decisions of the courts are concerned as much with reconciling the parties as with awarding damages or punishing offences" (p. 149; see also Lloyd, 1962, p. 18; Ottenberg, 1960, p. 59). Unlike psychologists, who focus on the responses of individuals to mainly hypothetical situations, anthropologists analyze the characteristics of judicial procedures in contrasting settings in terms of the functioning of real-life social systems. This appears to me far more illuminating than a psychological approach that in essence merely confirms the existence of well-known "differences."

The burden of the arguments in this section will now be briefly summarized. Much of the journal literature in experimental social psychology deals with issues that are both trivial in a wider context and specific to contemporary American culture. In spite of this provincialism, limitations to generality are hardly ever acknowledged, and cross-cultural verification of claims is not only seldom attempted, but the need for it is not even recognized.

FUNDAMENTAL FALLACIES

Underlying the prevailing stance in experimental social psychology are a number of tacit assumptions that remain unquestioned by the in-group. What seem to be three of the most important and closely related ones will be briefly examined.

The Individuocentric Bias

Deaf to the voices of critics like Tajfel (1972) or Pepitone (1981), mainline social psychologists cling to Allport's conception of psychological processes internal to the individual as the central focus, so-called situational factors being treated as secondary and derivative. It seems to me that many experimental social psychologists are like people living on a high plateau who have discovered that water boils at 90° C; they are unwilling to listen to objections from the valley, because for them the boiling point is axiomatically a property of water and not of the ecological context in which it is boiled!

It would seem that this kind of belief about the individual is a "cultural truism" (McGuire & Papageorgis, 1961) shared by most Westerners but probably most deep-rooted among Americans. In the case of psychologists with the aspiration to be "scientific," it is probably reinforced by the tendency to put emphasis on the individual as a biological unit; hence the attempt to identify uniform internal processes that can account for social behavior. Other cultures often have very different and more socially oriented notions of what constitutes a person. This has been very fully documented by White and Kirkpatrick (1985), who go so far as to suggest that many of our psychological theories are little more than elaborations of Western "folk models." Such a view is not confined to anthropologists and has recently been powerfully argued by Valsiner (1985).

Culture as a Veneer

When experimental social psychologists dismiss any overtures from their cross-cultural colleagues, it is in the belief that culture is peripheral to their main concerns, which is of course closely related to what has just been said. If the internal processes governing social behavior are essentially the same in all humans, then any member of the species will do as a subject. This standpoint has been expressed with amazing ingenuousness by Gerard and Conolley (1972):

> Social influence phenomena occurring anywhere and at any time can be interpreted within the same basic conceptual framework. . . . Given the abiding faith in basic universals of humankind, the social psychologist might just as well work with the subject population he knows something about and that is close at hand—the students in his classes. (p. 242)

Such a simple faith is more appropriate in the religious sphere, and no attempt was made to spell out what the "basic universals" are supposed to be. The problem of universals is certainly a difficult one (Lonner, 1980) and cannot be adequately discussed here. It should be noted, however, that, *pace* Gerald and Conolley, their existence does not preclude the influence of culture. As a prominent human biologist put it, "The demonstration of cross-cultural universals is not in itself adequate for, or even indicative of, a need for a resort to biological explanation" (Reynolds, 1976, p. 175). Generally biologists are in agreement with anthropologists who hold that for humans the creation and acquisition of culture is a fundamental mode of adaptation. In recent years there has been increasing interest in the relationship between genetic and cultural evolution (Boyd & Richerson, 1985; Cavalli-Sforza & Feldman, 1981), and the view that culture is merely something superficial is sheer nonsense.

The Shibboleth of "Process" versus "Content"

This dichotomy is, as in the above illustration, commonly used as a stick with which to beat cross-cultural psychologists while telling them that their work is pointless. The case has probably been most cogently presented by Faucheux (1976), but there is no space here to rehearse his arguments and my subsequent discussion of these problems (Jahoda, 1980, 1986). Instead, I propose to approach the issue via another field of psychology.

The process/content dichotomy seems often to be viewed in rather simplistic terms, as though the relationship were like that between, say, a shredder and the things one puts into it. Thus it does not matter whether these are apples or cabbages—the way the mechanism operates is exactly the same. What this ignores is that psychological processes are not the result of parts put together from a blueprint, but the product of *development*.

When Piaget first put forward his theory, it was essentially psycho-biological, structures developing out of the activities of the organism in relation to the environment. He initially regarded the latter, in both its physical and its social aspects, as sufficiently similar everywhere to be quite content to confine his work to Genevan children. His awareness of the relevance of cultural variations seems to have resulted from an encounter with the formidable Margaret Mead in the course of a series of interdisciplinary discussions during the 1950s. Thereafter he encouraged some of his students to undertake cross-cultural studies and this changed his previous position so extensively that he later wrote:

> Psychology elaborated in our environment, which is characterized by a certain culture and a certain language, remains essentially conjectural as long as the necessary cross-cultural material has not been gathered as a control. (Piaget, 1966)

Since then extensive cross-cultural research has shown that while the sensory-motor stage seems closely similar everywhere, thereafter increasing divergence is observed. Such work has led to substantial modifications of Piagetian theory away from the notion of a universally homogeneous pattern of development that is uniform across domains (Dasen, 1982).

It should be evident from this line of work that no clear separation of process and content can reasonably be maintained: The input from the actions directed toward the environment will differentially affect the nature of cognitive structures and functioning. If that be granted, then surely there is no reason to think that social cognition and behavior develop in a different and more uniform manner! On the contrary, it ought to be obvious that in the social sphere cultural variations are likely to have an even more profound influence, yet experimental social psychologists have steadfastly refused to acknowledge their importance.

CONCLUSION

I accuse mainstream social psychology of being guilty of *suggestio falsi*. Both textbooks and journal articles commonly imply universality without seeking to provide any grounds for the implicit claims, a position that appears to me indefensible. This state of affairs (admittedly not wholly confined to social psychology) has some unfortunate consequences. American psychology enjoys an unrivaled prestige and, in the words of Koch (1985), by the 1920s "it had become an American export commodity that commenced virtually to flood the world market" (p. 25). As a teacher and examiner in Third World countries I can confirm this diffusion and have noted that students have to learn by rote a good deal of material that makes little sense to them. It is thus not surprising that sophisticated indigenous social psychologists have good reason to complain about Western ethnocentrism (e.g., Ho, 1980; Zaidi, 1979).

What, then, can be done? Above all, one should be honest. This means acknowledging openly that most of current experimental social psychology is essentially concerned with sophomores, its range of generality being largely unknown. If it is felt that a particular theory is applicable globally, then some evidence for such a claim should be provided. This would admittedly be a difficult task, requiring considerable resources. One would have to study not only students in other cultures, but ordinary people; and not only urbanites, but people in small village communities, who still constitute a substantial part of the world population. It is questionable whether, in the case of most current theories, such an undertaking would be worthwhile. As I have argued elsewhere (Jahoda, 1979), most theories of experimental social psychology depend critically on certain sociocultural features such as literacy, universalism as distinct from particularism, and a relatively wide range of social behavior, beliefs, and attitudes not governed by social norms. Moreover, the most popular methods of experimentation would not be feasible in a small community: It would be hard, if not impossible, to assemble a group of strangers and to obtain the services of confederates. Thus, in my view, such an enterprise would be doomed before the start.

There are of course less ambitious alternatives, compatible with the well-known thesis put forward by Gergen (1973) to the effect that social-psychological theories are relative to time and place. For instance, by replications with student subjects in other cultures one could gain information about range of applicability. Unfortunately, such work as has been done along these lines is hardly encouraging, even in a culture similar to the American (Amir & Sharon, 1987).

Although preferable to mere assertion, verification attempts as such are not enough to escape from the myopic vision of current mainstream social psychology, since such attempts are constrained by theoretical formulations of Western origin. What is needed is more exploratory work that may initially be mainly descriptive but at a later stage could also serve to generate hypotheses. It is here that cross-cultural psychologists can help to provide a broader perspective in such important areas as the psychological consequences of social change and modernization (e.g., Berry, 1980). Since much of the research of cross-cultural social psychologists employs methods that presuppose literacy (Segall, 1986), most of the information about social behavior in preliterate cultural settings will come from anthropologists. An understanding of "love relationships," as promised in extract B above, could hardly be achieved by relying on social-psychological studies in the United States!

It seems to me that the aspiration of social psychology to be taken seriously as a discipline cannot be fulfilled by an excessive reliance upon experimentation and a failure to recognize its limitations. Social psychology ignores at its peril the immense richness and variety of social behavior across the globe. The comments by Poincare (1908, n.d.), while referring to astronomy and geology in relation to our understanding of the physical world, apply equally well to the social sciences:

> By making long excursions in space and time, we may find our ordinary rules completely upset, and these great upsettings will give us a clearer view and better comprehension of such small changes as may occur nearer us, in the small corner of the world in which we are called to live and move. We shall know this corner better for the journey we have taken into distant lands where we had no concern. (p. 21)

NOTE

1. There is no intention to pillory particular individuals and references are therefore omitted.

8

CROSS-CULTURAL REPLICATIONS
A Prerequisite for the Validation
of Social-Psychological Laws

IRIT SHARON
YEHUDA AMIR

Frijda and Jahoda (1966) claimed that the majority of cross-cultural studies aim at uncovering causal relationships and that this kind of research is in principle merely an extension of comparisons of intra-cultural groups. The ultimate goal in both cases is the elaboration of general behavior laws. Frijda and Jahoda included within this framework cross-cultural replications that are carried out merely to make sure that particular generalizations were not restricted to one specific culture. However, they emphasized that "it cannot be taken for granted that all experiments do lend themselves to direct cross-cultural replication" (Frijda & Jahoda, 1966, p. 111).

Various approaches have been raised relating to methodological problems in cross-cultural research. Berry (1978) stressed the issue of "dimensional identity" of a common underlying process across cultures as a prerequisite for methodological and conceptual comparability. One of the ways to demonstrate dimensional identity is an empirical demonstration of equivalence in the data collected from various cross-cultural samples. Berry and Dasen (1974) distinguished between three kinds of equivalence, each one providing evidence for dimensional identity: functional, conceptual, and metric.

Functional equivalence exists when two or more behaviors (in two or more cultural systems) are related to functionally similar problems (Berry, 1978, p. 98). The same term was used by both Frijda and Jahoda (1966) and Goldschmidt (1966). The former authors stressed that cross-cultural research assumes the existence of dimensional identity, yet specific cultures sometimes need different conceptual systems to describe them fully and adequately: "Concepts and dimension developed within the context of Western culture need by no means to be the most appropriate to describe human behavior in general" (Frijda & Jahoda, 1966, p. 15). These authors claim that similar activities have different functions in different societies and therefore the same activities cannot be used for comparative purposes. Functional nonequivalence is an issue in sampling problems, in testing procedures, in language data, and so forth, and actually "there is not one single operationalization that would work in every culture" (Frijda & Jahoda, 1966, p. 116).

As a result of the above problems, the research strategies of cross-cultural studies are quite complicated and therefore should be based on elaborate designs. Frijda and Jahoda (1966) claim that "cross-cultural comparisons may have to be supplemented by intra-cultural comparisons, in order to ascertain the intra-cultural variability due to variables which could not be controlled cross-culturally" (p. 123). Other supplements should be cross-cultural comparisons on other dimensions (to rule out alternative interpretations of results) and intracultural comparisons along the same, or similar, dimensions.

The problem of cross-cultural research in social psychology was especially stressed in relation to experimental social psychology. Jahoda (1979) claimed that much of social psychology consists of inductive generalizations, the limits of which need to be established by cross-cultural work. Jahoda tried to refute possible arguments questioning the need for cross-cultural research. According to such arguments, social psychologists deal with basic universals of humankind or with the relationship between conceptual variables abstracted from the totality of human behavior, and therefore uncontaminated by culture. Jahoda disagreed with the fact that such variables and relations exist.

Faucheux (1976) has claimed that the generality of a theory is a theoretical question and only a theory can define the generality of the proposition it asserts. This assertion means that a specific theory can be tested with any human subjects, irrespective of culture, with the only concern being the operational translation of the concepts underlying the experiment. Jahoda (1979) disagreed with this claim and stated that "it is by no means self-evident that a concept embodied in a theory that has its origins within a particular culture can necessarily be operationalized into a conceptual equivalent in a different culture" (p. 143). He also emphasized that as no strong hypothetico-deductive theories exist in social psychology, rather only broad theoretical orientations, Faucheux's assumption cannot be sustained (see also Jahoda, Chap. 7, this volume).

Jahoda (1979) argued that the theories prevalent in experimental social psychology are the products of a specific cultural milieu. In different cultures it would be difficult even to test these theories, as they would not be relevant there. Some theories contain presuppositions about social relations that do not hold in other cultures. This fact of life underscores even more the crucial need for replications as a precondition for drawing conclusions from the "antiseptic laboratory" to real and diverse cultures.

The principal, and striking, conclusion from an extensive literature survey is that there is practically no research the starting point of which is an attempt to validate findings, or the purpose of which is to see how many findings from one culture can be generalized or "recreated" in others. Numerous research projects have compared cultures, taking as their starting points the hypothesis that specific differences exist between cultures, differences that are related to differences in the psychological phenomena being studied.

The literature contains one instance of a basic research study that attempts to challenge cross-cultural findings on a wider than usual scale. Rodrigues (1982) carried out a replication of a number of central studies in social psychology for Brazilians. The advantage of Rodrigues's research as opposed to others is in the "open" approach taken to the question of whether the findings can be replicated. However, the studies to be replicated were chosen in a nonrandom manner, and thus the findings fail to provide a general answer to the basic question, namely, whether social psychological findings can, in general, be replicated across cultures.

A survey of the comparative research studies in the literature presents a distorted picture of the extent of similarity or difference between cultures, or of the replicability or nonreplicability of findings, due to a number of "external" factors:

(1) It is reasonable to assume that findings that are published in the scientific literature are not a representative sample of research findings. They overrepresent differences between cultures and underrepresent findings that have failed to prove hypothesized cross-cultural differences. This is primarily a result of publication policies that prefer results showing differences. Representative research is needed that would sample a broad range of findings, attempt to replicate them, and publish the rate of replication without distorting it by withholding "no difference" findings. Only then can we learn which findings have general and which have only isolated validity.

(2) The reported replication studies make use of instruments that are operationally similar or conceptually equivalent to the instruments employed in the original studies. Had the operational definition of the variables investigated been changed, for example, by means of a change in research instruments, the results of such studies might have been different, in the direction of either more or of less generality.

It must be emphasized that replications in which a "multimethod" approach is taken are necessary in order to ensure conceptual or theoretical generality of the aspects under examination. Research of this kind is practically nonexistent today.

THE POSSIBLE CONTRIBUTION
OF CROSS-CULTURAL RESEARCH
TO SOCIAL PSYCHOLOGY

The need for cross-cultural research and validation is raised every few years in articles published in leading social psychological journals calling for changes in the research approach taken by psychologists. The authors of these articles (e.g., Gergen, 1978; McGuire, 1973) advocate carrying out research on new aspects of various psychological variables, or, alternatively, investigating relations between the variables themselves. Yet even if such lines of thought are pursued, the preference of journal editors to publish only reports that show differences eliminates the possibility of publishing findings that replicate results of earlier studies. Therefore, replication research is rarely carried out today. Instead, it is assumed that a finding has general validity.

In the natural sciences, a basic/fundamental condition for the publication of any research paper is that its findings be replicated several times. However, in psychology, as in the behavioral sciences in general, no tradition of replication of findings exists. This is particularly surprising in light of the fact that it is more difficult to formulate precise operational definitions of psychological variables than of those variables that are studied in the natural sciences. Perhaps this very difficulty makes such replications less likely to be undertaken.

The difficulty involved in operationalizing psychological variables should compel researchers in the field of psychology to replicate their findings a number of times in order to establish their reliability. This strategy, however, is rarely used in psychological research in general or social psychological research in particular. On the contrary, a single sample drawn from a given population usually serves as a basis for determining psychological reliability. No attempts are made to increase the number of samples—either within the same subpopulation or in other populations, and sometimes not even in cases in which the circumstances or research methods differ.

At this juncture, the important exception should be noted, namely, the research method adopted by Byrne in his research on the effects of similarity on interpersonal attraction (1971). Byrne carried out numerous replications of his findings on different populations, in different contexts, and on different areas of similarity. In this manner, he succeeded in "sharpening" his findings, clarifying their exact significance, and distinguishing which types of similarities were involved and how they act to strengthen interpersonal attraction. This type of research paradigm, which asks if a certain finding is still obtained when certain elements of the research procedure are altered, is rare in social psychology. He thereby succeeded in discovering relevant variables that influence the phenomenon of interpersonal attraction.

Given the rarity of replications of intracultural research, it is not surprising that intercultural replications, which do not hypothesize specific differences but attempt to verify the validity of findings, are practically nonexistent, or at least are not reported in the literature.

The contextual approach to social psychological research propounded by McGuire (1983) may serve as a guideline for the development of the cross-cultural validation approach. According to McGuire, the cultural context within which the psychological phenomenon occurs is only a particular case of the context within which the phenomena occur. Cross-cultural validation research can be used to study these phenomena and psychological variables because it is possible to learn more about them from the contexts in which they occur. Furthermore, it will be possible to characterize these contexts and to analyze the dimensions along which they differ. Cultural variables can be located, variables that are related to the phenomena under discussion, affect them, or interact with the independent variables that affect them. In this way, cross-cultural validation research can advance our knowledge of the phenomena and psychological variables that have been studied.

CROSS-CULTURAL VALIDATION
OF SOCIAL-PSYCHOLOGICAL FINDINGS
THROUGH REPLICATION

The present authors conducted an extensive project on the cross-cultural validation of social-psychological findings through replications. This project will be briefly described and the main findings and conclusions will be presented thereafter. In the following section the methodological difficulties that were encountered by the researchers will be elaborated, and some possible solutions will be considered.

The purpose of this study was to evaluate the reproducibility of social-psychological findings across cultures and subcultures. The basic approach adopted was that of a validation research. Specifically, the question dealt with was that of cross-cultural validity *in general* and no attempt was made to deal with a specific psychological phenomenon or with a specific minitheory. The authors strongly believed that what was needed were studies about the general validity of social-psychological findings geared to test whether such findings could be reproduced at all in different cultures. No specific hypotheses about phenomena that should or should not be reproduced were proposed.

Three aspects of cross-cultural validity were investigated in the study: The influence of culture itself on psychological laws; the influence of specific subpopulations within a culture; and the combined influence of culture and the specific population studied. (For an extensive report of this study, see Amir and Sharon, 1987.) Henceforth, this research selected studies conducted in other (than Israel's) cultures and replicated them in Israel on a population similar to the original one (influence of culture), as well as on a different population (combined influence of culture and population). Thus it was possible to evaluate both the importance of culture *per se* and the combined effects of both inter- and intracultural factors on research results and on the establishment of scientific laws.

The Method of the Study

From all the studies that were published in four top journals in social psychology during the period from January 1, 1973, to April 1, 1975, 35 studies were randomly sampled. From this primary sample six studies were selected for replication in Israel.

The requirement of adequacy and comparability of descriptive categories served as a major criterion for the inclusion of a specific study in this research. The reasoning behind this decision was, as Frijda and Jahoda (1966) had stated, that concepts and dimensions developed within the context of one culture need not be the most appropriate to describe behavior in another culture. If this criterion could not be met, the study was not included. Generally, it was necessary to decide in advance if the original dependent variable could be replicated or had to be changed in order to be of the same meaning in the other culture.

Special emphasis was given to meet the requirement of functional equivalence of the type of behavior studied in the other cultural setting. In cases of doubt in this respect, the particular study was not replicated. The method employed for the selection of studies for replication thus involved a very conservative procedure. It weeds out strong emics and biases the selection in favor of replicability. This is important, especially in light of the subsequent findings in this study.

Each study was prepared for two replications: (1) on a sample of university students, which in most cases constituted a replication on a similar sample to the one used in the original study, and (2) on a sample of high school students, which may be considered a somewhat different subculture.

Results and Conclusions

Twelve replications were analyzed and compared with the results of the original six studies. Since the main purpose of the project was the cross-validation of social-psychological findings in general and not a test of a specific hypothesis in a specific content area, the findings of the project will be presented in a summary way, that is, collapsed across studies.

Very generally, we classified the findings into seven categories:

(1) results replicated in each of the experiments (original experiment and both replications)
(2) results found only in the original experiment and in the replication on a similar sample
(3) results found in the original experiment and in the replication on a different sample
(4) results found in the original experiment only
(5) results found in the two replications only, that is, the same culture, different from the original one
(6) results found only in the replication on a similar sample
(7) results found only in the replication on the different sample

These seven categories can be regarded as follows: Category 1 gives optimal indication for the cross-cultural validity (or lack of validity) of the findings. Results in Category 2 also show cross-cultural validity, but no cross-sectional validity within the receiving culture itself. Category 3 shows validity that is "beyond" the cultural and intergroup differences (though it would be hard to interpret).

The results in the following categories stress, mainly, the lack of cross-cultural validity: Category 5 includes results found in both replications and, therefore, apparently expresses phenomena characteristic only of the specific culture in which the replications were carried out. Categories 4, 6, and 7 present results specific to certain subpopulations in a specific culture.

The first analysis of the results was a quantitative one. A total of 64 results from the original studies were compared to those of the two replications by classifying them into the seven aforementioned categories. Out of the 64 results found in the original studies, only 16 (25%) repeated themselves in both replications. These results indicate optimal cross-cultural replicability. Another eight results (12.5%) indicate partial replication. Those results are replications of findings in another culture, but only with regard to the same kind of population. Only one result (1.6%) indicated a replication between the original study and the replication on a different population in a different culture. Five results (7.8%) indicated intracultural without cross-cultural replicability (Category 5). The remainder of the results (53%) indicates lack of any kind of replicability of the data (Categories 4, 6, and 7).

In addition to the quantitative aspect, the results can also be classified qualitatively. Such a classification may sharpen the examination of the relationship between the type of results and the degree of replication. For this purpose, the following two categories were proposed: (1) Results that deal with the central hypothesis of the research as compared with additional results that have only secondary importance, and (2) results that deal with the main effects of the independent variables as compared with results that deal with interactions between these variables.

The following conclusions can be drawn from the application of this categorization to the findings: Regarding the first category, it was found that in most of the cases in which the results of the replications were similar to those of the original study, they were related to the central hypothesis of the research. As for the additional results, in general they were not replicated and in those cases in which the replications produced additional results, these were different from the original ones. Yet it is important to note that in all the replications the analysis of the data was geared only to test the original hypotheses and the additional findings that were reported in the original experiment. Hypotheses that were not reported in the original experiments or those that arose during the experiment were not examined. Therefore, it is possible that additional differences between the original studies and the replications that have not been examined actually do exist.

As reported, additional results were found in the replications that had not been reported in the original experiments (in spite of a report that the analysis was undertaken). These results were regarded as cases of "dissimilar" results because it was assumed that no report on these results testifies to their not having been statistically significant in the original experiments. It should be noted that we refer to the effects of independent variables alone and not to the manipulation checks and/or reliability checks of the variables.

As to the classification between results of main effects and those of interactions, the picture here is much clearer. Out of the 16 optimally replicated results (Category 1), 14 (87.5%) are main effects, and in these cases the main effects in the replications were generally in the same direction as in the original experiments. Categories 2, 3, and 5 include results that were similar in any two samples. These categories also comprise mainly (85.7%) main effects. The third group of categories comprises specific results (results that were found in only one sample). This group includes 44% interactions and 56% main effects. This distribution points to the basic conclusion that most of the truly replicated results comprise main effects and not interactions. One should note again that the main effects in the replications were generally in the same direction as in the original experiments.

For the interactions obtained, the overlap between results from the original experiments and those of the replications was very small. Even when interactions were obtained between the same independent variables in the replications and in the original experiments, they indicated *different directions*. Furthermore, *new* interactions were obtained in the replications and some interactions that were found in the original experiments were not replicated at all. All this points to the specificity of the findings regarding interactions and the lack of correspondence between the original studies and both replications. Nisbett (1977) came to similar conclusions with regard to personality research, claiming that most findings of interactions are not replicable. Rodrigues (1982), in his replication studies, did not differentiate between the replicability of main effects and interactions. However, from a careful analysis of his results (p. 105), it turns out that the great majority of his replicated results were main effects. Only a few interactions were found in the replications, some of them not in the direction of the original findings.

One of the reasons for the strong emphasis of the present researchers on the exclusion of "noise" (i.e., incidental inclusion of irrelevant stimuli in the 12 replications not necessarily present in the original studies) was the desire to exclude possible alternative explanations to the major findings of this study. Therefore, it seems that, for instance, the general trend found with regard to interactions (i.e., the many *new* interactions found in the replications as well as those *not* found, as compared with the original studies) cannot be explained in terms of unintentional variations (i.e., noise) in the replicated studies. Most probably, these findings point to some general trend indicative of cross-cultural social psychological behavior.

METHODOLOGICAL DIFFICULTIES AND DILEMMAS

In this section the methodological and technical difficulties that confronted the authors in the study described earlier will be elaborated. We will present some different solutions to these problems and consider their consequences for cross-cultural research.

On the topic of the *selection of studies*, many questions arose. When sampling six studies out of hundreds, one can hardly speak of a representative sample. Rather, there is a selection according to some technical criteria. These criteria should be well checked for their relevance to cross-cultural replicability. One should be especially careful to exclude neither the emic nor the etic studies from the sample of replications.

A specific problem the present authors encountered in their research was the inability either to locate or to elicit responses from the original researchers in order to get the material needed for the replications. In some cases the original researchers were unable to deliver this material. As these studies were not replicated, one wonders if this exclusion caused any bias. There is no reason to assume a specific direction, yet the problem should be dealt with somehow. Of course, this problem would not have occurred had the replication been planned from the outset.

The issues regarding the *preparation of test materials* were more complicated. In most cases the information published in the articles was not sufficient for an adequate replication. At times, even additional information, directly supplied by the original researcher, was not detailed enough to ensure a precise replication. This obstacle is naturally solved in simultaneous planning of cross-cultural replications.

Problems that cannot be solved by simultaneous planning are mainly those connected with the issues of equivalence. This issue, raised by most cross-cultural researchers, has no clear-cut answers or criteria and much is left to the researcher's judgment. A relevant example in the authors' study is the replication of Newtson and Czerlinsky's (1974) study. These researchers investigated shifts in the communication of attitudes according to the assumed attitude of the audience. The specific attitudes employed by the original researchers were political attitudes, on a scale of liberal versus conservative. The attitudes were relevant to the political issues in the United States when the original study was carried out, that is, dovish versus hawkish attitudes toward the war in Vietnam. It is obvious that the same issue would not have any equivalence in the Israeli culture a number of years later.

The solution to this problem was found by constructing an attitude scale relevant to the Israeli political life at the time the replication was conducted, that is, attitudes favoring or opposing the return to Arab hands of the territories occupied since the Six Day War. There was sound basis to assume that this attitude is conceptually equivalent to the one used in the Newtson and Czerlinsky (1974) experiment, but this was merely our assertion.

The third type of methodological issues is the *sampling of subjects*, which is also related to the notion of equivalence. When one intends to use the same type of subjects as in the original study, equivalence cannot always be complete and one should decide which characteristic of the subjects is most crucial to meet the demands of equivalence. Thus, for instance, first- (or second-) year students in the United States (where most of the original studies were conducted) are chronologically and emotionally younger than the same "type" of students in Israel, all of whom have already served in the army for a number of years. On the other hand, if 19-year-olds were selected, no occupational equivalence would be obtained, as one cultural group comprises students and the other one soldiers. There seems to be no fully satisfactory solution to this dilemma. So, in the studies conducted by the present authors, the replication on a "similar" sample comprised local students similar to those used in the original studies on the dimension of educational situation (e.g., first-year psychology students in both samples).

The question of *procedure* also raises a number of problems. These problems may sometimes seem minor or even trivial. One should, however, pay attention to their effect on the reproducibility of results, as they may interact with the independent variables. Following are two examples.

In replications it is practically impossible to produce a physical setting identical to that of the original study. This may affect the findings directly, since it was experimentally found (i.e., Biggers & Preyor, 1982) that various features of the physical setting have direct influence on the results. These variables may interact with other independent variables and produce totally different results that might be mistakenly attributed to the influence of culture. According to Biggers and Preyor, the physical setting influences the mood of the subject. If the dependent variable is related to the mood of the subject, as, for example, in measures of aggression or measures of interpersonal attraction or of endorsement of leaders, the effect of the physical setting produces "noise." The interaction with the independent variables might manifest itself mainly by intensifying or diminishing the effect of an independent variable. As stated above, there is no way to solve these problems entirely. One should only be aware of them and try to minimize their possible effect by trying to get as much detailed information as possible about the procedure of the original experiment.

The second example in this domain concerns the identity of the experimenter. It is common knowledge today that the experimenter's identity (i.e., age, sex, ethnic origin, etc.) or conduct has crucial influence on the results of the experiment. While the conduct of the experimenter is sometimes described and the instructions he or she gives the subjects are sometimes quoted (or are otherwise available from the original researcher), details about his or her identity are practically never provided. Information about the age or sex of the experimenter or of his or her similarity or dissimilarity to the subjects in other respects may be especially important to consider in cross-cultural replications, since these variables may have different relevance in different cultures. If so, one must vary the experimenter's identity from the original experiment to achieve equivalence.

The last issue concerns the *analysis of results*. In the project done by the authors of this research, the principle was to analyze the results in exactly the same way as in the original investigation. This was the policy adopted, since the purpose of the project was merely to determine whether results were similar or dissimilar in different cultures. Therefore, no additional analyses were made. This may have biased the results toward more similarity. It is probable that results not mentioned in the original article were not significant and therefore a significant result found in a replication is unique and constitutes cultural specificity. However, if a specific analysis was not done for some reason by the original researcher, this assumption does not hold true. This issue, too, can be solved only by simultaneous planning of a study and its replication, by simultaneously conducting the experiments, and by simultaneous analysis of the results.

CONCLUSION

The general conclusion that may be derived from this chapter relates to the critical necessity for conducting replications of studies in various cultures. Only if studies are replicated under different conditions, such as different populations, different situations, and, of course, different cultures, may one come to general and universal conclusions regarding a social psychological variable or phenomenon.

Just as one should not construct social psychological theories based upon studies using n = 1 subjects, likewise one cannot confirm them on the basis of a single study in which the number of investigated situations is 1. This is especially true when the generalization beyond the population studied is to a different cultural group.

As to the methodological issues related to cross-cultural replications, it seems doubtful whether "cookbook recipes" of how to conduct validation studies can at present be suggested. Problems raised in this chapter should be taken into account when planning replications. Only additional empirical efforts with different types of replication studies with diverse solutions to the inherent methodological problems will yield more clear-cut directions about how to conduct cross-cultural validation studies. At any rate, the recommendation is unequivocal that such studies should be carried out and published. We should avoid the present-day practice of simply ignoring the problem of drawing generalized conclusions from research findings in a single sample—in psychology in general, and in social psychology in particular.

9

PUTTING THE ETIC TO WORK
Applying Social Psychological Principles in Cross-Cultural Settings

JOSEPH E. TRIMBLE

Time and again, psychologists have displayed a tendency to be so absorbed in their own abstractions that they have lost sight of vitally important factors in real life.

—Mazafer Sherif (1951)

The words of the eminent social psychologist Mazafer Sherif, writing in the fifties, were no more than an echo of another social psychologist, Kurt Lewin. Writing at about the same time, Lewin noted: "Research that produces nothing but books will not suffice" (1948, p. 203). Both Sherif and Lewin, along with a few other social scientists of their time, argued for relevancy and applicability of research in terms of both the subject matter and the generalizability of the results. The theoretician and the practitioner need to collaborate, Lewin maintained, and this "can be accomplished . . . if the theorist does not look toward applied problems with highbrow aversion or with a fear of social problems and if the applied psychologist realizes that there is nothing as practical as a good theory" (1951, p. 169).

To promote the application of social science, Lewin (1948) coined the phrase "action research," which, from his perspective, called for the application of general laws to the understanding of social conditions. If done properly, presumably the results would lead to social action.

Action research, as conceived by Lewin, never really caught on in social psychology; however, it did find its way into the fields of criminology and social work (Sanford, 1970). Today we find social psychologists striving to fulfill Lewin's dream in the rapidly emerging field of applied social psychology. Evidence of that effort can be found in the publications of the *Applied Social Psychology Annual, Progress in Applied Social Psychology*, the *Journal of Applied Social Psychology*, and the *Journal of Social Issues*. Publication topics are impressive and far reaching in their coverage.

WHAT IS THE APPLIED PERSPECTIVE?

A number of social psychologists have offered several definitions of the applied perspective. Rutter and Robinson (1981) point out that applied social psychology "is practical: it tries to help solve and prevent a range of problems in everyday life" (p. 345). It is also theoretical and, as such, attempts should be made "to test and extend existing theories by taking them outside the laboratory and . . . to use everyday problems as its source of new issues and theory" (p. 345). Arguing that a singular definition for the area is difficult, Bickman (1980) states, "Basic research is aimed toward accumulating knowledge about fundamental principles of behavior, while . . . applied research is intended to provide input into problem solving" (p. 11). Pulling the definitions together one would conclude that laboratory-grounded theory *can* be put to some use in understanding real world problems and that social science research methods can be applied to studying social issues.

Applying social psychological theory and research methods to real world problems gives the researcher an opportunity to determine the viability of current knowledge. Putting theory into practice can serve to establish its predictive validity and stimulate additional research. From what we are led to believe about the field, the applied researcher can also approach real world problems with the utmost of confidence since "no empirical evidence has been forthcoming to support the hypothesis that a laboratory science can produce theoretical truths which do not extend to real life" (Turner, 1981, p. 4).

STATUS OF CROSS-CULTURAL
AND APPLIED TOPICS
IN SOCIAL PSYCHOLOGY

An analysis of the contents of 14 prominent social psychology texts yields some interesting findings about the field and its emphasis on cultural and applied topics. Slightly more than 7,600 pages were written between 1982 and the present in an effort to present the current level of interest of perceived importance in the field. Less than 1% of the pages gave the concept of culture attention in any form; even less was given to the condition and status of the major ethnic-minority populations in North America. When there was such material, it almost made exclusive reference to Blacks—one typically finds this group discussed in sections dealing with racism, prejudice, and discrimination. Research citations are also minimal for American Indians, Asian Americans and Pacific Islanders, and Hispanic populations. Material dealing with applied social psychology consumed close to 5% of the pages—such material was usually covered in sections dealing with health behavior, legal and environmental topics, and in specifically prepared inserts typically labeled "Applications." Two texts (Fisher, 1982; Cvetkovich, Baumgardner, & Trimble, 1984) wove the applied perspective throughout the various chapters and interestingly contained more references to culture and ethnic matters than all of the other 12 texts combined. Finally, all of the texts devoted some attention to the topics of prejudice and racism, areas in which one would naturally expect a good deal of discussion about ethnic minorities and cultural matters.

One could argue that not enough published material is available on cultural and applied topics to warrant adequate textbook coverage. Much to the anticipated chagrin of the textbook authors, that is not the case. An examination of the publication topics found just in the *Journal of Cross-Cultural Psychology* from 1970 to 1980 alone shows that 43% were devoted to social psychological and personality topics and overall 514 articles dealt with more than 42 ethnic and nationalistic populations; for the latter, some 10% contained research findings on North and Central American ethnic populations (Lonner, 1980). If textbook authors were so inclined, there is ample information on the subjects of culture and ethnicity available for inclusion in textbooks.

Now what about the limited coverage given to the application of social psychological research findings and the use of its methods? In all fairness to the textbook authors, efforts were made by some of them to include material that draws attention to the application of social psychological principles, even though it was restricted to certain areas (i.e., health, law, and environment). Nonetheless, there is room for improvement given the rapid and accelerating interest in the applied field, as evidenced by the growing number of publications. Future textbook authors would serve the discipline well if they would attempt to strike a reasonable balance between the theoretical and applied perspective.

APPLYING SOCIAL PSYCHOLOGY
IN CROSS-CULTURAL SETTINGS

Given the current interest in applied social psychology, it would be safe to conclude that more and more studies will be directed to culturally different populations, not only in North America but probably for other nation states as well. As a consequence, social scientists will face a multitude of theoretical and methodological concerns quite often presented by indigenous peoples whose cultures are unique in contrast to the dominant groups in North America. Predictably, the work of cross-cultural psychologists will be a source for guidance and direction. In the main, applied researchers will be confronted with the vicissitudes of "putting the etic to work," as the title of this chapter suggests.

To put the etic to work first and foremost will require researchers to examine the methodologies of cross-cultural psychologists and cultural anthropologists. One should be aware that cross-cultural psychology is defined more by methodology than by findings (Berry, 1980). Knowledge of the empirical findings in both fields may prove useful, but not nearly as useful as the methods.

Putting the etic to work also implies that researchers should place an emphasis on what cross-cultural psychologists refer to as "universals"— not universal psychological constructs or similarities in behavior, but universally acceptable methods of generating empirical data. A discussion of universal psychological processes has itself received a good deal of attention (see Jahoda, 1980). The basic challenge for an applied approach to cross-cultural social psychology is to identify useful and appropriate *methodological etics*—research technologies that are both sensitive and appropriate for use in all cultural groups. It would be naive for one to assume that a methodological etic is sufficient to collect data from different cultural folk—other intercultural matters may exist that could affect data collection and use of results. In an attempt to highlight issues and problems, the remaining sections of the chapter will focus on a few examples of applied social psychological studies conducted among culturally unique groups, an assortment of methodological concerns, the influence of researchers as agents of sociopolitical change, and the ethical and social responsibilities of applied researchers.

Doing Applied Cross-Cultural Social Psychology

In applying social psychological techniques with culturally distinct ethnic-minority groups, the would-be researcher sets a process in motion that of necessity must take into consideration the *ethos* and *eidos* of the cultural group in question. Not to do so could lead to an early death of the project and likely alienate the research team from future work with the community. In turn, as has happened far too often, community members receive further substantiation for their levels of distrust toward research and its progenitors. Lack of cultural sensitivity and awareness of community dynamics sets up a "no-win" situation—science receives a bad reputation (often much deserved) and the community problem continues to go unsolved.

What can one do to minimize cross-cultural conflicts accruing from the researcher-community interface? Fortunately, owing to the growing body of research in cross-cultural settings, a good deal can be learned from successful efforts. Where space is insufficient, detailed references will be made in the following sections to assist the reader in obtaining additional information.

Gaining entry in the field. Whether social scientists wish to accept it or not, their presence in culturally distinct—especially certain ethnic-minority—communities in North America is cause for considerable suspicion. Often the mere suggestion that one is an academic is enough to spark controversy—this is apparently even true for researchers who share the same ethnicity as members of the host community. The origins of the suspicions derive from two sources—a community's lack of experience with the research process, and previous relationships with researchers.

Many ethnic-minority and culturally distinct communities, especially rural ones, have little or no understanding or appreciation for aca-demics-grounded research—science and all its trimmings are foreign to the residents. Researchers are often viewed by themselves and com-munity residents as socially and culturally marginal to the society they presume to study. As a consequence, "no matter how skilled he is in the native tongue, how nimble in handling strange social relationships, how artistic in performing social and religious rituals, and how attached he is to local beliefs, goals, and values, [the researcher] rarely deludes himself into thinking that many community members really regard him as one of them" (Freilich, 1970, p. 2).

Regardless of his or her affinity and expressed understanding of the community, the researcher often stands to be accused as some kind of government agent or a spy—"He is not what he pretends to be and that he is gathering information for some purpose harmful to the com-munity" (Freilich, 1970, p. 3), an outsider looking for a place to establish a permanent residence, a missionary sent in to convert the residents, or another social scientist whose prime interest may be to gain prestige and a promotion.

Because of the recent concern about the presence of researchers, a number of American Indian communities in the United States and Canada have issued edicts prohibiting and restricting any form of research in their respective communities. One Indian reserve in British

Columbia, after learning of a researcher's interpretations of life in the community, issued an ordinance that flatly forbids any form of research involving its residents. A similar ordinance was issued by a polar slope village in Alaska after learning that the results of a study they initiated with a psychiatrist were released to the newswire services. The findings from the study were apparently very condemning, as they presented a view of village life that many residents did not want openly discussed. Some Indian reservation communities in the continental United States require all outside researchers to present a prospectus to the tribal council for review and sanction. If sanctioned, researchers are granted what is equivalent to a solicitor's license that carries with it a number of contingencies, which typically include (1) the assignment of a knowledgeable tribal member to monitor all research activities, (2) restrictions on the nature and composition of potential respondents (this restriction makes random sampling almost an impossibility), (3) the right to review all original and completed research questionnaires, interview schedules, and field notes, (4) the right to review any documents submitted for publication with the understanding that the tribe has the right to reject such documents, and (5) the right to review, comment, and pass judgment on any final reports. Add to these contingencies the procedures for receiving informed consent and protecting the rights of all respondents and one could readily surmise that conducting field research is much more complex than randomly pooling college students in quasi-laboratory settings.

Collecting data in the field generates many more psychosocial problems than besets the theoretically oriented, laboratory-grounded social psychologist. Field-oriented social scientists are likely to deal with at least four types of problems, namely "(1) physical survival, (2) psychological comfort, (3) everyday pragmatics, and (4) moral dilemmas" (Freilich, 1970, p. 19). Accounts of the experiences of field researchers, especially cultural anthropologists, are widespread and truly illuminating (see Freilich, 1970; Wax, 1960; Henry & Saberwal, 1969). Wintrob (1969) maintains that the field experience is likely to create a "dysadaptation syndrome" characterized by periods of withdrawal, anxiety, feelings of rejection and helplessness, emergence of dependency feelings toward key informants and hosts, intense vacillation of affect, frustration, self-doubt, and expressed feelings of loneliness. Wax (1960), while spending time in a Japanese-American relocation center, commented, "At the conclusion of the first month of work I had obtained very little data and I was discouraged, bewildered and obsessed by a sense of failure" (p. 168). On the same theme, Freilich (1970) remarks, "Each field trip is thus, in part, a mystical experience and a sacred ritual" (p. 16), for in the process the field researcher is pushed to carefully assess his or her presence within the context of the host culture and his or her goals as a scientist.

Gaining entry into the field, whether invited by the host culture or not, carries an enormous responsibility. This responsibility not only extends to the residents and respondents, but also to the maintenance of one's scientific integrity. More important, the applied researcher should recognize that mistakes, errors in protocol, and violations of cultural norms, beliefs, and values are not easily forgiven by members of the host and scientific communities. Impetuously and boldly rushing into a community for the sheer sake of advancing one's pet theory and hopefully promoting science is unconscionable, intolerable, and indeed disrespectful.

Before setting foot into a culturally different community for the purposes of conducting applied research, researchers would do well to heed the recommendations of those who have been there before. After spending some five years conducting research on the aging process in numerous ethnic minority communities in the United States, Bengston, Grigsby, Corry, and Hruby (1977) drew up the following considerations for future applied oriented researchers, as follows:

(1) Research should be multidisciplinary. If not possible, the solitary researcher should seek the consultation of other social scientists and persons who have some working knowledge of the community in question. Advice and assistance should be solicited to focus on methodological and procedural matters; receptivity of community focus; knowledge of community dynamics, including potential key informants and community leaders; and knowledge concerning the essence of basic and applied literature in the disciplines that touch on the research theme.

(2) Conventional research strategies are not easily "translated to action research with a policy-oriented focus" (p. 88). Too many constituencies are involved, as the number of stakeholders inevitably expands to include members of both the lay and the scientific communities. The scientific community will be concerned with methodological soundness and the lay community will want "to be assured that they are not getting ripped off, that their collective voices will be heard, and that they will share in monetary remuneration" (p. 89).

(3) Because of the number of potential stakeholders, the potential for conflict is considerable. Bengston et al. (1977) argue that "the nature of the conflct between the lay community and professional researchers demands that strategies for conflict resolution be given consideration equal to that directed toward design criteria and methodological procedures" (pp. 89-90).

(4) Above all the considerations applied, action researchers must be prepared to adapt to many changes that could occur in the course of the effort. They must be prepared to revise strategies and tactics to accommodate the changing concerns of community life.

Cultural equivalence of research tools. Applied social psychologists typically rely on the use of the survey approach and the structured interview format to collect information. To a lesser extent, some researchers make use of case study approaches, meta-analytic procedures, secondary data analytic methods, and, to a very limited extent, quasi-experimental approaches. In the domain of policy research "there is no single, comprehensive methodology for doing the technical analysis of policy research [therefore] . . . policy researchers have been free to pursue a variety of methodological directions in technically analyzing social problems" (Majchrazak, 1984, p. 58). Nonetheness, there are policy research approaches that have proven their effectiveness, including focused synthesis (actually a literature review), secondary analysis, field experiments, qualitative methods, surveys, case studies, and cost-benefit and cost-effectiveness analyses. For all intents, the aforementioned approaches could be referred to as "methodological etics," for it is tacitly assumed that the techniques could be used with any group, regardless of its cultural background.

Methodological etics are akin to what cross-cultural psychologists refer to as "cultural equivalence"—phenomena that are consistent across all human beings and all human groups. Malpass and Poortinga (1986) argue that essentially three kinds of *equivalences* can exist: (1) Functional equivalence exists when behaviors emitted by people from different cultures occur in response to similar problems; (2) conceptual equivalence exists when people from different cultures share a common meaning about specific stimuli; and (3) metric equivalence exists when the psychometric properties of one's data obtained from different cultures reveals a comparable pattern. The nature of functional and conceptual equivalences present real problems for applied researchers— exclusive reliance on methodological etics without regard for these concepts could invalidate an entire research venture.

On more than one occasion social scientists assumed that a form of equivalence existed for the major research topic, only to discover after spending countless hours in organizing the research effort that a form of conceptual nonequivalence existed that created a bias. Two examples will serve to illustrate the significance of the latter occurrence.

More often than not, researchers assume that their respondents and subjects share common ethnic and nationalistic origins. In the cross-cultural literature, studies abound in which researchers purport to be studying such groups as the Japanese, Israeli Jews, Mexican Americans, Hong Kong Chinese, American Indians, Canadians, Australian aborigines, Greek Australians, Nigerian Ibos—this list could continue, comprising a multitude of nationalistic and hyphenated ethnic populations. Researchers assume with confidence that their sampled subjects "have an equal understanding of behavior or concepts pertaining to behavior"(Malpass & Poortinga, 1986, p. 66). They also assume that the subjects share a common understanding of their own ethnicity and nationalist identification. There is evidence though that suggests that the assumption may not be altogether valid.

Marin and Marin (1982) cite a problem that illustrates how the use of an ethnic category created an instance of conceptual nonequivalence. The two investigators searched the records of 500 patients at a clinic in East Los Angeles, California, an area heavily populated with people of Hispanic origin. Marin and Marin expected to find mostly Hispanics in their sample. To their surprise, they found that some patients *with Spanish surnames* actually checked the "white" and "other" ethnic identification categories on the medical form. When they examined the "other" category, they found that 3% of the patients wrote in specific ethnic identifiers, such as "Mexican-American" and "Chicano," and designations that indicated they were of Hispanic origin. All in all, some 12 to 13% made classification errors even though they had a Spanish surname. Clearly, the use of "Hispanic" as a means to identify a sample population is insufficient, as the ethnic category means quite different things to people with Spanish surnames. As an alternative, Marin and Marin suggest that researchers rely on surname lists to identify their samples; however, this technique is not without its problems.

The other sample concerns a study we initiated several years ago that focused on the adaptive strategies taken by ethnic-minority elderly toward a natural disaster. Our ethnic samples consisted of 689 rural Black, Caucasian and American Indian elders from 11 states (Trimble, Richardson, & Tatum, 1982). To identify the elderly samples initially, we planned to use the age of 55 as a cut-off point, a standard recommended by the National Institute on Aging. However, after carefully reviewing our decision, we realized that Blacks and American Indians used different criteria for defining elderly status. Our research showed that both ethnic groups perceived the onset of elderly status as occurring at a younger age than Caucasians by as much as 12 years (Trimble, 1981). Many of the ethnic respondents (about 40%) preferred to define their elderly status not in terms of age but in terms of their perceived roles and responsibilities within their families and respective communities. Caucasians tended to rely more on age criteria (typically 65 years of age) than did the ethnic samples. In short, we discovered *after the fact* that a general pattern of disagreement existed as to what actually *best* describes or determines elderly status; this was even true for the three samples residing in the same community. The lesson to be learned from this study is fairly straightforward. Researchers are advised to include a subjective measure of age, especially among elderly populations, when studying different ethnic and cultural populations.

Discussions concerning the equivalence topics, strategies for building culturally sensitive research instruments, and matters concerning establishing collaborative arrangements with host cultures abound in the literature. On topics dealing with issues in cross-cultural research, readers are advised to consult Warwick and Osherson (1973), Bulmer and Warwick (1983), and Triandis and Lambert (1980). Concerning methodological and procedural matters, works written and prepared by Lonner and Berry (1986) and Triandis and Berry (1980) should be checked.

In closing out this section, it would be instructive to point out that cross-cultural psychological research often generates unwanted and undesirable variables—subtle variations that are not a part of the original design and thus are overlooked. Specifically, Sargent (1977) defines these variables "as any factors that interfere with meaningful comparisons and conclusions in cross-cultural research" (p. 712). Such variables can be prevented provided researchers carefully review a host of potent sources before they enter the field.

Sargent (1977) suggests that the following sources are worthy candidates for preventing the researcher from uncovering the specious variables:

(1) the motivation of the researcher to arrive at a conclusion that would support a pet theory. Closely tied to this is the "researcher-as-crusader" effect, which is often the "unconscious motivation" of policy and social action researchers.

(2) the perceptual orientation of the researcher, often expressed through ignorance, naivete, inadequate preparation, and inconsistent frames of reference. In applied research particularly, researchers should be fairly knowledgeable about social change, modernity, and acculturative processes occurring within a culture.

(3) unbridled trust in data produced by questionnaires and survey instruments. Put another way, do the data accurately represent social conditions, opinions, and the ethos of a culture? In the earlier example concerning our study on the elderly, it was clear to us that survey responses were not comparable if we persisted in using age as our criteria for defining subgroups.

(4) All or any one of the previous sources of unwanted variables can lead to unwarranted interpretations. In the final analysis, this source of

speciousness should be avoided *at all costs*, especially in policy and action-oriented research.

Often "pesky," unwarranted variables can be discovered by examining the accuracy of the original data. Sargent cites the example of a Russian researcher who had conducted extensive interviews with centurions in the Caucasus region of the Soviet Union. In part of his presentation, the researcher showed a picture of a 138-year-old woman and her 85-year-old son. Sargent points out that "it probably did not occur (to the researcher) that (the woman) would have been 53 when the son was born, which would have been almost a miracle" (1977, p. 713). Sargent goes on to point out that birth dates and records are almost nonexistent in the study area, but nonetheless a tradition of longevity is associated with the native residents. Given the likely encouragement of Soviet propagandists, the researcher pursued his research faithfully, but in the end aroused suspicion about his total effort.

APPLIED RESEARCH
AS SOCIOPOLITICAL CHANGE

Applied and policy-oriented research is highly political. By its very nature, the field focuses on topics that are an intimate part of the everyday activities of the community, the state, and the nation. Hence, applied research is not value-free, since the topic selected for study may represent a major source of concern and interest in a community of interest. Whether one is invited to explore the topic or it is self-initiated, the researcher and the methods and procedures can rapidly become quite visible, possibly disruptive, and consequently very politicized.

On the surface, many applied topics can appear benign. In time, however, the significance and importance they receive through the organization of a research effort brings otherwise suppressed attitudes and feelings to the surface. Even hiding behind the objective goal of research invariably is not sufficient to suppress the affective elements lodged in a topic—research may be guided by objectivity, but policy-oriented topics in the eyes of a community's residents are fueled by affect.

As researchers plan and organize the field-based research around a sensitive topic, they will cause residents to reflect upon the issues. In time, residents will be reminded of their deep-seated feelings and frustrations, and what was once a suppressed and repressed topic of discussion rapidly surfaces to become an everyday point of concern. The researchers and their hired locals soon can become the target of controversy to the extent that the success of the research effort could be placed in jeopardy.

Often researchers are invited to study a persistent problem in a community that has been the interest of previous researchers in the same community. The presence of the new research team reminds the community of the need for intervention and policy and the real possibility that, despite continuing research efforts, the problems are not likely to disappear. Countless communities have witnessed the "comings and goings" of research experts to the extent that many have become complacent and apathetic about change and the resolution of conditions that persistently cause frustration, bitterness, and suppressed hostilities. Under these conditions, researchers can expect to find a community that is reluctant or unwilling to cooperate and may even set up insurmountable barriers in hopes of sabotaging the project.

During the 1960s and 1970s, numerous "impoverished" Black, Hispanic, and American Indian communities were the subject of intense research on poverty, sponsored, in a large majority, by the U.S. government. The researchers arrived, consorted with local community leaders, conducted their interviews, snapped countless photos, and left, in many instances never to be heard from again. Many community residents were reminded of their impoverished status, the deeply embedded prejudice of those in more affluent communities, and their seemingly hopeless conditions. A decade or so has elapsed and the conditions for many have not changed.

What has changed though are communities' concern about policy-oriented researchers. The so-called "safari-scholar" era has come to an end and "data mining" is no longer tolerated (Hursh-Cesar & Roy, 1976). More than ever, many leaders in ethnic-minority and culturally distinct communities view researchers, regardless of their intent, as elitists and, in more accurate terms, colonialists. Consequently, the rules have changed and social science researchers can no longer count on the bind of cooperation they are accustomed to when it comes to soliciting support.

Many applied researchers are aware of the newly found and long overdue stance that the ethnic-minorities have taken toward research. However, knowledge of the politics surrounding the conduct of action research does not warrant the use of tactics to work one's way around them. In 1986, a researcher interested in collecting data from residents in a small Cree Indian village in Canada's Manitoba province knew that the tribal leaders would be reluctant to sanction his effort. The tribe's research policies were fairly well known. Stimulated by the possibility of a large federal grant, he sought cooperation from a local nonnative school principal. The principal consented, assuming that the researcher had the tribe's blessings. Several days later, over lunch, the principal happened to mention his excitement about the pending research project to a few tribal leaders. In a matter of a few hours, the researcher and all his instruments were escorted to the reserve's boundaries. A week later, the researcher's university received a heated letter essentially declaring the reserve "off-limits" for anyone remotely connected to the institution.

Applied cross-cultural researchers are not immune from the ethics governing research in general and those that may take place in another country or in a community that is culturally different. Many cultural enclaves may not comprehend the necessity for informed consent, for example. Nonetheless, a researcher is obligated to protect and honor the rights of the participants.

All social psychologists are aware of the ethical principles governing the research process and a vast majority dutifully and faithfully honor the code. Yet many ethnic-minority psychologists have at least one tale to tell about someone who violated the code when studying a culture other than his or her own. The magnitude and seriousness of these tales actually led to the development of the Advisory Principles for Ethical Consideration in the Conduct of Cross-Cultural Research, spearheaded by a number of prominent American social psychologists (Tapp, Kelman, Triandis, Wrightsman, & Coelho, 1974). The principles expand upon the standards established by the American Psychological Association to include: "(1) the inherent ethical acceptability of the actions undertaken in the research, (2) respect for the host culture, (3) open communication, (4) respect for subjects' rights, (5) protection of subjects' welfare and dignity, and (6) benefit to the participants" (Warwick, 1980, p. 361). Readers are encouraged to review the principles for more details concerning each of these six points.

Most Third World communities don't understand the rules and goals of science, the rationale behind random selection, the structure and format of interview schedules and questionnaires, academic freedom, the publication process, and the ethical standards governing the research process. What they understand best, though, are the many problems they face as they learn more and more about their social conditions relative to other countries and communities. Cross-cultural psychology has achieved a level of sophistication in which enough accumulated knowledge exists to offer conscientious and culturally sensitive skills to those communities interested and willing to sponsor policy-oriented research that could lead to proactive forms of socio-cultural change.

10

CROSS-CULTURAL CONTRIBUTIONS TO THEORY IN SOCIAL PSYCHOLOGY

HARRY C. TRIANDIS

The validity of social psychological theories varies with the populations to which they are supposed to apply. One of the realities of human behavior is selectivity in perception. We perceive what we have categories for, what is salient, and what is most useful to us. But what is most useful in New York is obviously not what is most useful in Beijing or Zanzibar.

Starting with such fundamental differences in what is likely to be perceived, we move to what is likely to become classically conditioned, to what is instrumentally reinforced, to what motives are likely to be aroused, and so on. It is obvious that since such fundamental processes are affected by culture, our theories will be culture-bound. But exactly how? The message of this chapter is that while the fundamental mechanisms of social psychology are valid across the world, some very important details about the way these mechanisms work are very different, reducing the validity of many of our theories.

In order to survey the way culture results in the differential validity of theories, we will begin with the most abstract theoretical viewpoints and examine how they are likely to be affected by culture. We will then move from the abstract to the more concrete. We will discover that culture reduces the validity of the more specific theories much more than it reduces the validity of the more abstract theories. For example, Skinner's notion that behavior is a function of its consequences is valid everywhere, but *what* behavior and *what* consequences may be culturally unique.

As we survey the field, we will discover that social behavior is immensely more variable than the behaviors that have been studied by Western social psychologists. We have been using blinders and filters provided by our culture. This is not too surprising, since social psychology itself is a cultural product (Hogan & Elmer, 1978), much as religions, political structures, or legal systems are cultural products.

General Structure of the Chapter

First we will use McGuire's (1985) masterful summary of social psychological theories and ask: In what ways is culture likely to be implicated in the way that type of theory is operating, and hence how culture is likely to increase or decrease its validity? In so doing we will order the theories from the most general, hence valid around the world, to the most likely to be modified by local conditions. Obviously, in this undertaking I will use my judgment, since there are no empirical tests of the various types of theories in the diverse cultures of the world.

When using my judgment, I will rely primarily on information from comparative psychology (if a theory applies to apes, it is very likely to be universal) and cross-cultural psychology (if I know of studies that cast doubt on the generality of a theory, I will so indicate), and secondarily on my own observations of social behavior in such diverse setting as Argentina, Aboriginal Australia, Japan, India, Greece, Nigeria, and so on.

Incidentally, when we talk about cultures, we mean "the human made part of the environment," which consists of both objective products (roads, tools) and subjective elements (norms, roles, laws, values). We will view cultural differences as the products of differential rates of interaction among humans. Those who share a language and live in the same time period and geographic location are more likely to interact and hence develop such subjective elements and objective products.

Variations in culture can be viewed as occurring in distinct geographical regions. The most variation will arise from contrasts across seven regions: northwestern Europe and North America; the Mediterranean, including North Africa; Africa south of the Sahara; South Asia; East Asia; the Pacific Islands; and South and/or North American Indians. Within these regions separations caused by national boundaries, language, and geography reduce the unity of culture and foster the development of distinct cultures. Within each of these smaller regions differences due to age, sex, social class, urban-rural domicile, religion, race, and other demographics that tend to segregate people will produce subcultures. For our purposes the seven major regions of the world will be the testing grounds of our theories.

Our survey will show that social behavior varies along several dimensions. Some of these dimensions, as far as we can tell, are universals (Triandis, 1978). These universal dimensions will be augmented by dimensions that Deutsch (1982) posited should exist in most social situations.

We will then survey how the various elements of subjective culture (Triandis, 1972), such as norms, roles, values, locally developed self-concepts, and the like, affect social behavior (Triandis, 1977, 1980). In so doing we will consider the major ways in which cultures differ.

In the final section of the chapter we will examine how the various dimensions of social behavior will affect social psychological theories. Thus we will attempt to distinguish broadly valid from more limited theories of social psychology.

SECTION 1: SOCIAL PSYCHOLOGICAL THEORIES

The most abstract elements of social psychological theories, as argued by McGuire (1985), involve four views of human nature. These four views form 2^4 = 16 cells, each cell including a particular type of theory. McGuire's four abstract contrasts were:

(1) *being* versus *becoming*: the person acting to maintain equilibrium versus the person striving to attain new levels of complexity, growth, or transcendence
(2) *active* versus *reactive*: behavior activated by internal needs versus behavior elicited as a reaction to environmental events
(3) *cognitive* versus *affective goals*: goals that have ideational elements, such as consistency or meaning, versus goals that have affective elements, such as maintaining self-esteem or tension reduction
(4) *internal* versus *external adjustments*: the person acts to achieve internal adjustments versus adjustments made to accommodate person-environment relationships.

McGuire argues, correctly in my view, that complex and mutually contradictory determinants of social behavior coexist, so that each of the 16 views of human nature advanced by these four contrasts is valid under some conditions and invalid under other conditions. The experience of humans with diverse ecologies/cultures is one of these limiting conditions. Thus a main task of this chapter becomes the exploration of the relative validity of McGuire's 16 types of theory in various cultural environments. We will argue that the validity of these theories will be high in some and low in other environments, depending on the type of behavior under study. Thus (a) culture, (b) role, (c) situation, (d) person, and (e) type of behavior must be considered when we examine the validity of a theory. We wish to partition the variance of social behavior across individuals (motivational systems), category of behavior(s), situations (e.g., public-private), roles, and cultures. To the extent that such partitioning shows that cultures account for some of the variance, the construct of culture is useful for social psychology.

Unfortunately, when testing theory, social psychologists have usually taken two positions: (a) Most have presumed that what is valid in their culture is valid everywhere (Pepitone, 1986); (b) the opposite stance is radical cultural relativism, that is, what is valid in one culture is invalid every place else. Neither of these extremes is generally justified. One might concede that for some behaviors (e.g., psychophysical judgments) position (a) may be reasonable, and for some individuals-in-culture (e.g., highly frustrated persons running amok in the Philippines) position (b) may be reasonable. But for most behaviors, roles, situations, and persons, the validity of a theory will vary with culture. Thus cross-cultural work is essential if a truly scientific social psychology, one that accounts for the social behavior of all humans, is to be developed.

In this exploration we should keep an eye on the kinds of distortions that modern social psychology is likely to introduce. Hogan and Elmer (1978) have pointed out that individualism and rationalism are among the important values that Western social psychologists use without conscious awareness. These values result in underestimation of the influence of groups, norms, culture, and emotion or impulse on social behavior. Also, while social behavior consists of interaction, negotiation, and dialogue, and is influenced by rich paralinguistic stimuli, most laboratory work consists of experimenter-manipulated stimuli and responses of the subjects to these stimuli. Thus much of the substance in social interaction is missed and hence is not the concern of mainstream social psychological theories.

In undertaking the task of determining the validity of theories, it is useful to remind ourselves of Klineberg's idea (1954) that motives can be called "dependable" when they occur universally and in both lower and higher animals. Klineberg used the criteria of physiological basis, phylogenetic continuity, and universality to determine the "dependability" of motives. It seems reasonable to adopt Klineberg's strategy and argue that when a behavior has a physiological basis, shows phylogenetic continuity, and is universal, it will be determined by the same psychological laws worldwide. If we do not know of a physiological basis, or do not see the behavior patterns in lower animals, or do not find it in every culture, the probability that we will be required to modify our psychological laws increases. Furthermore, if only one of the three criteria is absent, the modification of the psychological laws can be minor, but as more of the three criteria are absent, the required modifications will become major.

McGuire's Table 2 (p. 295) is reproduced as our Table 1. The order of the cells has been rearranged, for purposes that will become clear later. The lack of tests for such theories in the diverse regions of the world will force me to use the phylogenetic continuity criterion to order them from (a) high probability of universal validity through (b) medium to (c) low probability of universal validity.

TABLE 1

	Action Initiation vs.			
	Need for Stability (being)		Need for Growth (becoming)	
	Reactive	Active (Internal instigation)	Reactive	Active
		Instigation	Instigation	
Action Termination				
Affective goals				
internal (change self)	Ego-defense	Tension Reduction	Identity	Attraction
external (change environment)	Repetition	Expression	Contagion	Assertion
Cognitive goals				
internal (change self)	Categorization	Consistency	Utilitarian	Stimulation
external (change environment) relationship	Induction	Hermeneutics	Template	Autonomy

SOURCE: Reorganized from McGuire's Table 2 (1985, p. 295).
NOTE: Double underlining means that the theory is probably equally valid in all cultures; single underlining means that the theory is probably somewhat different across cultures; no underlining means that the theory is probably greatly different (less valid in some than in others) across cultures.

(a) High Universal Validity

Repetition. Theories that deal with habits, such as Skinner's, are probably equally valid worldwide. I do not take a position concerning the validity of Skinner's theory in our culture. I assume that it is reasonably valid and all I am claiming is that it will not lose its validity elsewhere. On the other hand, details about the way the theory operates in different cultures will allow slight modifications and improvements. For example, Haruki and Shigehisa (1983) and Haruki, Shigehisa, Nedate, Wajima, and Ogawa (1984) have shown that while both Japanese and U.S. subjects learn equally well when the experimenter rewards them when they make a correct response, the Japanese learn just as well when the experimenter rewards himself (or herself) when they make a correct response. Subjects from the United States learn something under the latter condition, but significantly less than the Japanese. So *what* is reinforcing, or the *conditions* under which a signal is reinforcing, depends on culture. The more collectivistic Japanese learn as well when someone else gets rewarded as when they get rewarded, while the individualistic American subjects learn less well when someone else gets rewarded than when they get rewarded.

Tension reduction. These theories argue that reduction of tension is relevant to behavior. Again, *if* such theories are valid in our culture, they should also be valid elsewhere. I see no reason for differential validity. Of course, culture again modifies the specifics—for example, when we examine tension reduction in a hungry person, what to eat, when to eat, with whom to eat, and so on are influenced by culture. However, that is not a change in the structure of the theory.

Contagion. Theories that depend on modeling, and modifications proposed by LeBon, Tarde, and others, are worldwide. For instance, blind following of a leader whom everyone else is following may be explained by such a theory.

Expression. These theories emphasize play, acting out on impulse, and exercising a function. Since play is found universally (Sutton-Smith & Roberts, 1981) and in higher primates, we expect such theories to be equally valid in our culture and in other cultures.

(b) Moderate Universal Validity

Categorization. All humans use categories (see Triandis, 1964, for a review), that is, they make responses to discriminably different stimuli. However, cultures differ very widely in what they categorize, in how many distinctions they make across particular domains of meaning, in the speed of reaction to a particular category, the boundaries and fuzziness of categories, and so on (Price-Williams, 1980; Triandis, 1964). So if the theory emphasizes the importance of categories, prototypes, the selectivity of perception and the like, it will be equally valid in all cultures; but if it emphasizes some details of the categorization content, its validity will be reduced.

Assertion. These theories argue that power is a key motive and war of each against all is the natural state of humans. Since dominance is one of the phenomena widely observed in higher primates, it seems likely that these theories have validity to more or less the same extent worldwide. Of course, we know that cultures differ in the amount of stratification and in the extent differences in power are acceptable (Hofstede, 1980). In cultures low in stratification or in "power distance," these theories may be less valid than in cultures high in stratification. It may even be the case that different "theories of power" will be needed for cultures high and low in stratification or "power distance."

Utilitarianism. Theories that use utility as a variable appear to deal with cognitive epiphenomena of reinforcement events. In short, they reflect, at the cognitive level, events in the stimulus-response-reinforcement sequence. Their validity will thus be equal to the validity of repetition theories discussed above, that is, if they are valid in our culture, they will also be valid elsewhere. However, we expect some modifications in the relative validity of these theories because information processing requires the use of categories, which are linked to language. Since languages differ in the availability of their categories, the modifications are likely to be nontrivial.

Stimulation. The need for stimulation has been observed in higher apes and even in rats. Theories that use this construct are likely to be equally universal. However, we know that the amount of human-made stimulation is greater in cultures of high complexity (e.g., that of the ancient Egyptians) than in simpler cultures (e.g., that of the pygmies). Thus we expect that the level of adaptation for stimulation (Helson, 1964) will differ across cultures. Thus the amount of stimulation that will prove satisfactory in one culture will be different from that in another.

Identity. Theories that utilize roles, in-groups, and the like, have some abstract elements that are universal. For example, roles as constellations of behavior that are appropriate for a person in a particular position in a social system are recognized worldwide (see Triandis, 1972, for review). However, the content of the roles differs drastically from culture to culture (Triandis, Vassiliou, & Nassiakou, 1968).

Template theories. This class of theory may be represented by Miller, Galanter, and Pribram's (1960) TOTE (test-operate-test-exit). Such theories are used to explain how behavior is regulated. The argument is that the person has a standard or ideal or goal. The person tests the situation and determines how much still needs to be done to reach the standard, operates to reach it, tests again, and when the standard is reached, stops. Templates probably exist equally in all cultures. However, the content of each template will vary with culture. Obviously, the standards or goals will be different, the intensity of the desire to meet the standards will be different, the operations one may undertake to reach the goals will be different, and the criteria for meeting the standards will be different. Given so many areas of possible difference, the validity of the theories may well be somewhat lower in some cultures than it is in others.

(c) Low Universal Validity

Attraction. While attraction is a universal phenomenon, and may be a function of the extent one is reinforced less the costs of the relationship, there are so many factors that determine attraction that the validity of their contents is likely to be low in some cultures. Specifically, while aesthetic judgments have some universal attributes (e.g., stimuli that are too complex or too simple are less satisfying) (Berlyne, 1980), there are specific aesthetic elements that differ widely across cultures. For example, fat women are preferred by some African tribes (they even use fat-houses to increase their weights before they are presented as desirable brides). The relative importance and attraction of in-groups (e.g., castes) and the like must be considered in many cultures and often override simple considerations of reward-cost factors (Hogan & Elmer, 1978).

Induction. These theories utilize different selves under different conditions to predict different behaviors. The definition of the self is quite different from culture to culture (see Marsella, DeVos, & Hsu, 1985). In some cultures the person is seen as a satellite of the in-group, hence not as an independent entity. For example, in Bali people use teknonyms as names (e.g., father of X; grandmother of Y), a usage that obviously implies that the person as such is not important but the relationship with others is. One does not behave "as an individual" but as a representative of a group. Thus it is dangerous to assume that findings obtained with one kind of self will necessarily generalize.

Hermeneutics. These theories use *both* unconscious inferences and interpretations of the social situation, and assume that the person is an implicit theorist (Kelley, Heider, and others). In the case of interpretations of the social situation by the person, the theory uses the interpretation as its element. Such elements require the assumption that humans are self-conscious. Yet there is much doubt that this is universally the case. At least some theorists see humans as automatons, reacting to stimulus patterns. Jaynes (1977), for instance, has argued that the pre-Homeric Greeks were not self-conscious. They acted like automatons responding to inner voices, which they interpreted as the voices of the gods. This view seems to have received favorable comment by some classicists (see Smith, 1980). Mindless behavior, for example, obviously would be outside the bounds of such theories.

Ego-defensiveness. Such theories assume that the ego need to protect the ego is more or less similar around the world. Yet many aspects of the self are rather different across the world (Marsella, DeVos, & Hsu, 1985). In some cultures (e.g., the Buddhist), the ideal is to have no ego. To what extent people achieve that ideal is something we do not know, but presumably such an ideal will reduce the validity of the theory for some of these persons.

Consistency. These theories make the assumption that inconsistency is noxious. Yet some social scientists (Hiniker, 1969) have argued that consistency is a Western ideal, derived from Aristotelian thinking. For example, Bharati (1985) maintains that in India contradictions are not disturbing; one might be a "vegetarian who eats meat." Such a construct is impossible by definition, according to Aristotle, but not according to Hindu thinking, in which the two contradictory qualities are seen as facets of the same transcendental reality. Or, to take another Asian example, Iwao (1986) argues that in Japan inconsistency is a sign of sophistication. Only simple, naive people behave according to their attitudes. The sophisticated behave according to the situation, and their attitudes are irrelevant (it reminds us of Snyder and Gangestad's, 1986, high self-monitors). Finally, Pelto (1968) argues that in "loose" societies consistency is not desirable.

Control or *autonomy.* These theories specify that people seek to control their environments and if they do not manage to do so they feel depressed (Langer, 1983). However, some theorists have argued that people want the security provided through control by authorities (e.g., Fromm, 1941). In my opinion the need for control is high worldwide, as witnessed by the extensive use of magic and religious practices to influence the environment. However, people do differ in how much control they expect to have and how much they value autonomy (Burger, 1985). There is much evidence that child-rearing patterns differ widely in their emphasis on autonomy versus obedience (see Berry, 1979). Thus autonomy theories will have less validity in those cultures where autonomy is not expected or valued, and so, like theories of power, they will differ across cultures.

Some Evidence of Differential Validity of Theories

I must admit at the outset that the evidence here is indirect, and rival hypotheses have not been eliminated. But that is not surprising. As far as I am aware, this is the first article that has attempted to explore the question of the differential validity of social psychological theories in different cultures. What we can present as "evidence" will have to be tentative.

McGuire's 16 types of theories are quite abstract. The problem with abstractions is that while they allow us to communicate they miss too much detail. For example, to discuss under the abstraction "political behavior" the British parliamentary system, the Nigerian *oba*, and the Soviet local committee misses some rather major differences. Similarly, the theories that are universally valid are stated at a high level of abstraction, thereby sacrificing important detail.

At a lower level of abstraction are several well-known social psychological theories, such as attribution, congruity, dissonance, social comparison, reward-cost balances, equity, the contingency theory of leadership behavior, and so on. Here we find cross-cultural replications that, broadly speaking, support the theories but provide important modifications in certain instances.

For example, attribution theory in its most abstract version may have universal validity, but we must note some important ways in which attributions will be affected by culture (Holloway, Kashiwagi, Hess, & Azuma, 1986). To take just one example, consider the following: The word *mamihlapinatapei* means, in the language of the Indians of the Tierra del Fuego, "looking at each other hoping that either one will offer to do something that both desire but are unwilling to do." It does not require an experiment to suggest that this is likely to be a more common attribution among the Fuegans than among Kansas farmers. In fact, I rather doubt that there are *any* Westerners who make this attribution! Doubts about the generality of attribution theory are also cast by Miller (1984) and others.

Consider the question of consistency as another example. Obviously, if cultures differ in consistency-seeking, that fact has major implications for many of our theories (see Abelson et al., 1968, for the full range of consistency theories). As stated earlier, Bharati (1985) has argued that Hindus are perfectly comfortable with inconsistency. If that is true, their behavior will show less consistency than the behavior of U.S. samples. In a study by Triandis (1968), which utilized the semantic differential (as a measure of affect in person perception) and the behavioral differential (as a measure of behavioral intentions toward the same stimuli), the U.S. judgments linking "evaluation" and "respect" (would admire the character, obey, believe the stimulus person) correlated .42, while the Indian judgments correlated .27. The standard error of measurement was only .06 because of the large Ns. So this is an enormous difference. However, the rival hypothesis that the Indians were simply careless in answering the instruments cannot be ruled out in this study. Furthermore, the Indians were students, and therefore familiar with Aristotelian logic. The "Westernization" of the Indians would increase their consistency, while their possible carelessness, or disinterest in the task, could decrease their consistency. Thus the Indians were under the influence of two competing pressures, and we do not know to what extent we can depend on the data. Nevertheless, as a minimum, the data suggest that Bharati may have a point.

Consider now, as another example, the notion of comparison level of alternatives in the Thibaut and Kelley (1959) theorizing. It assumes that individuals will stay in a relationship or will leave it, depending on whether they receive rewards that exceed their costs relative to the alternative rewards and costs they perceive from possible, alternative relationships. The assumption, of course, is that the individual will be free to move to another relationship. But in collectivist cultures (Hofstede, 1980) people do not believe that they have such freedom. They may feel trapped and regret their condition, but usually it would not occur to them to leave. One can argue that such people have such a high CLalt that they are anchored to their in-groups, but I wonder how useful the CLalt notion is with such elastic construction!

Still another example can be taken from equity theory. Marin (1985) reviewed the cross-cultural literature on equity theory. It is clear from his review of 14 studies that equity theory is supported only under some conditions. In exploring a number of possible moderator variables, Marin concluded that differences among the samples on the individualism-collectivism dimension can be advanced to account for the difference in support of equity theory. That is, in general, studies done in individualistic cultures such as the United States and Western Europe find support for equity theory. Studies done in Latin America, East Asia, or Southern Europe find support for equity theory under very restricted conditions—when the subject is interacting with an unknown other or with an in-group member but the subject's contribution (inputs) to the joint product is low.

In some studies reviewed by Marin, such as Triandis, Leung,

Villareal, and Clack (1985), a personality variable (idiocentrism versus allocentrism) that corresponds to individual collectivism was used. This is, then, a *within*-culture study with cross-cultural parallels. The evidence was that allocentrics were more likely to use the principles of equality or need rather than equity in making distributions of resources, while idiocentrics tended to use equity. Thus both culture and personality variables moderate the probability that equity theory will make correct predictions in situations of resource allocation.

In short, allocentrics or subjects in collectivist cultures use the equality and need principles more widely than the equity principle. On the other hand, idiocentrics or subjects in individualist cultures are more likely to use the equity principle. Thus cross-cultural studies and those they have inspired have identified that equity theory is supported under specifiable cultural conditions, but not under others.

A Model That Attempts to Integrate Several Theories

The reader is referred to Triandis (1972, 1977, 1980) for the presentations of a model that integrates several theories. The basic idea is that social behavior is determined by habits and behavioral intentions. Behavioral intentions are determined by social factors (self-definition, norms), the affect toward the behavior, and the perceived consequences of the behavior. Each of these constructs is differentially weighted. The weights are determined by cultural factors. For example, in cultures where the group exerts more influence than do individual goals, the social factor is weighted more heavily (see Davidson, Jaccard, Triandis, Morales, & Diaz-Guerrero, 1976). Both ecological (Berry, 1967) and social class (Kohn, 1969) variables are relevant to understanding whether the group goals or individual goals will be given primacy.

In other words, we can identify dimensions of cultural variation, such as individualism (giving more weight to personal than to collective goals), collectivism (internalizing collective goals), tightness (behavior must conform exactly to norms), or looseness (behavior can deviate a good deal from norms), that result in different weights for the components of the model.

SECTION 2: DIMENSIONS OF CULTURAL VARIATION

Limitations of space preclude description of the dimensions of cultural variation. However, we can refer the reader to some of the relevant literature. Individualism and collectivism have been discussed by Hui (1984), Hui and Triandis (1986), Triandis, Leung, Villareal, and Clack (1985), Triandis et al. (1986); cultural complexity by Carneiro (1970), Lomax and Berkowitz (1972), Murdock and Provost (1973); modernity by Yang (see Chap. 6, this volume); tightness versus looseness by Pelto (1968), Peabody (1985), and Robbins, DeWalt, and Pelto (1972).

The individualism-collectivism domain is of special interest. It has been discussed both theoretically (e.g., Parsons, 1951) and in the domain of values (e.g., Kluckhohn & Strodtbeck, 1961) as a major dimension of cultural variation. There are sensitive discussions (e.g., Lebra, 1976) of how the private self and the public self are affected by this dimension. There are numerous empirical investigations showing that particular cultural groups (e.g., Hispanics) differ from other cultural groups (e.g., mainstream North Americans in the United States) on dimensions relevant to this domain. Traditional Greeks (e.g., Triandis, 1972); Hispanics (e.g., Marin & Triandis, 1985; Triandis, Marin, Hui, Lisansky, & Ottati, 1984; Triandis, Marin, Lisansky, & Betancourt, 1984); Hong Kong Chinese (Bond, Wan, Leung, & Giacalone, 1985; Bond & Forgas, 1984; Leung & Bond, 1984); and Japanese (Mann, Radford, & Kanagawa, 1985) have been shown to have collectivist tendencies, while samples from the United States and Australia have been shown to have individualist tendencies.

Collectivism tends to be related to tightness (Boldt & Roberts, 1979). Among preliterate cultures, complexity is positively related to collectivism (Zern, 1983). But among literate samples, high complexity is related to individualism (Young, 1965). A moderate relationship between complexity (diversity of roles) and tightness of role expectations (Boldt, 1978) is expected. Parents who use much information in child rearing foster cognitive complexity (Harvey, Hunt, & Schroder, 1961; Thomas, 1972). Parents from tight cultures impose their tightness on their children (Lambert, Hamers, & Frasure-Smith, 1979).

Collectivism results in a sharper differentiation of social behavior across in-group-out-group boundaries than does individualism. Thus, among collectivists social behavior with in-group members tends toward greater levels of association, subordination, and intimacy, and toward out-group members it tends toward greater levels of dissociation, superordination, and formality than is found among individualists.

We also expect social behavior to be more intense and interdependent in collectivist cultures, and more distant and detached in individualist cultures, than in the cultures of the opposite pattern. Social relationships will be more enduring in simpler, collectivist cultures than in individualist cultures; conversely, in individualist cultures we will find more temporary relationships. We expect greater emphasis on large groups in complex collectivist cultures and greater emphasis on small groups in simple and in individualistic cultures, where privacy and being alone tend to be valued (see Wheeler, 1986, for support of these expectations).

SECTION 3: CULTURAL VARIATIONS AND SOCIAL PSYCHOLOGICAL THEORIES

We will follow the order of theory presentation that was used in Section 1 of this chapter. For each theory we will ask: What hypotheses concerning the modification of the theory seem plausible?

We start with McGuire's highest levels of abstraction.

Being versus becoming. It seems plausible that "becoming" will be emphasized in cultures that are complex, individualistic, and loose; "being," which reflects the stability associated with maintaining the current equilibrium, will be found more commonly in cultures that are simple, collectivist, and tight.

Action versus reaction. There may be a slight tendency for people in individualistic cultures to favor action over reaction, but the relationships should be weak. Research on internal locus of control suggests that individualism emphasizes action.

Cognitive versus affective goals. There may be a small tendency for individualists to favor cognitive over affective goals. Boykin (1983), for example, has argued that high evaluation of cognition and rationality is a Western pattern and that Africans value affect more.

Internal versus external adjustments. According to Diaz-Guerrero (1979), collectivist Mexicans tend to make internal adjustments while individualists from the United States tend to modify the environment to make it fit their situation. I expect that this contrast between individualism and collectivism will also be found in other cultures.

If we combine the four hypotheses just stated, we will conclude that *autonomy* will be the most important theory that accounts for the behavior of individualists and *ego-defensive*, which will become *in-group-defensive* in collectivist cultures, theories will account best for the behavior of collectivists. That is so because, in McGuire's placement of theories in the 16 cells, autonomy is at the intersection of the qualities becoming-active-cognitive-external, and ego-defensiveness at the intersection of being-reactive-affective-internal. Perhaps the extrapolation is too large, but one must admit that autonomy does seem like a central concern of individualists. In fact, the Triandis et al. (1986) study of the etics of individualism found "distance from in-groups" and "self-reliance" as the key ways to characterize individualism. Also, the extreme collectivist (e.g., isolated tribes) cultures tend to be ethnocentric and prejudiced, since only the in-group is valued, and such tendencies are associated with ego-defensiveness (Adorno, Frenkel-Brunswik, Levinson, & Stanford, 1950).

It would seem useful to test these ideas by developing competing predictions about autonomy and in-group-defensiveness, and testing them in extremely individualistic and extremely collectivist cultures. Presumably, in the individualistic cultures the autonomy-based predictions would be confirmed and in the collectivist the in-group defensiveness-based predictions would be supported.

Moving to the lower level of abstraction we may analyze each of McGuire's theories in cells 1 to 16.

Categorization. This cognitive activity ought to occur everywhere. However, it seems likely that the more complex the culture, the greater will be the cognitive complexity, and hence the number of categories will be greater. Tightness is probably associated with narrow categories (Detweiler, 1978, 1980). Detweiler found that people on Truk in the Pacific used narrower categories than people in the United States.

Stimulation. Complex cultures are likely to offer more variety and the level of adaptation for stimulation is likely to be higher. As a result we expect people in complex cultures to have a greater need for stimulation, and hence for stimulation theories to account for more of the variance in social behavior.

Templates. Theories like Miller, Galanter, and Pribram's (1960) that utilize the TOTE notion may not be changed by culture, except in details, such as the level of the threshold that is used to decide whether to "operate" or to "exit." It is conceivable that in tight cultures these thresholds will be more delicately adjusted so that slighter variations from a standard will lead to action.

Attraction. We hypothesize that in simple and in collectivist cultures attraction will be linked to attributes of the in-group and may be a less important attribute of people than in individualist cultures (Bond & Hwang, 1986). Emphasis on physical attraction, as a factor in attraction, is well established in Western social psychology. But in the East other variables are likely to overwhelm physical attraction. For example, Bond and Hwang discuss how in Chinese culture "collectivism and interpersonal 'dependency' are highly valued, and individual's concerns about establishing, maintaining, and improving interpersonal relationships can be viewed as desirable traits, which may make him attractive to others or to himself" (p. 241). The empirical work that they review suggests that while physical attraction is an important factor, other personal traits (e.g., friendly, enthusiastic to serve others, humble, altruistic, etc.) are even more important among collectivist Chinese subjects.

In complex and in individualist cultures multiple criteria may be used—for example, attraction toward the unusual, the exciting, the exotic, as well as agreement with values, cognitive similarity, and so forth.

Identity. In collectivist cultures the self is a bundle of roles. The use of teknonyms in some collectivist cultures, such as the Balinese (Geertz, 1963), is especially revealing about the importance of the group relative to the importance of the individual in such cultures. According to Geertz, a person's name in Bali is a nonsense syllable that is hardly ever used. When a child is born the name used is linked to the family name, e.g., "first-born," "fifth-born" and the like. After the person becomes an adult and gets married, the person's name becomes "father of X" and later "grandfather of Y." Thus identity is not personal, but group-linked. Social behavior in cultures such as the Balinese should be more under the control of the S-factors discussed earlier than the A- or C-factors. An excellent discussion of sociocentric conceptions of personhood is provided by Shweder and Bourne (1982), who contrast this view of the self against the views associated with autonomous individualism, and explore the advantages and costs of each view.

Greenwald (1982) has distinguished private, public, and collective self. The self as an aspect of the group will be common in collectivist and also tight cultures. Most social behavior in such societies is determined by roles, so that other theories of social behavior in such societies will have comparatively little validity. Thus we expect that in collectivist/tight cultures social identity theories will account for much of the variance in social behavior.

Contagion. Such theories should account for some of the variance in simple and collectivist cultures. Since modeling, vicarious learning, and the like are included in these theories, we expect behavior to be more a function of such processes when there are few models and there is strong loyalty to in-groups.

Tension reduction. It is unlikely that the cultural patterns will relate to these theories in a systematic way, although the type of perceived tensions may differ from culture to culture.

Repetition. Similarly, I expect repetition theories to be valid universally, with minor adjustments, such as the relatively greater rates of learning by collectivists when the experimenter reinforces him- or herself rather than reinforcing the subject.

Expression. We expect such theories to be valid universally, but there might be slight shifts in validity. For example, complex play may be more motivating in complex than in simple cultures; individual competitive sports may be more popular in individualist cultures, while group competitive sports may be more popular in collectivist cultures.

The remaining theories, with three exceptions, seem unrelated to our three cultural patterns. The exceptions are:

Autonomy. As mentioned above it is especially likely to account for the variance of social behavior in individualist cultures, particularly if they are complex and loose.

Assertion. Assertion theories may account for some of the variance in collectivist cultures where differences in power are large. Hofstede (1980) found correlations of the order of .7 between differentiation of levels of power and collectivism. We expect, thus, that assertion theories will be more valid in collectivist than individualist cultures. Also, very simple cultures, such as the pygmies, tend to be egalitarian, hence assertion theories will not be specially pertinent in such cultures. By contrast in complex cultures we find much social stratification, even in those cultures (e.g., the Soviets) in which the ideology is opposed to power differentials. We expect in such cultures assertion theories to be quite useful.

Ego-defensive and in-group-defensive theories. As stated earlier, our expectation is that theories of this class will have more validity in collectivist than in individualist cultures, though they will probably be substantially valid universally.

The model. The model mentioned earlier is designed to use dimensions of cultural variation as parameters. Specifically, the S-component's weight increases with cultural tightness and collectivism, and the number of different determinants of behavior increases with cultural complexity.

DISCUSSION

The social psychology that has been developed so far has depended much too much on the college sophomores (Sears, 1986) of Europe and North America. This is a severe limitation that must be overcome by utilizing cross-cultural data.

The central argument of this chapter has been that the immense variations of social behavior have not been examined, and certainly have not been studied systematically. In Table 1 we presented McGuire's 16 types of theories. In the main part of this chapter we argued that the validity of these theories is likely to be different in different types of cultures. Collectivism-individualism and the other two dimensions of cultural variation are our candidates as the moderators of the validity of theories.

Clearly, we do not have the data to tell which theories will be more or less valid in which types of cultures. Not yet, anyway. We must guess. If guessing has any utility, I suggest that the theories with two lines under them in Table 1 will be equally valid worldwide, those with one line will be differentially valid, and the ones without lines will be valid in some cultures and invalid in other cultures.

The second principle for guessing about validity is relevant to the way Table 1 has been rearranged from McGuire's original presentation. I suspect that the theories in the upper-left-hand corner will be found to be valid in simple, collectivist, tight cultures much more than in complex, individualistic, loose cultures; conversely, the theories in the lower-right-hand corner will be found to be more valid in the complex, individualistic, and loose than in the simple, collectivist, and tight cultures.

If the perspective that I have just outlined is even partially correct, what does it imply for contemporary social psychology? It is useful to recall that "scientific psychology advances only with the discovery of its limits" (Thorngate, 1976, p. 123). Thus the fact that some of our theories may be invalid in some settings is not a calamity. We should be proud that they are valid in *some* settings. Thorngate also points out that it is impossible to have theories that are simultaneously general (apply to all humans, all behaviors), simple (parsimonious), and accurate (valid, precise) in their predictions. He quotes Gardner's law that (Rigor) × (Relevance) = Constant (p. 126). He shows that similar relationships hold for generality, simplicity, and accuracy. Thus simple theories are not general, general theories are not accurate, and simple theories are not accurate except under very restricted (nongeneral) conditions.

Thorngate also makes a statement that is specially relevant to cross-cultural, social psychology. He claims that "most or all social psychological research may be viewed as an attempt to uncover and codify norms, be they norms of behavior or norms of thinking, motivation, etc." (p. 130). Since the essence of culture is shared norms, and values (Triandis, 1972), if Thorngate is correct, *all social psychology should be cross-cultural.*

Thus a way to do social psychology is to develop the best understanding of the relevant norms that dominate a particular behavior in a particular cultural context (Pepitone, 1976). Some elements of our theories may be sufficiently general (e.g., Skinner's statement "behavior is a function of its consequences") to be valuable in all settings; others will be valid in a family of settings, and so on. Given that perspective, Table 1 provides a map of hypotheses that will be supported in different settings.

CONCLUSION

The major contribution of cross-cultural psychology to social psychology is that it provides broader perspectives for understanding the probable limitations to our understanding of social behavior. Most contemporary social psychology has developed on the basis of data from complex, individualist, and loose cultures. As a result there has been a neglect of social behavior where there is a major difference of power (say, behavior of literate and illiterate subjects), of behaviors that occur in expressive settings (e.g., a one-month wedding in India), of behaviors that do not have as a goal a task accomplishment, but rather the maintenance of an existing social relationship, or of behaviors that are involved in long-lasting relationships. There is very little research on formal situations in which most of the behaviors are under the control of explicit norms. We have many studies that involve temporary, voluntary, licit social behavior in small groups, and few studies that involve enduring, involuntary, illicit social behaviors or behaviors involving large groups.

As we investigate such relationships, we will probably find that each of our theories has specific limits. Cultural dimensions, such as simple-complex, tight-loose, collectivism-individualism, will moderate the generality of our theories, in much the way Marin's (1985) review of equity theory suggested that in individualistic cultures the equity principle is widely used, while in collectivist cultures it is used only when the other person is an out-group member, or an in-group member, but the actor has contributed to the accomplishment of the task less than the in-group member. Clearly, this is a refinement of equity theory that adds a great deal to its utility. Many such refinements will be possible as social psychology becomes truly cross-cultural.

11

CROSS-CULTURAL PSYCHOLOGY IN A POST-EMPIRICIST ERA

ANDRÉ KUKLA

By "empiricism" I mean the view that questions of truth and falsehood are to be settled by an appeal to observation and experiment. Empiricism comes in various degrees. At one end of the continuum stands Skinner (1974), who considers logic to be a branch of the empirical science of behavior. At the other end is Plato, who regarded all sensory experience as an impediment to the apprehension of reality. In comparison to most places and times, the English-speaking world in the twentieth century has been marked by a relative extreme of the empiricist temper. But—inevitably—the pendulum has begun to swing the other way. Evidence of the decline of radical empiricism has been noted in virtually every academic discipline from physics (Bohm, 1971) to jurisprudence and literary criticism (Michaels, 1980). Within psychology, the postempiricist attitude is most apparent in the work of social-psychological theorists like Gergen (1978) and Sampson (1978), who emphasize the contractual nature of knowledge. The most broadly influential critiques, however, have come from philosophers of science working within the analytic tradition (Feyerabend, 1978; Hanson, 1969; Kuhn, 1970), who have uncovered enormous difficulties in the empiricist formulations of their immediate predecessors, the logical positivists (Ayer, 1952; Reichenbach, 1962).

In this article, I wish to explore some of the consequences of these trends in the philosophy of science for the discipline of cross-cultural psychology. Naturally, I will not be able to do full justice to the many contentious issues that are involved in this topic. My aim only is to delineate an important subject for further discussion.

THE CRITIQUE OF
CLASSICAL EMPIRICISM

I begin with a very abbreviated presentation of recent postempiricist arguments. These arguments purport to show that the differences

AUTHOR'S NOTE: Preparation of this article was supported by a Social Sciences and Humanities Research Council of Canada Leave Fellowship (451-86-0403) and by a University of Toronto Research Leave Grant.

between competing scientific theories often cannot be settled by an appeal to observational evidence.[1] The two most important reasons for this conclusion are the following. First, the extreme empiricism of the logical positivists requires that there be a universal *observation language* that can be used to describe data without any theoretical involvement. Such descriptions, if they were possible, could be used to evaluate the claims of any and all competing theories. But there is no universal observation language. Two theories may employ conceptual schemes that are *incommensurable,* in the sense that the data descriptions in one theory have no logical equivalents among the data descriptions of the other theory. In that case, the data that are relevant to each theory simply have no bearing on the other. Yet they may both be theories of one and the same realm of phenomena. Moreover, the deployment of different conceptual schemes can actually alter the qualitative content of our observations: Confronted with a reversible figure of a duck-rabbit, those who have only the concept "duck" will see a duck, and those who have only the concept "rabbit" will see a rabbit. In Kuhn's phrase, adherents to theories that employ incommensurable conceptual schemes "live in different worlds."

Second, even when theories share the same concepts, they may differ in their *presuppositions,* that is, assumptions that can neither be confirmed nor disconfirmed by evidence because they tell us what is to *count* as evidence in a particular domain. An ordinary scientific hypothesis may be overturned by the weight of accumulated evidence. But the rules whereby hypotheses are overturned cannot themselves be overturned. Indeed, attempts to submit these rules to empirical tests must inevitably fall into the logical error of begging the question. Investigators who begin with different presuppositions may very well arrive at conflicting theories. When this happens, they will not be able to settle their differences by an appeal to evidence. Furthermore, as in the case of different conceptual schemes, proponents of different presuppositions may obtain qualitatively different experiences of the world. This is due in part to the fact that our beliefs have an effect on our behavior, which in turn produces effects in the environment. Therefore, people who make different assumptions about the nature of things may be witness to different events. Rosenthal's (1966) work on the experimenter bias effect makes this point very forcefully.

When theories employ incommensurable conceptual schemes or incompatible presuppositions, they belong to different *paradigms.*[2] In psychology, S-R theory and the computational approach of cognitive science are timely examples of paradigms. S-R theory strives to explain behavior in terms of functional relations between stimuli and responses.

Computational theory explains behavior in terms of propositional attitudes like beliefs and desires. Empirical work undertaken from within the S-R paradigm leads only to ever more refined S-R theories. Computational research leads only to more refined computational theories. The differences between these two approaches are too fundamental to be settled by experiment. This is what makes them competing paradigms.

THE NATURE OF
NONSCIENTIFIC THOUGHT

The foregoing philosophical critique of classical empiricism has a direct bearing on the interpretation of cross-cultural studies. Students of other cultures regularly encounter beliefs in demons, ghosts, divination, magical spells, and countless other phenomena the reality of which is denied by the contemporary scientific worldview. The question is: What are we to say about beliefs like these? To oversimplify a complex piece of intellectual history, we may distinguish two different types of answers. The older account is that members of other cultures arrive at their unscientific opinions about the world because their mental processes are in some way defective:

> The whole mental furniture of the Kaffir's mind differs from that of a European. . . . He is a complete stranger to Western conceptions of clear thinking and is as ignorant of logic as he is of the moons of Jupiter. His conceptions of cause and effect are hopelessly at sea. (Kidd, 1905; cited in Jahoda, 1982, p. 167)

The newer and more liberal account of non-Western thought begins with a crucial distinction between collectively created systems of beliefs and the thought processes of individuals. On this view, the erroneous opinions of so-called primitives are due to their inheriting a less rational collective system. Within their own system, however, they operate very much as we do.[3] According to Horton, for example, both Westerners and primitives subscribe to their respective opinions about the world on the basis of an uncritical faith in received views:

> The layman's ground for accepting the models propounded by the scientist is often no different from the young African villager's ground for accepting the models propounded by one of his elders. In both cases the

propounders are deferred to as accredited agents of tradition. As for the rules that guide scientists themselves in the acceptance or rejection of models, these seldom become part of the intellectual equipment of members of the wider population. (Horton, 1970, p. 171)

Implicit in the passage by Horton is an important corollary to the liberal account of primitive belief systems. The liberal view differs from the older one in denying that there are qualitative differences in intellectual functioning between the modern Westerner and the primitive at the *individual* level. But it agrees with the older view that there is a qualitative difference between the collectively created belief system of Western scientists on the one hand and all nonscientific systems on the other. This purported difference can be stated in a fairly precise manner. In both the scientific and the nonscientific systems, it is true that no individual is in possession of enough direct evidence to warrant all of his or her beliefs: To some extent or other, we must all defer to "accredited agents." In the scientific system, however, there are always *some* individuals who have adequate evidence for any given belief. But in the systems of primitive societies, there are some beliefs for which *no one* has evidence.

From the viewpoint of the post-Kuhnian philosophy of science, this liberal account of the differences between scientific and nonscientific belief systems may not yet be liberal enough. If scientific paradigms contain presuppositions, then it is simply not true that every scientific belief is based on someone's possessing good evidence for it. At the very least, our principles about what constitutes good evidence cannot themselves be based on evidence. For example, the principles of statistical significance testing cannot be confirmed by experimental results, since they are the principles that tell us what to make of experimental results in the first place. Thus the fact that non-Western belief systems contain propositions for which no one has any evidence does not serve to distinguish these systems from science.

A non-Western example will clarify my point. According to the classic anthropological field study by Evans-Pritchard (1937), the African Azande obtained their answers to important questions by administering a special poison to a fowl. The answer was determined by whether the fowl lived or died. Now, from a scientific point of view, the efficacy of the poison oracle is a testable hypothesis, albeit an implausible one. A preliminary test might involve asking the oracle a question the answer of which is already known, and noting whether we obtain a correct reply. Suppose that such a test is conducted and that the oracle is found to make a mistake: When asked whether 2 + 2 = 4, the oracle answers no. Interestingly, this discovery would not have discomfitted the Azande, for according to their system of beliefs, some batches of poison might simply be defective. Indeed, the test of asking a question the answer to which is already known was routinely used by the Azande to distinguish good poison from bad. Evidently, belief in the oracle was not based on the collection of empirical evidence for its validity, nor even on the perception that such evidence had ever been collected. On the contrary, belief in the oracle was itself the basis on which certain events in the world could be construed as evidential in the first place: Without the prior assumption that the oracle works, there would be no way of testing whether a batch of poison was good or bad. In brief, the validity of the oracle was *presupposed* in the Azande system.

From the viewpoint of classical empiricism, the Azande committed an empistemological error in making their belief in the oracle immune from falsification (Popper, 1959). But we have seen that scientific theories also have unfalsifiable elements. The place of the poison oracle in the Azande system is roughly equivalent to the place in science of *induction,* that is, the principle that regularities in the past are predictive of future events. If we were not already committed to this principle, we might take every failure to replicate an experimental result as evidence that the past is *not* a reliable guide to the future, just as we suppose that every false reply by the oracle undermines its authority. Our practice, however, is to *presume* that the attempted replication failed to duplicate the value of some causally relevant variable, even if we have no idea what that variable might be (compare: the poison came from a bad batch). In this way, any finite number of observations, however chaotic they may be, can be made compatible with a continued belief in inductive reasoning (Kukla, 1978, 1980). Empirical research can call to question the validity of *particular* inductive claims, but not the validity of induction itself. Compare Jahoda's (1982) discussion of the poison oracle:

> There may have been, and often was, skepticism about specific oracles or verdicts, but not easily about the system as a whole because it formed the overall framework within which Azande thinking about the world was largely confined. (p. 181)

These considerations impel us toward a third view of nonscientific belief systems. To begin with, we must recognize that, underlying the particular paradigms that have come and gone in the history of science, there stands a superordinate paradigm employing fundamental concepts and presuppositions that are shared by all scientific theories. One of these presuppositions is that past regularities are predictive of future events. The belief systems of other cultures constitute *alternative paradigms* that are incommensurable with the scientific paradigm because they do not share all the same concepts and presuppositions. As is the case with competing scientific paradigms, the disagreements between science as a whole and the Azande system cannot be settled by an appeal to the evidence, because these two systems have radically different ideas about what *constitutes* evidence. Experimental tests of the poison oracle simply beg the question—one might as well ask the oracle about the validity of science. The results of such cross-paradigmatic investigations might be of interest to the investigators, but they need not concern the investigatees.

The incommensurability of alternative paradigms does not entail that we can have no basis for preferring one paradigm over another. The history of science shows that scientists do find reasons for changing their paradigmatic allegiances from time to time. The important point, however, is that these shifts cannot be justified on the basis of a purely rational assessment of the evidence. They are motivated rather by aesthetic, moral, political, or practical *values*. According to Kuhn, one of the most potent values in the history of science has been the desire to work on interesting and challenging puzzles. A paradigm that creates many questions requiring "further research" is likelier to gain adherents among scientists than one that provides definitive answers to most of its questions right from the start (Kuhn, 1970, p. 10). By this criterion, the poison oracle cannot hope to compete with contemporary physics. But this is not to say that physics is closer to the truth.

Evidently, the post-Kuhnian analysis of science leads to radical relativism. If adherents to different scientific paradigms "live in different worlds," then members of non-Western cultures must surely live in worlds that are even more different. There is no way to adjudicate the conflict between modern science and the Azande by an appeal to the properties of a transcendent reality, because every such appeal must already be embedded in the terms and assumptions of one of the competitors. There is no neutral court.

CROSS-CULTURAL PSYCHOLOGY
IN A POST-EMPIRICIST ERA

In this section, I will try to indicate what post-Kuhnian relativism might mean for the actual practice of cross-cultural psychology. My account can be no more than a starting point for further analysis and discussion, however. Its main function is to serve as a stationary target for critical reaction.

In Kuhn's writings, scientists are depicted as active members of one paradigmatic family or another. But what is the situation of post-Kuhnian scientists who comes to understand the relativity of every paradigm, including their own? One possibility—the least interesting—is that such scientists continue to inhabit the world of their origin, having changed only a superficial philosophical gloss that accompanies their research endeavors. A more intriguing possibility is that their new mental equipment enables them to shift at will from one paradigm to another—to see either the rabbit or the duck. At this moment in the history of ideas, it is by no means certain that these alternatives exhaust the range of post-Kuhnian options. Nevertheless, one point seems fairly clear: The dichotomous choice between "accepting" a belief system and "rejecting" it is an oversimplification that fails to capture the post-Kuhnian attitude toward alternative systems. A post-Kuhnian investigator of the Azande oracle, or the I Ching, or the Pantheon of the ancient world will not simply reject these systems because they conflict with modern science. But neither will he or she accept them in the same manner as an Azande, an indigenous Taoist, or an ancient Greek might accept them. Still, the post-Kuhnian is prepared to take these systems *seriously* in some sense that would be repudiated by a classical empiricist. A major task of the post-Kuhnian revolution is to explain what this attitude of taking a system "seriously," as distinct from simply accepting it, entails. Not actively *dis*believing the system is surely a necessary condition for taking it seriously; but it can hardly be sufficient.

To illustrate the issues involved here, consider the phenomenon of faith healing. Let us suppose, as most scientific investigators of this phenomenon have concluded, that faith healing is at least sometimes effective, and that its effectiveness depends partly on the client's prior *belief* that the cure will be effective (Frank, 1974). This means that the disagreement between believers and disbelievers in the faith cure is of paradigmatic proportions. Certainly it cannot be settled by the simple empirical procedure of trying out the cure, since both believers and disbelievers are liable to find their own presumptions justified by the outcome. In this case, proponents of the two paradigms "live in different worlds" in a particularly dramatic sense: One group finds its ailments cured by the faith healer, and the other does not.

Now what is the situation of a person who recognizes that the effectiveness of faith healing is contingent upon his own assumption about the process? Such a person is essentially in the position of a postempiricist who surveys the claims of two competing paradigms. He understands that each one is "correct" in terms of its own assumptions. But can he avail himself of the faith cure while simultaneously holding on to his postempiricist, relativistic understanding of the situation? Or must he make a forced choice between philosophical clarity and expanded health care services? Speaking of self-fulfilling prophecies generally, Watzlawick (1984) has written that "a prophecy that we know to be only a prophecy can no longer fulfill itself" (p. 113). If Watzlawick is right, then a person who understands the self-validating nature of beliefs about faith healing would be unable to benefit from the faith cure. But I see no compelling reason for adopting this point of view. On the contrary, it seems that at least some people who avail themselves of faith cures are aware of the role played in the process by their own beliefs, or else they would not agree to calling them *faith* cures. If the faith healing issue is representative of interparadigmatic conflict generally, we may at least tentatively hypothesize that the validating experiences of a paradigm are accessible not only to the true believer, but also to the post-Kuhnian for whom the paradigm in question contains only relative truth. In other words, we may be able to see the world as the Azande see it without being Azande.

This possibility of travel to distant mental realms suggests an intriguing way of doing cross-cultural research. In essence, the method involves learning to experience the world like a member of another culture in order to broaden one's first-hand knowledge of the varieties of mental life. An outline of this enterprise, which I call "ethnophenomenology," is sketched below.

First, a word about phenomenology generally. By this term I mean the practice of treating first-person reports of mental states as observational data. For example, we may entertain the hypothesis that a particular form of mental exercise causes us to experience a white flash (Bernard, 1950). Phenomenological research consists of the *investigator's* performing the specified exercises and reporting whether he obtains the expected mental results. The essence of the behavioristic position in psychology has been that phenomenological reports of this kind cannot be admitted into the data base of science. The reasons adduced for this restrictive policy, however, have by now largely been discredited.[4] To be sure, a phenomenological methodology is heir to a variety of problems relating to generalizability, communicability, and so on. But these issues all have equally problematic counterparts in the enterprise of observing and reporting on other people's behavior.

Ethnophenomenological research consists of two stages. First, one strives to become adept at employing another culture's paradigm. For example, one might learn to use and interpret the I Ching in the same way as a Taoist sage. This process would undoubtedly be expedited by actual contact with "accredited agents" of the other system. But useful work could also be based entirely on archival materials. The second stage is to introspect into one's mental processes and to note how they are affected by immersion in the alternative paradigm. It is this second stage that identifies the enterprise as psychological rather than anthropological. The traditional distinction between cultural anthropology and cross-cultural psychology is that the former takes a culture's collectively created system of beliefs and values as its subject matter, while the latter strives to ascertain how the experiences and actions of individuals are affected by these collective systems. According to this division of labor, the project I am describing definitely belongs to psychology. Like anthropologists, ethnophenomenologists begin by studying a collective system. But they do so only as a means to ascertaining the effect of this system on individual consciousness.

It is not strictly necessary to hold to the postempiricist philosophy of science to contribute to ethnophenomenology. But the range of ethnophenomenological experiments open to the classical empiricist is drastically limited by his or her assumption that the systems being studied are *false*—for instance, that shamans do not "really" communicate with demons.[5] Because of this attitude, the classical empiricist would be able to duplicate in her or his own person only the most superficial aspects of the shamanistic state of mind. If he or she tried to study faith healing in this manner, it is doubtful that a cure would be obtained; and in his or her studies of shamanism, the classical empiricist would probably fail to obtain the spine-chilling visions that validate the shaman's worldview. A post-Kuhnian investigator, however, would take the alternative paradigm seriously, which means at the very least that she or he would be able to recreate a fuller analogue of the shaman's mentality in her or his own person.[6]

To be sure, even a post-Kuhnian will be unable to duplicate the mentality of shamanism to perfection. For one thing, real shamans are not generally inclined to be post-Kuhnian relativists. No matter how completely and seriously one immerses oneself in the concepts, assumptions, and practices of shamanism, the ethnophenomenologist does not thereby become a full-fledged member of the shamanistic paradigm—at least not without a full-fledged conversion that entails ceasing to be a post-Kuhnian scientist. The ethnophenomenologist becomes instead a *quasi-shaman*—a member (perhaps the only member) of a view of the world that comes into being when a post-Kuhnian immerses him- or herself in shamanism. But this nonequivalence of shamanism and quasi-shamanism is not crucially important for psychology. In the last analysis, the aim of psychology is to formulate laws of behavior and mental life that are as fundamental as possible. The basic concepts in which these laws are to be framed have been variously conceived as stimulus and response, or as belief and desire. But no one has ever supposed that terms like "shaman" or "Azande" will appear in these laws, any more than "cup" or "saucer" appear in the laws of physics. From the standpoint of psychology (it may be different for another science), we study Azande mental states only incidentally, as a physicist might incidentally use a cup in a physical experiment. The physicist is interested in the cup only as it instantiates a theoretically relevant concept such as weight or volume. Similarly, the cross-cultural psychologist is presumably interested in the Azande because they instantiate some theoretically significant concepts in psychology. As for ethnophenomenology, the important thing is for the investigator to enter into a mental state that differs from his or her ordinary one along some theoretically significant dimension. Thus, even if quasi-shamanism had nothing in common with shamanism (which is highly implausible), its introspective study might still be important for psychology. Quasi-shamanism is after all a variety of mental life. The fact that this particular variety may be very rare, occurring only among a handful of ethnophenomenologists, is irrelevant to its importance in advancing the theoretical goals of psychology.

There are some studies already in existence that can be regarded as prototypes of ethnophenomenological research. Among these are Kapleau's (1966) account of Zen training, the descriptions of contemporary yogic Hinduism by Bernard (1950) and Ram Dass (1976), and Castaneda's (1968, 1971, etc.) volumes on Yaqui sorcery.[7] Each of these authors reports having learned to obtain the experiences that validate an alternative view of the world; each of them received direct instruction from accredited experts in the alternative paradigm; and each of them eventually received his own accreditation as an expert. Clearly, these results could not have been obtained without taking the alternative paradigms very seriously indeed. Yet the authors were also trained and accredited in the scientific paradigm. Finally, the main focus of their work is decidedly psychological as opposed to anthropological: Their writings are replete with phenomenological reports of their own experiences, from which they extract what lessons they can about the nature of the mind.

What kinds of results have issued from investigations like these? It is difficult to say a few words on this topic without feeling the need to say a great deal more by way of explanation. For example, Castaneda (1968) informs us that the Yaqui sorcerer don Juan taught him to fly like a bird. What are we to make of this observation? Castaneda himself was quite uncertain whether he "really" flew like a bird or suffered a hallucination. From a post-Kuhnian perspective, however, questions of the "reality" of phenomena can be answered only relative to a paradigm (see note 6). Evidently, flying like a bird is possible in don Juan's paradigm—don Juan's claim to that effect is confirmed by Castaneda's experience. This discovery does not speak in any direct manner to the question as to whether levitation is scientifically possible. But it does give us an inkling into the remarkable plasticity of human experience. Naturally, one would like a more precise statement here. But the task of writing an analytical review of the current state of ethnophenomenological research must be left for another occasion.

In summary, ethnophenomenology is the enterprise of immersing oneself in another culture's worldview in order to observe in oneself the effect of such an immersion. This is not exactly how cross-cultural psychologists have approached their subject in the past. But the enterprise is psychological, and it does involve the study of other cultures. These are reasons enough to call it a branch of cross-cultural psychology. In any case, somebody has to do it, for it is inconceivable that such personal explorations into alternative realities could have nothing of significance to teach us about the mind.

NOTES

1. See Suppe (1977) for an authoritative review. Suppe refers to the extreme empiricism of the previous generation as the "received view," on account of the near-unanimity with which it was held. Since the "received view" is now defunct among philosophers of science, I have called it "classical empiricism."
2. This definition of a paradigm is somewhat narrower than Kuhn's (1970) original notion.
3. Gardner (1985, pp. 232-233) attributes this view to Franz Boas.
4. See Kukla (1983) for a more extensive discussion of this claim and those immediately following.
5. "There is, I think, no theory-independent way to reconstruct phrases like 'really there'; the notion of a match between the ontology of a theory and its 'real' counterpart in nature seems to me to be elusive in principle" (Kuhn, 1970, p. 206).
6. Compare Cohen's view that the task of the historian of science is "to immerse himself in the writings of scientists of previous ages . . . so totally that . . . he can correctly apply the words Alexandre Koyre used to delight in using about a scientist of the past,

'And he was right!'"(1977, p. 346). Cohen also suggests that the same courtesy be extended to Babylonian astrology. This could be called an ethnophenomenological approach to the history of science.

7. A number of critics have accused Castaneda of fabricating his accounts (Noel, 1976). Even if this accusation is true, Castaneda's books can still be read with profit for their descriptions of how an ethnophenomenologist might operate and the kinds of issues he is likely to encounter.

12

ORGANIZATIONAL STRUCTURE AND PROCESSES

PETER B. SMITH
MONIR TAYEB

The extensive literature concerning cross-cultural studies of organizational behavior has been reviewed by Tannenbaum (1980), Child (1981), and, most recently, Triandis (in press). A critical review of five of the most substantial studies has also been provided by Roberts and Boyacigiller (1984). All of these commentators, and many others, have pointed out that what this field requires is not so much more findings as clearer conceptualization. Accordingly, this chapter will not attempt to survey existing work but to address some of the issues that continue to undermine our best endeavors. Roberts and Boyacigiller identify three such issues, namely, inadequate conceptualization of culture; the ignoring of time variables and of differences in its conceptualization around the world; and the use of static measures, particularly pencil and paper ones.

Since all three of these issues have also been problematic for researchers who are engaged in monocultural studies, it is immediately apparent that the problem is one of degree rather than kind. Conceptualization of culture might be thought of as *the* distinctively cross-cultural issue, but no one who has read the literature on organizational culture is likely to agree that the problem is confined to the *cross-*cultural literature (Frost, Moore, Louis, Lundberg, & Martin, 1985).

Diagnosing that the field has conceptual problems is something on which all can agree. The divergences start to arise when more precise remedies are prescribed. Child (1981), for instance, laments the low level of awareness that organizational researchers often have of relevant work on cultural issues by anthropologists, sociologists, and psychologists. Roberts and Boyacigiller (1984), however, while also arguing for a broader perspective, find little value in anthropologists' conceptions of culture, seeing them as too influenced by study of man-made artifacts.

In this chapter we shall not propose that one or the other adjacent academic discipline has the answer to our difficulties. Rather, we shall assert that conceptually parallel problems arise in many different areas of investigation. These problems are then conceptualized in ways that make them specific to a particular field. Such reifications are then enshrined as a distinctive problem of the field. One such issue, which bedevils work across much of the social sciences, is what we choose to call the "inside-outside" problem. A person's actions do not appear the same to the person doing those actions as they do to those observing them. Within the cross-cultural field, this conceptual issue appears as the "emic-etic" dilemma (Berry, 1969, 1980). Emic or intracultural studies do not necessarily yield the same picture of a society as do etic or comparative ones. To be sure, some of these differences are due to problems of translation and nonequivalence of measures. But some differences stem from the fact that members of a given culture share a complex system for decoding the meanings of one another's behavior that may be inaccessible to outsiders. Thus there is an apparent logical paradox, whereby the only wholly valid etic study might be one in which a series of noncomparable emic studies was undertaken. Here is not the place to explore the full range of the various attempts to escape this dilemma that have been proposed (Triandis & Brislin, 1980).

Students of organizational behavior have also been confronted by the inside-outside problem, which appears in this context as a debate both between and within two broadly separate groups of researchers. These are those who have treated the organization as a whole as the appropriate unit of analysis ("macro" researchers), and those who have treated the organization work group as the appropriate unit ("micro" researchers). In this chapter we shall consider work focussed at both of these levels of analysis, but let us first illustrate the nature of the debate at each level in turn.

At least in Western countries, outsiders who enquire about the nature of a particular organization are likely to be shown an organizational chart detailing a hierarchical structure. Insiders within organizations tend to be much more finely tuned to the processes that they see going on around them than to these structurally prescribed procedures. Their interpretations of processes occurring within the organization are dependent upon their knowledge of that organization's culture. Newcomers to organizations quite often need extended periods of time before they can become fully socialized to the local culture. Macro researchers into organizational behavior thus face a particular version of the emic-etic dilemma, which they would term the "structure-process" dilemma. The logic of etic studies is to go for those aspects of organizations that can be reliably measured comparatively, namely, their structural qualities. The hazard of such a strategy is that what is measured may give only a very partial view of the meaning of those structural dimensions to members of organizations in particular settings. As a consequence of this partial view, structural measures such as those of size or degree of centralization may prove to be only very weak predictors of organizational performance. In terms of the emic-etic dilemma, it could be the case that we can only understand the effects of structure through studying processes, such as those emphasized by those within the micro research tradition. We shall return to the study of organizational structure in the next section.

While macro researchers into organizational behavior have chosen to approach their subject through analyses of formally prescribed structures, such as departments and decision procedures, micro researchers have opted for a focus upon the nature of superior-subordinate relationships through studies of leadership and participation. In this latter field the inside-outside problem is also well apparent. At least in Western countries, leaders see their leadership as more participative than do their subordinates (e.g., Heller & Wilpert, 1981). Xu (1984) has reported data from mainland China that shows the reverse pattern: Superiors saw themselves as more autocratic than did their subordinates. However, in both instances there is a divergence of perceptions, as between superiors' "inside" view of their actions and subordinates' "outside" view of those same actions.

The inside-outside problem has not been as directly addressed by researchers into leadership and participation as it has by the more macroscopically-oriented researchers into organizational structures. It has appeared self-evident to some leadership researchers that insider or self-report measures of leader style are the most likely to be valid, while to others the only measures worth having are those that derive from outsider measures, such as subordinates' perceptions. One of the few leadership theorists to address the question directly is Misumi (1985). Drawing on the vocabulary of the geneticists, he distinguishes general or "genotypic" and specific or "phenotypic" aspects of leadership behavior. The general aspect of a leader's behavior is seen as an underlying dimension, inherent in the process of leadership, which will be present in all settings. The specific aspect concerns the manner in which that dimension will be perceived within a particular country and organization's culture.

In the sections of this chapter that follow, we shall first examine in more detail some of the work done by macro researchers into cross-cultural aspects of organizational structures, and then that done by micro researchers into leadership. We select the study of organization structures and of leadership because they provide well-worked-over examples of research within the macro and micro traditions. In either case our purpose will be to see how far the reifications of the inside-outside dilemma current in that particular field take us toward confronting the emic-etic dilemma.

CULTURE AND ORGANIZATIONAL STRUCTURE

Among the researchers who have studied organizations cross-culturally, two groups can be identified. The first group comprises those who have found culture to have little or no effect upon the interrelationship of different structural aspects of organizations (Hickson, Hinings, McMillan, & Schwitter, 1974; Hickson & McMillan, 1981; Lammers & Hickson, 1979). They see structure as contingent upon such environmental factors as technology, size, industry, and market, and consequently advocate a "culture-free" theory of organizational structure. The second group comprises those who have found culture to play an overarching role in the structuring of organizations (Crozier, 1964; Hofstede, 1980; Maurice, Sorge, & Warner, 1980; Pascale & Athos, 1981; Sorge, 1980). They consequently propose a "culture-specific" thesis.

The Culture-Free Thesis

Many studies have attempted to examine the relevance of the culture-free thesis for different types of organizations in Western and Eastern societies (Donaldson, 1986; Hickson et al., 1979; Kuc, Hickson, & McMillan, 1980). Some of these examinations have also involved at least one developing country (Ayoubi, 1975; Badran & Hinings, 1981; Conaty, Mahmoudi, & Miller, 1983; Shenoy, 1981). These studies, with a few exceptions (notably Maurice et al., 1980), have supported the view that there are culture-free relationships between context and structure.

The basic assumption of the culture-free thesis is that the relationship between organizational characteristics and their contextual factors is stable across societies:

> [Our] hypothesis rests on the theory that there are imperatives, or "causal" relationships, from the resources of "customer," of employees, of materials and finance etc., and of operating technology of an organization to its structure, which take effect whatever the surrounding social

differences. . . . Whether the culture is Asian or European or North
American, a large organization with many employees improves efficiency
by specialising their activities but also by increasing, controlling and
coordinating specialities. (Hickson et al., 1974, pp. 63-64)

The consistency with which the researchers cited above have found
support for the culture-free thesis is impressive. However, some of this
consistency may be attributable to the various methodological inade-
quacies from which they suffer. The particular weakness that concerns
us here is the way in which the aspects of organizations to be studied
were selected. The purpose of studies such as that by Hickson et al.
(1979) was to test the stability of relationships between organizational
structure and its environmental correlates (the etic aspects) across
countries, rather than to examine their underlying rationale (the emic
aspects). The structural characteristics studied were limited to only a few
dimensions, namely, centralization, formalization, and specialization.
As Maurice (1976) points out, however, these were operationalized in a
way that practically precluded any testing of the national or cultural
variables that lie behind them. Let us take centralization, for example.
This dimension was measured in the studies mentioned above using
Aston Programme items and procedures (Pugh, Hickson, Hinings, &
Turner, 1968). The Aston scale for this dimension measures only who
finally makes a decision; it does not capture the events that make up the
essence of decision making, such as the amount or direction of
consultation and communication, processes that are more likely to
reflect managers' and employees' attitudes and values. Tayeb (in press),
in a study of two matched samples of English and Indian firms, found
that although the organizations achieved in some respects a "universal"
configuration in response to similar contextual demands, the *means* by
which they had done so were different. For instance, both groups of
organizations were similar with regard to the extent of centralization.
However, the processes that lay behind this similarity were quite
different. In the English sample there was more consultation and
delegation before a final decision would be made at a senior level,
whereas in the Indian sample senior managers consulted their subordinates to a lesser extent. The study went on to show that these two
different means of achieving the same end were highly consistent with
the cultural characteristics of English and Indian samples.
    Even within the limitations of the Aston type of studies, recent data
indicate that substantial variation in organizational structure may be
explicable only in culture-specific ways. Pugh and Redding (cited by
Redding & Wong, 1986) indicate substantial differences in organiza-

tional structure between firms of similar size in Hong Kong and in Britain. The Chinese firms had less precisely defined roles, fewer standardized procedures, fewer staff functions, and more centralization. The culture-free thesis clearly requires some qualification once size of firm is held constant rather than treated as a predictor of structure. Redding and Wong also report that 92% of Hong Kong firms employ fewer than 50 people, so it could be that in a sample that contained more large firms, the culture-free thesis would gain more support. Earlier work by Negandhi (1973) showed that among firms in Taiwan that had been matched by size and market, there were substantial differences between the structures of locally owned, Japanese-owned, and American-owned firms.

A more recent study conducted by Negandhi (1985) in America and India found that Indian organizations tended to be more centralized than their equal-sized North American counterparts. However, in both countries smaller firms were likely to be more centralized than bigger ones. Thus the evidence was both for and against the culture-free thesis.

The Culture-Specific Thesis

The proponents of this thesis argue that culture determines organizational structures and processes through influencing employees' work attitudes and behaviors. By implication, they thus argue that there is a high degree of consistency between people's attitudes, values, and behaviors outside and inside work organizations. For instance, it is asserted that in those cultures in which children have a high regard and respect for their parents, and obey their seniors within the family setting, power and authority relationships within work organizations are also characterized by the concentration of power and command in the hands of seniors and the submission and obedience of subordinates (Davies, 1983; Hofstede, 1980; Kakar, 1971).

Cultural dimensions such as power distance, uncertainty avoidance, individualism, and masculinity (Hofstede, 1980); interpersonal trust, commitment, and hard work (De Bettignies, 1973; Tayeb, in press); and avoidance of face-to-face encounters in conflict situations (Crozier & Thoening, 1976), have been proposed. In many cases such process dimensions have been shown to be reflected heavily in management styles across different cultures. For instance, Hofstede argued that two major cultural dimensions, power distance and uncertainty avoidance, are conceptually linked with two organizational dimensions, concentration of authority and structuring of activities, respectively. Tayeb

(1979, in press), in studies of Iranian, Indian, and English organizations, found that two more cultural dimensions, commitment and trust, had strong associations with structural measures, especially of organizational centralization and of type of management control system used. For instance, those with lower commitment had less autonomy and were subject to more controls, such as being required to clock in, while those with higher commitment were not.

Cultural values and attitudes are only one of the various sets of factors that bear upon an organization. As we emphasized in the preceding section, advocates of the culture-free thesis have also shown that the organization's task environment and contextual factors, such as technology, size, industry and market, exert their own demands, and these may create strong pressure for particular structural forms. We discuss next how the tension between the culture-free and the culture-specific views may be best accommodated.

Emic and Etic Aspects
of Organizational Structure

In order to appreciate the significance of both structures and processes in organizational structure, we need a new definition of the concept that recognizes the role that each plays. This definition should then help us understand why some cross-cultural studies of organizational structure have not been able to unravel the complex relationships between culture and organization.

Organizational structure is therefore redefined here as *a framework for decision making and decision implementation.* An understanding of organizational structure requires references not only to dimensions such as centralization, formalization, specialization, and standardization (Pugh et al., 1968), but also to the processes, relationships, and actions that lie behind these dimensions. These organizational processes include power and authority relationships; the handling of uncertainty and risk taking; reliability, interpersonal trust, and honesty; dedication, loyalty, and commitment; motivation, reward, and inducement; control and discipline; coordination and integration; and communication, consultation, and participation.

Given this definition, it seems that environmental factors have implications primarily for formal organizational structure, or etic aspects, such as centralization, formalization, and specialization. The relationships between these features of organization and contextual factors are widespread but not universal, as the studies from Hong Kong and elsewhere indicate. It is indeed common sense to expect that beyond a certain point an increase in the number of employees will lead, one way or another, to an increase in the division of labor (functional specialization). It is here that the universality of the findings may end. Employees' behaviors and relationships with one another within the workplace, the emic aspects, are based on their work-related values and attitudes concerning such issues as power and authority, tolerance for ambiguity, commitment, and management philosophy and ideology. These values and attitudes have strong associations with the employees' cultural, occupational, educational, and social backgrounds, which, in turn, are rooted in their societies. In the limiting case of the data from Hong Kong, cultural values may ensure that firms remain small, thus circumventing the imperative that large firms must employ formalization and functional specialization. Within the size range of firms found in Hong Kong, there need be no clash between environmental imperatives and cultural values.

A reinterpretation of the findings of studies the authors of which supported either a culture-free or a culture-specific model of organizational structure in the light of the emic-etic distinction thus brings out a different conclusion. That is, both groups may be correct in their assumptions. Members of the former have studied the inherently etic aspects of organizational structure, and, not surprisingly, found them similar across different cultures. Members of the latter group have studied the inherently emic aspects of organizational structure and found that they varied considerably across cultures.

A more comprehensive approach to studying and understanding organizations in intercultural, and, indeed, intracultural, settings would employ a research design that enables the researcher to examine both emic and etic aspects of organizations. The conclusions thus arrived at would be more realistic than has hitherto been the case. Several implicitly monocultural researchers have attempted to do just this in recent years (e.g., Hunt & Osborn, 1982; House, in press), but we have some way to go in defining appropriate measures and research procedures.

CULTURE AND LEADERSHIP STYLE

In studies of organizational structure it has been the advocates of the culture-free model who have made most of the running. By contrast, in studies of work-group behavior advocates of culture-specific models have been far more influential. This may simply be because a more microscopic focus upon the behavior of particular leaders within an organization makes it increasingly difficult to formulate measures that are truly culture-free. Whether for this reason or not, early attempts to formulate universally applicable theories of effective leadership style (Bales, 1958; Blake & Mouton, 1964; Likert, 1961; Stogdill & Coons, 1957) have found inconsistent empirical support. Even within North America, environmental contingencies have been shown markedly to affect which styles of leadership are linked to high performance by subordinates (Bryman, 1986; Yukl, 1981).

Research in other parts of the world has frequently been influenced by the conceptualizations of leader style first formulated in the United States. For instance, most of the U.S. theorists listed above found it useful to distinguish two dimensions of leader style, one concerning the leader's attention to the task at hand and the other concerning the leader's attention to the maintenance of working relations among the work team. Similar distinctions are found in the work of Misumi (1985) in Japan and Sinha (1981) in India.

Studies of effective leader styles in Europe have yielded findings that are as inconsistent as those from North America. For instance, in Britain, Argyle, Gardner, and Cioffi (1958) found productivity higher in electrical engineering plants where supervisors were democratic and nonpunitive, whereas Cooper (1966) found the supervisors in an oil-processing plant who rated high on task relevance were the most effective ones. However, studies conducted in societies in other parts of the world have given much more consistent support to two-factor theories of leadership style. The research conducted by Misumi (1985) over 30 years in Japan has shown that effective supervisors in that country are those who score high both in orientation toward task performance (which he terms P) and in orientation toward team maintenance (M). This finding has been replicated in coal mines, shipbuilding yards, banks, local authority offices, bus companies, and many other workplaces. In a similar manner, Bond and Hwang (1986) review studies of leader style undertaken by Taiwan. Translations of the Ohio State leader style measure show positive relations between both consideration (similar to M) and initiating structure (similar to P) and performance measures in factories, local government offices, and schools. So too, Sinha's (1981) studies in India support the view that the effective leader is to be characterized as a nurturant task, or NT, leader. Furthermore, Ayman and Chemers (1983) found both Ohio State leadership scales related to productivity in a factory in Iran, although in this case both scales loaded on a single factor.

There is a certain irony about this pattern of findings. The theories first formulated in the United States would appear to be most strongly supported in those parts of the world that are less like the United States, and must be rejected in United States and in the countries in Europe and elsewhere that are most similar to it. We should nevertheless hesitate before accepting such a bold conclusion in its entirety. It is quite possible that the differences found are partially explicable through the use of more numerous and more tough-minded criterion measures in the North American studies. Furthermore, the measures used in many of these studies have been adapted for use in the non-Western countries concerned. Ayman and Chemers's questionnaire included the item "The supervisor is like a kind father." Sinha's nurturance scale includes the item "Does your superior help you to grow up and assume responsibility?" While these items may well be valid components of a consideration factor in the countries where they have been used, they are not likely to factor together with U.S.-based consideration items if used in Western countries. The fact that measures have been adapted for use within these various countries indicates that the surprising consensus of findings from non-Western countries may not be what Berry (1969) characterizes as an etic finding based on "imposed-etic" categories. It is better seen as an apparent consensus based upon the confounding of etic and emic approaches. What is therefore needed to gain a clearer comprehension of the divergence of findings from different countries is a further application of Misumi's (1985) distinction between general measures and specific measures, which was advanced earlier in this chapter.

It could well prove to be the case that leaders in organizations from all parts of the world do indeed need to attend both to the task at hand and also to the maintenance of good relationships within the work team. But *how* this is to be accomplished in each setting will be dependent upon the meanings given to particular leadership acts in that setting. A supervisor who frequently checks on which work is done correctly may be seen as a kind father in one setting, as task-centered in another setting, and as officious and mistrustful in a third. The meaning of acts is given by the cultural context within which they occur. In certain cultures—those that Hofstede (1980) characterizes as collective—the attribution of meaning is likely to be much more consensually shared than would be the case in more individualist societies. So one possible explanation for the more consistent findings on leadership in non-Western countries is that in collective cultures there is a much more unified view of what leaders should do. A second possibility is that the sharpness of the distinction that U.S. researchers made between "task" behavior and "group maintenance" is itself culture-bound and will be variously blended in a different manner in different cultures. Even within other cultures as individualistic as the United States, it could be that the boundaries between what is "task" and what is "maintenance" are drawn differently. On this view, whether or not the two dimensions come out as linked to high performance in any particular culture depends on the meanings given to specific behaviors within that culture. A third view would be the culture-specific view that different leader styles really are required in different cultures. Existing studies certainly provide some encouragement for this view, but substantial variability in the samples and types of measurement used in different countries requires our continuing caution.

A series of studies has recently been undertaken in an attempt to clarify these issues (Smith et al., 1987a, 1987b; Smith & Peterson, in press). In each of these studies subordinates have been asked to make ratings of the leadership style of their superiors, using one or another of the established measures of leader style. Such measures are largely composed of rather broad general characterizations of leader behavior. For instance, one Ohio State item used is, "Is your superior friendly and approachable?" Respondents are then asked to complete a further series of 36 specific questions, asking about the superior's behavior much more precisely. For example, they are asked when the superior comes to work, where he or she eats lunch, who he or she has meetings with, who he or he talks to and how often, and so forth. Correlations are then computed separately for each country's data between the perceived style of the supervisor and each one of the 36 specific behaviors. Data have been collected from shop-floor assembly workers in Britain, the United States, Hong Kong, and Japan, and from samples of middle managers in Britain, the United States, Japan, and India. Results are so far available for measures of Misumi's PM leadership styles and for Blake and Mouton's 9.9 and paternalism scales.

The overall pattern of findings is relatively clear. Eight of ten of the 36 behaviors prove to correlate consistently positively with one or another of the style measures in all the countries sampled. For instance, talking sympathetically with a subordinate who has personal difficulties is seen as considerate in all cultures, and frequency of talking about work progress is seen as task-centered in all cultures. But the remaining 26 behaviors show wide and frequently significant differences between countries in correlation with the style measures. For instance, it was found that a supervisor who talks about a subordinate's personal difficulties to his or her colleagues when the person is absent was deemed inconsiderate in Britain and the United States, but considerate in Hong

Kong and Japan. The supervisor who shows disapproval of latecomers to work is seen as task-centered in Britain and Hong Kong, unfriendly or inconsiderate in the United States, and neither of these things in Japan. Like these differences, many of the others found are readily explicable in terms of existing knowledge from emic studies of the cultures concerned.

This series of studies also showed that in all the countries included in the sample, subordinates who evaluated their current work situation highly also evaluated their supervisors as high on both P and M, just as Misumi's theory predicts. Western researchers might well argue that such a concordance of the various different ratings by the subordinates points to some kind of halo effect due to the use of a set of relatively similar rating scales. However, for the present purpose this need not be a problem. At the very least the study shows that in all four countries the scales measuring P and M leader styles have high social desirability. At the same time the data show that the specific meanings of the P and M styles vary by culture. These studies are therefore consistent with the second of the three possible views of conflict in the findings of previous leadership research. That is to say that while an etic view of leadership may indeed identify universals in the general manner in which supervisors are seen to behave, emic analyses will show that different specific behaviors mediate the effects of such styles in each culture.

CONCLUSION

The pattern of findings emerging from leadership studies reinforces the view discussed in the previous section concerning organizational structure. It is most unlikely to be the case that leadership processes in organizations can be comprehended solely in terms of an etic model. Neither is it the case that the best we can aspire to is a series of incommensurable emic analyses of cultural meanings. What can be accomplished is a series of comparably structured emic analyses, which will show us the range within which the effects of structures or leadership acts can be construed universally. If we were once able to do that, we might also be better placed to understand why our success has been so limited in understanding these same issues within our own society. We could, for instance, contribute from an informed base to debates about organizational culture. We could also place in context the individualistic manner in which leadership has been conceptualized in the West. In such ways can cross-cultural work not only derive but also feed back into what we are pleased to think of as the mainstream.

13
CULTURE AND INTERGROUP PROCESSES
WILLIAM B. GUDYKUNST

> During most of his [or her] life the adult acts not purely as an individual but as a member of a social group. However, the different groups a person belongs to are not equally important at a given moment. Sometimes his [or her] belonging to one group is dominant, sometimes his [or her] belonging to another... in every situation the person seems to know what group he [or she] belongs to and to what group he [or she] does not belong. He [or she] knows more or less clearly where he [or she] stands, and this position largely determines his [or her] behavior. (Lewin, 1948, p. 46)

As Lewin indicates, group memberships influence individuals' behavior. "Whenever individuals belonging to one group interact collectively or individually, with another group or its members *in terms of their group identifications,* we have an instance of intergroup behavior" (Sherif, 1966, p. 12). Tajfel (1978) argues that behavior can be viewed as varying along a continuum from purely interpersonal to purely intergroup. Recent conceptualizations, however, suggest that a single continuum may oversimplify the analysis. Stephenson (1981), for example, contends that both interpersonal and intergroup factors are salient in every encounter between two individuals and that interpersonal salience affects intergroup processes (and vice versa).

Brewer and Kramer (1985) draw a distinction between "process" and "outcome" intergroup research. Process-oriented research includes the "intraindividual and interpersonal *processes* underlying the formation and maintenance of intergroup orientations," while outcome-oriented research refers to studies "that are concerned with the perceptual and behavioral consequences or outcomes of such processes" (p. 220). The emphasis in this chapter is on process-oriented intergroup research concerning social identity and the consequences of the ingroup-outgroup distinction, but outcome-oriented research on intergroup contact also is discussed (see Brewer & Kramer, 1985; Gudykunst, 1986; Stephan, 1985; Tajfel, 1982; Wilder, 1986, for reviews). The argument

AUTHOR'S NOTE: The chapter benefited from the comments and suggestions of Michael Bond, Harry Triandis, and Stella Ting-Toomey.

throughout is that culture strongly affects intergroup processes and that dimensions of cultural variability must be taken into consideration if the influences of culture on intergroup processes are to be fully understood.

CULTURAL VARIABILITY

Culture as a Theoretical Variable

Culture provides individuals with a *"theory of what his [or her] fellows know, believe, and mean. . . .* It is this theory to which a native actor *refers* in interpreting the unfamiliar or the ambiguous, in interacting with strangers" (Keesing, 1974, p. 89). Culture, therefore, influences how individuals deal with members of different groups. Cultural differences per se, however, are not important in explaining variations in intergroup processes across cultures; rather, it is necessary to treat cultures as operationalizations of *dimensions* of cultural variability. As Foschi and Hales (1979, p. 246) argue, culture is treated as a theoretical variable only when "culture X and culture Y serve to operationally define a characteristic, *a*, which the two cultures exhibit to different degrees." Foschi and Hales's position is consistent with Doise's (1986) contention that different levels of analysis (e.g., kinds of explanation) must be "articulated" (i.e., interlinked) in order to provide the most complete account of any specific process. The focus of this chapter is on utilizing Doise's ideological level processes (i.e., cultural variability) to explain processes occurring at the positional level (i.e., intergroup processes). Both of these levels, in turn, can be used to explain the other levels (i.e., intrapersonal and interpersonal/situational levels).

Dimensions of Culture

Individualism-collectivism is the major dimension of cultural variability isolated by theorists across disciplines as a dimension affecting intergroup processes (Hofstede, 1980; Kluckhohn & Strodtbeck, 1961; Marsella, DeVos, & Hsu, 1985; Triandis, 1986). Hui and Triandis's (1986) research indicates there is general agreement on the meaning of individualism-collectivism among researchers around the world. Individualistic cultures emphasize the individual's goals, while collectivistic cultures stress that group goals have precedence over individual goals. In individualistic cultures, individuals take care of themselves and members of their immediate family, while in collectivistic cultures, the ingroups to which individuals belong take care of them in exchange for loyalty (Hofstede, 1980). People in individualistic cultures tend to be universalistic and apply the same value standards to all. People in collectivistic cultures, in contrast, tend to be particularistic and apply different value standards for members of their ingroups and outgroups.

Triandis (1986) sees the key distinction between individualistic and collectivistic cultures as the focus on the ingroup in collectivistic cultures. Collectivistic cultures emphasize goals, needs, and views of the ingroup over those of the individual; the social norms of the ingroup, rather than individual pleasure; shared ingroup beliefs, rather than unique individual beliefs; and a value on cooperation with ingroup members, rather than maximizing individual outcomes. Triandis points out that ingroups have different rank-orders of importance in collectivistic cultures. Some, for example, put family ahead of all other groups, while others rank their company first. People in collectivistic cultures also draw sharper distinctions between members of ingroups and outgroups than do people in individualistic cultures. Finally, Triandis argues that different types of collectivism exist, that is, "contextual" collectivism involves ingroup influence that is specific to an ingroup, while "simple" collectivism allows individuals to choose how to behave when multiple ingroups are relevant.

Work by Triandis and his associates (1985, 1986) demonstrates that there is a psychological level (i.e., personality dimension) equivalent to the cultural level dimension of individualism-collectivism. Idiocentrism reflects an individualistic orientation, while allocentrism reflects a collectivistic orientation. Triandis et al.'s (1985) research in the United States revealed that idiocentrism is correlated positively with perceived loneliness and placing emphasis on achievement, while allocentrism is correlated positively to social support and negatively with anomie. These findings were replicated in the collectivistic culture of Puerto Rico by Triandis et al. (1986). This study also supports Kluckhohn and Strodtbeck's (1961) argument that all cultural variations exist within any specific culture. Specifically, Triandis et al.'s data indicate that idiocentrics exist in collectivistic cultures and allocentrics exist in individualistic cultures.

Several other dimensions of cultural variability also can influence intergroup processes. Hofstede (1980), for example, empirically derived four dimensions: individualism-collectivism (discussed above), power distance, uncertainty avoidance, and masculinity-femininity. High power distance cultures value an order of inequality, with everyone having a rightful place where the hierarchy reflects existential inequality.

Uncertainty avoidance involves the lack of tolerance in a culture for uncertainty and ambiguity. Cultures high in uncertainty avoidance have high levels of anxiety, a great need for formal rules, and a low tolerance for groups that behave in a deviant manner. High masculinity, according to Hofstede, involves valuing things, money, assertiveness, and unequal sex roles, while cultures in which people, quality of life, nurturance, and equal sex roles prevail are feminine.

Relatively little cross-cultural research on intergroup processes has been conducted to date. Interest in cross-cultural variations in intergroup behavior, however, appears to be on the rise (see Hewstone, 1985). Unfortunately, the majority of research does not treat culture as a "theoretical" variable. The purpose of the remainder of this chapter is to examine intergroup research across cultures and proffer theoretical explanations for the role of culture. Two types of hypotheses regarding the influence of culture on intergroup processes are generated whenever possible: hypotheses of cultural differences (HD) and hypotheses involving potential "universals" across cultures (HU).

SOCIAL IDENTITY

Group Membership and the Self-Concept

An individual's self-concept includes both private and public components. The private self is what individuals think about themselves, while the public self is the way they present themselves to others. The private and public selves both comprise personal and social identities. Personal identity is that part of the self-concept that drives from unique characteristics of the individual (e.g., intelligence, body build, interpersonal skills, etc.). Social identity, according to Tajfel (1978, p. 63), is "that *part* of an individual's self-concept that derives from his [or her] knowledge of his [or her] membership in a social group (or groups) together with the value and emotional significance attached to that membership."

Tajfel (1978) focuses on social identity in explaining intergroup processes. Social identity theory begins from the assumption that individuals seek positive social identities in their interactions with others. Individuals compare their group(s) with other groups and interact with members of these groups in a way that creates a favorable distinction for their group on positively valued dimensions (e.g., economic position, power, etc.). When the ingroup is considered superior to the relevant outgroup, a positive social identity emerges for members of the ingroup.

There is evidence to suggest that group memberships are more important for self-conceptions in collectivistic cultures than in individualistic cultures (see Marsella et al., 1985). Gabrenya and Wang's (1983) research, for example, revealed that Chinese utilized more group-oriented self-conceptions than people in the United States. This suggests that collectivistic cultures emphasize social identity, while individualistic cultures focus on personal identity. This conclusion appears to be supported by cross-cultural studies of the spontaneous self-concept (Bond & Cheung, 1983; Driver & Driver, 1983). Bond and Cheung's research, however, suggests that a simple collectivistic-individualistic distinction may not fully explain the differences that emerge; they found that Hong Kong Chinese and North Americans mentioned family roles more than Japanese, while Japanese mentioned sex and age more than the other two. These patterns correspond more closely to Hofstede's (1980) masculinity dimension of cultural variability. Other social roles, such as hierarchical group memberships (e.g., caste, social class), likewise should be influenced by cultural variations in power distance.

Cross-cultural research also suggests that there is consistency in the emphasis placed on ethnic identity for majority and minority groups across cultures. Hofman (1985), for example, found that blacks in the United States emphasize ethnic identity more than whites, and that Arabs in Israel place more importance on ethnic identification than Jews. This finding is consistent with both Brewer's (1979) conclusion and Bond and Hewstone's (1986) research in Hong Kong. Hofman also found greater cohesion in the identities of majority group members than in the identities of the minority group members in both cultures. Given the research cited, six hypotheses appear warranted:

HD1: Group memberships are a more important part of the self-concept in collectivistic cultures than in individualistic cultures.

HD1A: Sex identification is a more important part of the self-concept in collectivistic cultures that are high on masculinity than it is in collectivistic cultures that are low in masculinity or in individualistic cultures.

HD1B: Family is a more important part of the self-concept in collectivistic cultures that are low in masculinity than it is in collectivistic cultures that are high in masculinity or in individualistic cultures.

HD1C: Social class and other hierarchical group memberships dealing with power are more important aspects of the self-concept in collectivistic cultures that are high in power distance than they are in collectivistic cultures low in power distance or in individualistic cultures.

HU1: Identities of majority group members are more cohesive than identities of minority group members across cultures.

HU2: Members of minority groups emphasize ethnic identity as part of their self-concept more than members of majority groups across cultures.

Social and Ethnolinguistic Identity

While social identity theory was developed in an individualistic culture, it appears to be generalizable to collectivistic cultures (Bond & Hewstone, 1986; Ghosh & Huq, 1985; Hewstone, Bond, & Wan, 1983; Majeed & Ghosh, 1982). Majeed and Ghosh, for example, examined social identity in three ethnic groups in India, discovering differential evaluations of self, ingroup, and outgroups in High Caste Hindus, Muslims, and Scheduled Castes. Their research suggested also that the more common attributes were shared, the less the differentiation between ingroups and outgroups. Ghosh and Huq found similar results for Hindu and Muslim evaluations of self and ingroup in India and Bangladesh. Brewer and Campbell's (1976) research on ingroup-outgroup evaluations in Africa and Peabody's (1985) research in Europe supports these findings. Brewer and Campbell's cross-cultural study further suggests that the more group identities based on several categories (e.g., race, religion, economic condition) coincide, the greater the similarity assumed among members of the ingroup. Bond and Hewstone (1986) found that British high school students in Hong Kong perceive social identity and intergroup differentiation to be more important than do Chinese high school students. The British students also perceive group membership to be more important and have a more positive image of the ingroup than do the Chinese. The results for the Chinese, however, do not contradict social identity theory, but they do suggest that social differentiation in Hong Kong is "relatively muted," according to Bond and Hewstone (see also Bond, in press).

Closely related to work on social identity theory is research on ethnolinguistic vitality and ethnolinguistic identity. Ethnolinguistic vitality is the vitality associated with a particular ethnic group's language (it can be objectively or subjectively based), while ethnolinguistic identity refers to those aspects of an individual's social identity that are based on language. Giles, Bourhis, and Taylor (1977) argued that perceived ethnolinguistic vitality influences the degree to which members of a group will act based on group membership in intergroup situations. Bourhis and Sachdev (1984) examined Italian and English Canadians in both majority and equal situations. They found that both groups had more realistic perceptions in the majority than the equal setting. English Canadians, however, were more biased against the Italian language in the equal than in the majority setting. Giles, Rosenthal, and Young (1985) studied Greek- and Anglo-Australian perceptions of ethnolinguistic vitality. Both groups agreed about some aspects of each other's vitality, but disagreed about each other's position in Australian society. The Anglos' perceptions accentuated differences between ingroup and outgroup vitalities, while the Greeks attenuated the differences. Finally, Young, Pierson, and Giles (in press) found that perceptions of ingroup vitality are associated with the amount of exposure to the outgroup language in Hong Kong.

Preliminary research suggests that ethnolinguistic identity influences competence in the outgroup language in intergroup situations. Giles and Johnson (1987), for example, found that three of the five components of ethnolinguistic identity (ingroup identification, interethnic comparisons, and ingroup boundaries) were related to outgroup language competence in bilingual Welsh adolescents (perceived ingroup vitality and multiple group memberships did not have an effect), thereby supporting Giles and Byrne's (1982) intergroup theory of second language ability. Similar results were obtained in Hall and Gudykunst's (1986) study of the English ability of international students in the United States.

The preceding research on social identity and ethnolinguistic vitality/identity was conducted with one cultural group each time. Gudykunst (1987), however, studied the ethnolinguistic identity of international students in the United States. The results of this study revealed that members of collectivistic cultures identify with groups other than the ingroup more than do members of individualistic cultures; members of high uncertainty avoidance cultures make less secure intergroup comparisons than do members of low uncertainty avoidance cultures; members of feminine cultures identify less with the ingroup than do members of masculine cultures; and members of feminine cultures perceive softer boundaries between groups than do members of masculine cultures. He also found that perceived ethnolinguistic vitality is highest in individualistic cultures that are high in uncertainty avoidance and are also masculine. Eight hypotheses emerge from the research on social identity theory and ethnolinguistic vitality/identity:

> *HD2:* Members of high uncertainty avoidance cultures make less secure intergroup comparisons than members of low uncertainty avoidance cultures.

HD3: Members of feminine cultures perceive softer boundaries between groups than do members of masculine cultures.

HD4: Members of collectivistic cultures identity more with groups other than their ingroup than members of individualistic cultures.

HD5: Perceived ethnolinguistic vitality is higher in individualistic cultures that are high in uncertainty avoidance and masculine than in collectivistic cultures that are low in uncertainty avoidance and feminine.

HU3: Ingroup self-judgments are more favorable than judgments about outgroups across cultures.

HU4: The more group identities based on several categories coincide, the greater the perceived similarity of ingroup members across cultures.

HU5: The greater the perceived ethnolinguistic vitality, the more the intergroup differentiation across cultures.

HU6: The stronger the ethnolinguistic identity, the less the outgroup language competence across cultures.

CONSEQUENCES OF THE
INGROUP-OUTGROUP DISTINCTION

Ingroup Bias

Social categorization of individuals into distinct social groups results in the assignment of positive traits and rewards to the ingroup (Doise & Sinclair, 1973), as well as differential attitudes toward the groups involved (Doise et al., 1972). Ingroup bias occurs when negative interpersonal attraction is associated with category membership (Turner, Shaver, & Hogg, 1983) and occurs even when category membership is arbitrary and a member of the outgroup is a close personal friend (Vaughan, Tajfel, & Williams, 1981). In-group bias is reduced when membership in social groups is "crossed," that is, situations in which others are members of an outgroup on one criterion and members of ingroup on another criterion (Deschamps & Doise, 1978).

Wetherell (1982) found that both Europeans (individualistic) and Polynesians (collectivistic) in New Zealand display bias in the minimal group situation, but Polynesians moderate their discrimination and show greater generosity to outgroup members (i.e., maximize joint profit) compared to Europeans. One interpretation of this study is that members of collectivistic cultures moderate their discrimination toward outgroups more than members of individualistic cultures. Triandis (1987) disagrees with this conclusion. He suggests, in contrast, that there is no difference between individualistic and collectivistic cultures in the way they deal with outgroups. Rather, the strength of the distinction between ingroup and outgroup is different. The distinction between family and neighbors, for example, in collectivistic cultures is large, but it is small in individualistic cultures. He, therefore, suggests an alternative hypothesis, that "there is more trust toward neighbors in individualistic than in collectivistic cultures" (p. 2).

The Wetherell (1982) findings, however, are compatible with Bond and Hewstone's (1986) research, which revealed that British high school students in Hong Kong endorse more intergroup differentiation than do Chinese students. Wetherell's results likewise appear to be consistent with Triandis, Vassiliou, and Nassiakou's (1968) study of role perception in ingroups and outgroups in Greece and the United States, as well as Feldman's (1968) field study in Paris, Boston, and Athens. Feldman found that outgroup members were "treated better" in Athens (the most collectivistic) than in Boston and Paris (both individualistic). Feldman's results, however, may be unique to Greece, where foreigners and guests fare perceived as potential members of the ingroup. Strangers in other collectivistic cultures generally are not viewed as potential members of the ingroup (Triandis, 1986). Bond, Hewstone, Wan, and Chiu's (1985) study further suggests that group serving attributions are maintained in the presence of an audience in individualistic cultures, but not in collectivistic cultures. They argue that this is due to collectivistic socialization for maintaining harmony by surprising open conflict compared to individualistic socialization for developing harmony by resolving conflict openly in public.

Several studies reveal that Chinese, Japanese, and Colombians (all collectivistic) use the equity norm with members of outgroups more than people in the United States (Leung & Bond, 1984; Mahler, Greenberg, & Hayashi, 1981; Marin, 1981). Congruous findings emerge when decision rules for ingroup and outgroup members are compared in Japan and Australia (Mann, Radford, & Kanagawa, 1985), as well as when the use of the equality norm in ingroups is examined in Hong Kong and the United States (Bond, Leung, & Wan, 1982; Leung & Bond, 1982); that is, Chinese use the equality norm more with members of the ingroup than do people in the United States. The results of these studies appear to be consistent with Triandis's (1986) conceptualization o ingroup-outgroup behavior in individualistic and collectivistic cultures. Sinha (cited in Triandis et al., 1986), however, argues that allocentrics in individualistic cultures yield to the ingroup more than idiocentrics in collectivist cultures.

Research further suggests that some ingroup-outgroup behavior is a function of combinations of dimensions of cultural variability. Bond,

Wan, Leung, and Giacalone (1985), for example, found that Chinese are less critical of insulters from an outgroup if they are higher in status than are people in the United States. No specific effect emerged for status or group membership in the United States. They argue this pattern emerges because Hong Kong Chinese are collectivistic *and* high in power distance, while people in the United States are individualistic *and* moderate in power distance.

Cross-cultural differences that emerge with respect to the ingroup bias may be moderated when members of one culture are sojourning in another culture. To illustrate, Bond (1986) found that both exchange students from the United States and Hong Kong Chinese students perceived members of the other group to be more beneficient than members of their ingroup. Seven hypotheses emerge from the preceding research on the ingroup-outgroup distinction:

> *HD6:* Discrimination against the outgroup is greater in individualistic icultures than in collectivistic cultures.
>
> *HD7:* There is more trust toward neighbors in individualistic than in collectivistic cultures.
>
> *HD8:* Group-serving biases are maintained in the presence of an audience more strongly in individualistic cultures than in collectivistic cultures.
>
> *HD9:* The equity norm is used more with members of outgroups in collectivistic cultures than in individualistic cultures.
>
> *HD10:* The equality norm is used more with members of the ingroup in collectivistic cultures than in individualistic cultures.
>
> *HD11:* Allocentrics in individualistic cultures yield to ingroup norms more than idiocentrics in collectivistic cultures.
>
> *H12:* Criticism of the ingroup by a higher-status member of an outgroup is tolerated more in collectivistic cultures high on power distance than in collectivistic cultures low on power distance or in individualistic cultures.

Ingroup/Outgroup Relationships

The specific relationships between members of an ingroup and an outgroup depends, at least in part, on the ingroup's attitude toward outgroups and the outgroups' perceived intention toward the ingroup. Gudykunst (1985) and Levine (1985) utilize these two dimensions to develop typologies of stranger-ingroup relationships (nine and six types, respectively). Gudykunst specifies how the normative power and conflict potential of ingroup-outgroup relationships varies depending upon the two dimensions (e.g., when the ingroup has a positive attitude toward the outgroup and the outgroup seeks to assimilate with the ingroup, normative power is moderate and conflict potential is high). Levine argues that there is cultural variability in the way ingroups deal with strangers. Wood (1934) suggests that the differences are related to the degree of homogeneity and heterogeneity and the composition of the group in terms of percentage of "natives" and "foreigners." While neither Wood nor Levine use the term, their discussions focus on individualism and appear to be consistent with the research cited above. A plausible hypothesis, therefore, can be proffered:

> HD13: Strangers establish relationships with members of the ingroup more easily in individualistic than in collectivistic cultures.

There also are cross-cultural studies that have examined communication in ingroup and outgroup relationships. Noesjirwan (1978), for example, found that the rule-guided behavior with respect to the ingroup in Indonesia (collectivistic) is that members of the group should adapt to the group so that the group can present a united front. In Australia (individualistic), on the other hand, members are expected to do their own thing, even if they must go against the group. Similarly, Argyle, Henderson, Bond, Iizuke, and Contarello (1986) found that rules regarding ingroups, such as maintaining harmonious relations, are endorsed highly in collectivistic cultures (Japan and Hong Kong), but not in individualistic cultures (Britain and Italy). These findings are consistent with Levine's (1985) discussions of the functions of direct and indirect forms of communication. Direct communication, which predominates in individualistic cultures, allows for open conflict. Indirect communication, which is used extensively in collectivistic cultures, in contrast, does not allow for open conflict, but allows individuals to allude to shared experiences and, at the same time, conceal what is on their mind.

Related research indicates that ingroup relationships are perceived as more intimate in collectivistic cultures than in individualistic cultures (Gudykunst & Nishida, 1986). Gudykunst, Yoon, and Nishida (1987) also found that members of collectivistic cultures (Japan and Korea) perceive greater social penetration (personalization, a focus on the individuals in the relationship, and synchronization, the degree of coordination in the relationship) in their ingroup relationships than do members of individualistic cultures (United States). Their data further revealed greater perceived personalization in outgroup relationships in collectivistic cultures than in individualistic cultures. This finding is consistent with research indicating there is less discrimination toward outgroups in collectivistic than in individualistic cultures (Wetherell, 1982). Three hypotheses appear warranted given this research:

> *HD14:* Communication in ingroup relationships is more harmonious in collectivistic cultures than in individualistic cultures.
>
> *HD15:* Communication in ingroup relationships involves greater social penetration (e.g., personalization and synchronization) in collectivistic cultures than in individualistic cultures.
>
> *HD16:* Communication with members of outgroups is more personalized in collectivistic cultures than in individualistic cultures.

Research suggests that when members of one culture travel to another culture (i.e., are members of an outgroup in the foreign culture), they experience difficulties in adjusting to the host culture. One of the major factors that explains the degree of difficulty is the similarity of the host culture and the sojourner's native culture. Babiker, Cox, and Miller (1980), for example, found a positive correlation between cultural dissimilarity and the anxiety sojourners experience. Stephan and Stephan (1985) discovered a similar relationship for intergroup contact in the United States. Similarly, Furnham and Bochner (1982) observed a positive relationship between cultural dissimilarity and the social difficulties sojourners have in a foreign culture. Cultural dissimilarity also interacts with the type of relationship to influence the communication sojourners have with host nationals. To illustrate, Gudykunst, Chua, and Gray (1986) found that cultural dissimilarities influence the degree of uncertainty present in nonintimate relationships (e.g., relative strangers) significantly more than in relationships (e.g., friends). Two plausible hypotheses about cultural universals, therefore, emerge:

> *HU7:* The greater the dissimilarities between the ingroup and the outgroup, the greater the anxiety associated with, and difficulty of, intergroup interaction across cultures.
>
> *HU8:* Dissimilarities between the ingroup and the outgroup increase uncertainty less as the intimacy of an intergroup encounter increases across cultures.

Attributions

Cultural variations influence the attributes on which individuals focus in making attributions. Bond (1979; Bond & Forgas, 1984), for example, found differences due to collectivism (Hong Kong) and individualism (Australia) in the salience of extroversion, goodnaturedness, and conscientiousness. Similarly, Miller (1984) found that people in India (collectivistic) make greater reference to contextual factors and less reference to dispositional factors than people in the United States (individualistic) when explaining others' behaviors. In related research, Forgas and Bond (1985) examined perceptions of episodes in Hong Kong and Australia. They found that Chinese in Hong Kong differentiate among episodes based on equal/unequal (power distance) and communal/individual (individualism) dimensions. Australians also used equal/unequal to differentiate among episodes, but interpretations placed on the dimension were different than those of the Chinese and consistent with the difference between the two cultures' scores on power distance.

Detweiler's (1975, 1978) research suggests that cultural variation (Truk Islands vs. United States) influences individuals' category width, which in turn affects their intergroup attributions. Category width refers to the tendency to classify somewhat discrepant objects in the same or different categories: Categorizing discrepant objects in the same category reflects a wide category width and placing these objects in different categories reflects a narrow category width. Detweiler (1978) found that people from the Truk Islands (collectivistic) use significantly narrower categories than do people in the United States (individualistic). His earlier work (1975) revealed that narrow categorizers make stronger and more confident attributions about members of outgroups who cause a negative outcome than do wide categorizers. The research on attributes and category width thus suggests the following hypotheses:

> *HD17:* Group membership is a more salient aspect of perceptions of social episodes involving intergroup behavior in collectivistic cultures than in individualistic cultures.
>
> *HD18:* When group membership is salient, stronger and more confident attributions about members of an outgroup who cause a negative outcome are made in collectivistic cultures than in individualistic cultures.

INTERGROUP CONTACT

The Contact Hypothesis

The majority of research in outcomes of intergroup behavior has focused on the "contact hypothesis." Based on the work of Williams (1947) and Allport (1954), this hypothesis suggests that it is not the amount of contact that increases favorable attitudes (e.g., decreases prejudice) between members of different groups, rather, it is the "nature of the contact" that occurs. For intergroup contact to reduce prejudice, Cook (1978) argues that it is necessary for five conditions to exist: (1) Individuals should have equal status, (2) negative outgroup stereotypes should be disconfirmed, (3) cooperation should exist (e.g., participants work on a joint goal), (4) the situation should have high "acquaintance potential," and (5) there should be a supportive social climate. The majority of models developed to explain how different types of intergroup contact influence intergroup attitudes are based on an interpersonal, not an intergroup, perspective. Miller and Brewer (1986), for example, focus almost exclusively on similarity at the interpersonal level in their models of intergroup contact, even though they begin from Tajfel's (1978) social identity theory. Hewstone and Brown (1986) also build on social identity theory, but in addition emphasize Tajfel's distinction between interpersonal and intergroup behavior. They argue that interpersonal interactions between members of different groups will produce only changes in stereotypes when categorization occurs (e.g., the other individual is viewed as a representative of the outgroup).

Pettigrew (1986, p. 179) argues that all of the major criticisms of social psychological theory in general apply to work on the contact hypothesis:

(1) they are more often loose frameworks than testable theories
(2) they have centered on cold cognition to the relative exclusion of affective considerations
(3) they stress similarities (mechanical solidarity) to the virtual exclusion of differences (organic solidarity) as social bonds
(4) they focus largely on isolated, noncumulative effects
(5) they too glibly assume universality across time, situations, and cultures
(6) they are narrower- to middle-range in scope with bold generic theory that links various levels of analysis conspicuous by its absence

In order to overcome these problems, the contact hypothesis must be incorporated into a broader theoretical perspective such as Tajfel's (1978) social identity theory, and the interpersonal and intergroup levels of analysis must be "articulated," to use Doise's (1986) term. Hewstone and Brown's (1986) model is a good beginning, but, as Pettigrew points out, they focus on cognitive factors to the relative neglect of affective factors. While Hewstone and Brown draw on social identity theory in developing their model, they do not include social identity per se. Its omission appears critical because "it is from contact with other groups that groups find the need to reaffirm or redefine themselves" (Salamone & Swanson, 1979, p. 169). The inclusion of social identity also adds an affective component to the model (Pettigrew, 1986).

Intergroup Contact and Affect

Affective reactions are one of the major by-products of intergroup contact (Pettigrew, 1986). Bobad and Wallbott's (1986) cross-cultural research in eight cultures, for example, reveals that there is greater fear associated with interactions with people who are unfamiliar (e.g., members of outgroups) than with people who are familiar (e.g., members of ingroups). Their research also demonstrates that there is less verbalization of, and less control over, expressing anger with people who are unfamiliar than with people who are familiar. There were cultural differences across the emotions experienced with strangers and depending on whether emotions are experienced with familiar or unfamiliar people (see Appendix D, Scherer, Wallbott, & Summerfield, 1986), but the researchers did not examine culture × familiarity interaction effects so cultural hypotheses cannot be generated from the data. A comparison of the eight cultures across Hofstede's (1980) dimensions of cultural variability, however, allows for a potential theoretical explanation to be derived. The eight cultures are all moderate to high in individualism, moderate in masculinity, and low to moderate in power distance, while five of the eight are high in uncertainty avoidance and the remaining three are low to moderate. Given that uncertainty avoidance is the dimension Hofstede relates to the expression of the emotion, the following hypothesis is plausible:

> *HD19:* Members of high uncertainty avoidance cultures express emotions more in intergroup encounters than members of low uncertainty avoidance cultures.

Intergroup Conflict

Contact also appears to influence specific aspects of social identity theory. Jaspars and Warnaen (1982), for example, found greater intergroup differentiation (e.g., more negative attitudes) in Jakarta, where the groups have a large amount of contact, than in provincial samples in Indonesia, where the groups have relatively low contact. Compatible findings emerge from Hamilton, Carpenter, and Bishop's (1984) study of residential desegregation in the United States. They discovered that white residents who have black neighbors, but have little contact with them, have positive changes in their social attitudes. Given that one study was conducted in a collectivistic culture and one in an individualistic, it appears reasonable to assume that contact is not a necessary condition for positive attitude change or a decrease in intergroup differentiation across cultures.

Research (e.g., Trew's, 1986, work in Northern Ireland, and Taylor, Dube, & Bellerose's, 1986, study in Quebec) indicates that harmonious interpersonal contact can take place between members of different groups, even in the presence of a long history of intergroup tension in the society. This does not always occur, however, as Foster and Finchilescu's (1986) research in South Africa demonstrates. As Pettigrew (1986, p. 191, italics omitted) points out, these studies document that "the use of intergroup contact as a means of alleviating conflict is largely dependent on the social structure that patterns relations between the groups." Are there, however, specific dimensions of cultural variability that are related to the aspects of the social structure that influence intergroup relations? There is no research to date directly bearing on this question. The three cultures cited are relatively individualistic and are similar (e.g., have moderate Hofstede, 1980, scores) on power distance, uncertainty avoidance, and masculinity. One plausible dimension of variability that might influence this process is the degree of structural tightness, the "degree of hierarchical structure among sociocultural elements in a society" (Witkin & Berry, 1975, p. 11). Boldt and Roberts (1979) argue that "role relatedness" (e.g., the degree to which roles are interrelated) defines a culture as "tight" or "loose." Ireland and Canada appear to have a high degree of role relatedness with respect to the roles members of different ethnic groups fill, while South Africa appears to have little black-white role relatedness. A tentative hypothesis, therefore, can be posited:

> *HD20:* Contact has a greater impact on reducing intergroup conflict in tight
> cultures than in loose cultures.

CONCLUSION

Hypotheses regarding the influence of culture on intergroup processes and hypotheses of cultural universals have been posited. Some hypotheses were based on data from several studies, others were generated logically. All hypotheses proffered, however, should be considered tentative and subject to further research. Taken together, the hypotheses emphasize the necessity of taking cultural variability into consideration when examining intergroup processes. Research conducted in highly individualistic cultures like the United States and England suggests that group memberships are less important than they are in influencing behavior, and that when group membership is salient, the outgroup is discriminated against. Studies in collectivistic cultures, however, demonstrate that group memberships play a large role in affecting behavior and that outgroups are not necessarily discriminated against simply because they are outgroups.

The research cited in this chapter clearly indicates that the vast majority of research on intergroup behavior across cultures has been conducted in the last decade. The citations also suggest that relatively few researchers have contributed to the study of culture and intergroup behavior. Taken together, these two trends yield a body of research with less breadth than many other areas of cross-cultural research. Given the importance of the ingroup-outgroup distinction for intergroup behavior and the fact that culture influences how this distinction is made, future research cannot afford to ignore culture as a theoretical variable in explaining intergroup behavior.

Future work on culture and intergroup behavior could profit from pursuing several directions for future research. First, the hypotheses posited in this chapter should be tested empirically. Second, a theory of intergroup behavior (e.g., Hewstone & Brown's, 1986, model of intergroup contact; Giles & Johnson's, 1987, ethnolinguistic identity theory; Tajfel's, 1978, social identity theory) can be tested systematically across cultures. Third, a theory of cultural variability (e.g., Triandis's, 1986, work on individualism) can be extended systematically to account for differences in intergroup behavior across cultures. These approaches are not mutually exclusive and research from the three approaches inevitably must be integrated. Further, Triandis and his associates' (1985) work on idiocentrism-allocentrism indicates that this personality dimension varies within cultures and future work also will have to consider variability along this cultural/personality factor to explain intergroup behavior fully. The hypotheses proffered also suggest that both cognitive and affective factors must be incorporated in any explanation of intergroup behavior. More importantly, the hypotheses clearly indicate that the various levels of analysis (e.g., cultural, intergroup, interpersonal) must be articulated if processes occurring at any of the levels are to be explained adequately.

14

CULTURAL INFLUENCES ON GROUP PROCESSES

LEON MANN

In this chapter I argue that a cross-cultural perspective is essential for the proper study of human groups. To the extent that social psychology has neglected the cross-cultural analysis of group behavior, it has fallen short of its promise as a field of enquiry.

The key areas of interest to scholars of group behavior include the following:

(1) the reasons why groups are formed—the conditions under which they are brought into existence (Zander, 1985)
(2) the most important groups governing people's lives—discovery of the ingroups that reliably command loyalty and allegiance of their members—such as the family, the classroom, friends, the work organization
(3) the power of the group to influence its members. Included here are questions relating to the group's power to enforce norms and punish dissidents, the measures members take to defend their group's reputation and interests, and how members react when they believe they have failed their group, or the group has disappointed them
(4) the extent to which groups can be created artificially and the extent to which they can be split and dismantled. This relates to the experimental manufacture of ad hoc groups in the laboratory and the extent to which "groupness" can be assumed for such aggregates. It also relates to the resistance of natural groups to attempts at imposing divisions between members, for example, the minimal group phenomenon (see Tajfel, 1970).
(5) the dynamics by which change occurs in groups. This issue addresses the roles played by majorities and minorities in producing change, and the tactics used by these entities to protect their perceived rights and resources within the group.

These matters are close to the very core of social psychology. I submit that the cross-cultural perspective has demonstrated its worth in addressing some of these questions, but is also essential for obtaining complete answers to these questions. Some of these questions have indeed guided scholarship in social psychology—for example, the group's power to influence its members has been a central concern of social psychologists beginning with the classic work of Sherif (1935) and Asch (1952). However, answers provided on the basis of Western, laboratory-dominated research are of necessity limited because they assume a universality of group behavior that may be quite unwarranted. Moreover, a single-culture focus that ignores the diversity of meanings and functions of group life may have prevented social psychologists from recognizing some of the exciting possibilities for studying and understanding groups.

In this chapter I will briefly review some major aspects of group behavior and point to cross-cultural analysis as a significant contributor to their understanding. Group processes to be discussed include conformity, minority influence, majority and minority claims to rights and resources, the minimal group phenomenon, and the risky shift phenomenon.

THE PREVALENCE OF GROUPS

The universality of small, primary groups—such as family, play, interest, and association groups—is noted by Mann (1980). The anthropologist Coon (1946) stated that natural groups are characteristic of human beings everywhere, but noted that groups are more prevalent in large, complex modern societies than in traditional societies. Zander (1985) also refers to the prevalence of groups in different cultures and postulates, "In the United States, groups are not as widespread as in Japan, but they are probably more frequent than in England, Norway, Italy, Libya or Iran" (p. 49). Now, differences in prevalence of groups across cultures is an interesting problem for social psychology because questions arise as to why groups occur more naturally or are formed more frequently in some places than in others, or at some times more than at others. If, as Zander claims, groups are formed more frequently in the United States than in England or Norway (and to my knowledge no evidence is available to support that claim), much can be learned from cultural comparisons about the conditions that create the formation and maintenance of groups. Such comparisons would provide a richer data base for examining the reasons why existing groups fail to meet needs, the significance placed on group membership, the power of groups to maintain loyalty, and the conditions, such as stress, conflict, and alienation, that promote the quest for membership in groups promising instant acceptance and gratification. Are these groups formed because of rapid social change, the breakdown of primary groups such as the family, or the failure of existing groups to maintain control over their members? Social psychologists interested in these questions would do well to turn to cross-cultural comparisons for useful clues. Unfortunately, as social psychologists tend to rely on the study of temporary, ad hoc groups created in the laboratory, the diversity of factors underlying the formation of groups in natural settings tends to be ignored.

An interesting possibility for studying the effect of culture on small group formation can be found in the work of Weyrauch (1971). In Weyrauch's research, a small group of volunteers is brought together to live for 3 months in an isolated penthouse as part of a study on food and diets. The point of the study, however, is to trace the evolution of group rules. The group soon formulates a kind of "basic law" or constitution to regulate social interaction and rights to privacy, and to provide sanctions for breach of rules. Use of this research procedure in different countries could provide insights into the effect of culture on the process of group formation and maintenance.

CULTURE AND CONFORMITY

Research on conformity to group pressure has benefited greatly from the cross-cultural perspective. Groups must require their members to adhere to norms if they are to survive and achieve their goals. The dark side of conformity is embodied in Asch's (1952, 1956) famous studies that examined the powerful pressures groups exert on their members to yield to false standards. Asch found in the early 1950s that 32% of American male students yielded to the majority against their own judgment on at least half of the pressure trials. Studies of conformity provide an impressive illustration of the importance of the cross-cultural method for the understanding of this striking phenomenon.

At issue are such questions as:

— Was the high level of conformity found by Asch a peculiarly American phenomenon confined to the repressive, McCarthyist era of the 1950s?
— Is the high level of conformity a "rock bottom" phenomenon, reflecting the power of group forces, irrespective of time and culture (see Moscovici, 1985)?
— To what extend do cultural factors affect level of conformity and influence the social conditions under which groups exact conformity (Mann, 1980)?

It has been argued that the Asch experimental paradigm is built upon a dubious analogue of the group, involving the manufacture of a fake "peer group" that conspires to pressure a stranger into judging something incorrectly without providing an opportunity for discussion and counterinfluence. It is of cultural significance that at least in Western settings an ad hoc, artificially formed group of strangers can have this effect.

Replications of the Asch experiment in 10 countries, including the United States, the United Kingdom, Belgium, Brazil, Lebanon, Hong Kong, Fiji, Rhodesia (Zimbabwe), Germany, and Japan reveal that:

— The disconcerting level of conformity found by Asch is not peculiar to the United States but is obtained in countries such as Belgium 30 years after Asch's original studies (Doms & Van Avermaet, 1981).
— The incidence of conformity is particularly high in cultures with stringent sanctions for nonconformity, for example, the Bantu from Rhodesia (Zimbabwe) (Whittaker & Meade, 1967).
— The conformity effect is not always found. For example, it was virtually absent in British students (Perrin & Spencer, 1980).
— Ingroup-oriented cultures such as Japan, the Asch procedure elicits a high level of conformity when the confederates are friends (Williams & Sogon, 1984), but strong anticonformity responses when the confederates are strangers (Frager, 1970).

We now review some of the research.

Whittaker and Meade (1967) studied conformity in four cultures— Brazil, Lebanon, Hong Kong, and Rhodesia (Bantu). In three of the four countries, the frequency of yielding was remarkably similar to that found by Asch more than a decade earlier in the United States (33%), namely, Brazil (34%); Lebanon (31%); and Hong Kong (32%). Only in Bantu subjects from Rhodesia, a tribe with extremely stringent sanctions for nonconformity, was yielding significantly greater (51%). Chandra (1973) found a conformity rate of 36% for Fijian students. However, replications conducted in Germany (Timaeus, 1968) and in Japan (Frager, 1970) obtained significantly less conformity than found among Asch's American students in the early 1950s. Timaeus's (1968) sample of University of Cologne students produced a relatively low conformity response (22%). Frager's (1970) study of Japanese conformity is surprising for two reasons. An analysis of the anthropological literature led him to expect that social pressures would be strong in Japan and therefore conformity responses prevalent. However, the frequency of conformity responses (25%) was relatively low. Further, a strong anticonformity response was shown by 34% of the subjects; this is the tendency for the subject on neutral trials to call the wrong answer deliberately when the majority give the correct answer—a phenomenon rarely observed in conformity research. This unexpected finding raises some important questions regarding the differing forms that conformity and anticonformity responses might take in various societies, for instance, whether such strong anticonformity is unique to Japanese populations and whether other (or similar) patterns have occurred but were not noticed or reported in other research.

An important consideration is the significance to a Japanese subject of an ad hoc group of strangers gathered together in the laboratory. Nakane (1970) and others have commented on the strong loyalty Japanese have to one group and to that group alone. It would be incorrect therefore to conclude on the basis of Frager's findings that the Japanese are, in general, nonconformist. This striking rejection of pressure mounted by the group of strangers leads us to conclude that in Japan conformity can be elicited only by the natural group to which the individual already owes strong allegiance. Indeed, Williams and Sogon (1984) found that when friends—other members of sports clubs—were used as accomplices, the level of conformity was very high (51%) for Japanese students.

Failure to find or replicate the Asch effect in the United States and Britain (Larsen, 1974; Nicholson et al., 1985; Perrin & Spencer, 1981) has revived earlier debates over the question of whether mindless conformity of the Asch type is a product of particular cultures at particular times or is a universal, timeless, "rock bottom" phenomenon (Doms & Van Avermaet, 1981). The outcome of the debate is important for social psychology. If the Asch effect (which has the status of a classic in social psychology textbooks) were limited in time and place, social psychology would face the prospect of remaking itself periodically and questioning the assumption of universality in laws of social behavior.

Eco-cultural model of conformity. An impressive example of the usefulness of the cross-cultural perspective for understanding social processes is found in John Berry's (1967, 1974) research into conformity in subsistence societies. Berry's work demonstrates how social psychological theory can be tested by the cross-cultural method, selecting different cultures to represent different levels of the independent variable. Berry took as his point of departure Murdock's categorization of subsistence societies into low and high food accumulators (hunters and fishers *versus* farmers and shepherds). He predicted that high food accumulators would exhibit greater conformity because, consistent with their interdependent economic systems, such societies adopt socialization practices that enforce compliance. In an Asch-type situation a high incidence of conformity would therefore be expected.

Berry (1967) thus looked for the antecedents of conformity behavior in two interrelated variables—the nature of the economy and the severity of socialization practices to elicit compliance. His study of conformity among the high food-accumulating Temne of Sierra Leone, the low food-accumulating Eskimos of Baffin Island (a society in which hunting is carried out independently in small family groups), and the intermediate Scots demonstrate show a culture-related hypothesis can be tested. Berry's procedure involves a "false-norm" pressure situation. Each subject takes a test in which a reference line is followed by eight lines of varying length. The subject is asked to say which of the comparison lines is the same length as the reference line. The experimenter offers to "help" the subject by suggesting that most people say it is the sixth line (or whatever). The maximum conformity score obtainable is 15. In support of the hypothesis, the high food-accumulating Temne had a mean score of 9.04, the Scots 4, and the low food-accumulating Eskimos a score of 2.5.

Berry (1974) extended research on the effect of eco-cultural settings on conformity by studying high and low food-accumulating cultural samples in Sierra Leone, Australia, New Guinea, and Canada. The hypothesis that high food-accumulating cultures would be associated with high conformity scores on the normative pressure task was again supported (see also Munroe, Munroe, & Daniels, 1973). However, a third study (Berry & Annis, 1974), which measured conformity in high and low food-accumulating cultures among the Northwestern American Indians, failed to support the hypothesis, possibly because of the narrow range of cultures investigated, or perhaps because the normative pressure task was unsuitable for the sample.

In sum, the eco-cultural model offers a theory of group behavior from which, given information about the ecology and food-gathering habits of a community, it is possible to predict how its members will respond to conformity pressures. The model could be extended by distinguishing between collectivist and individualist societies (see Hofstede, 1980) and by distinguishing between societies in which the peer group is an active socialization agent and those that are almost exclusively adult-dominated. The point of this discussion, however, is to argue that knowledge about basic group processes, such as conformity, has been advanced by creative use of the cross-cultural method.

MINORITY INFLUENCE

The reverse side of conformity in groups is the study of how minorities sometimes manage to persuade the majority to adopt their viewpoint or judgment. Numerous studies have supported the assumption that persistence by a minority has an effect on the majority, whereas inconsistency fails to change the majority's perceptions and attitudes (Maass & Clark, 1984; Moscovici, 1985).

The field of minority influence, no less than the field of conformity, stands to benefit from a cross-cultural approach. Indeed, it is surprising that little cross-cultural research on minority influence has occurred, given the intellectual tradition of the European social psychologists who have been leaders in the study of minority influence; it is they who have traditionally drawn upon the societal/historical context in their analysis of group phenomena.

It is reasonable to assume that factors such as cultural change and the status of ethnic and racial groups in society are relevant to the conditions governing minority influence. Paicheler (1976, 1977), for example, found that changes in cultural attitudes relating to the issue on which the majority and minority disagree is important in determining whether a minority is able to persuade feminist issues. The minority took a position that was either in line with the *Zeitgeist* (profeminist) or opposed to the *Zeitgeist* (antifeminist) in French society. The minority was highly influential when it persisted in arguing for the profeminist position, but produced total breakdown of negotiation or a hardening of opposition when it persisted with the antifeminist position. These laboratory findings have implications for understanding why minority groups in certain countries at different times in history are more or less successful in producing change.

For example, blacks had considerable influence in the United States in the 1960s and 1970s, when the *Zeitgeist* moved toward interracial tolerance, while the racist Ku Klux Klan and the conservative John Birch Society had little influence at that time. Thus minority influence is at least partially determined by contemporary cultural norms and values relating to the issue. It is important to test the strength of the *Zeitgeist* factor by conducting studies in countries with different ideologies to determine the relationship between cultural *Zeitgeist* and effectiveness of minority influence on a particular issue.

The ethnic or racial identity of the minority attempting to influence the majority may also have a bearing on its success or failure. For example, if the minority viewpoint in a group discussion is espoused by "natural" minorities, such as blacks (in the United States), Tamils (in Sri Lanka), or Maoris (in New Zealand), will this weaken minority influence? Maass and Clark (1982) refer to such minorities as "double minorities" in that they differ from the majority in both ethnic membership and beliefs. Research evidence suggests that double minorities exert less influence than single minorities. However, no cross-cultural research has been conducted on this problem, which touches on the important question of the ability of actual minorities in multicultural societies to exert influence, even when their views are firmly and consistently stated. The rationale for such cross-cultural research (as distinct from multiethnic research) is the opportunity to extend the range and variety of minorities studied, so as to broaden the data base and provide a more robust test of the experimental hypothesis.

In sum, the phenomenon of minority influence has been well established in research in a wide variety of experimental conditions in different countries of the Western world, including France, Belgium, Switzerland, and the United States (Maass & Clark, 1984). Systematic cross-cultural research is, however, essential to establish whether minority influence occurs widely, for example, in cultures with a strong emphasis on public display of group uniformity, such as Japan.

Another issue is the relationship between minority influence and conformity—whether they operate through the same processes (Tanford & Penrod, 1984) or different processes (Moscovici, 1985). Here again, studies examining the relative strengths of conformity effects and minority influence in a sample of cultures varying in collectivist-individualist values would help determine whether the two phenomena are naturally related or quite separate.

MAJORITY AND MINORITY RIGHTS

The question of how majorities and minorities resolve competing claims for rights and resources is another aspect of group behavior to benefit from the cross-cultural perspective. The study of social justice principles—how individuals allocate resources among themselves—is an important area of social psychology (see Leung, this volume). The cross-cultural study of how subgroups and factions within groups distribute power and resources when there is a conflict of interest has contributed to an understanding of the significance of ingroups in people's lives, the ease or difficulty with which intact groups can be split into competing factions, the influence of cultural values (such as collectivism-individualism) on the rules used for accommodating majority and minority interests, and the strategies used by minorities to protect their vulnerable position. An example of cross-cultural work in this area is my own research on the decision rules favored by school children for handling competing claims of majorities and minorities in school classrooms (Mann, 1986; Mann, Radford, & Kanagawa, 1985).

Hofstede's (1980) construct of collectivism-individualism is a useful dimension for comparing cultural values relating to decision rules. Collectivist cultures are concerned with maintenance of the entire social group over individual or sectional interests, whereas individualist cultures emphasize personal interests over group or collective interests. It is predicted that in cultures in which collectivism is a dominant value, the decision rules favored will be those that accommodate majority and minority interests—such as "equal say" or turn-taking—whereas in cultures in which individualism is a dominant value the decision rules favored will be those that safeguard the power of the majority—such as majority rule.

Research testing this cross-cultural hypothesis has been conducted in five countries located at different points on Hofstede's (1980) collectivist-individualist dimension—Australia and New Zealand (high on individualism), Israel (near the midpoint), and Japan and Hong Kong (relatively high on collectivism). Mann, Radford, and Kanagawa (1985) compared the decision rules used by 12-year-old children in Japan and Australia in resolving a conflict of interest between a classroom majority and minority. The procedure involved the formation of two unequal size groups within a school classroom and a request to the children to determine which group—large or small—should have the right to act as decision maker on each of six trials. Whichever group was given decision control would be responsible for determining how rewards would be distributed between groups. It was found that Japanese and Australian children favored quite different decision rules. Japanese children in both the large and small groups strongly endorsed the "equal-say" (3:3) rule (73% and 86%, respectively). Australian children, in contrast, were split in their preferred decision rules: In the large group, 37% favored the "equal say" rule and 37% favored the "majority" (6:0) rule. In the small group, 49% favored the "equal say" rule and 34% favored a "minority" (0:6) rule that prescribed total say to themselves!

Thus Japanese children resist the experimenter's attempt to create two opposing interest groups and maintain a single decision rule ("equal say") irrespective of group membership. Australian children, however, accept quite readily the arbitrary division of the classroom into two competing groups and favor a decision rule that recognizes the split.

INGROUP FAVORITISM
AND DECISION RULES

The Flinders studies on children's decision rules and research in Britain on the "minimal" group phenomenon (Tajfel, 1981) show that children in Western cultures readily accept division of their school class into subgroups and grasp the opportunity to give favored treatment to their new subgroup. Henri Tajfel found that arbitrary division of children in a classroom into two equal-size groups on the basis of tossing a coin or on the basis of a common preference for the same painter was sufficient to create a strong bias or favoritism in treatment of the manufactured "ingroup," as evident in greater allocation of rewards to ingroup members than to "outgroup" members. Margaret Wetherell (1982) found that New Zealand children also show this remarkable tendency to take on the identity and interests of a "manufactured" ingroup. She tested white Pakeha children (individualist culture), Polynesian children, and Samoan children (collectivist cultures) on the "minimal" group procedure and found that while all three culture samples showed "ingroup" favoritism, white Pakeha children showed more such favoritism than Polynesian and Samoan children (see also Gudykunst, Chap. 13, this volume). What is remarkable in Western research is the readiness with which children discard existing group loyalties and embrace a newly created subgroup the interests of which coincide temporarily with their own.

MINORITY CLAIMS

We have also found that children in small (minority) groups sometimes take a strong, uncompromising position when claiming their share of decision control and resources (Kirkby, 1986; Mann et al., 1985). Indeed, some minority subjects (34% of Australian subjects, 7% of Japanese subjects) advocate complete decision control for themselves and total exclusion of the majority group. In some cases, minority subjects appear to be acting out of wholly selfish interests. In other cases, minority subjects claim total decision control, as they do not trust the numerically superior majority to allocate resources fairly. The responses of these children provide interesting insights into strategies adopted by a minority to protect its perceived interest. An obvious extension is to study the decision rules advocated by children from ethnic minorities—especially economically deprived minorities—when required to share rights and resources with children from the majority culture. Another possibility is to study children from cultures whose citizens have little interpersonal trust, which, according to Hofstede (1980) are usually those countries in which a gulf exists between the powerful and powerless.

An experiment by Paicheler and Darmon (1975), using Tajfel's "minimal" group procedure, suggests that minority subjects are especially sensitive to their size and vulnerability in relation to the majority and make their claims accordingly. In Paicheler and Darmon's experiment, conducted with French children, subjects in the majority condition were led to believe they represented 82% of the class, while subjects in the minority condition were led to believe they constituted a mere 18% of the class. They found that only majority subjects showed "ingroup" favoritism. Minority subjects failed to show "ingroup" favoritism, but seemingly, against their own interest, allocated more rewards to the majority. This finding suggests the intriguing possibility that minorities of different sizes advocate different decision rules and allocation principles in recognition of the vulnerability of their position. By using variations in the relative size of ethnic minorities in different countries (e.g., Indians in Fiji are 50% of the population; Maoris in New Zealand are 8% of the population), it is possible to conduct an alternative test of the hypothesis that the most vulnerable minorities are most deferential to the majority in choice of decision rule and allocation principle.

DECISION RULES FOR DEALING WITH GENUINE OUTGROUPS

It cannot be assumed that the same decision rules tend to deal with a competing subgroup created from one's own classroom will be used in dealing with a natural outgroup, such as children from a rival school or from a stigmatized ethnic or religious minority. It might be expected that children from collectivist cultures will use quite different rules in dealing with natural outgroups, on the assumption that collectivists make a firmer distinction between ingroup and outgroup (see Triandis, Chap. 10, this volume).

Leung and Bond (1984) found that collectivists use quite different distributive justice principles in dealing with ingroup and outgroup members. Chinese students tended to use the equality rule when allocating rewards to an ingroup member, but the equity rule when working with an outgroup member. Which groups constitute ingroups in collectivist cultures? There is evidence that collectivist cultures vary in the kinds of groups that function as ingroups. In Chinese society, the family is a powerful ingroup that dominates social relationships (Bond, 1986). In Maori culture, the kinship group is a powerful ingroup (Metge, 1976). In Japan, family, school class, and work organization all constitute major ingroups (Christopher, 1983). Indians identify their ingroups as those into which they are born (e.g., family), whereas North Americans often identify groups in which they choose membership (e.g., friends) as their ingroups (Verma, 1985). It remains to be seen how children modify their decision rules when dealing with a genuine outgroup rather than a manufactured outgroup. Cross-cultural research is underway to study the decision rules used by children when the other group—majority or minority—is brought in from another classroom. Presumably, this should make little difference in cultures in which classroom is not important as an ingroup (e.g., Australia, Hong Kong, New Zealand), but should have a significant effect in cultures in which one's own classroom functions as an important ingroup (e.g., Japan). We expect that Japanese children will respond differently to children from another classroom by placing their own class interest above the interest of the other class.

In summary, research on decision rules conducted in school classrooms in several countries reveals that children in individualist cultures accept arbitrary division into competing groups, including majority and minority status; children in collectivist cultures favor the use of the equal say or turn-taking rule in resolving majority and minority claims; children in individualist cultures favor the use of majority rule or self-interest in resolving majority and minority claims; majorities and minorities, especially in individualist cultures, differ in the decision rules and distribution principles advocated to protect their interest (minorities are especially prone to make disproportionate claims on rights and resources). Thus research in this area has demonstrated that while the problem of resolving competing claims between groups occurs across cultures, how children attempt to resolve the problem is related to the dominant values of a culture, and therefore a cross-cultural perspective is imperative. The importance of culture and "subjective culture" (Triandis, 1972) in intergroup relations is implicitly recognized by Brewer and Kramer (1985) and is considered elsewhere in this volume.

RISKY DECISIONS IN GROUPS

Another example of the value of the cross-cultural method in social psychology is found in work on the risky shift in group decision making.

The traditional assumption, that groups tend to be more cautious than individuals as decision makers, was rejected in the 1960s following the discovery of the risky shift phenomenon, the tendency for members after participation in group discussions about hazardous alternatives to become riskier in their own preferences (Kogan & Wallach, 1967). The risky shift phenomenon has been found in many Western countries, including Canada (Vidmar, 1970), England (Bateson, 1966; Fraser, Gouge, & Billig, 1970), France (Kogan & Doise, 1969), Germany (Lamm & Kogan, 1970), Israel (Rim, 1963), New Zealand (Bell & Jamieson, 1970) and the United States (Stoner, 1961).

Many explanations for the risky shift phenomenon have been advanced. Brown's (1965) cultural value hypothesis is of most interest to cross-cultural research. According to this hypothesis, there is a cultural value for riskiness or for taking a chance in contemporary Western society. When group members discuss the hazardous alternatives, the information exchanged supports and reinforces this cultural value. This is because individuals want to be at least as risky as their peers. If, in the course of discussion, they learn that they were not as risky as they thought, they are moved to adhere to the value and shift to a riskier option. A derivation from the hypothesis is that in societies in which the dominant culture value is caution the group discussion should lead to a *cautious shift*, especially on the items for which there is a strong cultural "demand" toward wariness and conservatism.

A direct way to test the cultural value hypothesis is to replicate the group discussion procedure in two societies, one with a strong cultural value of riskiness, the other with a strong value of caution. Such a study was conducted by Carlson and Davis (1971), who compared the effect of group discussions on riskiness in the United States (a high-risk culture), and Uganda (a low-risk culture). The individual decisions of the Ugandan subjects were initially more conservative than those of the Americans, supporting the premise that Ugandans are less favorably disposed to risk taking than Americans. Consistent with the culture-value hypothesis, the group discussion produced evidence of a shift to caution in the Ugandan sample (conservative shifts on 2 of the 11 problems), but in the American sample there was evidence of a risky shift (significant risky shifts were found on 3 of the 11 problems). Gologor (1977) tested the risky shift hypothesis in Liberia, a conservative African culture. As predicted by the culture-value hypothesis, the majority of shifts were in the cautious direction.

The rather reliable risky shift phenomenon is associated then with the value system of Western culture. The Carlson and Davis study is a good example of how cross-cultural research can be used to test a social psychological hypothesis. Such research also serves as a corrective to the common assumption that all group phenomena must be universal.

CONCLUSION

I have reviewed several problems in group behavior that have been enriched by a cross-cultural perspective—conformity, minority influence, the resolution of majority and minority claims, the minimal group phenomenon, and the risky shift phenomenon. To this list could be added the study of leadership styles (Meade, 1967; Misumi, 1972), experiments on group rejection of deviate members (Schachter et al., 1954), and research on children's cooperation-competition (Madsen & Shapira, 1970), all of which reveal significant cross-cultural differences.

It was argued that the cross-cultural perspective has made a useful contribution to knowledge about group behavior. Five general contributions can be identified from the preceding discussion.

(1) Some social psychological processes, such as anticonformity, are not universal, therefore the conditions that produce some aspects of group behavior must be examined for societal influences.
(2) The incidence of some social behaviors, such as conformity and "in-group favoritism," varies across cultures; this prompts the fundamental question of what determines the strength of a group phenomenon, why groups have greater or lesser influence on their members in some societies.
(3) Cultural differences relating to such basic dimensions as collectivism-individualism significantly determine the decision rules used by groups for the resolution of competing interests.
(4) Cross-cultural research can produce novel and surprising findings, for example, anticonformity, that provoke fresh thinking about new or rare group phenomena.
(5) Some important hypotheses in social psychology, such as the eco-cultural model of conformity, can be tested most effectively by the cross-cultural method.

It is an indictment that most social psychology textbooks assume an acultural stance, ignoring the importance of a cross-cultural perspective for an understanding of social behavior. Notable exceptions are Lindgren (1973), Gergen and Gergen (1981), and Cvetkovich, Baumgardner, and Trimble (1984). The stance taken by social psychology suggests that cross-cultural comparisons are mundane parametric variations of little theoretical significance or interest. Such myopia deprives social psychology of a rich source of inspiration and knowledge.

15

INTERPERSONAL BEHAVIOR
Cross-Cultural and
Historical Perspectives

JOHN ADAMOPOULOS

> But mark my words. In the same way as Phoebus Apollo is robbing me of
> Chryseis, whom I propose to send off in my ship with my own crew, I am
> going to pay a visit to your hut and take away the beautiful Briseis, your
> prize, Achilles, to let you know that I am more powerful than you, and to
> teach others not to bandy words with me and openly defy their King.
> (*Iliad*; Rieu, 1950, p. 28)

Thus began, Homer tells us, the great feud between Agamemnon and
Achilles that led to the death of many kings and princes (including, of
course, Achilles) during the Trojan War. Jaynes's (1977) arguments
against the presence of conscious motives in the *Iliad* notwithstanding,
awareness of status, and of the importance of self-presentation, appears
to lie at the core of this unparalleled, if rather tragic, epic of social
behavior some three thousand years ago.

The possibility that human action is similarly organized and patterned
in different cultures and historical periods in an intriguing notion that
has been addressed only partially by cross-cultural psychology, and
generally ignored by social psychology. A substantial portion of the
following discussion will concern the validity of the controversial quest
for the establishment of "universals" of interpersonal behavior (intended
or overt). It will be apparent that even though I do not consider the
available evidence explicitly indicative of behavioral universals, I find it
overwhelmingly suggestive of their existence.

Briefly, the structure of interpersonal behavior in different cultures
has been conceptualized as a configuration defined by the dimensions of
association-dissociation (affiliation), superordination-subordination
(control), and intimacy-formality (Adamopoulos, 1984; Triandis, 1978).
Disagreements about structural details—such as unipolarity *versus*
bipolarity, and orthogonal *versus* correlated dimensions—have been
frequent, but divergent theoretical approaches and research styles have
generally resulted in a surprising amount of agreement about the basic

AUTHOR'S NOTE: I am grateful to Yiannis Pikrodimitris and Ruth Parvin for their
contributions to this manuscript.

characteristics of these dimensions (Benjamin, 1984; Triandis et al., 1984; Wish, Deutsch, & Kaplan, 1976). Lonner (1980) has provided a comprehensive and thoughtful account of much of this work.

Observed similarity in behavior patterns across time and cultures, however, does not entail identity of underlying structures. Self-presentation, for example, may have been a central—indeed, a necessary—aspect of social interaction in Homeric times (see Adamopoulos, 1982), but is frequently considered a nonfundamental, and altogether negative, pattern of behavior today (e.g., Schlenker, 1985). Consideration of the processes that *generate* behavior patterns across cultures and time (and thus account for similarity as well as change in human action) has been neglected in psychology despite its obvious significance for the establishment of general theories of behavior. The description of such cross-cultural and transhistorical processes will be a basic feature of the thesis developed here.

A Necessary Caveat

The widely acknowledged failure of social psychology to establish "universal" laws of human behavior (e.g., Gergen, 1982) appears to make any effort to elevate observed similarities in the structure of behavior across cultures to the level of general theory rather futile. Yet, as intimated earlier, the convergence of the findings from numerous cross-cultural investigations of this problem is impressive (Lonner, 1980; Triandis, 1978). We cannot easily avoid dealing with this conclusion, unless we assume that, at best, it reflects agreement only about abstract behavioral labels among researchers. I find such a position difficult to accept, however, especially in light of related findings within different psychological domains and populations (e.g., Goldberg, 1981; Hirshoren & Schnittjer, 1981; Wiggins, 1980). Therefore, I will use the term *universal* rather liberally to refer to hypothetical constructs that are good candidates for future inclusion in a culturally sensitive theory of social behavior.

SYNCHRONIC AND DIACHRONIC UNIVERSALS

Gergen (1984) has recently, and with good reason, chastised social psychologists for their obsolete preoccupation with models of human nature that emphasize behavioral stability, rather than change over time, and that therefore result in the distortion of social reality. Cultural psychologists concerned with the formulation of behavior universals are not immune to this criticism. Cross-cultural invariance in behavior is, surely, only one of at least two basic criteria for universality: relative stability across cultures must be accompanied by some notion of consistency across time before we can make a legitimate claim for the universal status of a construct. Considering the large volume and high quality of social psychology's self-criticism about the effects of parochialism on its view of human nature—most recently by McClintock (1985) and Sears (1986)—this point should now be taken for granted. Yet the field's ethnocentrism and ignorance of the importance of history curiously persist.

An additional criticism against a strictly monocultural—or even a nonhistorical, cross-cultural—social psychology is derived from the philosophy of science that lies at the core of our generally accepted methodological practices, and especially from the Duhem-Quine thesis (e.g., Harding, 1976). Implicit in much modern social psychology is the notion that basic psychological structures (e.g., attitudes) are identical in all people; they differ only in content. Environmental and cultural influences are believed to be filtered through this common psychological equipment, which, it is parsimonious to assume, is common to all. I suggest that this may be cultural parochialism masquerading as scientific parsimony.

This approach, naturally, creates a vicious cycle in which culture and history play an increasingly trivial role. By deemphasizing cultural factors, social psychologists develop theories that are based on minimalist abstractions from reality, and are, inevitably, free of all cultural considerations. Necessarily, predictions from such theories exclude all cultural and temporal influences on human behavior.

Cross-cultural psychology has offered an improvement on this cultural reductionism of experimental social psychology by distinguishing between culture-common (etic) and culture-specific (emic) constructs (Malpass, 1977). The former are assumed to reflect consistencies across cultures, presumably within a specific time-frame (i.e., "synchronic" universals), whereas the latter are thought to be unique cultural events. Despite its prevalence, this distinction is susceptible to the criticism that emics are considered local phenomena, not easily interpretable within the larger theoretical context.

An alternative approach may treat emics as the specific ways in which universal processes are manifested in different cultures (see Smith and Tayeb, Chap. 12, this volume). Consequently, the emphasis would be on diachronic, evolutionary processes that yield temporally localized consistencies in human behavior given certain environmental inputs.

Synchronic Universals
from Diachronic Processes

I have described a working model for the evolution of relatively stable social behavior structures through diachronic processes elsewhere (Adamopoulos, 1984; Adamopoulos & Bontempo, 1987). Following Foa and Foa (1974), social interaction is conceptualized as resource exchange limited by certain constraints that are basic to human nature. During interaction, for example, a resource that is either material (concrete) or symbolic (abstract) is given or denied to another person. Furthermore, the exchange is oriented toward a *specific* other (i.e., a person whose absence would affect significantly the emotional tone of the interaction), or a *general* other (changing bank tellers should be, after all, much easier to most of us than changing lovers).

Historians have linked these constraints, which may be characteristic of the nature of social beings, to major developments in civilization. For example, the ability to exchange symbolic resources (e.g., information) has often been associated with revolutionary shifts in culture, such as the dramatic changes in social communication following the invention of the printing press (e.g., Eisenstein, 1979; Etkin, 1954). In addition, the orientation of the social exchange, as defined previously, may have been of importance in the occupational specialization that followed changes from hunting and gathering to farming and trading modes of subsistence in ancient societies (Jones, 1960). Within social psychology, Berry (1979, p. 181) has pointed to "a high probabilistic relationship between the ecology and the traditional culture components, such that in hunting nomadic societies 'loose' sociocultural systems predominate, while in agricultural societies 'tight' systems are more common." In the present context, it may be argued that such shifts in sociocultural systems were the outcome of the increased importance of interpersonal orientation as a constraint of social interaction.

As shown in Figure 1, these constraints (facets) may be thought of as undergoing a process of differentiation over time in a discrete order. The products of this diachronic process are patterns of social behavior that are stable for certain periods of time, and constitute the synchronic universals uncovered by modern cross-cultural psychology. The order in which these facets are differentiated is important because it accounts for correlations between behavioral structures (e.g., intimacy is more similar to subordination than it is to trading). In other words, this model makes tentative predictions about the differential evolution of inter-personal behavior, and provides theoretical, rather than empirical, definitions of the meaning of social action. As I hope the following discussion will show, it can be a useful tool in the interpretation of findings about major categories of social behavior cross-culturally.

MAJOR DIMENSIONS
OF SOCIAL BEHAVIOR

Affiliation and
Positive Social Interaction

As described in Figure 1, affiliation depends primarily upon the differentiation of the resource exchange mode, and would thus be ubiquitous in interpersonal interaction. There can be little doubt that much of human behavior—especially altruism—can be located on this dimension. Interestingly, many constructs and theoretical models generated in the laboratory have found cross-cultural support in this area.

Recent empirical support for Weiner's (1980) attributional account of helping (Reisenzein, 1986) underscores the model's ability to explain a wide range of behavior. It is possible, for example, to interpret some of the findings in Feldman's (1968) important studies of helping in three cultures by the attributional scheme developed by Weiner. In one study, Feldman found that Athenians refused overwhelmingly to mail an envelope without a stamp for a compatriot, but were more willing to do so for a foreigner. This contrasted greatly with findings in Paris and Boston, and was interpreted on the basis of traditional Greek outgroup discrimination and hostility (where the outgroup was assumed to include unfamiliar compatriots but not foreigners). A less awkward, attributional account of the findings, however, would focus on the negative emotional reaction that Greeks might have to requests for help from individuals perceived capable of performing the task. In fact, Feldman (1968, p. 209) reported that Greek refusals to compatriots "were quite blunt and adamant."

Most cross-cultural differences in various forms of positive social interaction seem to be related to the presence of particular cultural conditions, such as the availability and distribution of resources in the population (e.g., Carment, 1974; Nadler, 1986; Walsh & Taylor, 1982). Triandis, Marin, Lisansky, and Betancourt (1984) have reported the existence of a "simpatia" script among Hispanics, which leads to expectations of positive social interaction, and is believed to be the result of a strong emphasis on interpersonal relations in Hispanic culture. A similar finding has been reported in Indonesia (Noesjirwan,

Facets	Elements							
Resource Exchange Mode	Giving				Denying			
Interpersonal Orientation	Particularistic		Universalistic		Universalistic		Particularistic	
Resource Type	Concrete	Abstract	Abstract	Concrete	Concrete	Abstract	Abstract	Concrete
Behavioral Features	Intimacy	Subordination	Formality	Trading	Trading	Formality	Superordination	Intimacy

←—— Association ——→   ←—— Dissociation ——→

Figure 1: The Differentiation of Interpersonal Behavior (adapted from Adamopoulos & Bontempo, 1986).

1978). In both cases, it appears that people in the two cultures rely on compatriots for their livelihoods much more than do North Americans. In other words, social interaction in Hispanic and Indonesian cultures involves a greater emphasis on the sharing and giving of resources, which, of course, results in more associative behavior. Any apparent differences among the three cultures may be simply the result of different environmental, and possibly ecological, inputs—such as economic and climatic conditions that promote cooperation—in the diachronic processes that generate social behavior.

Dominance and Subordination

There is considerable cross-cultural evidence that some form of dominance and dependency characterize much of human interaction today (e.g., Margalit & Mauger, 1985; Rump, Rigby, & Walters, 1985). Berry's (1979) finding of a strong relationship between "tight" (complexly organized) sociocultural systems and individual conformity (a type of subordination) again demonstrates the importance of ecology and general culture in the formation of social behavior.

There is also ample evidence for a similar connection between social systems and patterns of dominance in historical accounts of feudalism around the world. Bloch (1961, p. 443) has argued that "European feudalism . . . involved a far-reaching restriction of social intercourse, a circulation of money too sluggish to admit of a salaried officialdom, and a mentality attached to things tangible and local." Feudalism, perhaps more than any other social system, was based almost exclusively on the relation between subordinate and chief. Thus it can be seen as an early exemplar of this dimension of social behavior. Bloch's description of European feudalism clearly emphasizes the particularistic character of this social system, which, as seen in Figure 1, is the primary defining element of superordination-subordination. Even the reference to "things tangible and local" is to the feudal lord's ability to pay soldiers for status and power. Money was probably a relatively abstract resource in that historical context. As the availability of abstract resources (e.g., information) increased, power and authority relations in society became more clearly delineated and institutionalized.

Intimacy and Formality

The impressive level of cross-cultural similarity established with the two previous dimensions of social behavior is not found with intimacy.

There are reports of many substantial differences between Western and non-Western cultures (e.g., Bachtold, 1982; L'Armand, 1984; Simmons, Vom Kolke, & Shimuzu, 1986), and even some differences among Western cultures (e.g., Arenson, 1979) in eye contact, courtship, marriage, and the experience of romantic love. These large differences are more easily understood if intimacy is seen as a complex dimension of social behavior that emerged later, or more slowly, than the dimensions of affiliation and dominance.

Recent work on the related phenomenon of privacy regulation (Altman & Chemers, 1980) strongly suggests that patterns of behavior involving the concepts of openness and closedness to others—as intimacy surely does—are controlled by evolutionary processes. Therefore, we can safely expect that intimacy has developed considerably over the past few centuries. Evidence in literary sources from as far back as the eighth century B.C. supports this hypothesis, and suggests that early forms of intimacy involved a certain amount of ritualistic and formal behavior (Adamopoulos, 1982).

The model outlined previously in Figure 1 explains why this may be the case. The emergence of intimacy as a separate behavior pattern from formality involves the differentiation and ultimate combination of all constraints. This is in contrast to the association-dissociation or superordination-subordination behavior features, which differ primarily in the resource exchange mode that they involve. Furthermore, intimacy and formality are exact opposites of each other on more facets than any other set of semantically polar features. In other words, the differentiation of intimacy and formality over time may have been a particularly long-term and complex process.

Historical analyses of various intimate relationships in different eras generally support this notion of undifferentiated behavior. Lacey (1968), for example, has presented the theme of undifferentiated familial-intimate relations and control in classical Greece. The same idea has been developed by Stone (1977) in his articulate account of family life in sixteenth-century England. Jeay (1979) and Adamopoulos (1982) have reported undifferentiated intimacy and formality in fifteenth-century France and Homeric Greece, respectively. Finally, Brown (1986) has argued that sexual orientation in ancient Greece and Rome was much less differentiated than it is today.

CONCLUSIONS

Kuhn (1977) has admitted the possibility that general "laws" of social behavior may exist (though he believes that they have not been uncovered yet). I believe that the evidence I have so briefly reviewed here is certainly suggestive of this possibility, and perhaps even strong enough to overcome many objections of both methodological and philosophical character.

Human beings appear to exhibit similar patterns of behavior across cultures. Furthermore, one need not look for these patterns at trivially high levels of abstraction, or restrict their applicability to purely conceptual domains. It is not trivial to argue that all humans, in our era, are capable of intimacy but differ in the manner in which they exhibit it. On the practical side, knowing details of this patterning will have obvious benefits on intercultural interaction, marriage, conflict resolution, and so on. On the theoretical side, however, the issue is far more complicated.

Gergen (1982) has introduced a series of important arguments against the notion that the identification and elaborate description of conceptual dimensions of behavior across cultures entails the presence of universal patterns of overt behavior. This position is based on the assumption that the description of a conceptual universal may be a function of the cognitive skills of theorists, rather than the result of the objective observation of human activity. To assume otherwise, Gergen warns, "is to engage in the fallacy of misplaced concreteness" (1982, p. 50). This criticism of a basic approach to cross-cultural research—including, alas, the one taken here—has substantial merit. It behooves cross-cultural psychologists to define behavior patterns in terms that apply to all human beings. In other words, once the *possibility* of a universal has been established, an attempt to *explain* it must follow—even if we must rely, at least initially, on rather simplistic applications of evolutionary theory.

This raises the very important issue of the compatibility of any attempt to establish universals of human social behavior with evolutionary theory. Gergen (1982) argued that (a) historical diffusion may account for any similarities in behavior across cultures, and that (b) advocating the existence of behavioral universals goes against the generally accepted tenets of the theory of evolution.

Historical Diffusion

Arguments about historical diffusion, like those of "cultural" diffusion that plague the methodology of much anthropological work (Narroll, 1961), are clearly legitimate, though the substantive, as opposed to the methodological, problem may not be as bad as has been assumed in the past. Swartz (1982) has reported evidence that intracultural variance in sharing elements of culture is greater than intercultural variance. This seemingly paradoxical finding may reflect the fact that all cultures must possess certain fundamental, universal characteristics if they are to survive.

People often borrow the ideas and behavior of their neighbors. To argue that such ideas, or behaviors, are "universal" may be premature, if not foolhardy (though Herodotus himself had pondered about these matters with regard to customs shared by the Greeks, the Egyptians, the Phoenicians, and others, almost 2,500 years ago!). However, it is frequently forgotten in these discussions of diffusion that, quite often, neighbors borrow only those ideas that they find acceptable and compatible, or at least reconcilable within their own sociocultural system (see Gomperz, 1901). Thus, for example, although the early Greeks intensely disliked trading and commerce, they developed institutions to accommodate merchants from other lands (Curtin, 1984). Lest my argument be discounted because of my genetic affiliation with that fine old culture, let me hasten to add that Herodotus repeatedly spoke of the unwillingness of the Egyptians to adopt many of the Greek ways, despite extensive contact between the two groups (de Selincourt, 1954).

Along similar lines, an influential perspective in comparative mythology advocates the existence of a common core of "heritage" among Indo-European cultures. This heritage explains—over and above the processes of migration and diffusion—similarities among different cultures, and is reflected in the myths of these cultures (see Larson, 1974). Thus dismissing behavioral universals by invoking diffusional processes ignores the possibility that historical and cultural diffusion processes themselves may be determined by universal patterns, such as those that are assumed to underlie the emergence of the behavior dimensions described earlier (Figure 1).

Universals and
the Theory of Evolution

Only a very narrow definition of universals as rigid structures is incompatible with evolutionary theory. In fact, as discussed earlier, cross-cultural psychologists have, at times, speculated about the nature of general, perhaps universal, psychological processes the various components of which may change over long periods of time. Environmental, ecological, climatic, and historical changes may alter the emergence of different behavior patterns, but may do so in a predictable manner. The process, rather than the outcome, of change should, in such cases, be considered universal.

One of the implications of this position is that two cultures coexisting in time may be very different interpersonally, with certain characteristics of one matching those of the other in a *different* historical period. For example, although Japan boasts as robust an economy as any today, certain aspects of its interpersonal culture are much more similar to those of European cultures centuries ago. Morsbach's (1980) account of the ritualistic nature of social relations in Japan bears, in some ways, a striking resemblance to descriptions of social interaction in the *Iliad* (Adamopoulos, 1982).

In addition, according to Morsbach (1980), the basic characteristic of Japanese interpersonal relations stems from the rather universalistic orientation of social exchange in that culture: Role expectations, rather than unique individual attributes, guide relationships. This, of course, is in agreement with the framework described earlier, which assumes that formality is based on a universalistic orientation. But it also leads to the possibility that the meteoric economic growth of Japan may be due to this universalistic orientation, since the exchange of economic resources and trading are necessarily universalistic in nature (Foa & Foa, 1974, 1980). On the other hand, economic success in other societies may be due to an entirely different dynamic. In the context of the theoretical framework developed earlier, emphasis on particularism, and on the unique aspects of the *self*, as opposed to the *other*, in social interaction (possibly *individualism*; Leung & Bond, 1984) may have led to the development of behavioral systems based on the notions of power and superordination.

Much has been written in recent years about the possible emulation of those practices from other cultures that are thought to create favorable conditions for economic growth. The present analysis, however, implies that similar goals can be achieved by very different activities. Japan may very well owe its economic rise to cultural factors that resulted in the development of behaviors associated with trading (Figure 1). In contrast, the U.S. and, possibly, Western European nations may have achieved their leading economic positions by developing sociocultural institutions that transformed all resources—including money and information—to symbols of individual dominance and power over the environment.

I am proposing, then, that despite the methodological and philosophical problems associated with the study of transhistorical psychological processes, the theoretical and practical potential of such an approach holds enormous promise for contemporary psychology.

Unless we wish to make an important component of our field the exclusive domain of historians, or remain singularly insensitive—especially for such a multicultural society—to cultural and social (!) issues, we must begin developing evolutionary frameworks for the study of long-term stability and change in human behavior.

Perhaps a wiser beginning would utilize more explicitly the considerable theoretical clout of biological evolutionary models (e.g., Buss, 1984; Campbell, 1982; Osgood, 1969). For example, natural selection can be used to explain the predominance of certain forms of interpersonal behavior in most cultures. It appears obvious that cooperation (a form of association) can help human beings survive in adverse conditions, and, surely, superordination implies the assertion of individual mastery and control over the environment. On the other hand, it is often difficult to wed such attempts to specific empirical investigations, and, after all, there is no compelling reason to believe that models of biological development can explain psychocultural evolution adequately (see Durham, 1976). This smacks of a biological determinism against which Gould (1977) has repeatedly, and brilliantly, warned us.

More to the point, I have suggested throughout this chapter that there seems to be an accumulation of evidence from experimental, historical, and literary sources indicating subtle but consistent changes in some (but not all) aspects of social behavior over long periods of time. Such systematic and predictable changes cannot be explained easily and in a nontrivial manner by invoking natural selection. Rather, we need to develop quite specific models of evolutional processes that produce human social behavior through time. I have presented the outline of such a model here. Clearly, more will be created as we articulate other fundamental constraints of human nature, in addition to those I have discussed so far. It is these constraints, rather than the behavioral structures they generate, that ultimately must be found compatible with natural selection and the evolutionary perspective in science. I suspect that, in good time, it will be so.

16

CULTURAL ROOTS OF AGGRESSIVE BEHAVIOR

MARSHALL H. SEGALL

CROSS-CULTURAL RESEARCH: CHALLENGE AND CONFIRMATION

It is quite common for cross-cultural psychologists, when chiding their mainstream colleagues for perilously ignoring cross-cultural research, to warn them that data gathered in cultures other than the United States challenge the generality of their (the mainstreamers') putative universal principles of behavior. Less commonly voiced is the equally important (and so much friendlier) fact that cross-cultural research can provide compelling support for behavioral principles the validity of which is less secure without it. In the case of human aggression, cross-cultural research and mainstream social psychology are inevitable allies, with the cultural input providing mainstream paradigms a convincing validation that could come from nowhere else.

AGGRESSION AND SOCIAL LEARNING

At least since the classic Yale studies on frustration and aggression (Dollard, Doob, Miller, Mowrer, & Sears, 1939; Miller, 1941), a central theme in mainstream social psychology is that aggression is learnable behavior. This proposition elicits *no* argument from cross-cultural psychologists. How could it?

If aggression is learnable, it is *ipso facto* cultural. All human learning occurs in cultural contexts. Culture shapes what is to be learned by offering standards, norms, and models to be emulated. It provides the reinforcements and, through values, the broader socioeconomic, religious, and moral context that encourages some behaviors while discouraging others. Necessarily, then, to understand how humans learn which aggressive behaviors to display, toward whom and under what circumstances, and with what anticipated consequences, cultural variables must be included in the study of aggression.

Consider, for example, the following set of studies, both mainstream and cross-cultural, that deal with aggression, power, and status. The argument that some aggressive behaviors might better be thought of as attempts to exercise social control via coercion has been made by Tedeschi and colleagues (e.g., Tedeschi, Smith, & Brown, 1974; Tedeschi & Melburg, 1983). If some coercive acts are judged to be unjustified and committed with an intent to harm their target, they are likely to be judged "aggressive," but similar acts when committed by an acknowledged superior toward a subordinate might well be seen as the legitimate exercise of authority and not as aggression. Since societies vary in the extent to which subordinates accept their lower status (Hofstede, 1980, 1983), cross-cultural differences in the judgment of the aggressiveness of coercive acts have to be anticipated.

This line of reasoning led Bond, Wan, Leung, and Giacalone (1985) to predict that Chinese students in Hong Kong and American students in Albany, New York, would respond differently to verbal insults delivered by a superior to a subordinate, with the Chinese students (whose culture, in Hofstede's [1980, 1983] terms, is characterized by relatively high "power distance") less apt to characterize the insults as aggressive acts. The authors also expected that because Chinese culture is more collectivistic (Triandis, 1985) than U.S. culture, the Hong Kong students would differentiate more between in-group and out-group sources of insults, negatively sanctioning in-group insulters more than out-group insulters to a greater extent than would the students in New York.

The hypothesis that markers of status and group membership would be more influential in determining the responses of the higher power distance/higher collectivism Chinese students was confirmed. For example, for the Chinese students, the high-status, in-group insulter was perceived as less unlikable and his or her acts as less illegitimate than the Americans perceived them. The cross-cultural research in this instance both supported and expanded the mainstream paradigm.

Even with issues on which intracultural data seem compelling enough, cross-cultural data, if not essential, can be very helpful. For example, studies of mass media effects in societies other than the United States (Groebel, 1986) permit the separation of variables that are confounded in the U.S.—where there are so many different cues and reinforcements for aggression that the role of the media is difficult to isolate. Moreover, to test the simple proposition that fictional media violence is a cause of aggression, wouldn't it be useful to vary the degree of violence in the media? If it can't be done experimentally, we must seek existing real world variations and these surely can be found over a sample of societies.

CROSS-CULTURAL STUDIES
THAT NEED DOING

In social learning theories, aggression is considered an outcome of learning from others, primarily through socialization and enculturation, involving both teaching and learning by observation. Social learning theories of aggression would find implicit support in cross-cultural research data showing systematic variations in aggression, and when these variations are correlated with specifiable eco-cultural differences, just *how* aggression is learned may be spelled out.

For example, potential support for the social learning approach exists in cross-cultural variation of parental responses to infants when they display—as do all infants—proto-aggressive behavior (Segall, 1976, p. 201). Such behavior includes the intense, diffuse, need-signaling actions of the relatively helpless infant. When those needs (for water, food, relief from discomfort, etc.) are tended to, the infantile behavior that induced the parental caretaking is also rewarded and thereby strengthened. Since the characteristic modes of infant caretaking vary among societies—so that infants in some societies receive more reinforcement for their proto-aggressive behavior—and since strength of aggressive behavior in older children also varies across societies, social learning theory would garner support from cross-cultural studies that demonstrated a relationship between the two.

Similarly, certain variations in the training of older children would interest social learning theorists of aggression. Suppose, for example, that cultures differed in degree of parental consistency in socialization and that this was correlated with variations in overt aggression by the children. Such a correlation would be in accord with a social learning principle that might link inconsistent reinforcement schedules with frustration and aggression.

Because of the well-established empirical link between frustration and aggression, differences across cultures in their characteristic levels of inequality of opportunity would also reveal a social learning mechanism working at the societal level.

In these and other ways, cross-cultural data, rather than challenging mainstream social psychology, would support its prevailing view of aggression, as provided by one or another version of social learning theory.

CROSS-CULTURAL RESEARCH AND BIOLOGY

The cross-cultural perspective also clarifies biological contributions to aggression. It is perhaps especially important to study aggression in a cultural perspective because of the pervasive view, among both laypersons and among some serious students of human aggression, that aggression is biologically determined, even instinctive. Data collected in a single society never permit empirical resolution of nature/nurture arguments. Polemics prevail. On the other hand, cross-cultural psychology and anthropology have over the years contributed to a more balanced biosocial view by revealing both pancultural generalizations about aggression (e.g., a very consistent picture regarding sex differences in aggression) and some provocative cultural differences.[1]

This contribution may best be revealed by a close look at a cross-cultural analysis of sex differences in aggression, to which we will devote much of the balance of our limited space.

GENDER, CULTURE, SOCIAL LEARNING, AND AGGRESSION

Gender Differences in Aggression

In her review of many cross-cultural studies dealing with sex differences, the anthropologist Carol Ember (1981) noted, "the most consistent and most documented cross-cultural differences in interpersonal behavior appears to be that boys exhibit more aggression after age 3 or so" (p. 551). This is true in the United States (Maccoby & Jacklin, 1974), in the several societies studied in the Six Cultures study (Whiting & Whiting, 1975), and in 71% of 14 societies for which ethnographic reports on aggression by young children (2-6 years) were examined by Rohner (1976). In fact, in Rohner's survey of these societies, either males clearly out-aggressed females or no difference was detectable. It is virtually impossible to find a society in which young girls are more aggressive than young boys.

With regard to criminal behavior, the findings are consistent with the conclusion that males are the more aggressive sex. Bacon, Child, and Berry (1963) presented data from 48 nonindustrialized societies showing that males commit the preponderance of criminal acts. In the United States, it has long been the case that the best predictor of fluctuations in crime rates is the proportion of the population composed of adolescent males. As Goldstein (1983) has noted, "The 1960-1975 increase in violent crime and the stabilization of the crime rate since 1975 parallel directly the number of 14- to 24-year-old males in the United States" (1983, p. 439).

Age Effects

So there is a correlation between sex and aggression and it exists across most societies. There is also a relationship between age and aggression. The perpetrators of most crimes in the United States are best described as male adolescents. In other industrialized societies we find the same phenomenon. In Newmann's (1979) profile of the most typical violent individuals in a number of societies we find them to be 15- to 30-year-old males, with lower socioeconomic status, living in urban areas, and disproportionately likely to be a member of an ethnic group that is low in the social hierarchy in the country. Naroll (1983) compiled "juvenile criminal ratios" for 42 industrialized societies and found that, for all of them, at least a quarter and as many as half of all reported crimes were committed by adolescent males (p. 389).

Biological Input

Thus we have cross-cultural evidence for a panspecies generalization about aggression. Males of the species perform most aggressive acts and they are most apt to do so as adolescents. What should we make of these universal findings?

A possibly relevant biological fact is that circulating testosterone is related to dominance behavior. Mazur (1985) explicitly linked testosterone to male adolescent behavior: "As young primate males pass through adolescence, they often become more assertive with posturing and strutting that may be labeled "macho" in human terms. . . . They move rapidly up the group hierarchy, taking their place among the adult males. These changes may be a consequence of the massive increase in testosterone production that occurs during puberty" (p. 383). Since there is a surge of male testosterone at adolescence, that alone may produce an intensification of dominance-striving behavior among male adolescents, and if that behavior includes aggressive acts (which constitute one possible form of asserting dominance over others), then a sex-linked, age-related hormonal phenomenon could account for male adolescent aggression. The validity of this answer depends on how closely dominance and aggression are linked. Despite some evidence that testosterone-produced differences in early development made males both more dominant and more aggressive, Mazur noted that it is important to distinguish dominance behavior from aggressive behavior, a distinction which is particularly important for humans, "who often assert their dominance without any intent to cause injury" (1985, p. 382).[2]

Dominance-striving by male adolescents includes many nonaggressive behaviors (e.g., displaying expertise at games, problem-solving, acquiring valued goods, demonstrating sexual prowess, and more), and whether it includes aggressive acts probably depends, in the end, on cultural norms.

There would be a very simple answer to the question of why most aggressive acts are committed by male adolescents (an answer that leaves out biology altogether) if cross-cultural research showed that in most societies boys are encouraged more than girls to behave aggressively. Then we could say that male adolescents are more aggressive simply because they have been taught to be. But, as we shall now see, this answer is too simple.

Training Inputs

Barry, Josephson, Lauer, and Marshall (1976) scored nearly 150 societies drawn from the Standard Cross-Cultural Sample (Murdock & White, 1969) on inculcation (deliberate teaching and encouragement) of aggression among children. They found a sex difference *on the average* over all of these societies—more inculcation of aggression for boys than for girls—with this average sex difference more marked during later childhood. But the sex difference was significant in only 20% of these societies when they were examined singly; in most of the others it was very small and in some there was no detectable sex difference. So the cross-cultural consistency in greater male aggressive behavior cannot be explained solely on the basis of differences in inculcation of aggression. Other factors must be implicated in the phenomenon of greater aggressive behaviors among males than merely their hormones or the fact that generally they are subjected to more inculcation of aggression than are females.

A Biocultural Interactive Model

The cultural mechanisms that interact with biology to produce sex differences in aggression must be more complex than inculcation alone.

They probably include (a) division of labor by sex, (b) gender identity, and (c) gender-marking. Each of these, and the relationship among them, will be dealt with in turn.

(a) *Division of labor by sex.* Every society has some division of labor by sex and some modal sex differences in behavior (Munroe & Munroe, 1975, p. 116). Most pertinent is the notion, expressed most clearly by Barry, Bacon, and Child (1957), that the division of labor by sex sets the stage for differentiation between the sexes in socialization emphases and that this differentiation in turn functions as a means for preparing children to assume their sex-linked adult roles.

The clearest of all (and most nearly universal) sex-linked adult roles is child rearing itself. During socialization, females are taught traits that are compatible with child rearing and are later encouraged to assume that role. Males, on the other hand, are taught other traits during childhood, like independence, and encouraged later to assume roles and pursue activities (e.g., food-getting) that are largely incompatible with child rearing. Consequently, females do most of the child rearing in most societies and virtually all of it in some.

Whatever the reasons for this division, there results, in many societies—and perhaps in all in varying degree—a paradoxical state of affairs. Young males have restricted opportunities to observe adult males since their fathers tend to be nonparticipants in the child rearing. To the extent that gender-role learning involves modeling for learning by observation, boys' acquisition of masculine identity early in life will be attenuated.

(b) *Cross-gender identity.* The cutting edge of this paradox is that father-absence is most marked in societies with the sharpest division of labor by sex. Thus precisely in those societies in which the two sexes are expected to have the most distinct gender identities, young males are less likely to acquire their masculine identity by emulation of male models!

In societies with a particularly distinct division of labor by sex there is therefore a likelihood that young males will acquire a cross-sex identity. How ironic this crossover is, considering that in societies where there is a relatively sharp gender-role distinctiveness, the role of women is often regarded with contempt by males, whose own activities are accorded higher prestige. Consider the pressure that adult males in such societies must face to avoid behaving "in womanly fashion." Yet their sons, we are here suggesting, are likely, during childhood, to acquire a predominantly female identity, particularly if their mothers make no special effort to masculinize their sons.

(c) *Gender-marking aggression.* The Bacon et al. (1963) study of crime, as we saw, showed that males commit the preponderance of crimes in most societies. This same study also revealed that aggressive crimes, such as assaults, rapes, and murders, were more apt to occur in societies that provided exclusive mother-child sleeping arrangements. Such arrangements prevail, of course, in societies where fathers are not active participants in child rearing. Bacon et al. related this finding to the idea of "cross-sex identity" that had been introduced earlier (e.g., by Whiting, Kluckhohn, & Anthony, 1958; and Burton & Whiting, 1961) as a likely problem to be found in "low-male-salience" societies. Applying this idea to crime, Bacon et al. offered the hypothesis that aggressive crimes are part of a defense reaction against initial feminine identification in males.[3]

Extending the Bacon et al. hypothesis, the anthropologist Beatrice Whiting (1965) suggested that males reared primarily by females would be more susceptible to envy of powerful adult males, but could not become like them until escaping somehow from the early influence of their mothers. Whiting linked the young males' status envy to what she called "protest masculinity." She acutely observed, "It would seem as if there were a never-ending cycle. The separation of the sexes leads to a conflict of identity of the boy children, to unconscious fear of being feminine . . . , exaggeration of the difference between men and women, antagonism against and fear of women, male solidarity and hence to isolation of women and very young children" (p. 137). This identity conflict would obviously constitute a problem for societies that encourage sharply distinguished gender roles.

In some such societies, the problem is dealt with in an institutionalized manner, namely, by male initiation ceremonies. Severe male initiation ceremonies at puberty, often including tests of endurance and manliness, were found by Whiting, Kluckhohn, and Anthony (1958) to be correlated with exclusive mother-son sleeping arrangements and post-partum sex taboos, both indices of father-absence. The interpretation of this finding that is pertinent to our present discussion is that such ceremonies serve the function of stamping in masculinity for boys who need it due to inadequate opportunity to acquire such an identification in childhood. What happens, however, in societies which have this identity conflict but lack the initiation ceremony? To answer this question, I have proposed (Segall, 1988) a class of aggressive behavior I labeled "compensatory machoism."

In societies which have the preconditions requiring a stamping-in of masculinity—but which fail to achieve this via initiation ceremonies or other institutionalized practices—adolescent males will try on their own to assert their masculinity. They may do so in a variety of ways, but one of them might well be to behave aggressively. If a society is one in which aggressiveness and such allied traits as fortitude and courage are an integral part of the definition of manliness, boys approaching manhood will wish to display these characteristics.

The resultant aggression is called compensatory machoism to underscore that it is rooted not in anger but in a felt need to escape from womanliness and to mark one's masculine gender.[4] In other words, such aggression has the function of displaying that the actor is behaving like an adult male, in accord with his society's definition of the masculine gender. Examples of male adolescent aggression for which this model may hold the key may be found in various cultural groups in technologically developed societies like the United States, but in such a society, father absence is confounded with so many other variables that testing the model requires data from many societies.

The theory of male adolescent aggression as gender-marking behavior (compensatory machoism)[5] that was just described is not only a partial product of anthropological data, more importantly it raises questions about aggression that can be answered *only* by cross-cultural research; this consequence follows because the questions involve variables that take different values in different societies and because the relevant variables are differentially confounded in different societies. It is a theory that can be tested only by exploiting cultural variations in division of labor by sex, the role of fathers in parenting, presence/absence of male initiation ceremonies, and similar phenomena that are impossible to simulate in a laboratory and hard to find in sufficient variation within any single society.

Were we to test this theory cross-culturally, we would also probably support other related theories, such as Tedeschi, Smith, and Brown's (1974) view of *coercive action*. Most relevant is their notion that "failure to live up to culturally determined expectations and lack of a significant male model in the home are associated with low self-esteem and lack of self-confidence, which in turn predisposes the individual to use coercion as a means of gaining access to the rewards that he feels cannot be achieved by more acceptable means" (Tedeschi et al., p. 553). Also testable cross-culturally is Felson's (1978) notion of aggression as *impression management*, namely, "escalation occurs when a person has been cast into a negative situational identity of self-image and retaliates in order to save face" (p. 205). We might understand even more fully such supporting findings (Felson, 1982) that males in the United States are most apt to express anger when they are recipients of insults from same-sex peers *and* in the presence of onlookers.

I have argued in this conclusion that we cannot understand human aggression without viewing it from a cross-cultural perspective. While biology is surely implicated, it interacts with our culturally shaped experiences to lead us to react to frustration, to assert dominance, and to attempt to resolve conflicts in a diversity of ways. We are only at the beginning of what will have to be a systematic cross-cultural analysis of socialization practices, structural variables such as division of labor by sex, and other potentially related variables if we are to understand this pervasive human behavior in ways that are not constrained by factors that must remain invisible from a monocultural perspective.

NOTES

1. See Boyd and Richerson (1985) and Campbell (1965, 1975), for analogous features of (and differences between) biological evolution and cultural evolution. These perspectives deny the very meaningfulness of a nature versus nurture question but instead acknowledge the interaction of cultural variables with biological ones. Cross-cultural psychologists increasingly share these perspectives and it seems to help them to fend off attacks from intemperate sociobiologists.

2. Mazur also notes that at present there are no firm data on the effect of testosterone on dominance in humans. Also, the causal link between testosterone and dominance behavior may be in the opposite direction, with success in status competition producing increase in testosterone. So he refers to the relationship between testosterone and dominance behavior as "reciprocal" (1985, p. 383).

3. Long ago, a similar hypothesis was hinted at by students of crime and delinquency in the United States (e.g., Glueck & Glueck, 1950).

4. This concept, compensatory machoism, is clearly derived from Whiting's notion of "protest masculinity." Both concepts are concerned with attempts to resolve cross-sex identity problems. Compensatory machoism further specifies that these attempts will include aggression by adolescent males, especially in societies lacking gender-marking rituals.

5. Psychological anthropologists are less likely than mainstream social psychologists to feel uneasy with the psychoanalytic flavor inherent in a concept like "compensatory machoism." For the latter group of readers, it might be well to note that the argument I have made could just as well have been couched in cognitive social learning terms, stressing the tendency of adolescent males to exaggerate adult male behavior, which they try, unsuccessfully, to emulate before they have had sufficient practice. This reinterpretation (or, better, shift in theory language) was suggested to me by Harry Triandis at the 1987 Nag's Head Conference on Culture and Behavior.

17
THEORETICAL ADVANCES IN JUSTICE BEHAVIOR
Some Cross-Cultural Inputs

KWOK LEUNG

Social justice has been studied in philosophy (e.g., Rawls, 1971), anthropology (e.g., Nader & Todd, 1978), and sociology (e.g., Cook & Hegtvedt, 1983). Only recently, however, has justice been extensively studied by social psychologists (Deutsch, 1983). In this growing literature, two dimensions of justice can be distinguished. Distributive justice concerns the fairness of the relative proportion of valuable resources allocated to various participants, and the most important theory is undoubtedly Adams's (1963, 1965) equity theory. Procedural justice concerns the fairness of the method used in deciding how to distribute the resources, and the most influential theory is Thibaut and Walker's (1975, 1978) theory of procedure. Both theories have, however, been criticized as too narrowly reflective of the dominant historical, cultural, and ideological trends in American society (Hayden & Anderson, 1979; Hogan & Elmer, 1978; Pepitone, 1976; Sampson, 1975). The main purpose of the present chapter is to show how these two dominant theories of justice may be extended in light of the cross-cultural data available. Thus, rather than being a general review, the present chapter is mainly theoretical and only included data that are relevant to the arguments advanced.

EQUITY THEORY IN
CROSS-CULTURAL PERSPECTIVE

Since the seminal work of Homans (1961) and Adams (1963, 1965), a voluminous literature has accumulated on equity theory (for reviews, see Cook & Hegtvedt, 1983; Greenberg & Cohen, 1982; Walster, Walster, & Berscheid, 1978). Despite the theory's popularity, it has been argued that equity theory has ignored the normative basis of distributive justice, and consequently has viewed equity as an internal, needlike motivational force (Pepitone, 1976). Other authors have further suggested that equity theory reflects an ideological bias of self-contained individualism, a philosophy of life deemed to be typical of Americans (Hogan & Elmer, 1978; Sampson, 1975, 1977). Deutsch (1975) has advanced a similar argument that the dominance of equity theory in American social sciences is probably due to the pervasive influence of economic values on all aspects of social life in America. These authors seem to suggest that equity theory is valid only in North America and possibly in Europe, but not in the rest of the world. Unfortunately, cross-cultural justice research has not received much attention, making a rigorous evaluation of this speculation difficult (for reviews of the limited literature on cross-cultural works, see Gergen, Morse, & Gergen, 1980; Major & Deaux, 1982). In the words of Major & Deaux (1982), "Although a variety of observations and analyses suggest national differences in justice behavior, research on actual behavioral differences is as yet too sparse for strong conclusions to be made" (p. 59). However, several studies have been published subsequent to Major and Deaux's review and may lead to a more optimistic conclusion.

Multiprinciple Approach:
A Recent Development

Equity theorists, notably Walster et al. (1978), regard the proportionality rule specified in equity theory as the only principle of justice. Most other theorists, however, have instead advocated a multiprinciple approach (e.g., Deutsch, 1975; Leventhal, 1976; Sampson, 1969, 1975). Three major allocation norms have been identified: (1) the equity norm, (2) the equality norm, and (3) the need norm.

With the increasing acceptance of the multiprinciple approach, it becomes important to establish the boundary conditions within which the three norms operate. However, Cook and Hegtvedt (1983) have concluded within which the three norms operate. However, Cook and Hegtvedt (1983) have concluded that not much progress has been made in this direction. In the following section, the relation between values and distributive behavior will be examined, as this analysis is vital to establishing such boundary conditions.

Values and Distributive Behavior

Cross-cultural critics of equity theory argue that equity theory is only applicable to societies in which a particular set of values are upheld, such as self-contained individualism (e.g., Sampson, 1975) and marketplace economic values (e.g., Deutsch, 1975). To address these criticisms, equity theory must be expanded to specify the influence of values on distributive behavior. Value differences exist across individuals as well as across cultures. Thus the influence of values on distributive behavior may be studied within one society (e.g., Greenberg, 1978) or across cultures (e.g., Bond, Leung, & Wan, 1982). I would suggest that both approaches are essential. Cross-cultural studies can expose researchers to a wider range of variation in values that affect distributive behavior than can monocultural studies (see Triandis, 1980). In the following, I will draw from recent developments in the research on values to develop a theoretical framework for analyzing the impact of values on distributive behavior. The usefulness of this framework will then be demonstrated by integrating the relevant data collected from different cultures.

A Theoretical Framework for the Influence of Values

Among the many works on values, Rokeach's (1973) theoretical and empirical contributions have been highly influential. In Rokeach's framework, values concerning means or modes of conduct are called instrumental values; those concerning goals or end-states of existence are called terminal values. Instrumental values provide the means for the attainment of terminal values. Although Rokeach regarded instrumental values as providing specific guidelines for idealized modes of conduct, it is not clear from the survey that he created to measure values how instrumental values are linked to specific behaviors. For instance, assuming that we have measured a person's value profile with the Rokeach Value Survey, it is unclear how this information is related to what he or she will do when called upon to allocate a group reward, or how he or she explains the occurrence of poverty or unemployment. Thus, even though Rokeach regards instrumental values as dictating specific modes of conduct, these values appear to be measures of general orientations. Research on personality and on the relation between attitudes and behavior has clearly indicated that such global, abstract concepts are not very predictive of specific behaviors (Epstein, 1979; Fishbein & Ajzen, 1975).

In recognition of this problem, Feather (1975) has proposed a framework that links values with specific behavior. In this framework, which is based on expectancy-value theory, tendencies to perform an act depend on the strength of expectancies (perceived likelihood of occurrence) that this act will lead to specific outcomes and on the valences (perceived values) of these outcomes for the person. Values are regarded as exerting an effect on the valences assigned to potential outcomes, although Feather has actually shown that values affect people's cognitions about social events. For instance, values are found to be consistent with reasons people give for events (Feather, 1971), explanations given for poverty (Feather, 1974) and for unemployment (Feather, 1985), and reasons given by medical students for entering medical school (Feather, 1982).

Feather's theoretical scheme can be used to elucidate the effects of values on distributive behavior. In this framework, it is hypothesized that values affect the beliefs people hold about a distributive situation, and that these cognitions then affect the types of distributive behavior that are salient. Values also affect the valences associated with the outcomes brought by the various models of distributive strategy under consideration. In the following, this scheme will be used to integrate the monocultural as well as the cross-cultural on the relation between values and distributive behavior.

The Impact of Values on Cognitions about Distribution

Protestant Ethic and Distributive Behavior

Based on the famous thesis of Max Weber, Mirels and Garrett (1971) constructed a Protestant Ethic (PE) scale, which measures the extent to which ideals such as asceticism, hard work, and individuality are endorsed. A number of studies have found that people who endorse the PE scale strongly tend to prefer the equity rule over the equality rule (e.g., MacDonald, 1971). According to the framework proposed, this difference occurs because (1) the Protestant ethic leads to a set of cognitions about task performance, which in turn leads to the preference for equity, or (2) the Protestant ethic leads to higher valences associated with the outcomes arising from the application of the equity calculus.

Greenberg (1978, 1979) has conducted a set of experiments that help to differentiate these two possibilities. Greenberg (1979) found that both high and low PE subjects used the equity rule to distribute rewards among workers, but that high PE subjects tended to base the equity rule on both the quantity *and* the duration of a worker's performance, whereas low PE subjects used only the duration information in applying the equity rule. Furthermore, Greenberg (1979) also reported that high PE subjects tended to regard the use of internal factors (ability and effort) in applying the equity rule as fair, and the use of external factors applying the equity rule as fair, and the use of external factors (luck and task difficulty) as unfair. In contrast, low PE subjects regarded the use of internal factors as fair, but to a lesser extent than did high PE subjects. They were neutral toward the use of external factors.

These results suggest that the Protestant ethic is related to the relative weights assigned to different kinds of inputs in applying the equity rule in reward allocation. Endorsement of the Protestant ethic is associated with a higher emphasis placed on input dimensions that are under people's direct control, such as effort and ability. Other empirical evidence for this conclusion can be found in Greenberg (1978) and in Stake (1983).

The reason for the preference for equality among individuals low in PE (e.g., Mirels & Garrett, 1971; MacDonald, 1971) can also be explained by a similar process. The results reviewed above indicate that low endorsement of PE leads to a *lower* emphasis on internal input dimensions. This tendency results in higher perceived similarity of inputs among the participants and thus leads to a more egalitarian allocation.

Why do individuals high in PE place a higher emphasis on internal input dimensions in reward allocation and regard their use as more fair? At present, only speculations can be made. It is probably because high PE individuals perceive the use of internal input dimensions as more likely to lead to better performance and higher productivity, and hence prefer to use them in reward allocation. In other words, endorsement of PE leads to different instrumentality perceptions concerning the use of internal input dimensions. Obviously, more work is necessary to evaluate the validity of this notion.

In the above analysis, the expectancy framework is useful in highlighting the role of instrumentality perceptions in explaining the effects of PE on distributive behavior. At this point, it seems that the effects of PE may not be mediated by different valences placed on the outcomes arising from different patterns of allocation. The heuristic function of this framework will be demonstrated further in the different areas reviewed below.

Perceived Potency and Reward Allocation

Kahn, Lamm, and Nelson (1977) reported that German subjects regarded generous allocators—those whose inputs were high and who used the equality norm in reward allocation—as less potent than did American subjects. In the language of expectancy theory, this result suggests that German and American subjects had different instrumentality perceptions of this particular mode of allocation. Systematic investigation of the cultural differences between Germans and Americans in distributive behavior has not yet begun, but such differences, if uncovered, may be explained by this difference in instrumentality perception.

The Impact of Values on Valences

Is there any evidence for the influence of values on the valences associated with the outcomes following the use of different allocation rules? To my knowledge, no data exist in the monocultural literature that can be used to answer this question. We therefore have to turn to the cross-cultural literature. To sharpen the analysis, two types of outcomes are distinguished. Interpersonal outcomes refer to outcomes resulting from the use of a particular allocation rule and having effects on the group as a whole. In contrast, personal outcomes refer to outcomes that have a direct effect on one particular individual, but have no, or only indirect, effects on other participants.

Interpersonal Outcomes

Deutsch (1975) has proposed that interactional goals of a social context affect the preference for different allocation rules. Specifically, Deutsch suggests that equity will be preferred when the goal is to enhance productivity; equality will be preferred when the goal is to enhance enjoyable social relations; and the need rule will be preferred when the goal is to foster personal development. Subsequent empirical work has supported Deutsch's notions that concern for productivity is related to preference for equity, whereas concern for interpersonal relationships is related to preference for equality (Stake, 1983, 1985). Leung and Park (1986) further confirmed these two results with Korean as well as American subjects. It therefore seems reasonable to assume that people in general perceive the primary outcome of equality and equity as enhancing interpersonal harmony among the participants and the productivity of the group, respectively. The interactional goal behind the need norm has not been tested empirically, and Deutsch's (1975) proposal may be tentatively accepted. That is, the use of the need norm is employed in order to enhance the welfare and well-being of the participants. Thus, if values can affect the valences assigned to these three types of outcomes, they will affect the allocation norm used. For instance, if a certain value orientation leads to placing a higher value on one type of outcome, say interpersonal harmony, individuals who endorse this value orientation will prefer to use equality over the other two rules.

Personal Outcomes

Outcomes of an allocation may have a more direct effect on the individuals involved. Three major types of personal outcome may be identified. First, the use of different allocation rules may lead to different reward levels for the participants. That is, the size of the reward received depends on the rule used. Second, the use of a certain norm will convey a particular social image about the allocator and the recipient to observers and to other participants (see Reis, 1981). Third, the use of a particular allocation norm may have an impact on one's self-concept, such as an enhanced belief in one's fairness.

Values and Interperson Outcomes

The effects of collectivism. A major dimension of cultural variation is individualism-collectivism (Hofstede, 1980, 1983; Hsu, 1970; Triandis, 1987). Cultures that endorse individualism, such as countries in North American and in Europe, place a higher value on autonomy, competitiveness, achievement, and self-sufficiency. In contrast, cultures endorsing collectivism, such as countries in South America and Asia, place a higher value on interpersonal harmony and group solidarity. Based on this conceptualization of individualism and collectivism, it can be predicted that collectivists would prefer equality to a larger extent than would individualists, because they place a higher value on interpersonal harmony. On the other hand, individualists would prefer equity to a larger extent than collectivists because they value achievement and self-sufficiency more.

It has been pointed out that the distinction between ingroups and outgroups is more salient in collectivist cultures (e.g., Leung & Bond, 1984; Triandis, 1972). Thus Leung and Bond proposed that the above analysis may only be applicable to ingroup situations. When outgroup members are involved, collectivists may behave like individualists and use the equity norm. Consistent with this reasoning, Bond et al. (1982) and Leung and Bond (1982) found that Chinese subjects (collectivists) used the equality norm to a larger extent than did American subjects (individualists) in assigning rewards to classmates with whom they had finished a group project. This situation involved ingroup members and the pattern supports the previous analysis. When outgroup members were involved, however, there was evidence showing that collectivists tend to use the equity norm. For instance, Mahler, Greenberg, and Hayashi (1981) found no difference between Japanese and American subjects in their allocation of a profit between two carpenters who were acquaintances and invested together to buy a house. Marin (1981) found that Colombian subjects used the equity norm to a larger extent than did American subjects in allocating a reward between two strangers who worked together in a psychological experiment. Aral and Sunar (1977) found that Turkish subjects used the equity norm to a larger extent than did American subjects in allocating a reward between two architects who designed a project together. Judging from the scenario they used, these two architects were merely acquaintances and can be regarded as having an outgroup relationship. These three studies supported the argument that when outgroup members are involved, collectivists (Japanese, Colombians, and Turks) also used the equity norm, and may even use it to a larger extent than do individualists (Americans).

The more direct evidence for this reasoning comes from a study by Leung and Bond (1984) in which they explicitly manipulated the ingroup-outgroup variable. They found that with outgroup members (strangers), Chinese subjects followed the equity norm more closely than did American subjects. With ingroup members (friends), however, Chinese subjects preferred a norm that could benefit ingroup recipients. Note that in this study the allocators also received part of the reward.

Results from two recent studies seem to be inconsistent with the Leung and Bond formulation. Marin (1985) found no difference between Indonesian and American subjects in their allocation to ingroup recipients. However, this result must be interpreted with caution because the Indonesian subjects in the study were students studying in the United States and had stayed there for an average of 20 months. Leung and Iwawaki (1986) found that Japanese, Korean, and American subjects showed no difference in their allocation to ingroup recipients. However, Leung and Kwawaki argued the most probable reason for this result was that the three university student groups did *not* differ in their collectivism levels as measured by Hui's (1984) collectivism scale. Thus the results from these two studies can be explained and do not necessarily contradict the Leung and Bond framework.

The Leung and Bond formulation can easily fit into the expectancy framework discussed earlier. Because of their collectivist orientation, collectivists value interpersonal harmony more with ingroup members. This higher valence placed on interpersonal harmony leads them to prefer allocation rules than result in a larger share for the ingroup recipients. Thus the effect of collectivism on reward allocation is interpreted through its effect on the valence assigned to outcomes of reward allocation rather than the cognitions about the distributive situation.

The effects of resource scarcity. Murphy-Berman, Berman, Singh, Pachauri, and Kumar (1984) studied the extent to which the three norms (equality, equity, and need) were used by Indian and American subjects. They found that a larger proportion of Indian subjects used the need norm than did American subjects. This pattern was replicated in a similar study that also compared Indian and American subjects (Berman, Murphy-Berman, & Singh, 1985).

At this point, the reason for this cultural difference can only be surmised. After a review of the literature, Greenberg (1981) concluded that in allocating a scarce resource, the need norm predominates and is regarded as fair. It may be argued that the underdeveloped economic conditions in India produce a heightened awareness of the scarcity of material resources. Consequently, Indian subjects placed higher valence on the outcome arising fro the use of the need norm—protecting the well-being of the participants—and hence used the need norm more frequently. The effect of resource scarcity on the valence assigned to the welfare of group members should be further evaluated in future research.

Values and Personal Outcomes

Weick, Bougon, and Maruyama (1976) compared the preferences of Dutch and American subjects for different forms of equity and inequity. It was found that Dutch subjects preferred situations involving high inputs for self, whereas American subjects preferred high outcomes for self. Weick et al. (1976) explained this cultural difference as caused by a Calvinistic heritage in the Netherlands that places a high value on inputs and deemphasizes the importance of outcomes. This result fits nicely into the expectancy framework. The higher valence placed on high inputs, rather than different instrumentality perceptions of high inputs, led Dutch subjects to prefer situations involving high inputs.

Section Conclusions

A framework that clarifies the effects of values on distributive behavior was proposed and shown to be consistent with the monocultural as well as the cross-cultural literature. Specifically, cross-cultural data have extended the range of variables and processes considered, such as perceived potency, collectivism, resource scarcity, and Calvinism, and have opened up some new directions for future research.

CULTURE AND PROCEDURAL JUSTICE

This section reviews the inputs of cross-cultural data to advancing theories of procedural justice. The dominant theory here is Thibaut and Walker's (1975, 1978) theory of procedure. Their earlier works have focused on the perceptions of the characteristics of several legal procedures, and subsequent works have included nonlegal settings, such as organizational settings (e.g., Greenberg & Folger, 1983). The major finding in these studies is that procedures granting the disputants process control (control of the evidence and arguments presented in the course of the processing of the conflict) *and* place the decision making (control of the outcomes of the conflict) in the hands of a disinterested third party are preferred and regarded as most fair. An example embodying these characteristics is the adversary procedure used in the courts of English-speaking countries (Thibaut & Walker, 1978).

Because the adversary adjudicatory system is used in American courts, Thibaut and Walker (1975) suspected that the preference for it may be due to greater familiarity with the procedure, rather than to the process control accorded disputants under this procedure. To address this question, procedural research has been extended to societies in which other forms of legal procedures are used, such as France and West Germany. It turns out that adversary procedures are also preferred by French and German subjects (Lind, Erickson, Friedland, & Dickenberger, 1978). This result was interpreted as a strong support for the theory of procedure proposed by Thibaut and Walker.

Anthropologists, however, have reported findings inconsistent with the work of Thibaut and Walker (1975). For instance, Nader and Todd (1978) have argued that, for societies in which people's circle of social interaction is limited and interpersonal relationships are stable and ongoing, methods of dispute resolution such as mediation and negotiation that allow for compromise over the outcomes are preferred. In societies in which people's social sphere is large and constantly changing, methods such as adjudication and arbitration, which usually result in all-or-nothing outcomes, are preferred (for a similar argument, see also Bond, Wan, Leung, & Giacalone, 1985; Gulliver, 1979). Thus mediation is reported by anthropologists to be preferred in Japan (e.g., Henderson, 1975; Kawashima, 1963; Peterson & Shimada, 1979), Chinese societies (Doo, 1973; Lubman, 1967), and Mexico (Nader, 1969).

Values and Procedural Preferences

Leung and Lind (1986) argued that the inconsistent findings reported by Thibaut, Walker, and their associates and by anthropologists can be reconciled by taking into account a culture's collectivism. Thus the stronger preference for adversary procedures would be found in individualist cultures (United States, England, France, and West Germany), whereas preference for mediation would be found in collectivist cultures, such as Japan and Mexico.

How does collectivism affect procedural preference? The expectancy framework discussed before is also useful in explicating the effect of collectivism. First, collectivism may affect the valences people place on the outcomes resulting from the application of different procedures. Collectivism is often associated with a stronger emphasis on interpersonal harmony (e.g., Hofstede, 1980; Triandis, 1984). As mediation is more effective than adjudication in leading to animosity reduction (e.g., Pruitt, 1982; Rubin & Brown, 1975), collectivists' preference for mediation can be explained by their desire for animosity reduction.

A second explanation can also be generated. Collectivists do not value interpersonal harmony with outgroup members more than individualists (e.g., Bond & Wang, 1983; Kawashima, 1963), and disputants are likely to be perceived as outgroup members. Thus collectivists' preference for mediation may not reflect a higher valence placed on animosity reduction, but rather may reflect different instrumentality perceptions of these procedures. Collectivists may prefer mediation over adjudication because they believe that mediation is more likely than adjudication to lead to animosity reduction. No cultural differences in the valence placed on animosity reduction is assumed in this explanation.

These two explanations of collectivists' preference for mediation were evaluated in a recent study with Chinese and American subjects (Leung, in press). Results showed that Chinese subjects preferred mediation and negotiation to a larger extent than American subjects, and that Chinese subjects preferred mediation and negotiation because they perceived these procedures as more likely to lead to animosity reduction, but not because they valued animosity reduction more. Thus these results support the instrumentality explanation of collectivists' preference for nonbinding procedures.

Section Conclusions

Recent cross-cultural research has uncovered a number of factors that have been ignored in mainstream research on procedural justice (see Leung, in press). For instance, capacity for animosity reduction turned out to be an important factor that affects people's procedural preference (Lissak & Sheppard, 1983), and its importance is highlighted in cross-cultural studies (e.g., Leung, in press). Obviously, a comprehensive theory of procedural justice cannot ignore this factor. Finally, as in distributive justice, the expectancy framework is useful for explaining cultural differences in procedural preferences.

GENERAL CONCLUSIONS

In this chapter the two most researched areas in social justice were reviewed with an emphasis on the contributions of cross-cultural data to theory-building. A general framework, based on expectancy theory, was proposed and shown capable of procedural justice. This framework offers a systematic way to conceptualize cultural differences and is useful for guiding future research efforts.

In the present review, cross-cultural studies were used as tools to broaden and improve theories of justice. I hope that this chapter has alerted mainstream justice researchers to some important issues by introducing them to relevant cross-cultural research and theorizing. The area of social justice will definitely benefit from data collected in different regions of the world, where both social and economic conditions are so diverse.

18

ATTRIBUTION THEORY AND PROCESSES
A Cross-Cultural Perspective

GARTH J.O. FLETCHER
COLLEEN WARD

Attribution theory is primarily concerned with describing and explaining the cognitive processes involved in the layperson's causal explanations for human behavior. The major theoretical thrust in attribution theory has been provided by Heider (1958), Jones (Jones & Davis, 1965), Kelley (1967), and Weiner (Weiner et al., 1971). However, the genesis of attribution theory is usually traced to Fritz Heider (1958), who presented a brilliant pastiche of provocative ideas concerning the causal attribution process. Jones, Kelley, and Weiner developed and expanded some of Heider's key ideas and produced more explicit and testable attribution models. The result was an explosion of research in the 1970s as attribution theory became one of the dominant fields in social psychology.

Interest and research in attribution theory has continued apace in the 1980s, though moving in a number of different directions. In the classic attribution models the layperson is assumed to have aims similar to those of the scientist: explanation, understanding, prediction, and control. Many of the inevitable theoretical debates have concerned the appropriateness and validity of this "naive scientist" model (Buss, 1978; Fincham & Jaspars, 1980). In addition, a number of competing attribution models have been advanced, though these have invariably used important elements from the earlier classic models (Kelley, 1983; Reeder & Brewer, 1979; Trope, 1986).

Several major trends have also become apparent in recent attribution research. First, interest has shifted away from testing the earlier models to answering other basic questions, such as what motivates the search for causes (Weiner, 1985). Second, there has been increased interest in individual differences in attributional thinking, with scales being developed to measure a variety of constructs, including attributional

AUTHORS' NOTE: We would like to thank Julie Fitness and Miles Hewstone for their valuable comments on a draft of this chapter. We also thank Ming Singer for providing a translation of several articles written in Mandarin.

style (Peterson et al., 1982) and the complexity of attributional schemata (Fletcher, Danilovics, Fernandez, Peterson, & Reeder, 1986). Third, attribution theory has been exported and applied to a wide range of areas within psychology, including emotions (Weiner, Russell, & Lerman, 1978), close relationships (Fincham, 1985; Fletcher, Fincham, Cramer, & Heron, in press), education (Weiner, 1979), therapeutic interventions (Forsterling, 1986), depression (Peterson & Seligman, 1984), and cross-cultural psychology (Bond, 1983).

In a major review of attribution theory and research, Ross and Fletcher (1985) portrayed the classic attribution models as partial and oversimplified, but standing up rather well to the barrage of research; they concluded that "attribution research represents a dynamic and innovative area of astonishing diversity and intellectual vigor, from which much can be learned" (p. 114). These authors might well have added, however, that their conclusions applied principally to North American society, with perhaps a nod toward other Western cultures. The question posed in the current review is just how well the same attribution models fare when applied to other cultures. To what extent are attribution schemata and processes universal?

We trust that the above skeletal summary will give those readers who are not attribution aficionados enough background to make our review intelligible. Where necessary we will provide brief descriptions of the relevant attribution theories. For those who wish to know more, a number of extensive reviews of attribution theory and research are available (Harvey & Weary, 1984; Kelley & Michela, 1980; Ross & Fletcher, 1985).

Virtually all cross-cultural research investigating causal attributions utilizes the classic pioneering attribution models. In this chapter we shall first consider the cross-cultural research dealing with Kelley's attributional model. Second, we will review the work carried out concerning achievement attributions (Weiner's model). Third, we will cover the research dealing with intergroup attributions. Fourth, we shall attempt to answer the question of whether the underlying cognitive dimensions in attributional schemata are universal. Finally, we shall critically examine some of the major issues and problems confronting cross-cultural attribution research.

KELLEY'S CAUSAL ATTRIBUTION MODEL

In Kelley's (1967) model, people utilize information emanating from three different sources in determining causal judgments: consensus, consistency, and distinctiveness. Further, Kelley hypothesized that different levels of these information sources would produce causal attributions that ranged along the internal-external dimension. For example, suppose I like a restaurant, and I know that (a) other people like the restaurant (high consensus), (b) I always like the restaurant (high consistency), and (c) I seldom like restaurants (high distinctiveness): I should conclude that it is a good restaurant (an external attribution). Alternately, the combination of low consensus, high consistency, and low distinctiveness should produce an internal (person) attribution; for example, I am a glutton.

To our knowledge only one study has tested Kelley's model in a cross-cultural context. Cha and Nam (1985) replicated the methodology pioneered by McArthur (1972) with Korean subjects who were supplied with brief descriptions of behavioral episodes and information concerning consensus, distinctiveness, and consistency. The results were remarkably similar to those found by McArthur in the United States and supported Kelley's model. As usual in cross-cultural comparisons, some differences were found; for example, Korean subjects used more external attributions than subjects in the United States.

Although there is a paucity of experimental research dealing with Kelley's model, many anthropological accounts contain rich cultural descriptions that include material relevant to attributional thinking. A good example is found in Malinowski's (1948) study of the Trobriand Islanders. The Kiriwina, like people in some other traditional cultures, were not fully aware of the causal role that impregnation plays in reproduction. Malinowski reported that when seeking to convince his native informants of the true causal account, they occasionally challenged him to explain the fact that the supposed cause was repeated daily yet produced effects so rarely—clear evidence that these informants understood the covariation principle that is an underlying rule in Kelley's model. A second example relevant to Kelley's model comes from Jahoda's (1982) analysis of the Azande's ritual use of the poison oracle. This ritual involves using a poison of uncertain strength on a fowl. A question is then asked and whether the fowl dies or not determines the answer. However, new poison is first tested to determine that it kill some fowls and spare others, rather than being so strong that it kills all the fowls or so weak that it leaves them all living. In addition, the previous procedure is used on more than one fowl with the same question to determine reliability. In terms of Kelley's attribution model, we have two of the three information dimensions perfectly represented—distinctiveness and consistency. While a systematic analysis of the anthropological literature is beyond the purview of this chapter, the examples cited here suggest that Kelley's model has some generality across cultures.

ACHIEVEMENT ATTRIBUTIONS

A good deal of cross-cultural research has been directed at attributions for achievements. Heider (1958) proposed that an individual's level of performance on a task can be attributed to internal factors (ability or effort) or external sources (luck or task difficulty). In elaborating Heider's ideas, Weiner and his colleagues (Weiner et al., 1971) postulated three important dimensions underlying these causal attributions: stability, locus of causality, and controllability. Stability refers to temporal duration—for instance, ability is a stable dispositional attribution whereas effort is unstable and often short-lived. Locus of causality refers to spatial location—for instance, ability is internal and task difficulty is external. Controllability refers to the level of perceived control—for instance, effort is very controllable while ability is less controllable. The latter two dimensions compose the familiar internal-external dimension that is a fundamental component in the classic attribution models.

The methodologies used in cross-cultural research have largely been borrowed from mainstream research. Three techniques have predominantly been used to test Heider's or Weiner's model of achievement attributions in cross-cultural settings. Some studies have manipulated the causal attributions (e.g., ability and effort) in written scenarios and measured various outcomes, such as rewards or punishments and predictions of performance (Betancourt & Weiner, 1982; Gupta & Singh, 1981; Iida, Reeder, McCabe, Miura, & Goldstein, 1986; Singh & Bhargava, 1985). In other studies subjects have judged the importance of various factors (usually ability, effort, task difficulty, and luck) as causes of their own or others' successes and failures in various hypothetical or factual scenarios (Chandler, Shama, Wolf, & Planchard, 1981; Holloway, Kashiwagi, Hess, & Azuma, 1986; Kuo, 1983; Powers & Rossman, 1984; Sagatun, 1981; Smith & Whitehead, 1984; Watkins, 1982; Watkins & Astilla, 1984; Yang, 1982). Finally, a third group of studies has directly manipulated success and failure in laboratory tasks with the causal attributions treated as the dependent variables (Boski, 1983; Fry & Ghosh, 1980; Kashima & Triandis, 1986; Salili, Maeher, Sorensen, & Fyans, 1976).

A review of these studies suggests that two attribution patterns apply across a diverse range of cultures: (a) High ability and high effort (as compared to low ability and low effort) are rewarded and perceived as predictive of high achievement, and (b) success is explained by internal causes (ability and effort), whereas failure is related more strongly to external causes (such as luck and task difficulty). This latter tendency is often referred to as a self-serving or egocentric bias, though it is possible to explain it in colder, information processing terms (Ross & Fletcher, 1985).

Of course, the studies cited above have also uncovered a host of differences between cultures. For example, Japanese students (compared to United States subjects) put a higher value on the amount of effort expended and rather less importance on the actual outcome, whether it be success or failure (Iida et al., 1986; Holloway et al., 1986). In addition, running counter to the usual egocentric bias, Japanese adults seem to attribute failures as much as successes to their own abilities (Chandler et al., 1981; Kashima & Triandis, 1986). Kashima and Triandis argue that the self-serving bias is an individual coping strategy that is less likely to occur in societies in which collective coping is the norm. In Japan mutual support and effort toward a group aim are given more importance than individual achievement, whereas the United States is an individualistic culture in which self-reliance and individual competition and achievement are highly valued (Spence, 1985). One problem with this explanation is that other collectivist cultures, such as India, seem to produce strong self-serving attributional patterns (Chandler et al., 1981). Both the general finding and Kashima and Triandis's account clearly warrant further investigation.

One issue raised by the findings noted above concerning the Japanese is that caution should be exercised before labeling attribution tendencies as self-serving or otherwise. Whether an attributional bias is self-serving or not will presumably depend on the structure of the self being served, and given that concepts of the self seem to vary across cultures (Marsella, DeVos, & Hsu, 1985; Miller, Chap. 20, this volume), we cannot assume universality in this context. We can easily imagine a culture, for example, in which accepting equal responsibility for both positive and negative outcomes represents a powerful norm and is a central feature of the inhabitants' self concepts. In such a culture an even-handed attributional pattern could presumably be interpreted as self-serving.[1]

A second example of cultural differences has been documented by Singh and his colleagues (Gupta & Singh, 1981; Singh & Bhargava, 1985; Singh, Gupta, & Dalal, 1979), who have shown that Indian students combine ability and effort information in an additive fashion when predicting performance. In contrast, American students treat them in a multiplicative fashion: For example, a student of low ability is perceived as being restricted to a relatively narrow performance range no matter how much effort is expended; conversely, a student of high ability is seen as being capable of greater improvement in performance if more effort is made (Surber, 1981). Singh and Bhargava explain this difference in terms of the collectivism of Indian culture as compared to the individualism of North American culture, although they do not make it clear how this cultural variable is causally related to the attributional differences between the cultures. However, we believe the finding deserves further attention.

One problem with the research cited above (with a few notable exceptions, such as Kashima & Triandis, 1986, and Watkins & Astilla, 1984) is that the attribution dependent measures (ability, effort, task difficulty, and luck) were preselected on the basis of the intuitions of the pioneering attribution theorists concerning the attribution process as it operates within Western cultures. We suspect that researchers have simply borrowed an approach commonly used in mainstream psychology. Such procedures have problems enough carried out within Western cultures (Fletcher, 1984; Ross & Fletcher, 1985). Their use becomes doubly suspect when applied to cross-cultural research because it implies that the attribution categories are given the same meanings across cultures, that the response distributions are the same on each scale, and that the underlying attributional dimensions are the same.[2] Fortunately, more recent cross-cultural work has shown that these assumptions may not be completely wide of the mark. We describe this research below.

A number of cross-cultural studies have used a free-response approach to content analyze academic attributions offered by students for successes and failures. The cultures examined include whites, blacks, and Indians in South Africa (Louw & Louw-Potgieter, 1986), Japanese students (Kashima & Triandis, 1986), Indian students (Misra & Agarwal, 1985), and Sri Lankan students (Niles, 1985). These studies have shown that ability, effort, and task difficulty are commonly mentioned, while luck is a less popular category. However, other kinds of causes are often mentioned, such as attitudes, mood, and health. The results from these studies show a remarkable convergence with data collected using the same free-response methodology in North America (Weiner, 1979).[3]

In summary, the above research has shown a surprising degree of similarity in achievement attributions across cultures. One caveat to this conclusion is that the research cited above used samples of secondary (high) school or university students. In many non-Western societies, relatively few people progress through the education system to such a level. Hence it could be argued that such samples in non-Western societies form distinct subcultural groups that have relatively more exposure to Western values through an education system that is liable to reflect values and beliefs that are relatively individualistic and achievement oriented.

THE GROUP-SERVING ATTRIBUTION BIAS

We have previously described the self-serving or egocentric bias in attributions. The equivalent bias at the group level has been labeled the ethnocentric or group-serving bias. (See Hewstone & Jaspars, 1982, for a discussion of intergroup relations and attributional processes.) These terms refer to the tendency for ingroup members to attribute internal causes to positive ingroup behaviors and negative outgroup behaviors, whereas external causes are attributed to negative ingroup behaviors and positive outgroup behaviors. Many studies have established that this phenomenon is pervasive and relatively robust within Western cultures across various groups, including ethnic groups (Stephan, 1985). One reason for the importance of the group-serving bias is that it supplies a mechanism by which stereotypical beliefs and prejudices can be maintained in the face of apparently conflicting behavioral evidence. Hence this bias helps explain the persistence with which erroneous negative stereotypes of outgroup members are often maintained.

The cross-cultural evidence concerning the group-serving bias is iinconsistent. Several studies have found evidence for the existence of the group-serving bias in non-Western settings. Hewstone, Bond, and Wan (1983) reported that Chinese students from different universities in Hong Kong made group-serving attributions favoring members of their own universities. Taylor and Jaggi (1974) found that Hindu subjects attributed internal causes for socially desirable behaviors performed by ingroup members and external attributions for undesirable behaviors. The reverse pattern was found for attributions to behaviors performed by Muslim outgroup members. However, a number of studies have found evidence that the group-serving bias is either nonexistent or markedly attenuated in some non-Western cultures (e.g., Bond et al., 1985; Boski, 1983). Our analysis of this research has thrown up three factors that we think may be important in generating the group-serving bias: cultural values or beliefs, general sociocultural factors, and behavioral expectations based on underlying stereotypes of the in-groups and the outgroups. We will briefly discuss each set of factors in turn.

Cultural Values or Beliefs

It seems likely that there exist cultural values or beliefs, distnct from the wider societal context, that may accentuate or dilute the group-serving bias. The available research suggests, for example, that the Chinese are relatively resistant to the group-serving bias (Bond et al., 1985; Hewstone & Ward, 1985). One plausible explanation for this is the value placed on modesty and harmony in Chinese societies (Bond, Leung, & Wan, 1982).

Sociocultural Factors

Various authors have speculated on the impact that wider socio-cultural factors may have on the group-serving bias. Pettigrew (1979) suggests that this bias will be greater among groups with a history of conflict or in which racial and ethnic differences coincide with national or socioeconomic differences. Deschamps (1973-1974) has argued that these biases should be most prominent in socially dominant majority groups or groups of equal status; minority groups, by contrast, might be expected to display outgroup favoring attributions. In accord with the latter suggestion, Hewstone and Ward (1985) found that Chinese students in Malaysia, who belong to a politically threatened but economically stable minority, made favorable outgroup attributions and unfavorable ingroup attributions—a reversal of the usual group-serving bias. In contrast, the Malay students, who are members of the politically powerful but economically disadvantaged majority group, produced strong group-serving attributions. Hewstone and Ward then repeated the experiment in Singapore, where the Chinese are in the majority and where ethnicity appears to be a less salient issue than in Malaysia (Clammer, 1982; Ward & Hewstone, 1985). In line with predictions, the Chinese students exhibited a neutral pattern of attributions, neither derogating themselves nor favoring the Malays in their attributions. The Malays evinced a weaker, but still significant, group-serving bias.

Expectations and the Favorability of
Ingroup and Outgroup Stereotypes

A standard account for the group-serving attributional bias would be in terms of expectations based on ingroup and outgroup stereotypes or social categorizations (Jaspars & Hewstone, 1982; Tajfel, 1978). If we assume that stereotypes are positive for ingroups and negative for outgroups, then positive behaviors by ingroup members, being consistent with these dispositions, will be attributed to such dispositions. In contrast, positive behaviors by outgroup members will be inconsistent with these preconceived, negative, stereotypical dispositions, and hence will be attributed to external causes. The opposite pattern will pertain to negative behaviors. These expectancies do not need to be behaviorally specific but may consist merely of general affective attitudes (Greenberg & Rosenfield, 1979).[4]

Again, Hewstone and Ward's (1985) study reported evidence consistent with the above attributional model. The Chinese students in Malaysia who evinced a reversal of the group-serving bias also held negative Chinese stereotypes; however, they possessed more positive ingroup stereotypes in Singapore, where the bias reversal did not occur. The Malays living in Malaysia exhibited a pronounced group-serving bias and held strong negative Chinese stereotypes, whereas in Singapore the Malay's group-serving bias was diluted and the accompanying negative Chinese stereotyping was substantially weaker. Hewstone and Ward's study also importantly suggests that the relative favorability of ingroup versus outgroup stereotypes is causally connected to wider sociocultural factors.

To conclude, the existing evidence, though scanty, supports the view that similar attribution processes are involved across cultures in producing the group-serving bias. However, the group-serving bias seems malleable and influenced by a range of sociocultural factors. Our analysis highlights the need to consider general cognitive processes that may be universal but at the same time remain sensitive to local cultural influences. What begins as ingroup versus outgroup stereotyping frequently ends up as prejudice and intergroup conflict. There can be few areas more important for social psychologists and cross-cultural psychologists to study and understand.

ARE THE UNDERLYING DIMENSIONS
OF CAUSAL SCHEMATA UNIVERSAL?

The central causal dimension in the classic attribution models is the internal-external dimension. Cross-cultural researchers have sometimes simply assumed that the internal-external dimension applies cross-culturally and have created composite indices of internal or external attributions (e.g., Chandler et al., 1981). Surprisingly little attention has been paid to the question of whether the same dimensions underpin causal schemata in different cultures, and hence whether these procedures are justified.

What evidence there is suggests that the central causal dimensions, such as the internal-external dimension, may indeed be universal. Betancourt and Weiner (1982) had students from Chile and the United States make direct judgments of the stability, locus, and controllability of various causes that were contained in written scenarios. The results were in accordance with Weiner's model for both samples. In a rare factor analytic study, Watkins and Astilla (1984) found clear evidence for the existence of the stability and controllability dimensions in the causal judgments of Filipino high school students. Again, these results are consistent with factor analytic studies carried out with North American students (Ross & Fletcher, 1985).

Miller (1984) obtained open-ended explanations of prosocial and deviant behaviors from Indian Hindus and North American subjects. The causal attributions were placed in different categories using a taxonomy based on the familiar internal-external dimension. The major difference found between cultures was the Indian adults of all socioeconomic levels made less reference to personal dispositions (Indian $M = 20\%$, U.S. $M = 40\%$) and more reference to external factors (Indian $M = 40\%$, U.S. $M = 18\%$), particularly social roles and interpersonal relationships. Miller's explanation, in a similar vein to those already described, is in terms of the more individualistic conception of the person in Western cultures, whereas the individual in non-Western cultures is conceived of in a more holistic fashion, and as more closely linked to the social and nonsocial environment. Perhaps such non-Western beliefs are realistically grounded in the fact that in collectivist cultures, compared to noncollectivist cultures, the external roles and norms actually have a more substantial causal impact on the individual's behavior (Jahoda, 1982). However, given that both cultures produced similar numbers of attributions overall and that a reasonably fine-grained coding taxonomy of attributions appeared to be meaningful and applicable across both cultures, one could reasonably conclude that the two cultures share the same general features of attribution schemata.

This apparent preference for external attributions in Indian society has also been found by Dalal, Sharma, and Bisht (1983). Their findings and Miller's results are relevant to a much studied social perception bias dubbed the "fundamental attribution error" by Ross (1977). This bias consists of the tendency to underestimate the causal role of situational determinants of behavior and overestimate the causal role of the internal determinants. An impressive array of research has confirmed the existence and pervasiveness of this phenomenon in Western cultures (Jones, 1979; Reeder, 1985). However, doubts have been raised concerning just how fundamental the "fundamental attribution error" is (Harvey, Town, & Yarkin, 1981). The cross-cultural findings noted above reinforce these doubts.

Cross-cultural work like Miller's is also relevant to how such biases may be explained within Western cultures. A popular explanation for the fundamental attribution error, though not the only one, is couched in terms of basic perceptual processes (Ross & Fletcher, 1985). Heider (1958) writes, "Behavior in particular has such salient properties it tends to engulf the total field, rather than be confined to its proper position as a local stimulus whose interpretation requires the additional data of a surrounding field—the situation in social perception" (p. 54). The cross-cultural findings suggest either that these perceptual processors are not centrally involved with the bias in Western settings or that other culturally derived processes or beliefs are quite capable of reversing or altering their impact. Either way, further cross-cultural research holds the promise of increasing our understanding of attribution processes within specific cultures and at a universal level.

Finally, indirect evidence concerning the cross-cultural viability of the internal-external dimension comes from research dealing with a topic not usually classed with attribution theory, namely, Rotter's concept of locus of control. Rotter's (1966) original scale was intended to be a measure of the generalized expectation for internal versus external control of reinforcement. Factor analytic studies have shown that both Rotter's scale and other scales developed to measure the same construct (e.g., Levenson, 1972) are not unidimensional (see Hui, 1982, for a review). One commonly found structure was reported by Collins (1974), who labeled the factors as difficult-easy world, predictable-unpredictable world, just-unjust world, and politically responsive-unresponsive world.

A good deal of research has compared the externality scores (either using the total or subscale scores) across cultures. Not surprisingly, given the kind of methodological problems already described, direct comparisons of scores derived from the same scales across cultures have not produced consistent results (Hui, 1982). For example, when compared to Caucasians, Hispanics have been reported as having higher externality (Castro, 1976; Kagan, 1976; Pehazur & Wheeler, 1971), lower externality (Cole & Cole, 1974, 1977; Garza & Ames, 1974), and the same levels of externality (Alvarez & Pader, 1978; Cole, Rodriguez, & Cole, 1978; Jessor, Graves, Hanson, & Jessor, 1968). The results have been mixed when scores were derived from the subscale dimensions (Buriel & Rivera, 1980; Reitz & Groff, 1972).

Comparisons between the factorial structures across cultures have also produced inconsistent results. However, our review of the literature has shown that of Collins's four factors described above, the most consistently replicated have been the predictable-unpredictable world and difficult-easy world constructs (Barling, 1980; Hui & Triandis, 1983; Munro, 1979; Nagelschmidt & Jakob, 1977; Ryckman, Posen, & Kulberg, 1978; Trimble & Richardson, 1982). This is significant because our reading of the items loading on these two factors, compared to the other items in the scale, suggests they represent constructs that are close to the traditional internal-external control dimension so beloved of attribution theorists.[5]

CROSS-CULTURAL RESEARCH: PROBLEMS AND PROSPECTS

In evaluating the challenge that cross-cultural psychology presents to mainstream social psychology in this area, we need to consider the major problems and lacunae inherent in cross-cultural attributional research. We have previously alluded to some of these points; here we shall briefly summarize and explicate the major issues.

It is clear from our review that cross-cultural research has been concerned with a rather narrow range of issues and questions (Bond, 1983). For example, without any particular rationale being offered, researchers have concentrated on two particular aspects of attribution theory: causal attributions for achievements and the individual difference construct of internal-external locus of control. These emphases have a haphazard ring about them. Kelley's model of causal attributions is probably the most influential and general causal theory within mainstream psychology (Ross & Fletcher, 1985). Given this model's potential cross-cultural applicability, it is not obvious why it has received so little attention from cross-cultural psychologists. In addition, most of the research has focused on cross-cultural comparisons between ratings of specific causes, such as ability or effort attributions. Little interest has been shown in the underlying causal dimensions that are central to the classic attribution formulations. We think that it is important for cross-cultural comparisons to be carried out at this deeper level of cognitive structure.

A further set of issues concerns how general cultural differences in beliefs or values are typically used by researchers to explain attributional differences between cultures. In the literature already cited, for example, the individualistic nature of Western cultures, as against the more collective nature of non-Western cultures, was often invoked to explain attributional differences concerned with topics as varied as the way effort and ability information are combined, the proportion of attributions given to the person or the situation, and the extent of the self-serving or group-serving attribution bias. Such general cultural variables are extremely vague and can be plausibly linked to an innumerable number of cultural differences. In short, such accounts lack explanatory and predictive power.

There are of course any number of ways to test these cultural explanations. We will suggest two general strategies. First, we think there is a need to develop more precise and powerful models linking general cultural variables, such as beliefs, values, or behavioral patterns, with subsequent attributional judgments by the postulation of intermediary cognitive components. A simple example is the model described earlier, dealing with group-serving attributional biases, that links ingroup and outgroup stereotypes and behavioral expectations with subsequent attributions. However, to our knowledge this model has not been explicitly tested in cross-cultural settings.[6]

The second strategy we propose is a methodological one, namely, measuring the hypothesized intervening cultural or cognitive variables as well as the dependent attribution variables. This enables path analytic or multiple regression procedures to be used in order to estimate the causal impact of such intervening variables. Although this is potentially a powerful design, we know of only a few cross-cultural studies that have used such techniques in the attribution realm (Detweiler, 1978; Schneider, Borkowski, Kurtz, & Kerwin, 1986).[7]

We shall close this section with a few general points concerning an attributional cross-cultural agenda. First, many of the criticisms that can be leveled at cross-cultural attributional work can be, and have been, directed at mainstream social psychology. Second, in line with other prescriptive agendas offered for cross-cultural attribution research (e.g., Bond, 1983), our recommendations involve a one-way traffic, namely, developing theories and methodologies within Western contexts and transporting and applying them within other cultures. In this respect our agenda is consistent with current attributional research, indeed with cross-cultural work generally. However, we believe that a two-way approach may be a more productive strategy. Moreover, it seems to us an open question whether or not the cultural origin of the original theory will influence the results of subsequent cross-cultural comparisons, even when the same methodologies are used. One promising direction for attribution theory, then, may be the development of indigenous attribution theories within non-Western cultures. A rare example of this approach is exemplified by Yang and Ho's (in press) intriguing Heiderian analysis of *Yuan* attributions, which are common attributions for relationship outcomes in Chinese society.

Finally, despite the limitations and problems associated with the extant cross-cultural attribution research, we believe it makes a significant contribution to our understanding of attribution processes. The findings reveal an interesting and important pattern of similarities and differences across cultures. The similarities suggest that the fundamental features of causal schemata are universal. However, this does not mean that the differences found between cultures are merely cosmetic; for example, the self-serving and group-serving attribution biases and the fundamental attribution error represent two of the most robust and well-replicated attributional phenomena in Western cultures. Yet, as we have seen, the cross-cultural evidence indicates these phenomena are not universal. Attempting to understand why such differences exist between cultures holds the promise for a deeper understanding of attribution processes and how they function within Western and non-Western cultures alike.

NOTES

1. We are indebted to Ming Singer for raising this particular issue.

2. These difficulties are not confined to this body of research but are recognized as general problems within cross-cultural psychology (Ward, 1987). Hui and Triandis (1983) give an excellent account of these and other methodological issues and present strategies to deal with them.

3. Louw and Louw-Potgieter (1986) claim their results do not replicate the North American data. However, their study used 36 coding categories—a much finer set of categories than used in other research. It is true that "academic ability" attributions are scarcely mentioned by their subjects. However, these authors have included five other categories in their taxonomy, such as "understanding the subject matter" and "English speaking ability," that would usually be classified as ability attributions. Suitably recast, their data look similar to results reported in other research.

4. The question of why attitudes toward ingroups are characteristically more positive than out-groups has attracted a good deal of theorizing and research, with a number of motivational and information processing explanations being advanced (Stephan, 1985).

5. There is evidence that some cultures embody finer distinctions in the external

control category (as defined in Rotter's scale) than in North American culture. For example, Nagelschmidt and Jakob (1977) reported that Brazilian women distinguish a sense of fatalism from the other external factors, and Munro (1979) argued that Africans make a distinction between supernatural forces and chance, more commonly utilizing the former.

6. There exist other, more complex attribution information processing models that utilize mediating cognitive components (e.g., Trope, 1986), and these could also be of value in future cross-cultural research.

7. The results from Detweiler's study are problematic because the "attribution"-dependent variables are idiosyncratic and, in our view, do not represent attributional questions. Using causal modeling techniques, Schneider et al.'s study found that the effort attributions of German children and North American children were related in somewhat different ways to recall performance, use of recall strategies, and the presence of metacognitive knowledge about memory states and processes.

19

PERSON PERCEPTION IN CROSS-CULTURAL PERSPECTIVE

LESLIE ZEBROWITZ-McARTHUR

What one notes about one's fellow men varies, of course, with the culture. (Bruner & Tagiuri, 1954, p. 640)

Current theorizing in person perception is concerned primarily with the *processes* of perceiving and judging persons, and scant attention is paid to the *content* of these perceptions, to the *stimulus information* on which they are based, or to the *functions* which they serve. As a result, U.S. research on person perception is marked by an inadequate taxonomy for representing the content of our perceptions of other people; an inadequate specification of the stimulus information that gives rise to these perceptions; and an apparent disinterest in developing general theories from which to predict what attributes will be perceived in a particular person by a particular observer.

In contrast to the mainstream focus on process, the ecological theory of social perception, proposed by McArthur and Baron (1983), does focus on the content and function of perceptions. More specifically, the ecological theory holds that social perceptions serve an adaptive function—either for the survival of the species or for the goal attainment of individuals. It further holds that a person's directly perceptible attributes, such as movements, vocal qualities, and facial appearance, provide useful knowledge about that person's behavioral "affordances" which are the opportunities for acting and being acted upon that the person provides. The particular affordances that are detected are assumed to depend upon the perceiver's attunements, which may be innate or conditioned by the perceiver's social goals, behavioral capabilities, or perceptual experience. While the ecological theory assumes that social perceptions will typically be accurate, it also considers the issue of error. One reason proposed for erroneous perceptions is impoverished stimulus information. Another source of error proposed by McArthur and Baron (1983) is the overgeneralization of perceptions that are usually adaptive. Such errors are assumed to derive from the greater utility of overdetecting certain affordances than of underdetecting them.

The tenets of the ecological theory of social perception highlight a number of theoretically important issues that cross-cultural research can address, and the purpose of the present chapter is to consider cross-cultural research in person perception within the ecological framework. One topic to be considered is research concerning the contents of person perception. The ecological assumption that what people perceive about others is their behavioral affordances suggests that the basic categories of person perception may vary across cultures if there are cultural variations in what constitute important affordances. Another topic to be considered is the stimulus information for person perception. The assumption that affordances are communicated by people's directly perceptible attributes suggests that cross-cultural agreement will be manifest in response to nonverbal stimulus information that reveals affordances with universally adaptive value. The additional asumption that perceptual attunements, derived from social goals and perceptual experience, may vary across cultures suggests that cultural specificity may be manifested in divergent affordances perceived in the same information. Finally, the assumption that errors sometimes derive from the overgeneralization of adaptive perceptual attunements suggests that certain errors will be culturally universal.

CONTENTS OF PERSON PERCEPTION

Several important questions remain unanswered by U.S. research on the contents of person perception. One question concerns the salient categories of person perception: To what extent are people perceived in terms of their traits, their behaviors, their social roles, their appearances? A second question concerns the specific qualities that are perceived in people: What traits, behaviors, and social roles are people perceived to have? A third question concerns the origins of person perception categories and qualities: What experiential or innate factors lead us to perceive people as we do? Because of its focus on process, these questions have been largely ignored in U.S. research. Cross-cultural research, on the other hand, has been more concerned with describing the content of person perception, perhaps because researchers in an unfamiliar culture acknowledge that they probably do not know what that content is. Furthermore, in discovering cultural similarities and differences, cross-cultural research sheds light on the origins of person perception content. When there are similarities in the contents of person perception across a variety of cultures, this suggests an origin in some specieswide behavioral evidence or cognitive organization. Alternatively, cultural differences in the contents of person perception suggest origins in some culturally transmitted view of people. Moreover, an analysis of the cultures that differ from one another may shed light on the specific modes of cultural transmission, including our own.

Salient Categories of Person Perception

With few exceptions, U.S. research on the contents of person perception has largely ignored the important question of what are the preferred concrete categories of person description. Cross-cultural research, on the other hand, has addressed this question, a focus that has undoubtedly been occasioned by researchers' exposure to very different conceptions of persons than those manifest in the United States. In identifying cultural variations in the primary categories of person description, this research highlights Western biases that would otherwise go unnoted. For example, Korten (1974) examined U.S. versus Ethiopian differences in the categories that people employ to describe other persons. The results revealed that American college students focused on abstract, enduring aspects of the person, such as abilities and knowledge, cognitive-emotional style, interpersonal style, and global characterizations. Ethiopian students at the same U.S. college employed more concrete descriptive categories that involved specific interpersonal interactions, interests and activities, and opinions and beliefs. Bond and Cheung (1983) have found similar cultural differences in the open-ended self-descriptions of Japanese and American students. The Americans gave greater weight to general psychological attributes, while the Japanese made more use of specific events, preferences, and goals. Korten (1974) suggested that American-Ethiopian differences in usage of the abstract abilities and knowledge category may reflect the fact that status has traditionally been ascribed rather than achieved in Ethiopia, which makes ability and knowledge less salient in person descriptions. She further suggested that cultural differences in the concreteness of descriptors could reflect a lower frequency of cognitive inferences among Ethiopians.

Miller (1984) proposed an alternative explanation for cultural differences in the abstractness of person descriptors, hypothesizing that these differences result from more individualistic conceptions of the person in Western cultures, as opposed to more holistic conceptions in non-Western cultures. More specifically, she argued that, whereas Western conceptions of the person operate on the premise that enduring dispositions regulate behavior across contexts and that the autonomous individual is the primary unit of moral responsibility, non-Western cultures emphasize the interdependence of the person and the social context, treating the social role rather than the individual as the primary unit of responsibility.

Miller's (1984) findings revealed that American adults gave greater weight to general dispositions than did adult Hindus, and most of the cultural differences were in the subcategory of personality traits. Hindu adults, in contrast, gave more weight to contextual factors, and most of these cultural differences were in the subcategory encompassing references to social roles and to patterns of interpersonal relationships, as well as references to the placement of persons, objects, or events in time or space. Moreover, Miller's (1984) data revealed no evidence that cultural differences in cognitive capacities or socioeconomic factors were responsible for the differences in person perception. This strongly suggests that cultural differences in basic conceptions of the person account for the differences in the abstractness of descriptors.

It should be noted that the cultural differences that become manifest when open-ended questions are given to assess the categories of person perception that people spontaneously use do not appear when more traditional closed question methods are employed. For example, Shweder and Bourne (1982) reported that multidimensional scaling analyses of Indians' sortings of trait terms revealed two abstract dimensions that are comparable to the conceptual organization of personality revealed in research with U.S. subjects. This finding provides additional evidence that the cultural differences do not derive from differences in conceptual abilities. Rather, they seem to reflect true cultural differences in conceptions of the person. However, a simple distinction between Western and non-Western views of the person may prove inadequate to account for the range of cultural differences. For example, Bond and Cheung (1983) found more similarity between the self-descriptions of Americans and Hong Kong Chinese students than between the Chinese and the Japanese.

Specific Qualities Perceived in People

While some research has identified cultural differences in the types of categories used in person perception, there is less definitive evidence pertaining to the specific content of perceptions. What are the abstract dispositions that Americans employ as descriptors and do they differ from the dispositions that Hindus employ, albeit with less frequency?

Similarly, what are the social roles that Hindus employ as descriptors, and do they differ from the roles that Americans employ? The latter question has received little if any attention, but there is some research bearing on the former question.

Factor analyses of the behavioral associations manifested in person descriptions generated by Norman (1963) have yielded the factors of agreeableness, extroversion, and conscientiousness for Filipino, Japanese, Hong Kong Chinese, and U.S. college students, and the factors of emotional stability and culture for all but the Filipinos (Bond, 1979). For the latter sample, cultured behaviors loaded on the conscientiousness factor, and behaviors indicative of emotional instability loaded on two separate factors—psychosomatic stability and mood stability (Guthrie & Bennett, 1971). Finally, Yang and Bond (1985) studied the factor structure of Chinese students' person descriptions, utilizing ratings on indigenous Chinese trait adjectives rather than translations of Norman's (1963) behavioral descriptions, and they found three factors that are very similar to those that are common to the other four cultures.

In addition to the foregoing cross-cultural commonalities in the specific dimensions along which people are perceived, there were some noteworthy differences. More behaviors loaded on the agreeableness factor in the Philippine sample than in the others, suggesting cultural differences in the degree to which behaviors will be interpreted in terms of their agreeableness. Also, as noted above, the conscientiousness factor for Philippine subjects included the items which loaded on the culture factor in the United States. There were also some other cultural differences in the particular items loading on each factor. In particular, for all groups but Americans, "intellectual" was found to load on the conscientiousness factor, along with "responsible" and "persevering." For Americans, it loaded on the culture factor, along with "artistically sensitive" and "polished." Another interesting cultural difference was the relatively weak loading of "tidy" on the conscientiousness factor for Japanese subjects compared with the other groups. These findings suggest that the meaning of a given behavior may differ from culture to culture, with resultant differences both in evaluations of the behavior and in the estimated probability of other, associatively linked, behaviors.

The foregoing factor analytic research reveals that specific behaviors are similarly associated across diverse cultures. It also suggests that people in varied cultures perceive in others the qualities of agreeableness, extroversion, conscientiousness, and stability. However, it may not be appropriate to conclude that these are universally perceived *traits*. Rather, it may be that in some cultures the factors that have been labeled "agreeableness," and so forth, reflect particular *social roles* that generate particular behaviors. For example, Guthrie and Bennett (1971) noted that the behaviors loading on the conscientiousness factor for Filipinos characterized a rural, unsophisticated person. Methodologies other than inductive factor-analytic techniques, such as open-ended person descriptions, are needed to directly establish the salience of specific traits or social roles in perceptions of people across various cultures.

Additional research is also needed to ascertain cultural similarities and differences in the specific descriptors that are applied to people. With the exception of Yang and Bond (1985), who used indigenous Chinese trait labels, investigators have all used Norman's (1963) behavioral descriptors, and these were not even translated into the national language for the Filipino and Hong Kong samples. Indeed, the obstacles to such translation were noted by Guthrie and Bennett (1971), who stated that "many Tagalog terms which are of great importance in the interpersonal behavior of Tagalogs did not have clearly equivalent counterparts in English." Thus the question remains as to which behavioral descriptions and trait adjectives have counterparts across diverse cultures, and which are culturally specific.

Recent research by John, Goldberg, and Angleitner (1984) begins to address the question of cross-cultural equivalence in specific person descriptors. In particular, the self-ratings of bilingual Americans and Germans on a series of English trait-terms were significantly correlated with their self-ratings on the German translations of these terms. Moreover, when the trait terms were grouped to form the five dimensions established in the aforementioned factor analytic research, the English-German correlations within each dimension were highly significant. These findings indicate that specific person descriptions have the same meaning in German and English. Whether or not the various descriptors are equally salient in the two cultures remains to be shown.

Factor analyses of Japanese and English mood terms by Watson, Clark, and Tellegen (1984) have also established the cross-cultural equivalence of person descriptors. Mood terms derived from Japanese students' self-descriptive diaries together with a set of English self-reported mood terms were sorted into synonym groups by bilingual judges. A factor analysis of the resultant cooccurrences revealed a large set of mood categories with both Japanese and English markers, as well as very similar loadings of the Japanese and English mood terms on "positive" and "negative" affect factors. One interesting exception was the factor loading for the Japanese word for "sleepy." Although the

Japanese word had the same denotative meaning as the English word, it was not negatively associated with positive affect in Japanese, as it was in English. Thus, while people may be perceived as "sleepy" in Japan as well as in the United States, this perception will have different associations in the two cultures. In interpreting this result, the authors noted that, in Japanese culture, sleeping is a favored indulgence . . . one of the most accomplished arts. Other cultural differences suggested that people may be perceived as experiencing certain moods in one culture but not in the other. More specifically, English terms that were not well-represented in a list of Japanese mood descriptors reflected contempt, shyness, fear, blameworthiness, rage, pride, and torment. Japanese terms that were not well-represented in a list of English mood descriptors denoted nostalgia, irritability, reluctance, general unpleasantness, and pain.

Asch's (1958) research on metaphorical descriptions of persons also considers the cross-cultural equivalence of person descriptors. This work investigated cross-cultural similarities in the tendency to describe people with terms that describe properties of the physical world. He examined languages that belonged to different families and were widely separated in time and space. Asch reported that all of these languages possessed terms that simultaneously describe both physical and psychological qualities in the same manner as English. For example, the word for "straight" universally designates "honesty," "righteousness," and "correct understanding," while the word for "crooked" means "dishonesty" and "wile." Asch argues that metaphorical descriptions of persons reflect similarities in the functional properties of persons and things. For example, he notes that to call a physical object "hard" is to describe a mode of interaction with it—the object resists physical change when it is physically pushed or pressed. To call a person "hard" describes a similar interaction—the person will resist psychological change when pushed or pressed with psychological force. In terms of the ecological framework, the metaphor gains its meaning by virtue of similarities in the affordances of both objects and persons.

The functional analysis of metaphorical descriptions of persons helps to account for some cultural differences in the specific qualities perceived in people, as well as the similarities. In some cultures a given affordance of people may not be relevant to perceivers' adaptive functioning and hence should not be perceived or metaphorically described. For example, Asch suggests that if the category of intelligence is not of importance, then one will not find terms such as *penetrating* or *bright* to describe it. Clearly, more research is needed to address adequately the question of what specific qualities are perceived in people and why. Cross-cultural research will be invaluable in addressing the latter question, provided that the documentation of cultural variations in the specific qualities perceived in people can be linked to cultural variations in their affordances.

Origins of Person Perception Categories and Qualities

Asch's research on metaphorical descriptions of persons suggests that our perceptions of people may sometimes reflect universal dimensions of judgment about any stimulus object. The fact that agreeableness, extroversion, and conscientiousness are the three primary dimensions of person perception in very diverse cultures also provides evidence for the universality of qualities perceived in people. Moreover, Bond (1979) has noted that these factors are similar in meaning to Osgood's dimensions of evaluation, activity, and potency, which suggests that cross-cultural agreement in behavioral associations may reflect universal dimensions of human judgment about any stimulus objects. However, it should be noted that the intercultural agreement at the level of person perception *factors* may obscure important differences at more concrete levels of analysis. As Shweder and Bourne (1982) have observed, Osgood's research finds universals by moving to a level of generality that makes "God" equivalent to "ice cream"—both are perceived as good, strong, and active.

Attention to cultural variations within a universal factor structure may provide important insights into the origins of person perception content. Moreover, cross-cultural research provides an ideal natural experiment for investigating what factors affect the salience of the various qualities we perceive in people. Bond and Forgas (1984) have recently explored this question in a cross-cultural investigation of the link between dimensions of person perception and behavioral intention.

In keeping with the ecological theory's assumption that people's perceptual attunements vary with their social goals, Bond and Forgas (1984) hypothesized that the extent to which a perceiver's behavioral intentions are influenced by specific behavioral information about a target person will vary with the adaptive relevance of that information within the perceiver's culture. More specifically, they argued that information about a target person's agreeableness and conscientiousness is more adaptively relevant to Chinese perceivers than to Australians because the former live in a collectivist culture in which people have less privacy and are more interdependent. Consistent with this proposal, they found that behavioral information loading on the factor of agreeableness in earlier studies had more impact on Chinese than Australian perceivers' expressed willingness to associate with the target person, and information loading on the factor of conscientiousness had more impact on Chinese than Australian perceivers' expressed willingness to trust the target person.

Another cultural difference reported by Bond and Forgas (1984) was that Australian perceivers expressed more willingness to trust an extroverted than an introverted target person, while extroversion had no impact on Chinese perceivers' trust. This effect cannot be attributed to an indifference to extroversion among the Chinese since, like the Australians, they did express more desire to associate with an extroverted target. An understanding of differences between the Chinese and Australian cultures is necessary to explain the failure of extroversion to predict Chinese perceivers' trust. One possibility is that the access to internal states that is provided by an extrovert is so commonplace in Chinese society, where privacy is minimal, that it is not diagnostic of trustworthiness.

Further evidence that the relative salience of different categories of person perception derives from the attunement to socially useful information is provided by Miller's (1984) research on the development of person perception across cultures. Early research in the West had revealed that children's descriptions of people stress concrete actions, interpersonal relationships, and other contextual factors, and that references to abstract, general dispositions increase with age. These developmental changes have long been attributed to children's inability to abstract general traits from behavioral regularities, just as parallel cross-cultural differences have been attributed to variations in cognitive capacities. However, Miller (1984) found that while U.S. children showed increased frequency of dispositional descriptions with increasing age, there was no such trend for Hindus. To the contrary, Hindus showed an increased frequency of more concrete, contextual descriptions with increasing age, a trend that did not obtain for Americans. If one makes the reasonable assumption that children in both cultures become more socially adept with increasing age, it would appear that perceiving persons in terms of abstract dispositions fosters adaptive behavior in the United States while perceiving persons in a more contextual fashion fosters adaptive action in India. In short, the culturally divergent perceptions of people may reflect the education of attention to different realities.

In addition to the evidence for cultural variations in the salience of different person perception categories and qualities, differences have been found in the associations among specific qualities. Cross-cultural research can address the relatively neglected question of what experiences influence such associations. For example, one might test Bond's hypothesis that when educated people have strong social obligations, as they do in Japan, China, and the Philippines, due to the their relatively small numbers, then intellectual behavior will be more strongly associated with conscientiousness than it is in the United States, where higher education is more widely available. Similarly, one might test the hypothesis that for the Japanese, "tidy" behavior is relatively undiagnostic of conscientiousness because tidy behavior is so endemic in the Japanese culture. In keeping with this argument, considerable research has demonstrated that distinctive qualities are more salient elements in person descriptions (McArthur, 1982).

Summary

Although the data are limited in the number of cultures sampled, the research that has been reviewed suggests that there are both universal and culturally specific elements in the contents of person perception. The specific categories of person perception emerging in free response descriptions appear in all cultures studied. There also seems to be cultural universality in at least some of the specific qualities ascribed to people. Finally, there is universality in the basic structure of person perceptions, with various behaviors and traits similarly associated across diverse cultures. These cultural commonalities must be qualified by some significant differences. Although the specific categories of person perception appear in all cultures, there are great differences in the frequency with which various categories are employed. There is also some evidence for cultural differences in the salience of particular qualities. And certain behaviors have different meanings—that is, different associations—in some cultures than in others.

The research reviewed in this section does more than establish some contents of person perception that are universal and some that are culturally specific. It suggests some tentative answers to theoretically important questions and highlights the need for additional cross-cultural research to answer them. For example, cultural variations in the frequency of various descriptive categories suggest that the bias to perceive behavior as caused by stable dispositions, which has been called the "fundamental attribution error" in U.S. research, reflects a culturally transmitted view of people, rather than some fundamental human perceptual or cognitive process. These cultural variations further suggest the fruitfulness of research devoted to ascertaining the experiential determinants and the behavioral consequences of perceiving people in terms of their abstract dispositions versus more specific, contextually embedded attributes. Similarly, cultural differences in the meanings assigned to certain behaviors draw attention to the relatively neglected question of what experiential factors influence people's implicit personality theories. At the same time, cultural similarities in behavior and trait associations, as well as the perception of specific metaphorically described qualities, suggests that certain contents of person perception have their origins in specieswide patterns of behavior or cognitive organization.

Existing research on the contents of person perception can be incorporated into the framework of the ecological theory of social perception. Cultural variations in the frequency of descriptive categories may reflect cultural variations in the categories that communicate various affordances. It seems reasonable to argue that in the United States and other Western cultures, where behavior is relatively unconstrained by social roles, a person's affordances for a perceiver will vary significantly with the person's dispositional traits, making such descriptive categories very useful for adaptive action (see Bond, 1983, p. 145, for elaboration of this argument). On the other hand, traits may be less diagnostic of important affordances in cultures in which behavior is severely constrained by social roles, rendering contextual descriptive categories more adaptively relevant. Cultural variations in the meanings assigned to certain behaviors may reflect differences in perceptual attunements derived from cultural variations in social goals or perceptual experience. For example, as argued earlier, "intellectual" may be associated with conscientiousness in Japan but not in the United States because Japanese social goals emphasize the responsibilities of intellectuals. And "tidy" may be associated with conscientiousness in the United States but not in Japan because perceptual experiences reveal great variation in the tidiness of Americans, but not in that of the Japanese. Finally, cultural universals in the contents of person perception indicate that certain descriptors have specieswide, adaptive value.

STIMULUS INFORMATION
FOR PERSON PERCEPTION

In its preoccupation with process, U.S. research on person perception has neglected not only the contents of person perception but also the stimulus information that gives rise to particular perceptions. The stimulus information provided to perceivers in the vast majority of studies has been trait adjectives in a written format. As such, important questions that remain to be answered include (1) what different kinds of stimulus information influence impressions? (2) what is the relative salience of different information? and (3) what are the origins of perceivers' responsiveness to various kinds of stimulus information? A cross-cultural perspective will facilitate research that addresses these questions. The prospect of conducting person perception research in an unfamiliar culture, coupled with translation difficulties, should make salient to investigators their implicit, and questionable, assumption that trait adjectives are the proper information to provide. The discovery of cultural similarities and differences in responsiveness to various types of information will shed light on the biological and cultural origins of this responsiveness. Such cross-cultural data will also contribute to a more general theory of person perception that can explain why particular stimulus information has an impact on impressions.

Although there are not much data regarding the stimulus information that gives rise to particular perceptions, ecological theory provides some general predictions. People's directly perceptible attributes—their faces, voices, gestures, sex, age—are assumed to provide the necessary information for social perceptions. Moreover, the postulate that people will be attuned to adaptively relevant information suggests three possible cultural differences in the stimulus information for person perception. First, there may be cultural differences in the stimulus information that reveals the same affordance. For example, in Oriental cultures, age-related stimulus information may reveal a person's dominance status whereas job-related stimulus information may be more important in Western cultures. Second, there may be cultural differences in the affordances that are revealed in the same stimulus information. For example, research by Triandis, Vassiliou, and Nassiakou (1968) suggests that the voices, gestures, and facial expressions during an argument may reveal positive behavioral affordances to Greeks and more negative ones to Americans. A third possible difference is that people in different cultures will be attuned to different information in their attempts to detect different affordances. Finally, cultural similarities should be manifest in perceptions derived from stimulus information that reveals affordances with universal adaptive value. Two areas of research that have investigated the impact on perceptions of directly perceptible stimulus information will be considered in this section: physical attractiveness and trait perception. One other area of research that has given considerable emphasis to the informational bases of person perception is emotion perception.

Although this research will not be discussed in the present chapter due to space limitations, it should be noted that the cross-cultural perspective is well represented in research on emotion perception, undoubtedly because this perspective has enabled researchers to address the content and function questions that they posed.

Physical Attractiveness

A recent and comprehensive review of research on physical attractiveness concluded that "today, scholars have admitted defeat in their search for a universal beauty. . . . Anthropologists have ended where they began—able to do no more than point to the dazzling array of characteristics that various people in various places at various times, have idealized" (Hatfield & Sprecher, 1986, p. 12). Although these authors are technically correct, their conclusion does not do justice to significant cross-cultural similarities in perceptions of attractiveness, and it does not provide sufficient encouragement to scholars who would endeavor to understand the cross-cultural differences as well as the similarities.

Ethologists and evolutionary biologists have proposed that attractiveness may be related to reproductive fitness (e.g., Guthrie, 1976). If so, then people should be perceived as attractive to the extent that their vocal, facial, and bodily characteristics reveal them to be of reproductive age, healthy, prototypical for their gender, and receptive. Most of these indicators of reproductive fitness should be universal. Moreover, culturally specific norms of attractiveness may derive from their indication of reproductive fitness in that culture, rather than reflecting an arbitrary array of characteristics. For example, Darwin (1891) proposed that local variations in standards of beauty might be based on locally adaptive variations in morphological traits, and Crognier (1977) interpreted the admiration of long, slender limbs in an equatorial tribe as based on their value for heat dissipation.

Exotic definitions of beauty notwithstanding, cross-cultural research has revealed considerable agreement in attractiveness ratings. Ford and Beach (1951) reported that health, feminine plumpness, and cleanliness are attractive across a wide range of cultures. Although plumpness is no longer an indicator of health in economically developed societies, extreme emaciation remains an indicator of ill-health in modern as well as more traditional cultures. As such, it is noteworthy that both Kenyan and British subjects perceived extremely thin female body shapes as unattractive while the Kenyans found the fatter shapes more attractive than did the British (Furnham & Alibhai, 1983). Further evidence for cross-cultural agreement in the perceived attractiveness of various body types has been provided by Gitter, Lomranz, Saxe, and Bar-Tal (1982), who found that both Israeli and U.S. students perceived female bodies with the distinctly feminine characteristics of large breasts or an hourglass shape as more attractive than the less distinctively feminine small breasts and a pillar shape. Interestingly, research on the perceived attractiveness of male body types has not yielded such strong effects for distinctively masculine characteristics (e.g., Lavrakas, 1975), a result that may indicate that the bodily appearance of the male is less diagnostic of reproductive fitness than that of the female.

Research on facial determinants of attractiveness has also provided evidence consistent with the argument that attractiveness is related to areproductive fitness. Cunningham (1986) found a strong positive correlation between men's ratings of women's facial attractiveness and perceptions of their general health and fertility, and Deutsch, Clark, and Zalenski (1983) found that the perceived facial attractiveness of men and women across the lifespan corresponds with their reproductive capacity. There is also evidence that faces prototypical for their gender are more attractive than those that are not. In particular, babyish features are perceived as less attractive in adult male faces than in adult female faces, which typically retain more infantile characteristics (McArthur & Berry, 1987). Cunningham (1986) has further shown that certain mature facial characteristics also contribute to female attractiveness, and he suggested that the combination of childlike and mature features may signal that the female is at an optimal age for mating. Finally, Cunningham (1986), as well as others, has demonstrated that transient facial characteristics indicative of receptivity, such as a smile, are positively related to perceived attractiveness.

While the foregoing studies of facial attractiveness did not directly assess cross-cultural agreement, Cunningham (1986) found that the features of Black and Oriental beauty pageant contestants devited from Caucasian norms in the same manner as more attractive Caucasians differed from their less attractive counterparts. Of course, it is possible that the selection of Black and Oriental beauty contestants was influenced by Western standards of beauty. However, the existing research evidence does suggest that faces viewed as attractive in Western cultures are in fact seen as attractive by non-Westerners as well (Martin, 1964; McArthur & Berry, 1987; Thakerar & Iwawaki, 1979).

Although there is not much research that systematically investigates the determinants of physical attractiveness across a variety of cultures, the work that has been reviewed casts considerable doubt on the validity of the assertion that beauty is culturally specific. Additional research to ascertain what facial, vocal, and bodily characteristics are perceived as attractive across cultures certainly seems warranted. So does research that seeks to find cultural differences in definitions of beauty that can be predicted from cultural variations in the adaptive value of the features and/or from cultural variations in perceptual experience. In systematically investigating the contribution of culture to perceived attractiveness rather than merely asserting it, researchers will shed new light on the question of what features are attractive within a given culture and why they are attractive.

Trait Perception

If psychologists have been skeptical of the proposition that there are pancultural determinants of perceived attractiveness, they have rarely even considered the possibility that there are pancultural determinants of perceived *traits*. However, research has established considerable consensus within cultures in the impact of facial and vocal information on perceptions of a person's stable dispositions (see Kramer, 1963; McArthur, 1982). One problem with most of this research is that it has lacked a guiding theory as to what specific facial and vocal characteristics communicate what psychological traits and why they do so. As such, cultural specificity has often been assumed, but rarely tested. Recent work by McArthur and her colleagues has attempted to remedy this state of affairs by considering the question of what facial and vocal characteristics yield what impressions within the framework of the ecological theory of social perception.

As noted earlier, ecological theory holds that social perceptions will be influenced by facial or vocal characteristics that typically reveal attributes the detection of which is essential for adaptive behavior. Among these characteristics are those that distinguish infants from more mature individuals, and considerable research has established that the facial characteristics that identify infants do in fact reveal their dependency and approachability. The ecological theory further predicts that a strong attunement to adaptively significant facial characteristics may be overgeneralized. In particular, it has been hypothesized that adults with immature facial or vocal qualities are perceived to have childlike psychological attributes. Considerable research in the United States has provided strong support for this prediction (McArthur & Berry, 1987).

Facial determinants. According to ecological theory, perceptions of adults with babyish facial features or childlike voices should be culturally universal. Since maturational changes in craniofacial appearance are very similar for all humans, as well as for a variety of other species, there should be cross-cultural consensus in the identification of babyfaced adults. Similarly, since at least some "age markers" in speech are biologically given, there should be cross-cultural consensus in the identification of adults with childlike voices. Moreover, if the documented perceptions of adults with babyish facial features or childlike vocal qualities do derive from the overgeneralization of analogous perceptions of real babies, then there should be pancultural generality in impressions of the psychological qualities of such adults.

McArthur and her colleagues investigated these predictions by replicating earlier studies with samples of Korean college students. Korean students' impressions of schematic, Western faces whose features varied in babyishness provided strong evidence for the cross-cultural generality of reactions to babyfaced adults (McArthur & Berry, 1987). In addition to the cultural commonalities in perceptions of the schematic faces, there were also some interesting differences that may be attributed to the effects of perceptual experience on perceivers' attunements. Variations in nose length alone had no significant impact on Korean trait ratings, and this was attributed to the fact that relative nose length is not a salient marker of the maturational status of Oriental faces. Variations in eye size alone also revealed some cultural differences. Inasmuch as age-related transformations of relative eye size hold true regardless of racial variations in eye structure, it was suggested that the failure of eye size to predict certain of the Korean subjects' impressions may have been due to the staring quality of the "supranormal" babyish eyes in the schematic faces.

In keeping with this explanation, a second study revealed that ratings of real Caucasian male faces, which represented natural variations in eye size, yielded the same strong positive correlation between eye size and perceived childlike qualities that had been observed in U.S. samples (McArthur & Berry, 1987). This study further revealed near perfect agreement between U.S. and Korean subjects regarding the relative babyfacedness of 20 young American males, as well as a strikingly similar impact of perceived babyfacedness on trait ratings. Finally, the same facial features that were correlated with U.S. ratings of babyfacedness were also correlated with Korean ratings, and a physiognomic composite of the features that had best predicted U.S. babyface and trait ratings also predicted Koreans' ratings. However, the predictive power of these features was not so great for Korean as for U.S. trait perceptions, and further research is needed to determine whether this reflects the relative unfamiliarity of Korean subjects with Western faces and / or whether it reflects some cultural differences in the facial features that are perceived as babyish.

While McArthur and Berry's (1987) work compared only two cultures, additional evidence for the generality of appearance-based trait perceptions has been provided by Keating (1985) and her colleagues. These authors investigated the physiognomic communication of dominance in 11 cultures by asking people which of two paired adult faces of the same sex was the most dominant. The results revealed considerable cross-cultural agreement in dominance choices for face pairs that included Caucasian pairs, Black pairs, and Oriental pairs. The physiognomic features that characterized the faces perceived as dominant across all 11 cultures were receding hairlines, thin lips, and broad chins. Keating also found that a nonsmiling expression is perceived as more dominant than a smile across the same 11 cultures and that lowered brows are also perceived as dominant across 7 of these cultures. These findings were interpreted in light of Guthrie's (1976) evolutionary-based postulates concerning the facial characteristics that communicate threatening qualities. However, the data are also quite consistent with hypotheses regarding impressions communicated by age-related facial qualities. Children have proportionately larger lips and smaller chins than adults, and it has been noted that high eyebrows are another sign of youth (Guthrie, 1976). I know of no data on the frequency of smiling across the lifespan, but I would not be surprised to learn that children also smile more than adults.

Vocal determinants. Like the research documenting cross-cultural agreement in the perception of personality in faces, there is evidence for cross-cultural agreement in the perception of stable dispositions in voices. For example, Scherer (1972) found that American and German raters showed high agreement in their perceptions of both American and German speakers on dimensions reflecting competence, power, and warmth. While Scherer's research did not investigate what specific vocal characteristics yielded this cross-cultural agreement in impressions, a recent study by Montepare and McArthur (1987) tested the hypothesis that such agreement may result from cross-cultural similarities in responses to vocal immaturity. More specifically, they compared Korean and U.S. subjects' impressions of American speakers reciting the alphabet. The results revealed substantial agreement regarding the relative power, competence, and warmth of the speakers, which indicates that prosodic vocal qualities convey the same information regarding behavioral propensities to perceivers from diverse cultures. Agreement regarding the relative childlikeness of the young adult

American voices was also highly significant, indicating a cross-cultural generality in age-related paralinguistic information. Finally, the same childlike vocal qualities predicted both groups' trait ratings, revealing a cross-cultural generality in the tendency for childlike adult voices to elicit reactions paralleling those elicited by the young.

It is interesting to note that the significant U.S.-Korean agreement regarding the relative childlikeness of American speakers' voices was not as strong as the near perfect agreement regarding the relative babyishness of American faces that had been observed by McArthur and Berry (1987). This suggests that vocal maturity may be more culturally specific than facial maturity, a conclusion that would not be surprising inasmuch as the maturation of facial structure is more fixed than that of vocal characteristics. Indeed, even pitch can be influenced by social factors. Further research is clearly needed to determine whether some components of a childlike voice are culturally specific and whether particular prosodic qualities have a different impact on impressions across various culture groups. Such research will elucidate the poorly understood informational bases of trait perceptions within cultures as well as across cultures.

Although it has been argued that Scherer's (1972) data may reflect cross-cultural similarities in impressions of speakers whose voices vary in vocal maturity, Scherer was interested in investigating the *accuracy* of these impressions. To do so, he compared the trait ratings made by acquaintances of the speakers with those made by strangers. It should be noted that agreement between strangers and acquaintances could conceivably reflect shared vocal stereotypes rather than indicating accurate perceptions by strangers. Moreover, the lack of agreement could reflect inaccurate perceptions by acquaintances, by strangers, or by both. However, if acquaintance ratings are accepted as accurate indices of personality, then Scherer's data reveal some interesting cultural differences in attunements to vocal indicators of personality. In particular, the trait ratings of Germans who were strangers to the speakers were more likely to be accurate—that is, to agree with acquaintance ratings—than were the ratings of American strangers. This trend held true when Germans were rating Americans as well as when they were rating Germans. Further research addressing the question of cultural differences in the accuracy of voice-based impressions may reveal some of the factors that contribute to the development of variations in accuracy both within as well as across cultures.

Behavioral determinants. In addition to cross-cultural similarities in the facial and vocal bases of trait perceptions, research by Young (1980) has documented cross-cultural similarities in the behavioral bases of trait perceptions. In particular, Hong Kong students and American students showed significant agreement when they were asked which of 19 behaviors are associated with 12 different traits. One shortcoming in this research was the short list of behaviors, and future research employing a more extensive survey of behaviors may uncover cultural differences in behavior-trait associations, in addition to the similarities.

A recent study by Hoffman, Lau, and Johnson (1986) has demonstrated that behavior-based trait perceptions do differ across culture when there is a trait label for the target's behavior in one culture but not in the other. Bilingual subjects' impressions of people were different when they had read a series of descriptive statements that could be economically labeled with a term from the language in which the description was written than when there was no such label in the language. More specifically, the existence of a label facilitated "going beyond the information given" and generating schema-congruent traits that were not in the original descriptions. On the other hand, the presence or absence of a labeled schema had no effect on impressions of attributes that were directly presented in the original descriptive statements.

Summary

The few studies that have systematically investigated trait perceptions reveal impressive agreement across a variety of cultures. Additional research in search of pancultural agreement in the impressions created by various facial, vocal, bodily, and behavioral characteristics should prove fruitful not only in the empirical findings that it will provide, but also in the theoretical development that will be required to predict such agreement. Similarly, research investigating cultural differences in the impressions created by various types of nonverbal information will teach us much about the origins of meaning in this information and the experiential and situational factors that influence information salience. Finally, it should be noted that cross-cultural research on the informational bases for impressions should pay heed to cultural differences in the *contents* of impressions. In particular, the assessment of trait perceptions should be supplemented with measures designed to assess more contextually bound impressions, such as perceptions of people's social roles, specific activities, and interpersonal interactions. Measures designed to tap the concept of affordance may prove useful in bridging the different descriptive domains, inasmuch as trait descriptors may be used in one culture because they reveal affordances that are revealed in another culture by social role descriptors.

CONCLUSIONS

What can we add to Bruner and Tagiuri's (1954) assertion that what one notes about one's fellow human varies with the culture? We have learned that in many cultures people are described in terms of their concrete, contextually embedded behaviors and roles more than in terms of the abstract traits that dominate Western descriptions, and it has been argued that this cultural divergence reflects the education of attention to those attributes that communicate important behavioral affordances within a given culture. We have also learned that the meaning of certain behaviors varies across cultures, that descriptors occurring in one culture sometimes have no counterpart in another, that certain attributes are more readily perceived in one culture than another, and that certain stimulus information is more salient in some cultures than others. Unfortunately, with few exceptions, these findings lack a coherent theoretical foundation. We are consequently left with a potpourri of cross-cultural differences that provides little understanding of why these particular differences exist or what other differences one should expect.

An ecological theory of social perception has been offered to explain some of the documented cultural differences in person perception as well as to suggest other similarities and differences that might obtain. However, this theory, or any other, is not itself sufficient to generate specific predictions about cultural variations in person perception. An additional, very necessary requirement is an understanding of the cultures under investigation. Such understanding is not essential to study cross-cultural similarities, and it is for this reason that existing research has done more to elucidate cultural similarities than differences in the contents of person perception, judgments of physical attractiveness, and trait perception.

The theoretical emphasis on similarities in much of the research can be attributed at least in part to social psychology's cultural isolation. As Jones (1985) stated in his review of major developments in social psychology during the past five decades, "Social psychology . . . is largely a North American phenomenon" (p. 47). Yet the understanding of other cultures is something that should be viewed as central to the subdiscipline of social psychology, which is ostensibly concerned with the impact of the social environment on behavior. And the scattered but tantalizing data regarding cultural differences reviewed here indicate that person perception researchers will be well rewarded if they acquire sufficient acquaintance with other cultures to explicate these differences further. More specifically, one can hope to learn answers to important "what" and "why" questions that have been slighted in the U.S. focus on the "how" of person perception: What are the specific qualities perceived in people and why? What stimulus information communicates these qualities and why?

20

BRIDGING THE CONTENT-STRUCTURE DICHOTOMY
Culture and the Self

JOAN G. MILLER

Concepts of the self stand at the center of much current social psychological as well as anthropological research. In both disciplines, this interest has reflected, in part, the recent "cognitive revolution" in the social sciences. Mainstream social psychologists, for example, have supplemented their interest in more reactive concepts, such as self-esteem, with attention to the self as an active processor of information (e.g., Greenwald & Pratkanis, 1984; Markus & Wurf, 1987). Psychological anthropologists[1] similarly have gone beyond traditional areas of anthropological inquiry, such as kinship or religion, to focus on indigenous conceptions of the person and of the self (e.g., Heelas & Lock, 1981; White & Kirkpatrick, 1985). Despite this congruence of concern, however, there has been relatively little interchange between the two traditions.

The present chapter will consider some of the reasons for the relative isolation of work in these two disciplines and will underscore the value of greater interchange between them. In particular, Part I of the chapter will highlight ways in which the limited interchange between social psychologists and psychological anthropologists reflects their contrasting paradigmatic assumptions. It will be argued that whereas many psychological anthropologists have tended to dismiss social psychological theories as ethnocentric, many social psychologists have assumed a reductionist stance toward cultural considerations—treating cultural content as subordinate to universal properties of human psychology and/or to properties of the objective environment. In reviewing cross-cultural research on social perception and affect, Part II of the chapter, in turn, will document the importance of taking cultural factors into account in understanding the self. The research will be shown to suggest that the nature of psychological processes and structures may be understood only in relation to cultural content and may even, in part, be constituted by such content. Finally, the essay will consider broader theoretical implications of an attention to cultural considerations for social psychological research. It will be argued that an attention to cultural factors may make it possible to treat content and structure in a less dichotomous manner and contribute to a deparochialization of social psychological theory.

CONTRASTING THEORETICAL PRESUPPOSITIONS DISTINGUISHING PSYCHOLOGICAL ANTHROPOLOGY AND MAINSTREAM SOCIAL PSYCHOLOGY

The perspectives of social psychology and of psychological anthropology differ from each other in many of the ways that theorists have identified as distinguishing alternative scientific theories (Carey, 1985; Suppe, 1974). At perhaps the most obvious level, the two subfields differ in their aims. Whereas the interest of social psychologists is in characterizing processes at the individual or psychological level, the concern of psychological anthropologists is in characterizing collective or cultural phenomena. It might appear then that the two perspectives could be relatively easily integrated as distinct yet interrelated levels of analysis. Such an integration, however, is made somewhat problematic by the divergent views emphasized in each field concerning the nature and origin of culture and concerning the goals and procedures of scientific inquiry.

Conceptions of Culture and of Science Within Psychological Anthropology

Psychological anthropology is distinguished by its view of culture as a system of meanings. Geertz (1973), for example, conveys the dominant perspective of this tradition in his definition of culture as "an historically transmitted pattern of meanings embodied in symbols, a system of inherited conceptions expressed in symbolic forms by means of which men communicate, perpetuate, and develop their knowledge about and attitudes toward life" (p. 89). Whereas early work by psychological anthropologists emphasized the representational and normative aspects of cultural meaning systems (e.g., Tyler, 1969), more recently greater recognition has been given to the constitutive functions of cultures (e.g., Quinn & Holland, 1987). As shared "definitions, premises, statements, postulates, presumptions, propositions, and perceptions about the nature of the universe and man's place in it" (Schneider, 1976, p. 203), cultural rules are seen as creating social forms. Such culturally created realities, in turn, are often experienced as facts of nature:

> It seems to be the case that people have a tendency to treat culturally created things as if they were natural things. . . . For example, as Schneider (1968) has pointed out, the "observation" that kinship is made of flesh and blood contains the verdict that the physical facts of biological relatedness count as shared identity, which then entails the presumption that certain kinds of rights and duties will be assumed between "kin" as a matter of course. (D'Andrade, 1984, p. 92)

Central to this anthropological conception of culture is the notion of arbitrariness. Cultural meaning systems are viewed as bearing an indeterminate relationship to objective patterns of covariation existing in the natural world and as analytically irreducible to other systems, such as features of the ecology or biological requirements. As Sahlins argues, culture must be seen as bearing a hierarchical relationship of appropriation rather than a subordinate relationship of causality to these latter factors:

> The objectivity of objects is itself a cultural determination, generated by the assignment of a symbolic significance to certain "real" differences even as others are ignored. . . . A law of nature stands to a fact of culture only as a limit does to a form. . . . A limit is only a negative determination; it does not positively specify how the constraint is realized. (Sahlins, 1976a, pp. 62-64)

An example of the indeterminant relationship between biological predispositions and cultural forms may be found in work on color universals (e.g., Berlin & Kay, 1969). Whereas the biological structure of human perception enables distinctions to be made between the complementary hues of red and green and of yellow and blue, cultures exist that do not encode such distinctions in their set of basic color terms (Sahlins). The arbitrary relationship of cultural forms to objective patterns of covariation also may be illustrated in the presence of cultural representations that have no objective reference (e.g., "unicorn") or that share the same objective reference (e.g., "morning star," "evening star") (Tyler, 1978).

Certain epistemological and methodological commitments follow from the symbolic conception of culture under consideration. In particular, psychological anthropologists have tended to abandon, as a normative ideal, the search for universal generalizations. Explanation is modeled instead after that in the humanities. As Geertz (1973) has argued, the psychological anthropologist engages in a form of "thick description": "Rather than beginning with a set of observations and attempting to subsume them under a governing law, such inference begins with a set of (presumptive) signifiers and attempts to place them within an intelligible frame" (p. 26). Explanations offered by psychological anthropologists then tend to be particularistic and contextual rather than nomothetic and predictive. Explanatory force is achieved through producing an interpretive account that reveals meaningful order in a diverse set of local phenomena, rather than through producing generalizations that predict to other cases.

Finally, in having the exigesis of symbolic meaning as their primary goal, psychological anthropologists frequently employ hermeneutical methodological strategies. It is assumed that interpretation is required to read the variable forms in which cultural meanings are expressed and that ethnographic interpretation therefore is "essentially contestable" (Gallie, 1964, cited in Geertz, 1973, p. 29). Constraints on such interpretation are introduced, however, by increasing the range of phenomena taken into account. Thus, in contrast to the "detachable" conclusions of physical science, anthropological interpretations derive validity by providing a holistic account of diverse domains of behavior.

Concepts of Culture and of Science
Within Mainstream Social Psychology

The concept of culture has tended to be much less clearly elaborated within mainstream social psychology than within psychological anthropology. In particular, the dominant approach to culture assumed within mainstream social psychology has been an ecological view (e.g., Barker, 1968; in anthropology, see Whiting, 1980). Central to this perspective is the notion of adaptation: Cultural forms are interpreted as functional accommodations to objective constraints, given in the structure of the environment and/or the human information processing system.

In contrast to the symbolic view of culture emphasized within psychological anthropology, the ecological perspective tends to portray cultures as nonarbitrary. It is assumed that the nature of cultural forms may be causally explained by reference to objective properties of a particular environmental milieu and/or by reference to universal, biologically given constraints. For example, Super, Harkness, and Baldwin apply such a model in arguing that cultural differences in the use of taxonomic as contrasted with functional categories arise from the contrasting ecologies of different cultures:

> When there are many similar or identical objects in a class, several related classes, and a need for choosing varying combinations of items selected

from these classes, the most efficient method of organization is by class, that is by taxonomic group. Otherwise, efficient grouping amounts to physical proximity of things that will be used together. Cultures or subcultures that are materially simple will rarely require categorization organization. (Super, Harkness, & Baldwin, 1977, p. 5)

This view of culture may be seen to be compatible with a covering law model of scientific explanation, focused on the formulation of universal generalizations. In particular, it is assumed that causal connections exist between biological constraints, ecological conditions, and cultural meanings, and thus that cultural considerations may be accommodated within a predictive model. Also, since functional constraints may be analyzed in objective terms, cross-cultural comparison is considered possible in terms of an observer-free, scientific language.

Finally, unlike psychological anthropology, mainstream social psychology may be seen to emphasize methodologies, modeled after those in the natural sciences. It is maintained that the constructs under study may be defined in such a way that they are relatively unambiguously linked to overt behavioral or verbal manifestations and thus require relatively little interpretation to employ.

Factors Contributing to the Limited Interchange Between Psychological Anthropology and Mainstream Social Psychology

The limited interchange between the disciplines of psychological anthropology and of social psychology may be traced, in part, to these contrasting aims, concepts, and procedures that, it has been seen, characterize each discipline. In particular, it will be argued, many psychological anthropologists have viewed the notion of culture adopted within social psychology as overly narrow and have challenged its predictive power. In turn, in many cases social psychologists have assumed that the influence of cultural factors on social psychological phenomena may be explained in terms of more fundamental noncultural phenomena.

One objection raised by psychological anthropologists to an ecological view of cultures is the tendency of this approach to portray cultures in somewhat vacuous terms. As Shweder and Bourne (1982) note, to discover cross-cultural commonalities, investigators typically identify highly abstract functional equivalences between populations, while overlooking the many differences distinguishing these populations. Also, in many cases universals are discovered by methodological procedures focused on only a relatively small subset of the potentially relevant data. Thus it is argued that cross-cultural ecological comparisons of cultures often fail to capture the richness of cultural forms and are of limited value to the anthropologist interested in ethnographic illumination.

A second objection raised by psychological anthropologists to an ecological explanation of culture is that such an approach, while claiming to be predictive, in fact is indeterminate. It is noted that a wide range of functional adaptations may evolve to satisfy any given objective constraint and that it is not possible to predict what *specific* cultural form will evolve by reference to such objective considerations alone (Sahlins, 1976a; Shweder, 1979). For example, whereas an existing birth control program may be explained as a functional response to the problem of overpopulation, it must be recognized that cultural practices ranging from economic reform to warfare might equally have evolved as responses to such a problem.

Theorists have argued, furthermore, that, along with functional considerations, many nonrational factors must also be taken into account in order to explain the nature of cultural forms. As Sahlins (1976b) illustrates in discussing American food customs, considerations of functionality are frequently subordinated in cultural practices to nonrational considerations, such as conceptions of personhood:

> The tabu on horses and dogs ... renders unthinkable the consumption of a set of animals whose production is practically feasible and that are nutritionally not to be despised. Surely it must be practicable to raise *some* horses and dogs for food in combination with pigs and cattle. There is even an enormous industry for raising horses as food for dogs. But then, America is the land of the sacred dog. (Sahlins, 1976b, p. 171-172)

It is maintained as well that even in cases in which cultural practices are adaptive or functional, they operate within the context of cultural values or presuppositions that are themselves nonrational. Levine (1984), for example, gives an illustration of such an effect in discussing the Nyakyusa practice of segregating adult generations in different villages. Whereas such a practice is adaptive in avoiding inconvenience associated with intergenerational avoidance taboos, the taboos themselves, it is argued, reflect arbitrary cultural values, not a response to objective environmental contingencies.

Within the discipline of mainstream social psychology, in turn, the cultural considerations raised by psychological anthropologists are frequently regarded as of secondary importance. The structuralist premises characterizing much social psychological inquiry have led investigators to maintain that to explain a phenomenon is to understand it in terms of a general structure or process. Cultural variation then tends to be regarded as a factor to be controlled (e.g., in "culture-fair" tests) in the search for invariant psychological structures or processes and/or merely as the content to which such structures and processes are applied.

In assuming that cultural meanings are analytically reducible to meanings derived from individual observation of experience, social psychologists have also at times argued that cultural meanings are nonessential influences on individual conceptualization. From this perspective, then, cultural meaning systems are treated as communal derivations of individual knowledge, rather than as prerequisites for individual knowledge.

CULTURAL CONCEPTIONS OF THE PERSON
AS CONSTITUTIVE OF SOCIAL EXPERIENCE

Variation in Cultural Conceptions of Personhood

Conceptions of personhood have been documented to vary markedly across different cultural groups. Whereas all cultures recognize the individual as empirical agent, most cultures do not retain the individualistic conceptions of the person emphasized in the United States. As Geertz argues:

> The Western conception of the person as a bounded, unique, more or less integrated motivational and cognitive universe, a dynamic center of awareness, emotion, judgment and action organized into a distinctive whole and set contrastively both against other such wholes and against its social and natural background, is, however incorrigible it may seem to us, a rather peculiar idea within the context of the world's cultures. (Geertz, 1974, p. 225)

Theorists have noted that this emphasis on the autonomy of the individual represents a relatively recent notion, originating with the modern state (Dumont, 1965; Mauss, 1938/1985; Read, 1955). From a holistic conception of the person as inherently social emerged, in natural law theory, a conception of the individual as prior to the collective. In this modern view, individuals came to be accorded value as separate beings, rather than as occupants of social roles.

The present Western conception of the person has frequently been contrasted, in a dichotomous way, with both its historical predecessors and with conceptions of the person found currently in many non-Western cultures. Cultures are seen as conforming either to the Western, individualistic pattern, or to an alternative pattern, variously termed "holistic," "sociocentric," "collectivist," and so forth (e.g., Dumont, 1970). Whereas the first pattern is seen as stressing values such as egalitarianism, voluntarism, and independence, the second pattern is viewed as emphasizing values such as hierarchy, paternalism, and interdependence. Although this typology may be defensible at a highly global level of generality, it fails to capture both the variation in conceptions distinguishing different Western or non-Western cultures and the subtleties of conceptions held in particular cultures. Thus recent ethnographic work has documented marked variability in cultural conceptions found among different populations, even from the same regional area (e.g., Ostor, Fruzetti, & Barnett, 1982; White & Kirkpatrick, 1985).

As theorists have argued, Western cultural views tend to emphasize the separation and independence of the self from the environment (Dumont, 1965; Lukes, 1973). Conceived as existing in an original hypothetical state free of society, the "true" self tends to be identified with that which is unique to the agent, relatively enduring, and independent of social role. Such a conception of self may be seen to embody the dualism between nature and culture distinctive to much of Western thought:

> An analytic framework that equates "self/individual" with such things as spontaneity, genuine feeling, privacy, uniqueness, constancy, the "inner" life, and then opposes these to the "persons" or "personae" shaped by masks, role, rule or context, is a reflection of dichotomies that constitute the modern Western self. (Rosaldo, 1984, p. 146)

In such a cultural view, the mature self tends to be portrayed as a firmly bounded entity, capable of functioning autonomously and of resisting social pressures and other contextual influences.

In contrast to this Western notion, non-Western cultural conceptions tend to be less boundary-oriented (e.g., Lee, 1979; Marsella & Hsu, 1985). The self tends to be conceived as inherently social and as permeable, if not constituted, by contextual influences. Geertz (1974), for example, illustrates how Balinese, Moroccan, and Javanese cultures, though differing, each portray the self as constituted by social context rather than by an individuated psychological core. Conceptions of the self in Balinese culture, for example, it is argued, emphasize the self's placement in an unchanging and hierarchical social order:

> There is in Bali a persistent and systematic attempt to stylize all aspects of personal expression to the point where anything idiosyncratic, anything characteristic of the individual merely because he is who he is physically, psychologically, or biographically, is muted in favor of his assigned place in the continuing and, so it is thought, never-changing pageant that is Balinese life. It is dramatic personae, not actors, that endure; indeed it is dramatic personae, not actors, that in the proper sense really exist. (Geertz, 1974, p. 228)

In contrast, concepts of self stressed in Moroccan culture, it is maintained, are more contextual and fluid—tending to downplay that which is enduring. Finally, still a third cultural view of self may be seen in the Javanese tendency to portray subjectivity as fundamentally identical across individuals and to regard overt behavior as fully scripted and thus also as invariant across actors.

Indian cultural views of the self may also be briefly considered as another example of conceptions differing markedly from those emphasized in the West (Bharati, 1985; Dumont, 1980; Ostor, Fruzetti, & Barnett, 1982). In contrast to the more dualistic Western views, Hindu conceptions of self reflect a fundamentally monistic outlook. This monism is evidenced, for example, in Hindu tendencies to identify the real with the One Absolute (*Brahman*) and to treat the phenomenal world of everyday reality and of the empirical self as only delusion (*maya*). In this cultural view, as Marriott (1976) argues, the self tends to be characterized as a relatively open entity, continually transformed by (and transforming) contextual influences. Reflections of this monistic outlook may be found, for example, in Hindu cultural beliefs that entities such as houses have moods and characters that affect their human occupants as well as in the myriad cultural practices, such as astrological forecasting, devoted toward harmonizing interchange with the surround (Daniel, 1984).

The Cultural Construction of Social Perception

Recent anthropological research indicates that the conceptions of self under consideration exist not only at a cultural level but affect as well individual social inference. Specifically, it has been ethnographically documented that, in accord with their more relationally oriented cultural conceptions of the self, adults from various non-Western cultures (Kirkpatrick, 1983; Rosaldo, 1984; Selby, 1975; Strauss, 1973) tend to place much greater attributional emphasis on conceptual factors relative to person factors than reported in Western samples (e.g., Fiske & Cox, 1979). Among the Cheyenne, for example, evidence suggests that "explanations of specific behaviors are generally in terms of relationships with other persons, not in terms of the inner core of traits of 'personality'" (Strauss, 1973, p. 333). Similarly, it is reported that the Zapotec of Mexico "remain adamant in their implicit insistence that one cannot go outside the taxonomic realm of kinds of persons to the realm of kinds of personality traits for explanation" (Selby, 1975, p. 21).

Such ethnographic findings are confirmed and extended in empirically oriented cross-cultural studies. Bond and Cheung (1983), for example, demonstrate that the open-ended self descriptions of Japanese college students tend to be more concrete than those of either American college students from the United States or Chinese college students from Hong Kong. In comparison to the other two cultural groups, the Japanese students are shown to describe themselves significantly more frequently by reference to "personal facts" (e.g., "I own a dog"; "I went to the cinema yesterday") and significantly less frequently by reference to general psychological attributes (e.g., "introverted"; "excited"). Other cross-cultural research documents that in describing their peers, Indian adults make significantly greater reference to actions (e.g., "he is hesitant to give away money to his family") and significantly less reference to personality traits (e.g., "he's selfish") than do American adults (Shweder & Bourne, 1982).

Developmental studies show as well that contrasting age trends may occur in individual attribution in different cultures, paralleling the cross-cultural attributional variation observed among adults from those cultures. In particular, it has been demonstrated that whereas Americans make significantly greater reference over development to personality traits in social explanation (e.g., "he is insecure"), Indians make significantly greater reference over development to contextual factors (e.g., "there was no one else about") (Miller, 1984). Also, whereas Americans' modes of person description become significantly more impersonal with increasing age (e.g., "she is kind"; "he is successful"), Indians' person descriptions become significantly more self-involved (e.g., "she listens to my problems"; "I admire his work") (Miller, 1987).

These various cross-cultural differences reported in attribution are interpreted as resulting, in part, from contrasting cultural conceptions of the person acquired over development in the various cultures (Bond & Cheung, 1983; Miller, 1984, 1987; Shweder & Bourne, 1982). In particular, acquisition of cultural views that stress individual autonomy and independence is seen as priming the more Westernized cultural groups to focus on abstract psychological properties in social attributions. In contrast, acquisition of cultural views that stress the fusing of self/ other distinctions in the case of the Indians or phenomenalism in the case of the Japanese is viewed as leading individuals to adopt a more context-sensitive attributional orientation. Direct support for this cultural interpretation is found in evidence that the observed attributional patterns vary with Westernization in values (Bond & Cheung, 1983; Miller, 1984, 1987), while showing no relationship to literacy, schooling, socioeconomic status, language, information, or cognitive facility in abstraction (Miller, 1984, 1987; Shweder & Bourne, 1982).

The impact of cultural views of the self on social perception may also be seen to be dramatically evidenced in everyday patterns of interaction, such as those between caregiver and child. Caudill and Schooler (1973), for example, document that, in holding culturally derived views of infants as potentially autonomous agents, American mothers encourage infants to express their own needs and desires. In contrast, in maintaining culturally based conceptions of infants as "extensions of themselves," Japanese mothers are shown to stress physical contact and to see little need to communicate through verbal expression. Similarly, Kakar (1978, 1979) links the more nurturant style of Indian as compared with American caregivers to their contrasting cultural presuppositions regarding the child's nature. It is argued that, reflecting their acquisition of cultural views of the self as inherently asocial and universal, American caregivers tend to assume an active role in "rearing" the child. In contrast, in conceiving the infant as naturally social and as possessing dispositions from its previous life, Indian caregivers are viewed as emphasizing the mutual learning and pleasure between adult and child and as experiencing little pressure to mold the child in a given direction.

Recent work on everyday language use also highlights the impact of cultural conceptions of the person on social perception (Schieffelin & Ochs, 1986). Ochs and Schieffelin (1984), for example, demonstrate that the simplified patterns of communication, or "baby talk," found among white middle-class American caregivers, and assumed by some psychologists to be necessary for language acquisition, are absent among caregivers studied in Papua New Guinea and in Western Samoa. In particular, caregivers in Papua New Guinea and Western Samoa do not expand childrens' utterances, ask leading questions, announce events, or use a simplified lexicon and grammar. Such findings are interpreted by Ochs and Schieffelin as reflecting the contrasting cultural presuppositions and normative expectations concerning the self held in each culture. For example, the Samoan pattern of language socialization, which involves the infant's accommodation to the requirements of the social context, is viewed as reflecting Samoan cultural presuppositions that the intentions and desires of the infant are not a subject for interpretation, as well as the cultural view of persons as socially stratified. In contrast, it is argued that the American pattern of accommodating speech to the infant derives, in part, from American cultural presuppositions that the infant is competent to serve as a communicative partner as well as from the American cultural ideology that stresses the intrinsic equality of all individuals and tends to mask evidence of social inequalities.

The Cultural Construction of Affective Experience

Although an interest in the relationship of culture to affective experience is longstanding among cross-cultural psychological and anthropological researchers, it is only relatively recently that investigators have examined ways cultural conceptions of the person may be, in part, constitutive of such experience (e.g., Heelas & Lock, 1981; Levy, 1973; Marsella & White, 1982; Shweder & LeVine, 1984; White & Kirkpatrick, 1985). Traditional approaches to culture and affect have tended to portray cultural norms, values, and beliefs as independent variables affecting universal psychological processes (e.g., Ekman, 1984; LeVine, 1973). As Lutz and White comment regarding this perspective:

> The mind-body dichotomy is particularly evident in what can be termed a "two layers" approach. In this, a distinction is made between natural, bodily, precultural emotion and ideal, cognitive cultural sentiment or second-order emotion. . . . Much like Freudian primary and secondary process thinking, the uniform or universal aspects of emotion are variously "shaped," "filtered," "channeled," "distorted," or "masked" by cultural "molds," "filters," "lenses," "display rules," or "defense mechanisms." (Lutz & White, 1986, p. 412)

In contrast, some recent work by psychological anthropologists has tended to maintain a more holistic perspective. It is assumed that no sharp boundary may be drawn between thought and affect or between culturally informed cognitive contents and "natural" psychological processes (Geertz, 1980; Kapferer, 1979). Rather, as shared representational, normative, and constitutive presuppositions, culture is seen as affecting "thought-feeling." It should be emphasized that investigators in this newer tradition of psychological anthropology acknowledge that affective experience may have physiological components that are universal. What is rejected rather is a view that portrays physiological responses as the essential defining aspect of affective experience.

Evidence obtained by psychological anthropologists, for example, suggests that emotion concepts vary markedly in relation to cultural differences in conceptions of the person (e.g., Keeler, 1983). In particular, such research indicates that the James-Langian or hydraulic view of emotion, dominant in both academic psychology and Western lay conceptions, does not adequately capture the ways affect is conceptualized and experienced in various non-Western settings, which hold more socially oriented cultural views of the self (Solomon, 1984; Yang, 1981).

One indication of this cultural variation in affective experience may be found in empirically based ethnosociological research on the meaning of emotion terms. Whereas studies suggest that among Americans, the primary referents of emotion terms are internal states (Davitz, 1969), studies among various South Pacific populations indicate that emotion terms are understood more relationally (White & Kirkpatrick, 1985). Lutz (1982), for example, shows that Ilafuk adults define and semantically sort emotion terms based on the situation in which such emotions typically occur, rather than on the basis of their internal referents. Gerber (1985) somewhat similarly finds that whereas Samoan adults group together emotion terms on a broad evaluative dimension, the referent of the terms are dissimilar from that in the American case. Thus, whereas Americans tend to link together, as semantically alike, emotions that give rise to egocentrically pleasant feelings, Samoans group together, as semantically alike, emotions based on their social good. Such cultural differences, in whether emotion is viewed principally in relation to the self or to the world, are interpreted as reflecting cultural variation in the value placed on cooperation, sharing, and hierarchical interdependence (Chan, 1985).

Other indications that contrasting cultural views of the self influence whether affect is experienced in James-Langian terms may be found in ethnographic accounts of everyday discourse and social action (Briggs, 1970; Harris, 1978; Lutz, 1985; Quinn & Holland, 1987; Rosaldo, 1980, 1984; Strathern, 1975). Lakoff and Kovecses (1987), for example, describe how "anger" is thought about (and, it is argued, in part experienced) by English speakers in terms of a hydraulic metaphor. English speakers, it is shown, tend to characterize anger as hot fluid in a vessel—that is, as an entity prone to "boil," "steam up," and "burst" out of its container. In contrast, emotions such as anger are conceptualized in more relational terms in various non-Western population. As Rosaldo illustrates, although the Ilongots of the Philippines maintain that "anger" may be hidden, they do not conceptualize "anger" as a potentially volatile entity, liable to explode, or as an entity whose nonexpression leads to ongoing inner turmoil. Rather "anger" is viewed as something that can be "paid for" and so dissolve or that can be "forgotten" without problematic psychological repercussions. Evidence for this interpretation is found in Ilongot understandings of events and in their everyday behavior—for instance, their puzzle at the ethnographer's desire to talk a feeling through instead of regarding a payment or a service as an "answer" to it or their acting on "anger" in ways that suggest that, as they claim, it has been "paid for" or simply "forgotten" and not, as Westerners would argue, denied. This view of emotion held among the Ilongots, evidence suggests, is linked to their culturally based views of the self. Unlike Western cultural assumptions, Ilongot cultural conceptions posit no necessary gap between the "presentation" and the "self" and thus do not portray emotions, like anger, as entities that originate in an asocial self and that must be controlled to meet the requirements of society.

Documentation that cultural views of the self result in divergent affective experience may also be found in ethnographically sensitive research concerning "mental health" and "mental disorder" (e.g., Bhattacharyya, 1977; Doi, 1973; Caudill & Lin, 1969; Kakar, 1978; Marsella & White, 1982; Westermeyer, 1976). Consonant with their individualistic cultural views, in Western societies mental health tends to be identified with autonomous functioning and self control (e.g., Kohut, 1971; Mahler, 1979). Mental disorder, in turn, tends to be regarded as primarily a psychological problem, requiring treatment focused on changing internal states and processes. In contrast, in accord with their more holistic cultural views, in many non-Western cultures the "mentally healthy" self is portrayed as a permeable entity, maintaining relationships of reciprocal interdependence with the social-natural-supernatural surround. As Clement illustrates in the case of Samoa, this cultural view of normality tends to be associated with a relational perspective on "mental disorder":

> Generally speaking, the Samoan concepts of mental disorders tend to focus upon conditions that are brought about by external, adverse circumstances and outside forces (e.g., *aitu*) rather than non-organic abnormalities internal to the afflicted person. . . . Those having what Americans might refer to as personality problems are not seen as having

mental problems but rather as being types of people who cause problems for others. (Clement, 1982, p. 203)

Reflecting their nondualistic outlook on mind/body/cosmos relations, treatments of "mental" disorders in many non-Western cultures, in turn, typically emphasize somatic and/or supernatural interventions designed to restore equilibrium with the surround, rather than psychological interventions oriented toward regaining "ego" control.

IMPLICATIONS OF A PSYCHOLOGICAL ANTHROPOLOGICAL PERSPECTIVE FOR MAINSTREAM SOCIAL PSYCHOLOGICAL RESEARCH

The anthropological work, reviewed in the last section, highlights the need to pay greater attention to cultural content in social psychological research on the self. In particular, the studies imply that cultural content must be regarded as an essential influence on the patterning of psychological structures and processes.

It was seen, for example, that age and cultural variation in everyday social attribution may reflect differences in individuals' culturally derived, conceptual assumptions, rather than differences in their cognitive capacities or objective adaptive requirements. Such results challenge the dominant cognitive developmental views of development, which have tended to focus exclusively on structural effects, such as changes in individuals' capacities for abstract thought. Rather the results indicate that cultural presuppositions may influence the directionality of developmental change and not merely the final endpoint reached along a universal developmental path.

On a more general level, the work discussed underscores the value of cross-cultural research in expanding and deparochializing psychological theory. Cross-cultural research has frequently been employed in a hypothesis testing mode. Studies of other cultural groups, for example, have made it possible to test the universality of existing psychological theories (e.g., Malinowski, 1927/1955; Spiro, 1982). In increasing the range of variation existing on particular variables, such studies also have served to uncover new relations between variables (e.g., Whiting & Child, 1953). The present review, in contrast, has documented the role of cross-cultural studies in hypothesis formulation. It has been shown that cross-cultural research may be valuable in revealing the implicit (and frequently culture-specific) norms, beliefs, and values that underlie any observed psychological effects. Such research then implies that cultural meaning systems must be taken into account in all social psychological theory formulation, even efforts limited to understanding a single social group.

NOTE

1. The designation "psychological anthropologist" is employed in this chapter to designate anthropological researchers whose work incorporates a symbolic view of culture, a concern with ethnographic illumination, and at least some attention to issues related to psychology. It should be noted, however, that some of the theorists discussed identify themselves principally as cognitive and/or symbolic anthropologists, rather than by the more narrow designation of psychological anthropologist.

21

A SECOND LOOK
AT THE PLATYPUS
A Reprise

JAMES T. TEDESCHI

In my earlier chapter in this book I raised questions for and about cross-cultural psychology. My state of naivete about this field has lessened by only two or three j.n.d.'s since writing the chapter. However, some sort of reprise is appropriate, since I spent four days in the summer of 1987 at the Nag's Head Conference Center in North Carolina with the editor and many of the contributors to this book. The editor told me that if a terrorist blew up the conference center, half of the world's best cross-cultural psychologists would be lost. Multiplying by two I arrived at the total of fewer than 50 productive cross-cultural psychologists in the world. Some subtraction is probably also appropriate, since a number of the participants at the conference were unwilling to assume the label or doubted that a separate discipline existed (at least at the present time).

If the number of cross-cultural psychologists is small, their goals are lofty and their problems are immense. The goal is to develop a theory of human behavior that includes cultural context. Whether such a theory will establish universal principles of psychology remains to be seen. Perhaps Gergen (1974) is correct that transhistorical universal laws of human behavior cannot be achieved, but that itself is a testable hypothesis. We can be sure that if we do not attempt to establish such principles, they will not be found. One message transmitted by cross-cultural psychologists is that the universal theories of human behavior cannot be established within particular cultural contexts. Scientists naturally (often without reflection) develop their descriptions and explanations of behavior within the linguistic and value contexts of their cultures. This does not mean that the resulting science is culturally restricted, as Gergen (1974) has concluded, but it would be wise to be suspicious about its universality.

Speculation about the important dimensions of culture (at least as cognized by individuals) has led to factor analytic studies (see Triandis,

1975). While there may be reservations about this method of discovery, including worries about building into the measures what intuitively is expected in the resulting factor structures, disputes about ways of rotating, interpretations of the resulting factors, and the willingness to draw causal inferences from correlational findings, it does represent some sort of beginning. The methodology provides a rough way of operationalizing the concept of culture and using it to test hypotheses about how the various dimensions of culture ought to affect psychological processes. It is probably much too early in the history of this way of proceeding to draw any conclusions of great significance for mainstream social psychology.

The sensitivity to cultural context, whatever that turns out to be, makes a cross-cultural psychologist much more oriented to theory than the typical mainstream psychologist. Triandis in this volume (Chap. 10) reflects the preoccupation of the cross-cultural psychologists in developing or modifying existing theories. Indeed, Yang has argued (Chap. 6, this volume) that a productive approach would be to study what is unique about human behavior in particular cultures. The development of indigenous psychologies would be productive of innovation in theories because the existing, presumably culturally dependent theories, originating for the most part in technologically and economically developed societies, would be unable to explain "exotic" forms of human behavior. Thus the study of filial piety, concern for face, and a self-concept rooted in the collective rather than the individual's sense of uniqueness may expand the range of psychological processes beyond that considered in mainstream research.

A finding that a psychological theory developed in one culture is disconfirmed in another culture certainly limits its range of generalization. It would be disconcerting to discover that the processes underlying human behavior vary from culture to culture. The typical way of proceeding in science has been to assume that some higher-order principle should allow us to explain such apparent inconsistencies. Unfortunately, social scientists in general have not built the conditions under which a process is assumed to operate into their theories. One reason for this oversight is that psychologists have largely been conducting research on a particular restricted population (i.e., college students) contained within a privileged white middle-class under conditions that are extremely limited in range (i.e., laboratory experiments). Critics of mainstream social psychology, such as Gergen (1974) and Harris (1981), have noted that cross-cultural variations in behavior over both geography and history are indefinitely large. Given that culture, which serves as the context or condition for given psychological phenomena, is itself undergoing continual and predictable change, a skeptic might well give up on the project of developing a general science of human behavior.

Cross-cultural psychologists are generally optimistic about the future development of our science, although they are skeptical about the merits of much that passes for current knowledge. Even among cross-cultural psychologists there is a lack of recognition of the need to build time as a condition into cross-cultural theories. Yang (Chap. 6, this volume) recognizes that historical development in the form of modernization may produce some homogeneous behavior patterns across cultures that before the cultural change were remarkably different. Building conditions of culture and temporal processes into theories of human behavior should extend the generality of scientific principles. Adamopoulous (Chap. 15, this volume) reports a historical study using content analysis that explicitly undertakes to study the evolution of psychological processes. While there may be reservations about the reliability and/or validity of the methods used, this research is important as a pioneering project because it explicitly incorporates temporal factors into the guiding theory.

While there are many pitfalls waiting for the cross-cultural psychologist (as there are also for the mainstreamer), a particularly noticeable one (to me) was the tendency to adopt the theoretical language of mainstream psychology for purposes of "describing" phenomena. Insofar as the theory adopted contains descriptions that are not value-free, excess baggage is being employed when looking at cultural comparisons. An example of this pitfall may be Segall's examination of aggression across cultures in the present volume (Chap. 16). I have argued in many places (Tedeschi, 1983, 1984; Tedeschi, Melburg, & Rosenfeld, 1984) that the term "aggression" is value-laden and that what it denotes is more dependent upon the values of the perceiver than the topology of behaviors. Segall applies the concept of "aggression" to a multitude of behaviors, but largely to antinormative conduct. Since the norms of the various cultures vary, the form of behavior denoted by "aggression" similarly varies.

If there is a lack of cultural universality in the principles governing "aggressive behavior," it may be in the ambiguity of the concept being used by the investigator to identify the relevant dependent variables rather than the lack of regularity of more specifically defined behaviors, such as contingent threats, or the use of punishments involving removal of material resources, and so forth. This is not a problem peculiar to cross-cultural psychologists. Theories constructed around ambiguous concepts do not work well within a given culture, either.

The problems and challenges ahead of the cross-cultural psychologists are formidable. I am now convinced that there is a vital need for theories in social psychology that incorporate cultural context and historical change in the explanation of human behavior. The few psychologists who are attempting to provide these contextual contingencies for scientific theories are embarked on an exciting and challenging course. I found them to be more open to new ideas and self-critical than is typical of mainstream psychologists. The birth pangs of cross-cultural psychology are just now receding and its development and growth are to be eagerly anticipated.

22

CODA

DAVID M. MESSICK

Having read many of the chapters in this book, in this brief coda I will outline answers to three interconnected questions. Would I change anything that I said in my earlier chapter now that I am less ignorant about what cross-cultural psychologists do and think? What is the challenge posed by the chapters in this book to mainstream social psychology? Finally, what can be done to make mainstream social psychologists more aware of the cultural context of their discoveries and theories?

In my earlier chapter I draw two conclusions, first that doing cross-cultural replications may be unwise because of the difficulty in interpreting failures to replicate, and, second, that cross-cultural work will have an impact only when it articulates clearly with social psychological theory. Nothing that I have read suggests that these conclusions are incorrect. However, many of the chapters (e.g., Jahoda, Leung, Mann, Triandis) stressed the importance of generalizing findings or hypotheses to culturally different subject populations. Were I to rewrite my first conclusion, I might place a bit more stress on the value, rather than the difficulties, of achieving this goal. My second conclusion I would not alter.

As I read these chapters, I tried to keep the title of this book in mind and to ask myself, "What is the challenge posed by this chapter to mainstream social psychology?" Let me summarize the conclusions I reached in terms of three overlapping categories: parochialism, methods, and theory.

(1) *Parochialism.* Possibly the most pervasive challenge, expressed most shrilly by Jahoda, is that mainstream social psychology is parochial because its subjects are typically North American college students and little or no thought is given to the generalizability of findings based on such samples. It is undeniable that most of the work reported in the major social psychological journals is experimental work using North American college students as subjects, but what can and must be denied is that most researchers do not think about the generality of their findings. In my experience, active researchers think about the generality of the work not only across different subject populations but also across different stimulus configurations. What we do not see in

great numbers are studies that have been performed in several cultural locations. However, I propose that this fact results from constraints on researchers' time, budgets, and international contacts rather than a lack of interest in generality or a glib assumption of the universality of the results. I disagree with the position that unless an article contains a specific disclaimer about generality ("these findings may characterize only UCSB students enrolled in Psychology 1") the article makes an implicit claim that the results are universal. The subject population is obvious and if a reader believes that different subject populations would manifest different sorts of behavior, the reader is free to develop the prediction and to test it. The additional expense, work, and time required to do cross-cultural replications have to be balanced against the potential returns that such replications promise. Cross-cultural psychologists may anticipate richer returns from such studies than other psychologists, but it is unfair for them to expect all psychologists to study variables that are important to the cross-cultural community. In short, I think most social psychologists agree that cross-cultural generality is desirable, but they think that other things are desirable as well. The decisions that they make about allocating their research time and money will reflect all of these factors. Intriguing proposals like that of Triandis, suggesting that social psychological theories may vary systematically in their cultural generality, are provocative, but it is unrealistic to think that psychologists who are interested in variables other than culture will test them.

(2) *Methods*. There was little that could be construed as a challenge to the methods of mainstream social psychology, aside from the paucity of cross-cultural replication. Jahoda and Miller suggest that social psychologists could improve their work if they paid more attention to cultural anthropologists; Adamopoulos might have us reading more history, especially the Homeric epics; and Zebrowitz-McArthur would not be disappointed if we read more sociobiology. As sources of hypotheses, I would not quarrel with any of these recommendations. One of the great strengths of social psychology is the inferential rigor that is afforded by its commitment to scientific methods, and these methods can be used to evaluate hypotheses of diverse origins. Other scholarly disciplines, including literary analysis, history, political science, ethology, sociology, and economics have made contributions using their own methods to the understanding of the social nature of human beings, and there is no more need for social psychology to ape these disciplines than there is for them to mimic social psychology.

(3) *Theory*. One challenge that seems contained in several chapters is the assertion that social psychological theory is unduly narrow because

it ignores cultural influences on behavior (Leung, Mann, Miller, Triandis). In one sense, I can agree with this claim, and that is in the sense that theory is always developing and it is the job of research to challenge theory. There is another sense in which I think the accusation is unwarranted, and that is the implication that at any stage in the development of a discipline, the theory that has been developed should be able to explain everything. The theoretical glass is half empty, but it is also half full. Social psychological theory has made impressive advances but we do not pretend to have a firm conceptual handle on everything. So while I will acknowledge that there is much conceptual work to be done before social psychology will have a good understanding of cultural influences on behavior, I would also expect an acknowledgment from cross-cultural psychologists that there have been advances within social psychology that make thinking about cultural processes clearer and easier.

Mann, for instance, notes that the hypothesis that groups become more risky than individuals holds only in cultures that value risk, and that in cultures that value conservatism, groups become more conservative. Both of these phenomena are subsumed under the group polarization hypothesis, which asserts that whatever the predominant tendency within a group, a group decision will tend to be more extreme in that direction than individual decisions. This generalization from the risky shift to the group polarization occurred primarily as a result of monocultural experimentation, but the generalization allows one to predict cultural differences.

In a similar vein, Leung finds Deutsch's generalization of equity theory useful in understanding how different cultures allocate resources among group members. The original version of equity theory may have seemed narrowly Western in outlook, but the more general structure, which also includes allocating equally and allocating according to needs, ties in nicely with the cultural continuum of individualism-collectivism. In modern theories of emotion, Miller notes, cognitive or interpretational factors play a large role in the expression or experience of emotion. Thus, to the extent that these cognitive meanings vary from culture to culture, theories of emotion that have been developed with little cross-cultural input would predict significant cultural variation in the expression and experience of emotion. Finally, Zebrowitz-McArthur's work on social perception is a brilliant illustration of how social psychological theory can indicate where cultural differences should and should not occur.

It is only fair to point out that mainstream social psychology poses a theoretical challenge to cross-cultural psychology as well as vice versa.

One of the persistent problems that social psychologists have grappled with is how to describe how internal qualities, for example, attitudes or personality dispositions, influence behavior. This, it appears to me, is an ominous challenge for cross-cultural psychologists. Whatever it is that we mean by culture—institutions, attitudes, personality traits, social environments, expectations, and so forth—what are the processes by means of which it influences behavior? This challenge involves an examination of what culture means psychologically, and of the mechanisms and processes that express culture through action. Only two of the chapters that I read, those of Leung and Zebrowitz-McArthur, deal explicitly with this challenge. Much of the cross-cultural data described in other chapters consist of pooled questionnaire responses. A social psychological theory will require a specification of how differences in these responses are related to the ways in which people evaluate, perceive, and interact in their social worlds.

Finally, if I were to advise cross-cultural psychologists on how to make mainstream social psychologists more sensitive to possible cultural influences or biases, I would recommend a three-point program. The first point would be to refrain from belittling or ridiculing the efforts of these psychologists. Doing good research, whether it involves culture or not, is never easy and hostile condescension to those who ignore culture may be counterproductive in that it reinforces whatever suspicions social psychologists may harbor that their cross-cultural colleagues have little but contempt and/or envy to offer. Second, I would advise highlighting examples of work that creatively combine cultural variables with social psychological concepts. I have already mentioned several chapters in this book that do a splendid job in this respect. Part of this effort should involve submitting papers on cross-cultural research or theory to mainstream journals. If most of them are rejected, consolation can be taken in the knowledge that most "mainstream" papers are also rejected. Finally, I would try to facilitate the logistics of getting research done in culturally disparate settings so that researchers who wished to replicate a study in Africa or Asia would not be faced with insurmountable problems. Having a research fund that could support this type of work would be a large step forward.

References

Abelson, R. P., Aronson, E., McGuire, W. J., Newcomb, T. M., Rosenberg, M. J., & Tannenbaum, P. H. (1968). *Theories of cognitive consistency.* Chicago: Rand McNally.

Adamopoulos, J. (1982). Analysis of interpersonal structures in literary works of three historical periods. *Journal of Cross-Cultural Psychology, 13,* 157-168.

Adamopoulos, J. (1984). The differentiation of social behavior: Toward an explanation of universal interpersonal structures. *Journal of Cross-Cultural Psychology, 15,* 487-508.

Adamopoulos, J., & Bontempo, R. N. (1987). Diachronic universals in interpersonal structures: Evidence from literary sources. *Journal of Cross-Cultural Psychology, 17,* 169-189.

Adams, J. S. (1963). Toward an understanding of inequity. *Journal of Abnormal and Social Psychology, 67,* 422-436.

Adams, J. S. (1965). Inequity in social exchange. In L. Berkowitz (Ed.), *Advances in experimental social psychology* (Vol. 2, pp. 267-299). New York: Academic Press.

Adorno, T. W., Frenkel-Brunswick, E., Levinson, D. J., & Sanford, R. N. (1950). *The authoritarian personality.* New York: Harper.

Albee, G. W. (1986). Toward a just society: Lessons from some observations on the primary prevention of psychopathology. *American Psychologist, 41,* 891-898.

Allport, F. H. (1924). *Social psychology.* Boston: Houghton.

Allport, G. W. (1954). *The nature of prejudice.* Reading, MA: Addison-Wesley.

Allport, G. W. (1968). The historical background of modern social psychology. In G. Lindzey & E. Aronson (Eds.), *The handbook of social psychology* (2nd ed.) (Vol. 1, pp. 1-80). Reading, MA: Addison-Wesley.

Almond, G. A., & Verba, S. (1963). *The civic culture: Political attitudes and democracy in five nations.* Princeton, NJ: Princeton University Press.

Altman, I., & Chemers, M. (1980). *Culture and environment.* Monterey, CA: Brooks/Cole.

Alvarez, C. M., & Pader, O. F. (1978). Locus of control among Anglo-Americans and Cuban Americans. *Journal of Social Psychology, 105,* 195-198.

American Psychological Association (1986). A disk equal to 80,000,000 words. *APA Monitor, 17,* 37.

Amir, Y., & Sharon, I. (1987). Are social-psychological laws cross-culturally valid? *Journal of Cross-Cultural Psychology, 18,* 383-470.

Apter, D. E. (1965). *The politics of modernization.* Chicago: University of Chicago Press.

Aral, S. O., & Sunar, D. G. (1977). Interaction and justice norms: A cross-national comparison. *Journal of Social Psychology, 101,* 175-186.

Arenson, S. J. (1979). Rankings of intimacy of social behaviors by Italians and Americans. *Psychological Reports, 44,* 1149-1150.

Argyle, M., Gardner, G., & Cioffi, F. (1958). Supervisory methods related to productivity, absenteeism and labour turnover. *Human Relations, 11,* 289-304.

Argyle, M., Henderson, M., Bond, M. H., Iizuka, Y., & Contarello, A. (1986). Cross-cultural variations in relationship rules. *International Journal of Psychology, 21,* 287-315.

Armer, M., & Schnaiberg, A. (1972). Measuring individual modernity: A near myth. *American Sociological Review, 37,* 301-316.

Armer, M., & Youtz, R. (1971). Formal education and individual modernity in an African society. *American Journal of Sociology, 76,* 604-626.

Asch, S. E. (1952). *Social psychology.* Englewood Cliffs, NJ: Prentice-Hall.

Asch, S. E. (1956). Studies of independence and conformity. A minority of one against a unanimous majority. *Psychological Monograph, 70,* No. 9 (Whole No. 416).

Au, T. K. (1983). Chinese and English counterfactuals: The Sapir-Whorf hypothesis revisited. *Cognition, 15,* 155-187.

Au, T. K. (1984). Counterfactuals: In reply to Alfred Bloom. *Cognition, 17,* 289-302.

Ayer, A. J. (1952). *Language, truth and logic.* New York: Dover.

Ayman, R., & Chemers, M. M. (1983). Relationships of supervisory behavior ratings to work group effectiveness and subordinate satisfaction among Iranian managers. *Journal of Applied Psychology, 68,* 338-341.

Ayoubi, Z. M. (1981). Technology, size and organizational structures in a developing country. In D. J. Hickson & C. J. McMillan (Eds.), *Organization and nation: The Aston programme IV* (pp. 95-114). Westmead, UK: Gower.

Babiker, I. E., Cox, J. L., & Miller, P.M.C. (1980). The measurement of cultural distance and its relationship to medical consultation, symptomatology, and examination performance of overseas students at Edinburgh University. *Social Psychiatry, 15,* 109-116.

Bachtold, L. (1982). Children's social interaction and parental attitudes among Hupa Indians and Anglo-Americans. *Journal of Social Psychology, 116,* 9-17.

Bacon, M. K., Child, I. L., & Barry, H. III (1963). A cross-cultural study of correlates of crime. *Journal of Abnormal and Social Psychology, 66,* 291-300.

Badran, M., & Hinings, C. R. (1981). Strategies of administrative control and contextual constraints in less-developed countries: The case of Egyptian public enterprise. *Organization Studies, 2,* 3-21.

Bagozzi, R. P., & Loo, F. V. (1978). Toward a general theory of fertility: A causal modeling approach. *Demography, 15,* 301-320.

Bales, R. F. (1958). Task roles and social roles in problem-solving groups. In E. E. Maccoby, T. M. Newcomb, & E. L. Hartley (Eds.), *Readings in social psychology* (pp. 437-446). New York: Holt.

Barker, R. G. (1968). *Ecological psychology: Concepts and methods for studying the environments of human behavior.* Stanford: Stanford University Press.

Barling, J. (1980). Multidimensional locus of control beliefs among English-speaking South African mothers. *Journal of Social Psychology, 111,* 139-140.

Barry, H. III, Bacon, M. K., & Child, I. L. (1957). A cross-cultural survey of some sex differences in socialization. *Journal of Abnormal and Social Psychology, 55,* 327-332.

Barry H. III, Josephson, L., Lauer, E., & Marshall, C. (1976). Traits inculcated in childhood: Cross-cultural codes V. *Ethnology, 15,* 83-114.

Bateson, N. (1966). Familiarization, group discussion, and risk taking. *Journal of Experimental Social Psychology, 2,* 119-129.

Beier, E. G., & Zautra, A. J. (1972). Identification of vocal communication of emotions across cultures. *Journal of Consulting and Clinical Psychology, 39,* 166.

Bell, P. R., & Jamieson, B. D. (1970). Publicity of initial decisions and the risky shift phenomenon. *Journal of Experimental Social Psychology, 6,* 329-345.

Bendix, R. (1967). Tradition and modernity reconsidered. *Comparative Studies in Society and History, 9,* 292-346.

Bengtson, V. L., Grigsby, E., Corry, E. M., & Hruby, M. (1977). Relating academic research to community concerns: A case study in collaborative effort. *Journal of Social Issues, 33*(4), 75-92.

Benjamin, L. S. (1984). Principles of prediction using structural analysis of social behavior. In R. A. Zucker, J. Aronooff, & A. I. Rabin (Eds.), *Personality and the prediction of behavior* (pp. 121-174). Orlando: Academic Press.

Bergmann, G. (1951). Ideology. *Ethics, 61,* 205-218.

Berlin, B., & Kay, P. (1969). *Basic color terms: Their universality and evolution.* Berkeley: University of California Press.

Berlyne, D. (1980). Psychological aesthetics. In H. C. Triandis & W. J. Lonner (Eds.), *Handbook of cross-cultural psychology* (Vol. 3, pp. 323-362). Boston: Allyn & Bacon.

Berman, J. J., Murphy-Berman, V., & Singh, P. (1985). Cross-cultural similarities and differences in perceptions of fairness. *Journal of Cross-Cultural Psychology, 16,* 55-67.

Bernal, M. E., & Padilla, A. M. (1982). Status of minority curricula and training in clinical psychology. *Amerian Psychologist, 37,* 780-787.

Bernard, T. (1950). *Hatha yoga: A report of a personal experience.* London: Rider.

Berry, D. S., & McArthur, L. Z. (1986). Perceiving character in faces: The impact of age-related craniofacial changes on social perception. *Psychological Bulletin, 100,* 3-18.

Berry, J. W. (1967). Independence and conformity in subsistence level societies. *Journal of Personality and Social Psychology, 7,* 415-418.

Berry, J. W. (1969). On cross-cultural comparability. *International Journal of Psychology, 4,* 119-128.

Berry, J. W. (1974). Differentiation across cultures: Cognitive style and affective style. In J. Dawson & W. Lonner (Eds.), *Readings in cross-cultural psychology* (pp. 167-175). Hong Kong: University of Hong Kong Press.

Berry, J. W. (1976). *Human ecology and cognitive style.* New York: Sage/Halstead.

Berry, J. W. (1978). Social psychology: Comparative, societal, universal. *Canadian Psychological Review, 19,* 93-104.

Berry, J. W. (1979). A cultural ecology of social behavior. In L. Berkowitz (Ed.), *Advances in experimental social psychology* (Vol. 12, pp. 177-206). New York: Academic Press.

Berry, J. W. (1980). Introduction to methodology. In H. C. Triandis & R. W. Brislin (Eds.), *Handbook of cross-cultural psychology: Vol. 2. Methodology* (pp. 1-28). Boston, MA: Allyn & Bacon.

Berry, J. W. (1980). Social and cultural change. In H. C. Triandis & R. W. Brislin (Eds.), *Handbook of cross-cultural psychology: Vol. 5. Social psychology* (pp. 211-279). Boston: Allyn & Bacon.

Berry, J. W., & Annis, R. C. (1974). Ecology, culture and psychological differentiation. *International Journal of Psychology, 9,* 173-193.

Berry, J. W., & Dasen, P. R. (Eds.). (1974). *Introduction to culture and cognition.* London: Methuen.

Betancourt, H., & Weiner, B. (1982). Attributions for achievement-related events, expectancy, and sentiments. *Journal of Cross-Cultural Psychology, 13,* 362-374.

Bharati, A. (1985). The self in Hindu thought and action. In A. J. Marsella, G. DeVos, & F.L.K. Hsu (Eds.), *Culture and self: Asian and Western perspectives* (pp. 185-230). New York: Tavistock.

Bickman, L. (1980). Introduction. In L. Bickman (Ed.), *Applied social psychology annual* (Vol. 1, pp. 7-18). Beverly Hills: Sage.

Biddle, B. J. (1979). *Role theory: Expectations, identities and behaviors.* New York: Academic Press.

Biddle, B. J. (1986). Recent developments in role theory. *Annual Review of Sociology, 12,* 67-92.

Biddle, B. J., Warneke, J., & Petty, R. (in press). Subject population, expectancy, modality, and cognitive dissonance. *Basic and Applied Social Psychology.*

Biggers, T. A., & Preyor, B. (1982). Attitude change as a function of emotion eliciting qualities of the environment. *Personality and Social Psychology Bulletin, 8,* 94-99.

Black, C. E. (1966). Change as a condition of modern life. In M. Weiner (Ed.), *Modernization: The dynamics of growth* (pp. 17-27). Washington, DC: U.S. Information Agency Voice of America.

Blake, R. R., & Mouton, J. S. (1964). *The managerial grid.* Houston, TX: Gulf.

Bloch, M. (1961). *Feudal society* (L. A. Manyon, Trans.). Chicago: University of Chicago Press.

Bloom, A. H. (1981). *The linguistic shaping of thought: A study of the impact of language on thinking in China and the West.* Hillsdale, NJ: Lawrence Erlbaum.

Blumer, H. (1969). *Symbolic interactionism: Perspective and method.* Englewood Cliffs, NJ: Prentice-Hall.

Bobad, E. Y., & Wallbott, H. G. (1986). The effects of social factors on emotional reactions. In K. R. Sherer, H. G. Wallbott, & A. B. Summerfield (Eds.), *Experiencing emotions: A cross-cultural study* (pp. 154-172). Cambridge: Cambridge University Press.

Bock, P. K. (1980). *Continuities in psychological anthropology.* San Francisco: W. H. Freeman.

Bohm, D. (1971). Quantum theory as an indication of a new order in physics: Part A. The development of new orders as shown through the history of physics. *Foundations of Physics, 1,* 359-381.

Boldt, E. D. (1978). Structural tightness and cross-cultural research. *Journal of Cross-Cultural Psychology, 9,* 151-165.

Boldt, E. D., & Roberts, L. W. (1979). Structural tightness and social conformity. *Journal of Cross-Cultural Psychology, 10,* 221-230.

Bond, M. H. (1972). The effect of an impression set on subsequent behavior. *Journal of Personality and Social Psychology, 24,* 301-305.

Bond, M. H. (1979). Dimensions of personality used in perceiving peers: Cross-cultural comparisons of Hong Kong, Japanese, American, and Filipino university students. *International Journal of Psychology, 14,* 47-56.

Bond, M. H. (1983). A proposal for cross-cultural studies of attribution processes. In M. Hewstone (Ed.), *Attribution theory: Social and applied extensions* (pp. 144-157). Oxford: Basil Blackwell.

Bond, M. H. (1986). Mutual stereotypes and the facilitation of interaction across cultural lines. *International Journal of Intercultural Relations, 10,* 259-276.

Bond, M. H. (Ed.). (1986). *The psychology of the Chinese people.* Hong Kong: Oxford University Press.

Bond, M. H. (1987). Intergroup relations in Hong Kong: The Tao of stability. In J. Boucher, D. Landis, & K. Arnold (Eds.), *Ethnic conflict: International perspectives* (pp. 55-78). Newbury Park, CA: Sage.

Bond, M. H. (1987). Old wine in new skins: Impressions about others can be disconfirmed by social reality! *Psychologia, 30,* 39-43.

Bond, M. H., & Cheung, T. (1983). College students' spontaneous self-concept: The effect of culture among respondents in Hong Kong, Japan, and the United States. *Journal of Cross-Cultural Psychology, 14,* 153-171.

Bond, M., & Forgas, J. (1984). Linking person perception to behavior intention across cultures: The role of cultural collectivism. *Journal of Cross-Cultural Psychology, 15,* 337-353.

Bond, M., & Hewstone, M. (1986). *Social identity theory and the perception of intergroup relations in Hong Kong.* Unpublished manuscript, Chinese University of Hong Kong.

Bond, M., Hewstone, M., Wan, K.-C., & Chiu, C.-K. (1985). Group-serving attributions across intergroup contexts: Cultural differences in the explanation of sex-typed behaviors. *European Journal of Social Psychology, 15,* 435-451.

Bond, M. H., & Hwang, K. K. (1986). The social psychology of Chinese people. In M. H. Bond (Ed.), *The psychology of the Chinese people* (pp. 213-266). Hong Kong: Oxford University Press.

Bond, M. H., Leung, K., & Wan, K.-C. (1982). How does cultural collectivism operate? The impact of task and maintenance contributions on reward allocation. *Journal of Cross-Cultural Psychology, 13,* 186-200.

Bond, M. H., Leung, K., & Wan, K.-C. (1982). The social impact of self-effacing attributions: The Chinese case. *Journal of Social Psychology, 118,* 157-166.

Bond, M. H., & Tornatsky, L. G. (1973). Locus of control in students from Japan and the United States: Dimensions and levels of response. *Psychologia, 16,* 209-213.

Bond, M. H., Wan, K.-C. Leung, K., & Giacalone, R. A. (1985). How are responses to verbal insult related to cultural collectivism and power distance? *Journal of Cross-Cultural Psychology, 16,* 111-127.

Bond, M. H., & Wang, S. H. (1983). Aggressive behavior in Chinese society: The problem of maintaining order and harmony. In A. P. Goldstein & M. Segall (Eds.), *Global perspectives on aggression* (pp. 58-74). New York: Pergamon.

Boski, P. (1983). A study of person perception in Nigeria: Ethnicity and self versus other attributions for achievement-related outcomes. *Journal of Cross-Cultural Psychology, 14,* 85-108.

Bourguignon, E. (1979). *Psychological anthropology: An introduction to human nature and cultural differences.* New York: Holt.

Bourhis, R., & Sachdev, I. (1984). Subjective vitality perceptions and language attitudes: Some Canadian data. *Journal of Social Psychology, 3,* 97-126.

Boyd, R., & Richerson, P. J. (1985). *Culture and the evolutionary process.* Chicago: University of Chicago Press.

Boykin, A. W. (1983). The academic performance of Afro-American children. In J. Spence (Ed.), *Achievement and achievement motives* (pp. 321-371). New York: Freeman.

Bradburn, N. N., & Berlew, D. E. (1961). Need for achievement and English industrial growth. *Economic Development and Cultural Change, 10,* 8-21.

Brewer, M. B. (1979). Ingroup bias in the minimal intergroup situation. *Psychological Bulletin, 86,* 307-324.

Brewer, M. B., & Campbell, D. T. (1976). *Ethnocentrism and intergroup attitudes: East African evidence.* Washington, DC: Halstead.

Brewer, M. B., & Kramer, R. M. (1985). The psychology of intergroup attitudes and behaviour. *Annual Review of Psychology, 36,* 219-243.

Briggs, J. (1970). *Never in anger.* Cambridge, MA: Harvard University Press.

Brislin, R. W. (1980). Introduction to social psychology, In H. C. Triandis & R. W. Brislin (Eds.), *Handbook of cross-cultural psychology: Vol. 5. Social psychology* (pp. 1-23). Boston: Allyn & Bacon.

Brislin, R. W., Lonner, W. J., & Thorndike, R. M. (1973). *Cross-cultural research methods.* New York: John Wiley.

Brown, R. (1965). *Social psychology.* New York: Free Press.

Brown, R. (1986). *Social psychology* (2nd ed.). New York: Free Press.

Bruner, J., & Tagiuri, R. (1954). The perception of people. In G. Lindzey (Ed.), *Handbook of social psychology* (pp. 634-654). Reading, MA: Addison-Wesley.

Bryman, A. (1986). *Leadership and organizations.* London: Routledge & Kegan Paul.

Bulmer, M., & Warwick, D. P. (Eds.). (1983). *Social research in developing countries.* New York: John Wiley.

Burger, J. M. (1985). Desire for control and achievement-related behavior. *Journal of Personality and Social Psychology, 48*, 1520-1533.

Buriel, R., & Rivers, L. (1980). The relationship of locus of control to family income and families among Anglo and Mexican-American high school students. *Journal of Social Psychology, 111*, 27-34.

Burton, R. V., & Whiting, J.W.M. (1961). The absent father and cross-sex identity. *Merrill-Palmer Quarterly, 7*, 85-95.

Buss, A. R. (1978). Causes and reasons in attribution theory: A conceptual critique. *Journal of Personality and Social Psychology, 36*, 56-71.

Buss, D. M. (1984). Evolutionary biology and personality psychology: Toward a conception of human nature and individual differences. *American Psychologist, 39*, 1135-1147.

Byrne, D. (1971). *The attraction paradigm.* New York: Academic Press.

Campbell, D. T. (1965). Variation and selective retention in sociocultural evolution. In H. R. Barringer, G. I. Blanksten, & R. W. Mack (Eds.), *Social change in developing areas: A reinterpretation of evolutionary theory* (pp. 19-49). Cambridge, MA: Schenkman.

Campbell, D. T. (1975). On the conflicts between biological and social evolution and between psychology and moral tradition. *American Psychologist, 30*, 1103-1126.

Campbell, D. T. (1982). Evolutionary epistemology. In H. C. Plotkin (Ed.), *Learning, development, and culture* (pp. 73-107). New York: John Wiley.

Cantril, H. (1965). *The patterns of human concerns.* New Brunswick, NJ: Rutgers University Press.

Carey, S. (1985). *Conceptual change in childhood.* Cambridge: MIT Press.

Carlson, J., & Davis, D. M. (1971). Cultural values and the risky shift: A cross-cultural test in Uganda and the United States. *Journal of Personality and Social Psychology, 20*, 392-399.

Carlson, R. (1984). What's social about social psychology? Where's the person in personality research? *Journal of Personality and Social Psychology, 47*, 1304-1309.

Carment, D. W. (1974). Indian and Canadian choice behaviour in a Maximizing Difference Game and in a game of Chicken. *International Journal of Psychology, 9*, 213-221.

Carneiro, R. L. (1970). Scale analysis, evolutionary sequences, and the rating of cultures. In R. Naroll & R. Cohen (Eds.), *A handbook of method in cultural anthropology* (pp. 834-871). New York: Columbia University Press.

Cassirer, E. (1944). *An essay on man.* New Haven: Yale University Press.

Castaneda, C. (1968). *The teachings of Don Juan: A Yaqui way of knowledge.* Berkeley: University of California Press.

Castaneda, C. (1971). *A separate reality: Further conversations with Don Juan.* New York: Simon & Schuster.

Castro, J. G. (1976). A Guttman facet design multidimensional attitude-behavior scale analysis of internal-external locus of control of Mexican American and Mexican nationals. *Dissertation Abstracts International, 36*(12-A), 7861.

Caudill, W., & Lin, T. (Eds.). (1969). *Mental health research in Asia and the Pacific.* Honolulu: University Press of Hawaii.

Caudill, W., & Schooler, C. (1973). Child behavior and child rearing in Japan and the United States: An interim report. *Journal of Nervous and Mental Disease, 157*, 323-338.

Cavalli-Sforza, L. L., & Feldman, M. W. (1981). *Cultural transmission and evolution.* Princeton: Princeton University Press.

Cha, J. H., & Nam, K. D. (1985). A test of Kelley's cube theory of attribution: A cross-cultural replication of McArthur's study. *Korean Social Science Journal, 12,* 151-180.

Chalkin, A. L., & Cooper, J. (1973). Evaluation as a function of correspondence and hedonic relevance. *Journal of Experimental Psychology, 27,* 184-189.

Chan, D. W. (1985). Perception and judgment of facial expressions. *International Journal of Psychology, 20,* 681-692.

Chandler, T. A., Sharma, D. D., Wolf, F. M., & Planchard, S. K. (1981). Multiattributional causality: A five cross-national samples study. *Journal of Cross-Cultural Psychology, 12,* 207-221.

Chandra, S. (1973). The effects of group pressure in perception: A cross-cultural conformity study. *International Journal of Psychology, 8,* 37-39.

Chapanis, A. (1967). The relevance of laboratory studies to practical situations. *Ergonomics, 10,* 557-577.

Child, J. (1981). Culture, contingency and capitalism in the cross-national study of organizations. In B. M. Staw & L. L. Cummings (Eds.), *Research in organizational behavior* (Vol. 3, pp. 303-356). Greenwich, CT: JAI Press.

Chinese Culture Connection (1987). Chinese values and the search for culture-free dimensions of culture. *Journal of Cross-Cultural Psychology, 18,* 143-164.

Chirot, D. (1976). *Social change in a peripheral society: The creation of a Balkan colony.* New York: Academic Press.

Chiu, H. Y. (1979). *A test of unidimensionality and universality of individual modernity in ten Taiwanese communities.* Unpublished doctoral dissertation, Indiana University, South Bend.

Christopher, R. C. (1983). *The Japanese mind.* London: Pan Books.

Clammer, J. (1982). The institutionalization of ethnicity: The culture of ethnicity in Singapore. *Ethnic and Racial Studies, 5,* 127-139.

Clark, L. A. (1987). Mutual relevance of mainstream and cross-cultural psychology. *Journal of Consulting and Clinical Psychology, 55,* 461-470.

Cohen, I. B. (1977). History and philosophy of science. In F. Suppe (Ed.), *The structure of scientific theories* (2nd ed.) (pp. 308-349). Urbana: University of Illinois Press.

Cole, D., & Cole, S. (1974). Locus of control and cultural conformity: On going against the norm. *Personality and Social Psychology Bulletin, 1,* 351-353.

Cole, D., & Cole, S. (1977). Counter normative behavior and locus of control. *Journal of Social Psychology, 101,* 21-28.

Cole, D., Rodriguez, J., & Cole, S. (1978). Locus of control in Mexicans and Chicanos: The name of the missing fatalist. *Journal of Counseling and Clinical Psychology, 46,* 1323-1329.

Cole, M. (1984). The world beyond our borders: What might our students need to know about it? *American Psychologist, 39,* 998-1105.

Collins, B. E. (1974). Four separate components of the Rotter I-E Scale: Belief in a different world, a just world, a predictable world and a politically responsive world. *Journal of Personality and Social Psychology, 29,* 381-391.

Conaty, J., Mahmoudi, H., & Miller, G. A. (1983). Social structure and bureaucracy: A comparison of organizations in the United States and prerevolutionary Iran. *Organization Studies, 4,* 105-129.

Conklin, H. (1955). Hanunoo color categories. *Southwestern Journal of Anthropology, 11,* 339-344.

Converse, P. E. (1986). Generalization and the social psychology of "other worlds." In D. W. Fiske & R. A. Shweder (Eds.), *Metatheory in social science: Pluralism and subjectivities* (pp. 42-60). Chicago: University of Chicago Press.

Cook, K. S., & Hegtvedt, K. A. (1983). Distributive justice, equity, and equality. *Annual Review of Sociology, 9*, 217-241.

Cook, S. W. (1978). Interpersonal and attitudinal outcomes in cooperating interracial groups. *Journal of Research and Development in Education, 12*, 97-113.

Cooley, C. H. (1902). *Human nature and the social order.* New York: Scribner.

Coon, C. S. (1946). The universality of natural groupings in human societies. *Journal of Educational Sociology, 20*, 163-168.

Cooper, B. (1966). Leader's task relevance and subordinate behaviour in industrial work groups. *Human Relations, 19*, 57-94.

Crognier, E. (1977). Assortive mating for physical features in an African population from Chad. *Journal of Human Evolution, 6*, 105-114.

Crozier, M. (1964). *The bureaucratic phenomenon.* Chicago: University of Chicago Press.

Crozier, M., & Thoening, J. C. (1976). The regulation of complex organized systems. *Administrative Science Quarterly, 21*, 547-570.

Cunningham, M. R. (1986). Measuring the physical in physical attractiveness: Quasi-experiments on the sociology of female facial beauty. *Journal of Personality and Social Psychology, 50*, 925-935.

Cunningham, W. A. (1972). *Modernity and academic performance: A study of students in a Puerto Rican high school.* Puerto Rico: University of Puerto Rico Press.

Curtin, P. D. (1984). *Cross-cultural trade in world history.* Cambridge: Cambridge University Press.

Cvetkovich, G., Baumgardner, S. H., & Trimble, J. E. (1984). *Social psychology: Contemporary perspectives on people.* New York: Holt, Rinehart & Winston.

Dalal, A. K., Sharma, R., & Bisht, S. (1983). Causal attributions of ex-criminal tribal and urban children in India. *Journal of Social Psychology, 119*, 163-171.

D'Andrade, R. G. (1984). Cultural meaning systems. In R. A. Shweder & R. A. LeVine (Eds.), *Culture theory: Essays on mind, self and emotion* (pp. 88-119). New York: Cambridge University Press.

D'Andrade, R. G. (1986). Three scientific world views and the covering law model. In D. W. Fiske & R. A. Shweder (Eds.), *Metatheory in social science: Pluralisms and subjectivities* (pp. 19-41). Chicago: University of Chicago Press.

Daniel, E. V. (1984). *Fluid signs: Being a person the Tamil way.* Berkeley: University of California Press.

Darwin, C. (1891). *The descent of man and selection in relation to sex.* London: John Murray.

Dasen, P. R. (1982). Cross-cultural aspects of Piaget's theory: The competence-performance model. In L. L. Adler (Ed.), *Cross-cultural research at issue* (pp. 163-170). New York: Academic Press.

Davidson, A. R., Jaccard, J. J., Triandis, H. C., Morales, M. L., & Diaz-Guerrero, R. (1976). Cross-cultural model testing: Toward a solution of the etic-emic dilemma. *International Journal of Psychology, 11*, 1-13.

Davies, J. A. (1983). Does authority generalize? Locus of control perceptions in Anglo-American and Mexican-American adolescents. *Political Psychology, 4*, 101-120.

Davitz, J. (1969). *The language of emotions.* New York: Academic Press.

Dawson, J.L.M. (1967). Traditional versus Western attitudes in west Africa: The construction, validation and application of a measuring device. *British Journal of Social and Clinical Psychology, 6*, 81-96.

De Bettingnies, H. C. (1979). Japanese organizational behaviour: A psychological approach. In D. Graves (Ed.), *Management research: A cross-cultural perspective* (pp. 75-94). Amsterdam: Elsevier.

Demo, D. (1985). The measurement of self-esteem: Refining our methods. *Journal of Personality and Social Psychology, 48,* 1490-1502.

Deschamps, J.-C. (1973-74). L'attribution, la categorisation sociale et les representations intergroupes (Attribution, social categorization and intergroup representations). *Bulletin de Psychologie, 27,* 710-721.

Deschamps, J.-C., & Doise, W. (1978). Crossed category memberships in intergroup relations. In H. Tajfel (Ed.), *Differentiation between social groups* (pp. 141-158). London: Academic Press.

De Selincourt, A. (Trans.). (1954). *Herodotus: The histories.* Baltimore: Penguin Books.

Detweiler, R. (1975). On inferring the intentions of a person from another culture. *Journal of Personality, 43,* 591-611.

Detweiler, R. A. (1978). Culture, category width, and attributions: A model-building approach to the reasons for cultural effects. *Journal of Cross-Cultural Psychology, 9,* 259-284.

Detweiler, R. A. (1980). Intercultural interaction and the categorization process: A conceptual analysis and behavioral outcome. *International Journal of Intercultural Relations, 4,* 275-295.

Deutsch, F. M., Clark, M. E., & Zalenski, C. M. (1983, April). *Is there a double standard of aging?* Paper presented at the 54th meeting of the Eastern Psychological Association, Philadelphia, PA.

Deutsch, M. (1975). Equity, equality, and need: What determines which value will be used as the basis of distributive justice? *Journal of Social Issues, 31,* 137-149.

Deutsch, M. (1982). Interdependence and psychological orientation. In V. J. Derlega & J. Grzelak (Eds.), *Cooperation and helping behavior* (pp. 15-41). New York: Academic Press.

Deutsch, M. (1983). Current social psychological perspectives on justice. *European Journal of Social Psychology, 13,* 305-319.

Diaz-Guerrero, R. (1979). The development of coping style. *Human Development, 22,* 320-331.

Dion, K. L., & Dion, K. K. (in press). Romantic love: Individual and cultural perspectives. In R. J. Sternberg & M. L. Barnes (Eds.), *The anatomy of love.* New Haven, CT: Yale University Press.

Doi, T. (1973). *The anatomy of dependence.* Tokyo: Kodansha.

Doise, W., & Sinclair, A. (1973). The categorization process in intergroup relations. *European Journal of Social Psychology, 3,* 145-157.

Doise, W. (1982). *L'explication en psychologie sociale.* Paris: Presses Universitaires de France.

Doise, W. (1986). *Levels of explanation in social psychology.* Cambridge: Cambridge University Press.

Doise, W., Csepeli, G., Dann, H., Gouge, C., Larsen, K., & Ostell, A. (1972). An experimental investigation into the formation of intergroup representations. *European Journal of Social Psychology, 2,* 202-204.

Dollard, J. (1935). *Criteria for the life history.* New Haven: Yale University Press.

Dollard, J., Doob, L., Miller, N., Mowrer, O., & Sears, R. (1939). *Frustration and aggression.* New Haven: Yale University Press.

Doms, H., & Van Avermaet, E. (1981). *The conformity effect: A timeless phenomenon?* Unpublished manuscript, University of Louvain.

Donaldson, L. (1986). Size and bureaucracy in East and West: A preliminary meta analysis. In S. Clegg, D. C. Dunphy, & S. G. Redding (Eds.), *The enterprise and management in South-East Asia* (pp. 67-92). Hong Kong: Hong Kong University Centre for Asian Studies.

Doob, L. (1973). Dispute settlement in Chinese-American communities. *American Journal of Comparative Law, 21*, 627-663.

Doob, L. W. (1980). The inconclusive struggles of cross-cultural psychology. *Journal of Cross-Cultural Psychology, 11*, 59-73.

Driver, E. D., & Driver, A. O. (1983). Gender, society, and self-conceptions. *International Journal of Comparative Sociology, 24*, 200-217.

Dumont, L. (1965). The modern conception of the individual: Notes on its genesis. *Contributions to Indian Sociology, 8*, 13-61.

Dumont, L. (1970). *Homo hierarchicus.* Chicago: University of Chicago Press.

Durham, W. H. (1976). The adaptive significance of cultural behavior. *Human Ecology, 4*, 89-121.

Eisenstein, E. L. (1979). *The printing press as an agent of change: Communications and cultural transformations in early-modern Europe* (Vol. I). Cambridge: Cambridge University Press.

Ekman, P. (1984). Expression and the nature of emotion. In K. Scherer & P. Ekman (Eds.), *Approaches to emotion* (pp. 319-343). Hillsdale, NJ: Lawrence Erlbaum.

Ekman, P., & Friesen, W. v. (1986). A new pan-cultural facial expression of emotion. *Motivation and Emotion, 10*, 159-168.

Ember, C. R. (1981). A cross-cultural perspective on sex differences. In R. H. Munroe, R. L. Munroe, & B. B. Whiting (Eds.), *Handbook of cross-cultural human development* (pp. 531-580). New York: Garland.

Epstein, S. (1973). The self-concept revisited: Or a theory of a theory. *American Psychologist, 28*, 404-416.

Epstein, S. (1979). The stability of behavior: I. On predicting most of the people much of the time. *Journal of Personality and Social Psychology, 37*, 1097-1126.

Etkin, W. (1954). Social behavior and the evolution of man's faculties. *American Naturalist, 88*, 129-142.

Evans-Pritchard, E. E. (1937). *Witchcraft, oracles, and magic among the Azande.* Oxford: Clarendon Press.

Faucheux, C. (1976). Cross-cultural research in experimental social psychology. *European Journal of Social Psychology, 6*, 269-322.

Feather, N. T. (1971). Organization and discrepancy in cognitive structures. *Psychological Review, 78*, 355-379.

Feather, N. T. (1974). Explanations of poverty in Australian and American samples: The person, society, or fate? *Australian Journal of Psychology, 26*, 199-216.

Feather, N. T. (1975). *Values in education and society.* New York: Free Press.

Feather, N. T. (1982). Reasons for entering medical school in relation to value priorities and sex of student. *Journal of Occupational Psychology, 55*, 119-128.

Feather, N. T. (1985). Attitudes, values, and attributions: Explanations of unemployment. *Journal of Personality and Social Psychology, 48*, 876-889.

Feldman, A. S., & Moore, W. E. (1962, September). *Industrialization and industrialism: Convergence and differentiation.* Paper presented at the Fifth World Congress of Sociology. Washington, DC.

Feldman, R. E. (1968). Response to compatriot and foreigner who seek assistance. *Journal of Personality and Social Psychology, 10*, 203-214.

Felson, R. B. (1978). Aggression as impression management. *Social Psychology Quarterly, 41*, 205-213.

Felson, R. B. (1982). Impression management and the escalation of aggression and violence. *Social Psychology Quarterly, 45*, 245-254.

Feyerabend, P. H. (1970). Against method. In M. Radner & S. Winokur (Eds.),

Minnesota studies in the philosophy of science (Vol. 4). Minneapolis: University of Minnesota Press.

Feyerabend, P. H. (1978). *Against method: Outline of an anarchistic theory of knowledge.* London: Verso.

Fincham, F. D. (1985). Attribution in close relationships. In J. H. Harvey & G. Weary (Eds.), *Contemporary attribution theory and research* (pp. 203-324). New York: Academic Press.

Fincham, F. D., & Jaspars, J. M. (1980). Attributions of responsibility: From man the scientist to man as lawyer. In L. Berkowitz (Ed.), *Advances in experimental social psychology* (Vol. 13, pp. 81-138). New York: Academic Press.

Findley, M., & Cooper, H. (1981). Introductory social psychology textbook citations: A comparison of five research areas. *Personality and Social Psychology Bulletin, 7,* 173-176.

Finison, L. J. (1986). The psychological insurgency, 1936-1945. *Journal of Social Issues, 42,* 21-33.

Fishbein, M., & Ajzen, I. (1975). *Belief, attitude, intention, and behavior: An introduction to theory and research.* Reading, MA: Addison-Wesley.

Fisher, R. J. (1982). *Social psychology: An applied approach.* New York: St. Martin's.

Fiske, D. W., & Shweder, R. A. (Eds.). (1986). *Metatheory in social science: Pluralisms and subjectivities.* Chicago: University of Chicago Press.

Fiske, S. T., & Cox, M. C. (1979). Person concepts: The effect of target familiarity and descriptive purpose on the process of describing others. *Journal of Personality, 47,* 136-161.

Flanagan, S. C. (1979). Value change and partisan change in Japan: The silent revolution revisited. *Comparative Politics, 24,* 253-278.

Flanagan, S. C. (1980). Value cleavages, economic cleavages, and the Japanese voter. *American Journal of Political Science, 24,* 178-206.

Fletcher, G.J.O. (1984). Psychology and common sense. *American Psychologist, 39,* 203-213.

Fletcher, G.J.O., Danilovics, P., Fernandez, G., Peterson, D., & Reeder, G. D. (1986). Attributional complexity: An individual differences measure. *Journal of Personality and Social Psychology, 51,* 875-884.

Fletcher, G.J.O., Fincham, F. D., Cramer, L., & Heron, N. (in press). The role of attributions in the development of dating relationships. *Journal of Personality and Social Psychology.*

Foa, E. B., & Foa, U. G. (1980). Resource theory: Interpersonal behavior as exchange. In K. J. Gergen, M. S. Greenberg, & R. H. Willis (Eds.), *Social exchange: Advances in theory and research* (pp. 77-94). New York: Plenum.

Foa, U. G., & Foa, E. B. (1974). *Societal structures of the mind.* Springfield, IL: Charles C Thomas.

Ford, C., & Beach, F. (1951). *Patterns of sexual behavior.* New York: Harper.

Forgas, J. P., & Bond, M. H. (1985). Cultural influences on the perception of interaction episodes. *Personality and Social Psychology Bulletin, 11,* 75-88.

Forsterling, F. (1986). Attributional conceptions in clinical psychology. *American Psychologist, 41,* 275-285.

Foschi, M., & Hales, W. H. (1979). The theoretical role of cross-cultural comparisons in experimental social psychology. In L. H. Eckensberger, W. J. Lonner, & Y. H. Poortinga (Eds.), *Cross-cultural contributions to psychology* (pp. 244-254). Lisse: Swets & Zeitlinger.

Foster, D., & Finchilescu, G. (1986). Contact in a "non-contact" society: The case of South

Africa. In M. Hewstone & R. Brown (Eds.), *Contact and conflict in intergroup encounters* (pp. 119-136). Oxford: Basil Blackwell.

Frager, R. (1970). Conformity and anti-conformity in Japan. *Journal of Personality and Social Psychology, 15,* 203-210.

Frank, J. D. (1974). *Persuasion and healing: A comparative study of psychotherapy.* New York: Basic Books.

Fraser, C., Gouge, C., & Billig, M. (1970). Risky shifts, cautious shifts and group polarization. *European Journal of Social Psychology, 1,* 7-30.

Freilich, M. (1970). Field work: An introduction. In M. Freilich (Ed.), *Marginal natives: Anthropologists at work* (pp. 1-37). New York: Harper & Row.

Freilich, M. (Ed.). (1970). *Marginal natives: Anthropologists at work.* New York: Harper & Row.

Frijda, N., & Jahoda, G. (1966). On the scope and methods of cross-cultural research. *International Journal of Psychology, 1,* 109-127.

Fromm, E. (1941). *Escape from freedom.* New York: Rinehart.

Frost, P. J., Moore, L. F., Louis, M. R., Lundberg, C. C., & Martin, J. (Ed.). (1985). *Organizational culture.* Beverly Hills: Sage.

Fry, P. S., & Ghosh, R. (1980). Attributions of success and failure: Comparison of cultural differences between Asian and Caucasian children. *Journal of Cross-Cultural Psychology, 11,* 343-363.

Furnham, A., & Alibbai, N. (1983). Cross-cultural differences in the perception of female body shapes. *Psychological Medicine, 13,* 829-837.

Furnham, A., & Bochner, S. (1982). Social difficulty in a foreign culture. In S. Bochner (Ed.), *Cultures in contact* (pp. 161-199). Oxford: Pergamon.

Gabrenya, W., & Wang, Y. (1983, March). *Cultural differences in self schemata.* Paper presented at the Southeast Psychological Association Convention, Atlanta, GA.

Gallie, W. B. (1964). *Philosophy and historical understanding.* New York: Schocken Books.

Gardner, H. (1985). *The mind's new science: A history of the cognitive revolution.* New York: Basic Books.

Garza, R. T., & Ames, R. E. (1974). A comparison of Anglo and Mexican college students on locus of control. *Journal of Counseling and Clinical Psychology, 42,* 919.

Gasmick, H. G. (1973). Social change and modernism in the American South. *American Behavioral Scientist, 16,* 913-933.

Geertz, C. (1963). *Peddlers and princes: Social change and economic modernization in two Japanese towns.* Chicago: University of Chicago Press.

Geertz, C. (1973). *The interpretation of cultures.* New York: Basic Books.

Geertz, C. (1974). "From the native's point of view": On the nature of anthropological understanding. In K. Basso & H. Selby (Eds.), *Meaning in anthropology* (pp. 221-237). Albuquerque: University of New Mexico Press.

Geertz, C. (1980). *Negara: The theatre state in nineteenth-century Bali.* Princeton: Princeton University Press.

Gerard, H. B., & Conolley, E. S. (1972). Conformity: In C. G. McClintock (Ed.), *Experimental social psychology* (pp. 237-263). New York: Holt, Rinehart & Winston.

Gerber, E. (1985). Rage and obligation: Samoan emotion in conflict. In G. M. White & J. Kirkpatrick (Eds.), *Person, self, and experience: Exploring Pacific ethnopsychologies* (pp. 121-167). Berkeley: University of California Press.

Gergen, K. J. (1974). Social psychology as history. *Journal of Personality and Social Psychology, 26,* 309-320.

Gergen, K. J. (1978). Experimentation in social psychology: A reappraisal. *European Journal of Social Psychology, 8,* 507-527.

Gergen, K. J. (1978). Toward generative theory. *Journal of Personality and Social Psychology, 36,* 1344-1360.

Gergen, K. J. (1982). *Toward transformation in social knowledge.* New York: Springer-Verlag.

Gergen, K. J. (1984). An introduction to historical social psychology. In K. J. Gergen & M. M. Gergen (Eds.), *Historical social psychology* (pp. 3-36). Hillsdale, NJ: Lawrence Erlbaum.

Gergen, K. J. (1984). Theory of the self: Impasse and evolution. In L. Berkowitz (Ed.), *Advances in experimental social psychology* (Vol. 17, pp. 49-115). New York: Academic Press.

Gergen, K. J., & Gergen, M. M. (1981). *Social psychology.* New York: Harcourt, Brace Jovanovich.

Gergen, K. J., Morse, S. J., & Gergen, M. M. (1980). Behavior exchange in a cross-cultural perspective. In H. C. Triandis & R. W. Brislin (Eds.), *Handbook of cross-cultural psychology: Vol. 5. Social psychology* (pp. 121-154). Boston, MA: Allyn & Bacon.

Ghosh, E., & Huq, M. (1985). A study of social identity in two ethnic groups in India and Bangladesh. *Journal of Multilingual and Multicultural Development, 6,* 239-251.

Giles, H., Bourhis, R., & Taylor, D. (1977). Towards a theory of language in ethnic group relations. In H. Giles (Ed.), *Language, ethnicty, and intergroup relations* (pp. 307-348). New York: Academic Press.

Giles, H., & Byrne, J. L. (1982). An intergroup approach to second language acquisition. *Journal of Multilingual and Multicultural Development, 3,* 17-40.

Giles, H., & Johnson, P. (1987). Ethnolinguistic identity theory: A social psychological approach to language maintenance. *International Journal of the Sociology of Language, 68,* 69-80.

Giles, H., Rosenthal, D., & Young, L. (1985). Perceived ethnolinguistic vitality: The Anglo- and Greek-Australian setting. *Journal of Multilingual and Multicultural Development, 6,* 253-269.

Gilmore, D. D. (1986). Mother-son intimacy and the dual view of woman in Andalusia: Analysis through oral poetry. *Ethos, 14,* 227-251.

Gitter, A. G., Lomranz, J., Saxe, L., & Bar-Tal, D. (1982). Perceptions of female physique characteristics by American and Israeli students. *Journal of Social Psychology, 121,* 7-13.

Goffman, E. (1959). *The presentation of self in everyday life.* New York: Doubleday Anchor.

Goldberg, D. (1974). Modernism: The extensiveness of women's roles and attitudes. *World Fertility Survey,* Occasional paper no. 14, International Statistical Institute.

Goldberg, D. (1975). Socioeconomic theory and differential fertility: The case of the LDCs. *Social Forces, 54,* 84-106.

Goldberg, L. R. (1981). Language and individual differences: The search for universals in personality lexicons. In L. Wheeler (Ed.), *Review of personality and social psychology* (Vol. 2, pp. 141-165). Beverly Hills: Sage.

Goldschmidt, W. (1966). *Comparative functionalism.* Berkeley: University of California Press.

Goldstein, A. P. (1983). United States: Causes, controls, and alternatives to aggression. In A. P. Goldstein & M. H. Segall (Eds.), *Aggression in global perspective* (pp. 435-476). Elmsford, NY: Pergamon.

Gologor, E. (1977). Group polarization in a non-risk taking culture. *Journal of Cross-Cultural Psychology, 8,* 331-346.

Gomperz, T. (1901). *Greek thinkers: A history of ancient philosophy* (Vol. 1). London: John Murray.

Gould, S. J. (1977). *Ontogeny and phylogeny*. Cambridge, MA: Harvard University Press.

Gouldner, A. W. (1960). The norm of reciprocity: A preliminary statement. *American Sociological Review, 25*, 161-178.

Gouldner, A. W. (1970). *The coming crisis in Western sociology*. New York: Basic Books.

Greenberg, J. (1978). Equity, equality, and the Protestant ethic: Allocating rewards following fair and unfair competition. *Journal of Experimental Social Psychology, 14*, 217-226.

Greenberg, J. (1979). Protestant ethic endorsement and the fairness of equity inputs. *Journal of Research in Personality, 13*, 81-90.

Greenberg, J. (1981). The justice of distributing scarce and abundant resources. In M. J. Lerner & S. C. Lerner (Eds.), *The justice motive in social behavior* (pp. 289-316). New York: Plenum.

Greenberg, J., & Cohen, R. L. (Eds.). (1982). *Equity and justice in social behavior*. New York: Academic Press.

Greenberg, J., & Folger, R. (1983). Procedural justice, participation, and the fair process effect in groups and organizations. In P. B. Paulus (Ed.), *Basic group processes* (pp. 235-256). New York: Springer-Verlag.

Greenberg, J., & Rosenfield, D. (1979). Whites' ethnocentrism and their attributions for the behavior of blacks: A motivational bias. *Journal of Personality, 47*, 643-657.

Greenwald, A. G. (1982). Ego-task analysis: An integration of research on ego-involvement and self-awareness. In A. Hastorf & A. M. Isen (Eds.), *Cognitive social psychology* (pp. 109-147). New York: Elsevier.

Greenwald, A. G., & Pratkanis, A. R. (1984). The self. In R. S. Wyer & T. K. Srull, *The handbook of social cognition* (Vol. 3, pp. 129-178). Hillsdale, NJ: Lawrence Erlbaum.

Groebel, J. (1986). International research on television violence: Synopsis and critique. In L. R. Huesman & L. D. Eron (Eds.), *Television and the aggressive child: A cross-national comparison* (pp. 259-281). Hillsdale, NJ: Lawrence Erlbaum.

Gudykunst, W. B. (1985). Normative power and conflict potential in intergroup relationships. In W. B. Gudykunst, L. Stewart, & S. Ting-Toomey (Eds.), *Communication, culture and organizational processes* (pp. 152-176). Beverly Hills: Sage.

Gudykunst, W. B. (1986). Toward a theory of intergroup communication. In W. B. Gudykunst (Ed.), *Intergroup communication* (pp. 152-167). London: Edward Arnold.

Gudykunst, W. B. (1987, July). *Cultural variability in ethnolinguistic identity*. Paper presented at the Social Identity Conference, University of Exeter, Exeter, England.

Gudykunst, W. B., Chua, E., & Gray, E. (1986). Cultural dissimilarities and uncertainty reduction processes. In M. McLaughlin (Ed.), *Communication Yearbook: 10*. Beverly Hills: Sage.

Gudykunst, W. B., & Nishida, T. (1986). The influence of cultural variability on perceptions of communication behavior associated with relationship terms. *Human Communication Research, 13*, 147-166.

Gudykunst, W. B., Yoon, Y. C., & Nishida, T. (1987). The influence of individualism-collectivism on perceptions of communication in ingroup and out-group relationships. *Communication Monographs, 54*, 295-306.

Gulliver, P. H. (1979). *Disputes and negotiations: A cross-cultural perspective*. New York: Academic Press.

Gupta, M., & Singh, R. (1981). An integration-theoretical analysis of cultural and development differences in attribution of performance. *Developmental Psychology, 17*, 816-825.

Gusfield, J. (1967). Tradition and modernity: Misplaced polarities in the study of social change. *American Journal of Sociology, 72*, 351-362.

Guthrie, G. M. (1970). *The psychology of modernization in rural Philippines.* Manila: Ateneo de Manila University Press.

Guthrie, G. M. (1977). A socio-psychological analysis of modernization in the Philippines. *Journal of Cross-Cultural Psychology, 8,* 177-206.

Guthrie, G. M., & Bennett, A. B. (1971). Cultural differences in implicit personality theory. *International Journal of Psychology, 6,* 305-312.

Guthrie, R. D. (1976). *Body hot spots: The anatomy of human social organs and behavior.* New York: Van Nostrand Reinhold.

Hall, B. J., & Gudykunst, W. B. (1986). The intergroup theory of second language ability. *Journal of Language and Social Psychology, 5,* 291-302.

Hamilton, D. L., Carpenter, S., & Bishop, G. D. (1984). Desegregation of suburban neighborhoods. In N. Miller & M. Brewer (Eds.), *Groups in contact* (pp. 97-122). New York: Academic Press.

Hanson, N. R. (1969). *Perception and discovery: An introduction to scientific inquiry.* San Francisco: Freeman.

Harding, S. G. (1976). *Can theories be refuted? Essays on the Duhem-Quine thesis.* Dordrecht, Holland: D. Reidel.

Harré, R. (1981). Psychological variety. In P. Heelas & A. Lock (Eds.), *Indigenous psychologies: The anthropology of the self* (pp. 79-103). New York: Academic Press.

Harris, G. (1978). *Casting out anger.* Cambridge: Cambridge University Press.

Harris, M. (1968). *Cultural materialism: The struggle for a science of culture.* New York: Vintage.

Harris, M. (1979). *Cultural materialism: The struggle for a science of culture.* New York: Vintage.

Haruki, Y., & Shigehisa, T. (1983). Experimental analyses of the types of reinforcement—with special reference to social behavior theory. *Waseda Psychological Reports,* Special Issue, 63-93.

Haruki, T., Shigehisa, T., Nedate, K., Wajima, M., & Ogawa, R. (1984). Effects of alien-reinforcement and its combined type of learning behavior and efficacy in relation to personality. *International Journal of Psychology, 19,* 527-545.

Harvey, J. H. (1987, February). *What's new in social psychology?* Paper presented at the annual meeting of the Council of Graduate Departments of Psychology, San Diego, CA.

Harvey, J. H., Town, J. P., & Yarkin, K. L. (1981). How fundamental is "the fundamental attribution error"? *Journal of Personality and Social Psychology, 40,* 346-349.

Harvey, J. H., & Weary, G. (1984). Current issues in attribution theory and research. *Annual Review of Psychology, 35,* 427-459.

Harvey, O. J., Hunt, D. E., & Schroder, H. M. (1961). *Conceptual systems and personality organization.* New York: John Wiley.

Hatfield, E., & Sprecher, S. (1986). *Mirror, mirror . . . The importance of looks in everyday life.* Albany: State University of New York Press.

Heyden, R. M., & Anderson, J. K. (1979). On the evaluation of procedural systems in laboratory experiments: A critique of Thibaut and Walker. *Law and Human Behavior, 3,* 21-38.

Heelas, P. (1981). Introduction: Indigenous psychologies. In P. Heelas & A. Lock (Eds.), *Indigenous psychologies: The anthropology of the self.* New York: Academic Press.

Heelas, P., & Lock, A. (1981). *Indigenous psychologies: The anthropology of the self.* New York: Academic.

Heider, F. (1958). *The psychology of interpersonal relations.* New York: John Wiley.

Heller, F., & Wilpert, B. (1981). *Competence and power in managerial decision-making.* New York: John Wiley.

Helson, H. (1964). *Adaptation level theory*. New York: Harper & Row.

Henderson, D. F. (1975). *Foreign enterprise in Japan*. Chapel Hill: University of North Carolina Press.

Hendrick, C. (1975). PSPB: Editorial comment. *Personality and Social Psychology Bulletin, 1,* 467-469.

Henry, F., & Saberwal, S. (1969). *Stress and response in fieldwork*. New York: Holt, Rinehart & Winston.

Hewstone, M. (1985). Social psychology and intergroup relations: Cross-cultural perspectives. *Journal of Multilingual and Multicultural Development, 6,* 209-215.

Hewstone, M., Bond, M. H., & Wan, K. C. (1983). Social facts and social attributions: The exploration of intergroup differences in Hong Kong. *Social Cognition, 2,* 142-157.

Hewstone, M., & Brown, R. (1986). Contact is not enough. In M. Hewstone & R. Brown (Eds.), *Contact and conflict in intergroup encounters* (pp. 1-44). Oxford: Basil Blackwell.

Hewstone, M., & Jaspars, J. (1982). Intergroup relations and attribution processes. In H. Tajfel (Ed.), *Social identity and intergroup relations* (pp. 99-133). Cambridge: Cambridge University Press.

Hewstone, M., & Ward, C. (1985). Ethnocentrism and causal attribution in Southeast Asia. *Journal of Personality and Social Psychology, 48,* 614-623.

Hickson, D. J., Hinings, C. R., McMillan, C. J., & Schwitter, J. P. (1974). The culture-free context of organization structure. *Sociology, 8,* 59-80.

Hickson, D. J., & McMillan, C. J. (1981). *Organization and nation: The Aston programme IV*. Westmead, UK: Gower.

Hiniker, P. J. (1969). Chinese reactions to forced compliance: Dissonance reduction or national character? *Journal of Social Psychology, 77,* 151-176.

Hirshoren, A., & Schnittjer, C. J. (1981). The use of the Behavior Problem Checklist with Greek deaf children in cross-cultural research. *International Journal of Psychology, 16,* 161-170.

Ho, D.Y.F. (1980). Face and stereotyped notions about Chinese face behavior. *Philippine Journal of Psychology, 13,* 20-33.

Hoffman, C., Lau, I., & Johnson, D. R. (1986). The linguistic relativity of person cognition: An English-Chinese comparison. *Journal of Personality and Social Psychology, 51,* 1097-1105.

Hofman, T. E. (1985). Arabs and Jews, Blacks and Whites: Identity and group relations. *Journal of Multilingual and Multicultural Development, 6,* 217-237.

Hofstede, G. (1980). *Culture's consequences: International differences in work-related values*. Beverly Hills: Sage.

Hofstede, G. (1982). Dimensions of national cultures. In R. Rath, H. S. Asthana, C. Sinha, & J.B.H. Sinha (Eds.), *Diversity and unity in cross-cultural psychology* (pp. 173-187). Lisse: Swets & Zeitlinger.

Hofstede, G. (1983). Dimensions of national cultures in fifty countries and three regions. In J. B. Deregowski, S. Dziurawiec, & R. C. Annis (Eds.), *Expiscations in cross-cultural psychology* (pp. 335-355). Lisse: Swets & Zeitlinger.

Hogan, R. T., & Elmer, N. P. (1978). The biases in contemporary social psychology. *Social Research, 45,* 478-534.

Holloway, S. D., Kashiwagi, K., Hess, R. D., & Azuma, H. (1986). Causal attributions by Japanese and American mothers and children about performance in mathematics. *International Journal of Psychology, 21,* 269-286.

Holsinger, D. B. (1973). The elementary school as a modernizer: A Brazilian study. *International Journal of Comparative Sociology, 14,* 180-202.

Homans, G. C. (1961). *Social behavior: Its elementary forms.* New York: Harcourt, Brace & World.

Hornstein, H. A. (1982). Promotive tension: Theory and research. In V. J. Derlega & J. Grazlak (Eds.), *Cooperation and helping behavior* (pp. 229-248). New York: Academic Press.

Horton, R. (1970). African traditional thought and Western science. In B. R. Wilsen (Ed.), *Rationality* (pp. 131-171). Oxford: Basil Blackwell.

House, J. S. (1977). The three faces of social psychology. *Social Psychology Quarterly, 40,* 161-177.

House, R. J. (in press). Power in organizations: A social psychological perspective. In J. G. Hunt, R. Balinga, H. P. Dachler, & C. A. Schriesheim (Eds.), *Emerging leadership vistas.* Boston: Lexington.

Hsu, F.L.K. (1970). *Americans and Chinese.* New York: Natural History Press.

Hsu, F.L.K. (1971). Psychosocial homeostasis and jen: Conceptual tools for advancing psychological anthropology. *American Anthropologist, 73,* 23-44.

Hui, C.C.H. (1982). Locus of control: A review of cross-cultural research. *International Journal of Intercultural Relations, 6,* 301-323.

Hui, C.C.H. (1984). *Individualism-collectivism: Theory, measurement, and its relation to reward allocation.* Unpublished doctoral dissertation, University of Illinois at Urbana-Champaign.

Hui, C.C.H., & Triandis, H. (1983). Multi-strategy approach to cross-cultural research: The case of locus of control. *Journal of Cross-Cultural Psychology, 14,* 65-84.

Hui, C. H., & Triandis, H. C. (1984). *What does individualism-collectivism mean: A study of social scientists.* Unpublished manuscript, University of Illinois Department of Psychology.

Hui, C. H., & Triandis, H. C. (1986). Individualism-collectivism: A study of cross-cultural researchers. *Journal of Cross-Cultural Psychology, 17,* 225-248.

Hunt, J. G., & Osborn, R. N. (1982). Toward a macro-oriented model of leadership: An odyssey. In J. G. Hunt, U. Sekaran, & C. A. Schriesheim (Eds.), *Leadership: Beyond establishment views* (pp. 196-221). Carbondale: Southern Illinois University Press.

Huntington, S. P. (1966). Political modernization: America vs. Europe. *World Politics, 18,* 378-414.

Hursh-Cesar, G., & Roy, P. (1976). *Third World surveys: Survey research in developing nations.* Delhi: Macmillan.

Ickes, W., Paterson, M. C., Rajecki, D. W., & Tanford, S. (1982). Behavioral confirmation and behavioral compensation: Alternative consequences for preinter-action expectancy. *Social Cognition, 1,* 160-190.

Iida, M., Reeder, G. D., McCabe, S., Miura, K., & Goldstein, M. (1986, September). *Moral evaluation of achievement outcomes in the United States and Japan.* Paper presented at the meeting of the American Psychological Association, Washington, DC.

Ike, N. (1973). Economic growth and intergenerational change in Japan. *American Political Science Review, 67,* 1194-1203.

Inglehart, R. (1977). *The silent revolution: Changing values and political styles among Western publics.* Princeton, NJ: Princeton University Press.

Inglehart, R. (1982). Changing values in Japan and the West. *Comparative Political Studies, 14,* 445-479.

Inkeles, A. (1966). The modernization of man. In M. Weiner (Ed.), *Modernization: The dynamics of growth* (pp. 151-163). Washington, DC: U.S. Information Agency, Voice of America.

Inkeles, A. (1969). Making men modern: On the causes and consequences of individual change in six developing countries. *American Journal of Sociology, 75,* 208-225.

Inkeles, A., & Smith, D. H. (1974). *Becoming modern: Individual change in six developing countries.* Cambridge, MA: Harvard University Press.

Iwao, S. (1986, July). *The pitfalls of cross-cultural attitude surveys.* Paper presented at the International Congress of Applied Psychology, Jerusalem, Israel.

Jacobs, R. C., & Campbell, D. T. (1961). The perpetuation of an arbitrary tradition through several generations of a laboratory microculture. *Journal of Abnormal and Social Psychology, 62,* 649-658.

Jahoda, G. (1979). A cross-cultural perspective on experimental social psychology. *Personality and Social Psychology Bulletin, 5,* 142-148.

Jahoda, G. (1980). Cross-cultural comparisons. In M. H. Bornstein (Ed.), *Comparative methods in psychology* (pp. 105-148). Hillsdale, NJ: Lawrence Erlbaum.

Jahoda, G. (1980). Theoretical and systematic approaches in cross-cultural psychology. In H. C. Triandis & W. W. Lambert (Eds.), *Handbook of cross-cultural psychology: Vol. 1. Perspectives* (pp. 69-142). Boston: Allyn & Bacon.

Jahoda, G. (1982). *Psychology and anthropology: A psychological perspective.* London: Academic Press.

Jahoda, G. (1984). Do we need a concept of culture? *Journal of Cross-Cultural Psychology, 15,* 139-151.

Jahoda, G. (1986). Nature, culture and psychology. *European Journal of Social Psychology, 16,* 17-30.

Jaspars, J., & Hewstone, M. (1982). Cross-cultural interaction, social attribution and intergroup relations. In S. Bochner (Ed.), *Cultures in contact: Studies in cross-cultural interaction* (pp. 127-156). New York: Pergamon.

Jaspars, J. M., & Warnaen, S. (1982). Intergroup relations, social identity, and self-evaluation in India. In H. Tajfel (Ed.), *Social identity and intergroup relations* (pp. 335-365). Cambridge: Cambridge University Press.

Jaynes, J. (1977). *The origins of consciousness in the breakdown of the bicameral mind.* Boston: Houghton Mifflin.

Jeay, M. (1979). Sexuality and family in fifteenth-century France: Are literary sources a mask or a mirror? *Journal of Family History, 4,* 328-345.

Jessor, R., Graves, T. d., Hanson, R. C., & Jessor, S. L. (1968). *Society, personality and deviant behavior.* New York: Holt, Rinehart & Winston.

John, O. P., Goldberg, L. R., & Angleitner, A. (1984). Better than the alphabet: Taxonomies of personality-descriptive terms in English, Dutch, and German. In H.C.J. Bonarius, G.L.M. Van Hecle, & N. G. Smid (Eds.), *Personality psychology in Europe: Theoretical and empirical developments* (pp. 83-100). Lisse: Swets & Zeitlinger.

Jones, E. E. (1979). The rocky road from acts to dispositions. *American Psychologist, 34,* 107-117.

Jones, E. E. (1985). Major developments in social psychology during the past five decades. In G. Lindzey & E. Aronson (Eds.), *The handbook of social psychology* (3rd ed.) (pp. 47-108). New York: Random House.

Jones, E. E., & Davis, K. E. (1965). From acts to dispositions: The attribution process in person perception. In L. Berkowitz (Ed.), *Advances in experimental social psychology* (Vol. 2, pp. 219-266). New York: Academic Press.

Jones, R. A. (1986). Social psychological research and clinical practice: An academic paradox. *Professional Psychology: Research and Practice, 17,* 535-540.

Jones, T. B. (1960). *Ancient civilization.* Chicago: Rand McNally.

Kagan, S. (1976). Preference for control in rural Mexican and urban Anglo-American children. *Revista Interamericana de Psicologia, 10,* 51-59.

Kahl, J. A. (1968). *The measurement of modernism: A study of values in Brazil and Mexico.* Austin: University of Texas Press.

Kahn, A., Lamm, H., & Nelson, R. E. (1977). Preferences for an equal or equitable allocator. *Journal of Personality and Social Psychology, 35,* 837-844.

Kakar, S. (1971). The theme of authority in social relations in India. *Journal of Social Psychology, 84,* 93-101.

Kakar, S. (1978). *The inner world: A psychoanalytic study of childhood and society in India.* Oxford: Oxford University Press.

Kapferer, B. (1979). Emotion and feeling in Sinhalese healing rites. *Social Analysis, 1,* 153-176.

Kapleau, P. (1966). *The three pillars of Zen: Teaching, practice, and enlightenment.* Tokyo: Weatherhill.

Karsh, B., & Cole, R. E. (1968). Industrialization and the convergence hypothesis: Some aspects of contemporary Japan. *Journal of Social Issues, 24,* 45-63.

Kashima, Y., & Triandis, H. C. (1986). The self-serving bias in attributions as a coping strategy: A cross-cultural study. *Journal of Cross-Cultural Psychology, 17,* 83-97.

Kawashima, T. (1963). Dispute resolution in contemporary Japan. In A. T. von Mehren (Ed.), *Law in Japan: The legal order in a changing society* (pp. 41-72). Cambridge, MA: Harvard University Press.

Keating, C. F. (1985). Human dominance signals: The primate in us. In S. L. Ellyson & J. F. Dovidio (Eds.), *Power, dominance, and nonverbal behavior* (pp. 89-108). New York: Springer-Verlag.

Keeler, W. (1983). Shame and stagefright in Java. *Ethos, 11,* 152-165.

Kessing, R. M. (1974). Theories of culture. *Annual Review of Anthropology, 3,* 73-97.

Kelley, H. H. (1967). Attribution theory in social psychology. In D. Levine (Ed.), *Nebraska symposium on motivation, 1967* (Vol. 15, pp. 192-238). Lincoln: University of Nebraska Press.

Kelley, H. H. (1983). Epilogue: Perceived causal structures. In J. Jaspars, F. Fincham, & M. Hewstone (Eds.), *Attribution theory and research: Conceptual developments and social dimensions* (pp. 343-369). London: Academic Press.

Kelley, H. H., & Michela, J. J. (1980). Attribution theory and research. *Annual Review of Psychology, 31,* 457-501.

Kennedy, S., Scheirer, J., & Rogers, A. (1984). The price of success: Our monocultural science. *American Psychologist, 39,* 996-997.

Kenrick, D. T. (1986). How strong is the case against contemporary social and personality psychology? A response to Carlson. *Journal of Personality and Social Psychology, 50,* 839-844.

Kerr, C., Dunlop, J. T., Harbison, F. H., & Myers, C. A. (1960). *Industrialism and industrial man.* Cambridge, MA: Harvard University Press.

Kidd, D. (1905). *The essential Kaffir.* London: Adam & Charles Black.

Kimble, G. A. (1984). Psychology's two cultures. *Amerian Psychologist, 39,* 833-839.

Kirkby, O. (1986). *The relationship between procedural and distributive justice in children's decision making.* Unpublished honours thesis, The Flinders University of South Australia.

Kirkpatrick, J. (1983). *The Marquesan notion of the person.* Ann Arbor: University of Michigan Press.

Klineberg, O. (1954). *Social psychology.* New York: Holt, Rinehart & Winston.

Klineberg, S. L. (1973). Parents, schools, and modernity: An exploratory investigation of sex differences in the attitudinal development of Tunisian adolescents. *International Journal of Comparative Sociology, 14,* 221-244.

Kluckhohn, F., & Strodtbeck, F. (1961). *Variations of value orientations.* Evanston, IL: Row, Peterson.

Koch, S. (1985). Foreword: Wundt's creature at age zero—and as centenarian: Some aspects of the institutionalization of the new psychology. In S. Koch & D. E. Leary (Eds.), *A century of psychology as a science* (pp. 7-35). New York: McGraw-Hill.

Kogan, N., & Doise, W. (1969). Effects of anticipated delegate status on level of risk taking in small decision making groups. *Acta Psychologica, 29,* 228-243.

Kogan, N., & Wallach, M. (1967). Risk-taking as a function of the situation, the person, and the group. In G. Mandler (Ed.), *New directions in psychology* (Vol. 3, pp. 111-278). New York: Holt, Rinehart & Winston.

Kohn, M. (1969). *Class and conformity: A study of values.* Homewood, IL: Dorsey.

Korten, F. F. (1974). The influence of culture and sex on the perception of persons. *International Journal of Psychology, 9,* 31-44.

Kramer, E. (1963). Judgment of personal characteristics and emotions from nonverbal properties of speech. *Psychological Bulletin, 60,* 408-420.

Kuc, B., Hickson, D. J., & McMillan, C. J. (1980). Centrally planned development: A comparison of Polish factories with equivalents in Britain, Japan and Sweden. *Organization Studies, 1,* 258-270.

Kuhn, T. S. (1962). *The structure of scientific revolutions.* Chicago: University of Chicago Press.

Kuhn, T. S. (1970). *The structure of scientific revolutions* (2nd ed.). Chicago: University of Chicago Press.

Kuhn, T. S. (1977). *The essential tension: Selected studies in scientific tradition and change.* Chicago: University of Chicago press.

Kukla, A. (1978). On the empirical significance of pure determinism. *Philosophy of Science, 45,* 141-144.

Kukla, A. (1980). Determinism and predictability: Reply to Dieks. *Philosophy of Science, 47,* 131-133.

Kukla, A. (1983). Toward a science of experience. *Journal of Mind and Behavior, 4,* 231-245.

Kuo, S. Y. (1983). Academic achievement and causal attributions of success and failure by success-oriented and failure-oriented children. *Bulletin of Educational Psychology* (Taiwan), *16,* 47-60. (Abstract only in English.)

Lacey, W. K. (1968). *The family in classical theory.* Ithaca, NY: Cornell University Press.

Lakatos, I. (1970). Falsification and the methodology of scientific research programmes. In I. Lakatos & A. Musgrave (Eds.), *Criticism and the growth of knowledge* (pp. 91-195). Cambridge: Cambridge University Press.

Lakoff, G., & Kovecses, Z. (1987). The conceptualization of anger in American English. In N. Quinn & D. Holland (Eds.), *Cultural models in language and thought.* Cambridge: Cambridge University Press.

Lambert, W. E., Hamers, J. F., & Fraser-Smith, N. (1979). *Child-rearing values: A cross-national study.* New York: Praeger.

Lamm, H., & Kogan, N. (1970). Risk-taking in the context of intergroup negotiation. *Journal of Experimental Social Psychology, 6,* 351-363.

Lammers, C. J., & Hickson, D. J. (Eds.). (1979). *Organizations alike and unlike.* London: Routledge & Kegan Paul.

Langer, E. (1983). *The psychology of control.* Beverly Hills: Sage.

L'Armand, K. (1984). Preferences in patterns of eye contact in India. *Journal of Social Psychology, 122,* 137-138.

Larsen, K. (1974). Conformity in the Asch experiment. *Journal of Social Psychology, 94,* 303-304.

Larson, G. J. (1974). Introduction: The study of mythology and comparative mythology. In G. J. Larson, C. S. Littleton, & J. Puhvel (Eds.), *Myth in Indo-European antiquity* (pp. 1-16). Berkeley: University of California Press.

Latané, B. (1986, March). Invited address, Southeastern Society for Social Psychology business meeting. Paper presented at the annual meeting of the Southeastern Psychological Association, Kissimmee, FL.

Lavrakas, P. J. (1975). Female preferences for male physiques. *Journal of Research in Personality, 9,* 324-334.

Lebra, T. S. (1976). *Japanese patterns of behavior.* Honolulu: East-West Center.

Lee, B. (Ed.). (1979). *Psychosocial theories of the self.* New York: Plenum.

Lerner, D. (1958). *The passing of traditional society: Modernizing the Middle East.* Glencoe, IL: Free Press.

Leung, K. (in press). Some determinants of reactions to procedural models for conflict resolution: A cross-national study. *Journal of Personality and Social Psychology.*

Leung, K., & Bond, M. H. (1982). How Chinese and Americans reward task-related contributions: A preliminary study. *Psychologia, 25,* 32-39.

Leung, K., & Bond, M. H. (1984). The impact of cultural collectivism on reward allocation. *Journal of Personality and Social Psychology, 47,* 793-804.

Leung, K., & Iwawaki, S. (1986). *Cultural collectivism and distributive behavior: A cross-cultural study.* Manuscript submitted for publication.

Leung, K., & Lind, E. A. (1986). Procedural justice and culture: Effects of culture, gender and investigator status on procedural preferences. *Journal of Personality and Social Psychology, 50,* 1134-1140.

Leung, K., & Park, H. J. (1986). Effects of interactional goal on choice of allocation rules: A cross-national study. *Organizational Behavior and Human Decision Processes, 37,* 111-120.

Levenson, H. (1972, August). *Distinctions within the concept of internal-external control: Development of a new scale.* Paper presented at the meeting of the American Psychological Association, Honolulu, HI.

Leventhal, G. S. (1976). Fairness in social relations. In J. W. Thibaut, J. T. Spence, & R. C. Carlson (Eds.), *Contemporary topics in social psychology* (pp. 211-239). Morristown, NJ: General Learning Press.

Levine, D. N. (1968). The flexibility of traditional culture. *Journal of Social Issues, 24,* 129-141.

Levine, D. N. (1985). *The flight from ambiguity.* Chicago: University of Chicago Press.

LeVine, R. A. (1973). *Culture, behavior and personality.* Chicago: Aldine.

LeVine, R. A. (1984). Properties of culture: An ethnographic view. In R. A. Shweder & R. A. LeVine (Eds.), *Culture theory: Essays on mind, self and emotion* (pp. 67-87). New York: Cambridge University Press.

Levine, R. V. (1984). Cross-cultural studies: A mad world. *APA Monitor, 15*(12), 5.

Levine, R. V., & Bartlett, K. (1984). Pace of life, punctuality and coronary heart disease in six countries. *Journal of Cross-Cultural Psychology, 15,* 233-255.

Levy, M. J., Jr. (1966). *Modernization and the structure of societies.* Princeton, NJ: Princeton University Press.

Levy, R. I. (1973). *Tahitians: Mind and experience in the Society Islands.* Chicago: University of Chicago Press.

Lewin, K. (1948). *Resolving social conflicts.* New York: Harper & Row.

Lewin, K. (1951). *Field theory in social science.* Chicago: University of Chicago Press.

Liebow, E. (1967). *Tally's Corner: A study of Negro street corner men.* Boston: Little, Brown.

Liebrand, W.B.G., Messick, D. M., & Wolters, F. (1986). Why we are fairer than others? A cross-cultural replication and extension. *Journal of Experimental Social Psychology, 22,* 590-604.

Likert, R. (1961). *New patterns of management.* New York: McGraw-Hill.

Lind, E. A., Erickson, B. E., Friedland, N., & Dickenberger, M. (1978). Reactions to procedural models for adjudicative conflict resolution: A cross-national study. *Journal of Conflict Resolution, 2,* 318-341.

Lindgren, H. C. (1973). *An introduction to social psychology* (2nd ed.). New York: John Wiley.

Linton, R. (1956). *The tree of culture.* New York: Knopf.

Liska, A. E. (1977). The dissipation of sociological social psychology. *American Sociologist, 12,* 2-8.

Lissak, R. I., & Sheppard, B. H. (1983). Beyond fairness: The criterion problem in research on dispute intervention. *Journal of Applied Social Psychology, 13,* 45-65.

Lloyd, P. C. (1962). *Yoruba land law.* London: Oxford University Press.

Lomax, A., & Berkowitz, N. (1972). The evolutionary taxonomy of cultures. *Science, 177,* 228-239.

Lonner, W. J. (1980). A decade of cross-cultural psychology: *JCCP,* 1970-1979. *Journal of Cross-Cultural Psychology, 11,* 7-34.

Lonner, W. J. (1980). The search for psychological universals. In H. C. Triandis & W. W. Lambert (Eds.), *Handbook of cross-cultural psychology: Vol. 1. Perspectives* (pp. 143-204). Boston: Allyn & Bacon.

Lonner, W. J., & Berry, J. W. (Eds.). (1986). *Field methods in cross-cultural research.* Beverly Hills: Sage.

Louw, J., & Louw-Potgieter, J. (1986). Achievement-related causal attributions: A South African cross-cultural study. *Journal of Cross-Cultural Psychology, 17,* 269-282.

Lubman, L. (1967). Mao and mediation: Politics of dispute resolution in Communist China. *California Law Review, 55,* 1284-1359.

Lukes, S. (1973). *Individualism.* Oxford: Basil Blackwell.

Lutz, C. (1982). The domain of emotion words on Ifaluk. *American Ethnologist, 9,* 113-128.

Lutz, C. (1985). Ethnopsychology compared to what? Explaining behavior and consciousness among the Ifaluk. In G. M. White & J. Kirkpatrick (Eds.), *Person, self and experience* (pp. 35-79). Berkeley: University of California Press.

Lutz, C., & White, G. (1986). The anthropology of emotions. *Annual Review of Anthropology, 15,* 405-436.

Lyons, J. O. (1978). *The invention of the self: The hinge of consciousness in the eighteenth century.* Carbondale: Southern Illinois University Press.

Maass, A., & Clark, R. D. III. (1984). Hidden impact of minorities: Fifteen years of minority influence research. *Psychological Bulletin, 95,* 428-450.

Maccoby, E. E., & Jacklin, C. N. (1974). *The psychology of sex differences.* Stanford: Stanford University Press.

MacDonald, A. P., Jr. (1971). More on the Protestant ethic. *Journal of Consulting and Clinical Psychology, 39,* 112-116.

Madsen, M. C., & Shapira, A. (1970). Cooperative and competitive behavior of urban Afro-American, Anglo-American, Mexican-American and Mexican village children. *Developmental Psychology, 3,* 16-20.

Mahler, I., Greenberg, L., & Hayashi, H. (1981). A comparative study of rules of justice: Japanese versus Americans. *Psychologia, 24,* 1-8.

Mair, L. (1972). *Introduction to social anthropology.* Oxford: Clarendon Press.

Majchrzak, A. (1984). *Methods for policy research.* Newbury Park, CA: Sage.

Majeed, A., & Ghosh, E.S.K. (1982). A study of social identity in three ethnic groups in India. *International Journal of Psychology, 17,* 455-463.

Major, B., & Deaux, K. (1982). Individual differences in justice behavior. In J. Greenberg & R. I. Cohen (Eds.), *Equity and justice in social behavior* (pp. 217-255). New York: Academic Press.

Malinowski, B. (1948). *Magic, science and religion and other essays.* Glencoe, IL: Free Press.

Malinowski, B. (1955). *Sex and repression in savage society.* New York: Meridian Books. (Original work published 1927)

Malpass, R. S. (1977). Theory and method in cross-cultural psychology. *American Psychologist, 32,* 1069-1079.

Malpass, R. S., & Poortinga, Y. H. (1986). Strategies for design and analysis. In W. J. Lonner & J. W. Berry (Eds.), *Field methods in cross-cultural research* (pp. 47-83). Beverly Hills: Sage.

Mann, L. (1980). Cross-cultural studies of small groups. In H. Triandis & R. Brislin (Eds.), *Handbook of cross-cultural psychology: Vol. 5. Social psychology* (pp. 155-209). Boston: Allyn & Bacon.

Mann, L. (1986). Cross-cultural studies of rules for determining majority and minority decision rights. *Australian Journal of Psychology, 38,* 319-328.

Mann, L., Radford, M., & Kanagawa, C. (1985). Cross-cultural differences in children's use of decision rules: A comparison of Japan and Australia. *Journal of Personality and Social Psychology, 49,* 1557-1564.

Margalit, B. A., & Mauger, P. A. (1985). Aggressiveness and assertiveness: A cross-cultural study of Israel and the United States. *Journal of Cross-Cultural Psychology, 16,* 497-511.

Marin, G. (1981). Perceiving justice across cultures: Equity vs. equality in Colombia and in the United States. *International Journal of Psychology, 16,* 153-159.

Marin, G. (1985). Validez transcultural del principio de equidad: El colectivismo-individualismo come una variable moderatora. *Revista Interamericana de Psycologia Occupational, 4,* 7-20.

Marin, G., & Marin, B. V. (1982). Methodological fallacies when studying Hispanics. In L. Bickman (Ed.), *Applied social psychology annual* (Vol. 3, pp. 99-117). Beverly Hills: Sage.

Marin, G., & Triandis, H. C. (1985). Allocentrism as an important characteristic of the behavior of Latin Americans and Hispanics. In R. Diaz-Guerrero (Ed.), *Cross-cultural and national studies of social psychology* (pp. 85-104). Amsterdam: North Holland.

Markus, H., & Wurf, E. (1987). The dynamic self-concept: A social psychological perspective. *Annual Review of Psychology, 38,* 299-337.

Marriott, M. (1976). Hindu transactions: Diversity without dualism. In B. Kapferer (Ed.), *Transaction and meaning* (pp. 109-142). Philadelphia: Institute for Study of Human Issues.

Marriott, M. (1979). *The open Hindu person and the human sciences.* Unpublished manuscript, University of Chicago, Department of Anthropology.

Marsella, A., DeVos, G., & Hsu, F.L.K. (Eds.). (1985). *Culture and self: Asian and Western perspectives.* New York: Tavistock.

Marsella, A. J., & White, G. M. (Eds.). (1982). *Cultural conceptions of mental health and therapy.* Dordrecht, Holland: Reidel.

Martin, J. G. (1964). Racial ethnocentrism and judgment of beauty. *Journal of Social Psychology, 63,* 59-63.

Maurice, M. (1976). Introduction: Theoretical and ideological aspects of the universalistic approach to the study of organizations. *International Studies of Management and Organization, 6,* 3-10.

Maurice, M., Sorge, A., & Warner, M. (1980). Societal differences in organizing manufacturing units: A comparison of France, West Germany and Great Britain. *Organization Studies, 1,* 59-86.

Mauss, M. (1967). *The gift* (I. Cunnison, Trans.). New York: Norton.

Mazur, A. (1985). A biosocial model of status in face-to-face primate groups. *Social Forces, 64,* 377-402.

McArthur, L. Z. (1972). The how and what of why: Some determinants and consequences of causal attributions. *Journal of Personality and Social Psychology, 22,* 171-193.

McArthur, L. Z. (1982). Judging a book by its cover: A cognitive analysis of the relationship between physical appearance and stereotyping. In A. Hastorf & A. Isen (Eds.), *Cognitive social psychology* (pp. 149-211). New York: Elsevier/North Holland.

McArthur, L. Z., & Baron, R. M. (1983). Toward an ecological theory of social perception. *Psychological Review, 90,* 215-238.

McArthur, L. Z., & Berry, D. S. (1987). Cross-cultural agreement in perceptions of babyfaced adults. *Journal of Cross-Cultural Psychology, 18,* 165-192.

McClelland, D. C. (1961). *The achieving society.* Princeton, NJ: Van Nostrand.

McClintock, C. G. (1985). The metatheoretical bases of social psychological theory. *Behavioral Science, 30,* 155-173.

McDougall, W. (1908). *Introduction to social psychology.* London: Methuen.

McGuire, W. J. (1967). Some impending reorientations in social psychology: Some thoughts provoked by Kenneth Ring. *Journal of Experimental Social Psychology, 3,* 124-139.

McGuire, W. J. (1973). The yin and yang of progress in social psychology: Seven koan. *Journal of Personality and Social Psychology, 26,* 446-456.

McGuire, W. J. (1983). A contextualist theory of knowledge: Its implications for innovation and reform in psychological research. In L. Berkowitz (Ed.), *Advances in experimental social psychology* (Vol. 16, pp. 2-47). San Francisco: Academic Press.

McGuire, W. J. (1985). Attitudes and attitude change. In G. Lindzey & E. Aronson (Eds.), *Handbook of social psychology* (3rd ed.) (Vol. 2, pp. 233-346). New York: Random House.

McGuire, W. J., & Papageorgis, D. (1961). The relative efficacy of various types of prior belief-defense in producing immunity against persuasion. *Journal of Abnormal and Social Psychology, 62,* 327-337.

McMurtry, L. (1968). *In a narrow grave: Essays on Texas.* Austin: Encino Press.

Mead, M. (1935). *Sex and temperament in three primitive societies.* New York: Morrow.

Meade, R. D. (1967). An experimental study of leadership in India. *Journal of Social Psychology, 72,* 35-43.

Merton, R. K. (1948). The self-fulfilling prophecy. *Antioch Review, 8,* 193-210.

Metge, J. (1976). *The Maoris of New Zealand.* London: Routledge & Kegan Paul.

Meyer, A. G. (1970). Theories of convergence. In C. Johnson (Ed.), *Change in communist systems* (pp. 113-129). Stanford: Stanford University Press.

Michaels, W. B. (1980). Against formalism: Chickens and rocks. In L. Michaels & C. Ricks (Eds.), *The state of the language* (pp. 410-420). Berkeley: University of California Press.

Milgram, S. (1974). *Obedience to authority.* New York: Harper & Row.

Miller, G., Galanter, E., & Pribram, K. H. (1960). *Plans and the structure of behavior.* New York: Holt.

Miller, J. (1984). Culture and the development of everyday social explanation. *Journal of Personality and Social Psychology, 46,* 961-978.

Miller, J. (in press). Cultural influences on the development of conceptual differentiation in person description. *British Journal of Developmental Psychology.*

Miller, N. E. (1941). The frustration-aggression hypothesis. *Psychological Review, 48,* 337-342.

Miller, N., & Brewer, M. B. (1986). Categorization effects on ingroup and outgroup perceptions. In J. F. Dorido and S. L. Gaertner (Eds.), *Prejudice, discrimination, and racism* (pp. 209-230). New York: Academic Press.

Mirels, H. L., & Garrett, J. B. (1971). The Protestant ethic as a personality variable. *Journal of Consulting and Clinical Psychology, 36,* 40-44.

Misra, G., & Agarwal, R. (1985). The meaning of achievement: Implications for cross-cultural theory of achievement motivation. In I. R. Lagunes & Y. H. Poortinga (Eds.), *From a different perspective: Studies of behaviour across cultures* (pp. 250-256). Lisse: Swets & Zeitlinger.

Misumi, J. (1972). *Group dynamics in Japan.* Kyushu University, Faculty of Education. Fukuoka, Japan: Japanese Group Dynamics Association.

Misumi, J. (1985). *The behavioral science of leadership.* Ann Arbor: University of Michigan Press.

Montepare, J. M., & McArthur, L. Z. (1987). Perceptions of adults with childlike voices in two cultures. *Journal of Experimental Social Psychology.*

Morsbach, H. (1980). Major psychological factors influencing Japanese interpersonal relations. In N. Warren (Ed.), *Studies in cross-cultural psychology* (Vol. 2, pp. 317-344). London: Academic Press.

Morse, C. (1969). Becoming versus being modern: An essay on institutional change and economic development. In C. Morse, D. E. Ashford, F. T. Bent, W. H. Friedland, J. W. Lewis, & D. B. Macklin (Eds.), *Modernization by design* (pp. 238-382). Ithaca, NY: Cornell University Press.

Moscovici, S. (1972). Society and theory in social psychology. In J. Israel & H. Tajfel (Eds.), *The context of social psychology: A critical assessment* (pp. 17-68). New York: Academic Press.

Moscovici, S. (1985). Social influence and conformity. In G. Lindzey & E. Aronson (Eds.), *Handbook of social psychology* (3rd ed.) (Vol. 2, pp. 347-418). New York: Random House.

Munro, D. (1979). Locus of control attribution: Factors among blacks and whites in Africa. *Journal of Cross-Cultural Psychology, 10,* 157-172.

Munroe, R. L., & Munroe, R. H. (1975). *Cross-cultural human development.* Monterey, CA: Brooks/Cole.

Munroe, R. L., Munroe, R. H., & Daniels, R. E. (1973). Relation of subsistence economy to conformity in three East African societies. *Journal of Social Psychology, 89,* 149-250.

Murdock, G. P., & Provost, C. (1973). Measurement of cultural complexity. *Ethnology, 12,* 379-392.

Murdock, G. P., & White, R. R. (1969). Standard cross-cultural samples. *Ethnology, 8,* 329-369.

Murphy-Berman, V., Berman, J. J., Singh, P., Pachauri, A., & Kumar, P. (1984). Factors affecting allocation to needy and meritorious recipients: A cross-cultural comparison. *Journal of Personality and Social Psychology, 46,* 1267-1272.

Nader, L. (1969). Styles of court procedure: To make the balance. In L. Nader (Ed.), *Law in culture and society* (pp. 69-91). Chicago: Aldine.

Nader, L., & Todd, H. F. (1978). *The disputing process: Law in ten societies.* New York: Columbia University Press.

Nadler, A. (1986). Help seeking as a cultural phenomenon: Differences between city and kibbutz dwellers. *Journal of Personality and Social Psychology, 51,* 976-982.

Nagelschmidt, A., & Jakob, R. (1977). Dimensionality of Rotter's I-E Scale in a society in the process of modernization. *Journal of Cross-Cultural Psychology, 8,* 101-112.

Nakane, C. (1970). *Japanese society.* Berkeley, CA: University of California Press.

Naroll, R. (1961). Two solutions to Galton's problem. *Philosophy of Science, 28,* 15-39.

Naroll, R. (1983). *The moral order: An introduction to the human situation.* Beverly Hills: Sage.

Negandhi, A. R. (1973). *Management and economic development: The case of Taiwan.* The Hague: Nijhoff.

Negandhi, A. R. (1985). Management in the Third World. In P. Joynt & M. Warner (Eds.), *Managing in different cultures* (pp. 69-97). Oslo: Universitetsforlaget.

Newman, G. (1979). *Understanding violence.* New York: Lippincott.

Newtson, C., & Czerlinsky, T. (1974). Adjustment of attitude communications for contrasts by extreme audiences. *Journal of Personality and Social Psychology, 30,* 829-837.

Nicholson, N., Cole, S. G., & Rocklin, T. (1985). Conformity in the Asch situation: A comparison between contemporary British and U.S. university students. *British Journal of Social Psychology, 24,* 59-63.

Niles, F. S. (1985). Attribution for academic success and failure in Sri Lanka. *Journal of Social Psychology, 125,* 401-402.

Nisbett, R. E. (1977). Interactions versus main effects as goals of personality research. In J. Magnusson & N. S. Endler (Eds.), *Personality at the crossroad: Current issues in interactional psychology* (pp. 235-242). Hillsdale, NJ: Lawrence Erlbaum.

Nishihira, S. (1974). Changed and unchanged characteristics of the Japanese. *Japan Echo, 1,* 21-32.

Noel, D. C. (1976). *Seeing Castaneda: Reactions to the "Don Juan" writings of Carlos Castaneda.* New York: Putnam.

Noesjirwan, J. (1978). A rule-based analysis of cultural differences in social behaviour: Indonesia and Australia. *International Journal of Psychology, 13,* 305-316.

Norman, W. T. (1963). Toward an adequate taxonomy of personality attributes: Replicated factor structure in peer nomination personality ratings. *Journal of Abnormal and Social Psychology, 66,* 574-583.

Ocha, E., & Schieffelin, B. B. (1984). Language acquisition and socialization: Three developmental stories and their implications. In R. A. Shweder & R. A. LeVine (Eds.), *Culture theory: Essays on mind, self and emotion* (pp. 276-320). New York: Cambridge University Press.

Osgood, C. E. (1969). On the whys and wherefores of E, P, and A. *Journal of Personality and Social Psychology, 12,* 194-199.

Ostor, A., Fruzetti, A. L., & Barnett, S. (Eds.). (1982). *Concepts of person.* Cambridge: Harvard University Press.

Otaki, M., Durrett, M. E., Richards, P., Nyquist, L., & Pennebaker, J. W. (1986). Maternal and infant behavior in Japan and America: A partial replication. *Journal of Cross-Cultural Psychology, 17,* 251-268.

Ottenberg, S. P. (1960). *Cultures and societies of Africa.* New York: Random House.

Paicheler, G. (1976). Norms and attitude change: I. Polarization and styles of behavior. *European Journal of Social Psychology, 6,* 405-429.

Paicheler, G. (1977). Norms and attitude change: II. The phenomenon of bipolarization. *European Journal of Social Psychology, 7,* 5-14.

316   THE CROSS-CULTURAL CHALLENGE TO SOCIAL PSYCHOLOGY

Paicheler, G., & Darmon, G. (1975). Representations majoritaires et minoritaires et relations intergroupes. Unpublished study cited in W. Austin & S. Worchel (Eds.) (1979), *The social psychology of intergroup relations*. Monterey, CA: Brooks/Cole.

Parsons, T. (1951). *The social system*. New York: Free Press.

Pascale, R. T., & Athos, A. G. (1981). *The art of Japanese management*. New York: Simon & Schuster.

Peabody, D. (1985). *National characteristics*. Cambridge: Cambridge University Press.

Pehazur, L., & Wheeler, L. (1971). Locus of perceived control and need achievement. *Perceptual and Motor Skills, 33*, 1281-1282.

Pelto, P. J. (1968, April). The difference between "tight" and "loose" societies. *Transaction*, 37-40.

Pepitone, A. (1976). Toward a normative and comparative biocultural social psychology. *Journal of Personality and Social Psychology, 34*, 641-653.

Pepitone, A. (1981). Lessons from the history of social psychology. *American Psychologist, 36*, 972-985.

Pepitone, A. (1986). Culture and the cognitive paradigm in social psychology. *Australian Journal of Psychology, 38*, 245-256.

Pepitone, A. (1986, July). *The role of culture in theories of social psychology*. Paper presented at the 8th International Congress of Cross-Cultural Psychology, Istanbul, Turkey.

Perrin, S., & Spencer, C. (1980). The Asch-effect, a child of its time? *Bulletin of the British Psychological Society, 32*, 405-406.

Perrin, S., & Spencer, C. (1981). Independence or conformity in the Asch experiment as a reflection of cultural and situational factors. *British Journal of Social Psychology, 20*, 205-209.

Peterson, C., & Seligman, M.E.P. (1984). Causal explanations as a risk factor for depression: Theory and evidence. *Psychological Review, 91*, 347-374.

Peterson, C., Semmel, A., von Baeyer, C., Abramson, L. Y., Metalsky, G. I., & Seligman, M.E.P. (1982). The attributional style questionnaire. *Cognitive Therapy and Research, 5*, 287-299.

Peterson, R. B., & Shimada, J. Y. (1978). Sources of management problems in Japanese-American joint ventures. *Academy of Management Review, 3*, 796-804.

Pettigrew, T. F. (1979). The ultimate attribution error: Extending Allport's cognitive analysis of prejudice. *Personality and Social Psychology Bulletin, 5*, 461-476.

Pettigrew, T. F. (1986). The intergroup contact hypothesis reconsidered. In M. Hewstone & R. Brown (Eds.), *Contact and conflict in intergroup encounters* (pp. 169-195). Oxford: Basil Blackwell.

Phares, E. J. (1978). Locus of control. In H. London & J. E. Exner, Jr. (Eds.), *Dimensions of personality* (pp. 263-304). New York: John Wiley.

Piaget, J. (1966). Necessite et signification des recherches comparatives en psychologie genetique. *International Journal of Psychology, 1*, 3-13. (English translation in J. W. Berry & P. R. Dasen (Eds.). (1974). *Culture and cognition*. London: Methuen.)

Poincare, H. (n. d.). *Science and method*. London: Constable. (Original work published 1908, Paris, Bibliotheque de Philosophie Scientifique)

Portes, A. (1973). The factorial structure of modernity: Empirical replications and a critique. *American Journal of Sociology, 79*, 15-44.

Powers, S., & Rossman, M. H. (1984). Attributions for success and failure among Anglo, Black, Hispanic, and Native American community college students. *Journal of Psychology, 117*, 27-31.

Price-Williams, D. (1980). Anthropological approaches to cognition and their relevance to psychology. In H. C. Triandis & W. J. Lonner (Eds.), *Handbook of cross-cultural psychology: Vol. 3. Basic processes* (pp. 155-184). Boston: Allyn & Bacon.

Proshansky, H. M. (1976). Environmental psychology and the real world. *American Psychologist, 31,* 303-316.

Pruitt, D. G. (1975). Call for "innovative" manuscripts. *Personality and Social Psychology Bulletin, 1,* 470.

Pruitt, D. G. (1982). *Negotiation behavior.* New York: Academic Press.

Pugh, D. S., Hickson, D. J., Hinings, C. R., & Turner, C. (1968). An approach to the study of bureaucracy. *Sociology, 1,* 61-72.

Pye, L. W. (1966). *Aspects of political culture: An analytic study.* Boston: Little, Brown.

Quinn, N., & Holland, D. (Eds.). (1987). *Cultural models in language and thought.* Cambridge: Cambridge University Press.

Ram Dass (1976). *The only dance there is.* New York: Jason Aronson.

Rawls, J. (1971). *A theory of justice.* Cambridge, MA: Belknap Press.

Redding, S. G., & Wong, G.Y.Y. (1986). The psychology of Chinese organizational behaviour. In M. H. Bond (Ed.), *The psychology of the Chinese people* (pp. 267-295). Hong Kong: Oxford University Press.

Reeder, G. D. (1985). Implicit relations between dispositions and behaviors: Effects on dispositional attribution. In J. Harvey & G. Weary (Eds.), *Attribution: Basic issues and applications* (pp. 87-116). Orlando: Academic Press.

Reeder, G. D., & Brewer, M. B. (1979). A schematic model of dispositional attribution in interpersonal perception. *Psychological Review, 86,* 61-79.

Reichenbach, H. (1962). *The rise of scientific philosophy.* Berkeley: University of California Press.

Reis, H. T. (1981). Self-presentation and distributive justice. In J. T. Tedeschi (Ed.), *Impression management theory and social psychological research* (pp. 269-291). New York: Academic Press.

Reisenzein, R. (1986). A structural equation analysis of Weiner's attribution-affect model of helping behavior. *Journal of Personality and Social Psychology, 50,* 1123-1133.

Reitz, H. J., & Groff, G. K. (1972, August). *Comparisons of locus of control categories among American, Mexican and Thai workers.* Paper presented at the meeting of the American Psychological Association, Honolulu, HI.

Reynolds, V. (1976). *The biology of human action.* San Francisco: W. H. Freeman.

Rieu, E. B. (Trans.). (1950). *Homer: The Iliad.* Harmondsworth, UK: Penguin.

Rim, Y. (1963). Risk-taking and need for achievement. *Acta Psychologica, 21,* 108-115.

Robbins, M. C., DeWalt, B. R., & Pelto, P. J. (1972). Climate and behavior: A biocultural study. *Journal of Cross-Cultural Psychology, 3,* 331-344.

Roberts, K. H., & Boyacigiller, N. A. (1984). Cross-national organizational research: The grasp of the blind man. In B. M. Staw & L. L. Cummings (Eds.), *Research in organizational behavior: Vol. 6* (pp. 423-475). Greenwich, CT: JAI Press.

Rodrigues, A. (1982). Replication: A neglected type of research in social psychology. *Intra-American Journal of Psychology, 16,* 91-109.

Rogers, A. (1969). *Modernization among peasants.* New York: Holt, Rinehart, & Winston.

Rohner, R. P. (1976). Sex differences in aggression: Phylogenetic and enculturation perspectives. *Ethos, 4,* 57-72.

Rokeach, M. (1973). *The nature of human values.* New York: Free Press.

Rosaldo, M. (1980). *Knowledge and passion: Ilongot notions of self and social life.* Cambridge: Cambridge University Press.

Rosaldo, M. Z. (1983). The shame of headhunters and autonomy of self. *Ethos, 11,* 135-151.

Rosaldo, M. Z. (1984). Toward an anthropology of self and feeling. In R. A. Shweder & R. A. LeVine (Eds.), *Culture theory: Essays on mind, self and emotion* (pp. 137-157). New York: Cambridge University Press.

Rosen, B. (1964). The achievement syndrome and economic growth in Brazil. *Social Forces, 42,* 341-351.

Rosen, B. (1971). Industrialization, personality, and social mobility in Brazil. *Human Organization, 30,* 137-148.

Rosenbaum, M. E. (1986). The repulsion hypothesis: On the nondevelopment of relationships. *Journal of Personality and Social Psychology, 51,* 1156-1166.

Rosenberg, S., & Gara, M. A. (1983). Contemporary perspectives and future directions of personality and social psychology. *Journal of Personality and Social Psychology, 45,* 57-73.

Rosenthal, R. (1966). *Experimenter bias effects in behavioral research.* New York: Appleton-Century-Crofts.

Ross, L. (1977). The intuitive psychologist and his shortcomings: Distortions in the attribution process. In L. Berkowitz (Ed.), *Advances in experimental social psychology* (Vol. 10, pp. 173-220). New York: Academic Press.

Ross, L., Greene, D., & House, P. (1977). The "false consensus effect": An egocentric bias in social perception and attribution processes. *Journal of Experimental Social Psychology, 13,* 279-301.

Ross, M., & Fletcher, G.J.O. (1985). Attribution and social perception. In G. Lindzey & E. Aronson (Eds.), *The handbook of social psychology* (3rd ed.) (pp. 73-121). New York: Random House.

Rotter, J. (1966). Generalized expectancies for internal versus external control of reinforcement. *Psychological Monographs, 80* (1, Whole No. 609).

Rubin, J. Z., & Brown, B. R. (1975). *The social psychology of bargaining and negotiation.* New York: Academic Press.

Rule, B. G. (1986). PSPB rejection rate lower than reported. *Society for Personality and Social Psychology Dialogue, 1,* 1.

Rump, E. E., Rigby, K., & Walters, L. (1985). The generality of attitudes toward authority: Cross-cultural comparisons. *European Journal of Social Psychology, 125,* 307-312.

Russell, B. (1945). *A history of Western philosophy.* New York: Simon & Schuster.

Rutter, D. R., & Robinson, B. (1981). An experimental analysis of teaching by telephone: Theoretical and practical implications for social psychology. In G. M. Stephenson & J. H. Davis (Eds.), *Progress in applied social psychology* (Vol. 1, pp. 345-374). New York: John Wiley.

Ryckman, R., Posen, C., & Kulberg, G. E. (1978). Locus of control among American and Rhodesian students. *Journal of Social Psychology, 104,* 165-173.

Sack, R. (1973). The impact of education on individual modernity in Tunisia. *International Journal of Comparative Sociology, 14,* 245-272.

Sagatun, I. J. (1981). Sex difference in attribution: A Norwegian study. *Scandinavian Journal of Psychology, 22,* 51-57.

Sahlins, M. (1976). *Culture and practical reason.* Chicago: University of Chicago Press.

Sako, S. (1979). *Asch experiment on conformity: A replication.* Unpublished master's thesis, University of Osaka.

Salamone, F. A., & Swanson, C. H. (1979). Identity and ethnicity. *Ethnic Groups, 2,* 167-183.

Salili, F., Maeher, M. L., Sorensen, R. L., & Fyans, L. J. Jr. (1976). A further consideration of the effects of evaluation on motivation. *American Educational Research Journal, 13*, 85-102.

Sampson, E. E. (1969). Studies on status congruence. In L. Berkowitz (Ed.), *Advances in experimental social psychology* (Vol. 4, pp. 225-270). New York: Academic Press.

Sampson, E. E. (1975). On justice as equality. *Journal of Social Issues, 31*, 45-64.

Sampson, E. E. (1977). Psychology and the American ideal. *Journal of Personality and Social Psychology, 35*, 767-782.

Sampson, E. E. (1978). Scientific paradigms and social values: Wanted—A scientific revolution. *Journal of Personality and Social Psychology, 36*, 1332-1343.

Sampson, E. E. (1981). Cognitive psychology as ideology. *American Psychologist, 36*, 730-743.

Sampson, E. E. (1985). The decentralization of identity: Toward a revised concept of personal and social order. *American Psychologist, 40*, 1203-1211.

Sampson, E. E. (1986). Justice ideology and social legitimation. In H. W. Bierhoff, R. L. Cohen, & J. Greenberg (Eds.), *Justice in social relations* (pp. 87-102). New York: Plenum.

Samuelson, C. D., Messick, D. M., Rutte, C. G., & Wilke, H. (1984). Individual and structural solutions to resource dilemmas in two cultures. *Journal of Personality and Social Psychology, 47*, 94-104.

Sanford, N. (1970). Whatever happened to action research? *Journal of Social Issues, 26*(4), 3-23.

Sarason, S. B. (1981). An asocial psychology and a misdirected clinical psychology. *American Psychologist, 36*, 827-836.

Sargent, S. s. (1977). Coping with unwanted variables in cross-cultural research: Examples from mental health and treatment of the aging. In L. L. Adler (Ed.), *Issues of cross-cultural research* (pp. 712-716). New York: New York Academy of Sciences.

Schachter, S., Nuttin, J., DeMonchaux, C., Maucorps, P. A., Osmer, D., Duijker, H., Rommetveit, R., & Israel, J. (1954). Cross-cultural experiments on threats and rejection. *Human Relations, 7*, 403-439.

Scherer, K. (1972). Judging personality from voice: A cross-cultural approach to an old issue in interpersonal perception. *Journal of Personality, 40*, 191-210.

Scherer, K. R., Wallbott, H. G., & Summerfield, A. B. (Eds.). (1986). *Experiencing emotions: A cross-cultural study.* Cambridge: Cambridge University Press.

Schieffelin, B. B., & Ochs, E. (Eds.). (1986). *Language socialization across cultures.* New York: Cambridge University Press.

Schlenker, B. R. (1985). Preface. In B. R. Schlenker (Ed.), *The self and social life* (pp. xi-xiii). New York: McGraw-Hill.

Schnaiberg, A. (1970a). Measuring modernism: Theoretical and empirical explorations. *American Journal of Sociology, 76*, 399-425.

Schnaiberg, A. (1970b). Rural-urban residence and modernism: A study of Ankara Province, Turkey. *Demography, 7*, 71-85.

Schneider, D. M. (1968). *American kinship: A cultural account.* Chicago: University of Chicago Press.

Schneider, D. M. (1976). Notes toward a theory of culture. In K. Basso & H. Selby (Eds.), *Meaning in anthropology* (pp. 197-220). Albuquerque: University of New Mexico Press.

Schneider, W., Borkowski, J. G., Kurtz, B. E., & Kerwin, K. (1986). Metamemory and motivation: A comparison of strategy use and performance in German and American children. *Journal of Cross-Cultural Psychology, 17*, 315-336.

Sears, D. O. (1986). College sophomores in the laboratory: Influences of a narrow data base on social psychology's view of human nature. *Journal of Personality and Social Psychology, 51,* 515-530.

Secord, P. F. (1986). Explanation in the social sciences and in life situations. In D. W. Fiske & R. A. Shweder (Eds.), *Metatheory in social science: Pluralisms and subjectivities* (pp. 197-221). Chicago: University of Chicago press.

Segall, M. H. (1976). *Human behavior and public policy: A political psychology.* Elmsford, NY: Pergamon.

Segall, M. H. (1979). *Cross-cultural psychology: Human behavior in global perspective.* Monterey, CA: Brooks/Cole.

Segall, M. H. (1986). Assessment of social behavior. In W. J. Lonner & J. W. Berry (Eds.), *Field methods in cross-cultural research* (pp. 265-290). Beverly Hills: Sage.

Segall, M. H. (1988). Psycho-cultural antecedents of male aggression: Some implications involving gender, parenting, and adolescence. In P. R. Dasen, J. W. Berry, & N. Sartorius (Eds.), *Health and cross-cultural psychology: Towards applications.* Newbury Park, CA: Sage.

Segall, M. H., Campbell, D. T., & Herskovits, M. (1966). *The influence of culture on visual perception.* Indianapolis: Bobbs-Merrill.

Selby, H. A. (1975). Semantics and causality in the study of deviance. In M. Sanches & B. Blount (Eds.), *Sociocultural dimensions of language use* (pp. 11-24). New York: Academic Press.

Sell, J., & Martin, M. W. (1983). An acultural perspective on experimental social psychology. *Personality and Social Psychology Bulletin, 9,* 345-349.

Shenoy, S. (1981). Organization structure and context: A replication of the Aston study in India. In D. J. Hickson & C. J. McMillan (Eds.), *Organization and nation: The Aston programs IV* (pp. 133-154). Westmean, England: Gower.

Sherif, M. (1935). A study of some social factors in perception. *Archives of Psychology, 27,* No. 187.

Sherif, M. (1936). *The psychology of social norms.* New York: Harper & Row.

Sherif, M. (1951). Light from psychology on intercultural relations. In K. W. Bigelow (Ed.), *Cultural groups and human relations* (pp. 110-126). New York: Columbia University, Teachers College.

Sherif, M. (1966). *In common predicament: Social psychology of intergroup conflict and cooperation.* New York: Houghton Mifflin.

Shweder, R. A. (1979). Rethinking culture and personality theory: Part II. *Ethos, 7,* 279-311.

Shweder, R. A., & Bourne, E. J. (1982). Does the concept of the person vary cross-culturally? In A. J. Marsella & G. M. White (Eds.), *Cultural conceptions of mental health and therapy* (pp. 97-137). London: D. Reidel.

Shweder, R. A., & Fiske, D. W. (1986). Introduction. Uneasy social science. In D. W. Fiske & R. A. Shweder (Eds.), *Metatheory in social science: Pluralisms and subjectivities* (pp. 1-18). Chicago: University of Chicago Press.

Simmons, D. H., Vom Kolke, A., & Shimuzu, H. (1986). Attitudes toward romantic love among American, German, and Japanese students. *Journal of Social Psychology, 126,* 327-336.

Singh, A. K., & Inkeles, A. (1968). A cross-cultural measure of modernity and some popular Indian images. *Journal of General and Applied Psychology, 1,* 14-26.

Singh, R., & Bhargava, S. (1985). Motivation, ability and exam performance: Tests of hypotheses of cultural difference and task difficulty. *Journal of Experimental Social Psychology, 21,* 466-479.

Singh, R., Gupta, M., & Dalal, A. K. (1979). Cultural differences in attribution of performance: An integration-theoretical analysis. *Journal of Personality and Social Psychology, 37,* 1342-1351.

Sinha, J.B.P. (1981). *The nurturant task manager: A model of the effective executive.* Atlantic Highlands, NJ: Humanities Press.

Skinner, B. F. (1938). *The behavior of organisms: An experimental analysis.* New York: Appleton/Century/Crofts.

Skinner, B. F. (1974). *About behaviorism.* New York: Knopf.

Smedslund, J. (1979). Between the analytic and the arbitrary: A case study of psychological research. *Scandinavian Journal of Psychology, 20,* 129-140.

Smith, D. H., & Inkeles, A. (1966). The OM Scale: A comparative sociopsychological measure of individual modernity. *Sociometry, 29,* 353-377.

Smith, M. B. (1980). Attitudes, values and selfhood. In H. E. Howe & M. M. Page (Eds.), *Nebraska symposium on motivation, 1979* (pp. 305-350). Lincoln: University of Nebraska Press.

Smith, P. B., Misumi, J., Tayeb, M. H., Peterson, M. F., & Bond, M. H. (1986). *On the generality of leadership style across cultures.* Unpublished manuscript, University of Sussex, School of Social Sciences, Brighton, UK.

Smith, P. B., & Peterson, M. F. (in press). *Leadership in context: A cultural analysis of organizational behaviour.* London: Sage.

Smith, P. B., Tayeb, M. H., Sinha, J.B.P., & Bennett, B. (1986). *Leader style and leader behavior: The case of the 9.9 manager.* Unpublished manuscript, University of Sussex, School of Social Sciences, Brighton, UK.

Smith, R. J. (1978). The future of an illusion: American social psychology. *Personality and Social Psychology Bulletin, 4,* 173-176.

Smith, S. H., & Whitehead, G. I. (1984). Attributions for promotion and demotion in the United States and India. *Journal of Social Psychology, 124,* 27-34.

Snyder, M., & Gangestad, S. (1986). On the nature of self-monitoring: Matters of assessment, matters of validity. *Journal of Personality and Social Psychology, 51,* 125-139.

Solomon, R. C. (1984). Getting angry: The Jamesian theory of emotion in anthropology. In R. A. Shweder & R. A. LeVine (Eds.), *Culture theory: Essays on mind, self and emotion* (pp. 238-254). New York: Cambridge University Press.

Sorge, A. (1980). *Cultural organization.* (Discussion paper 80-56). Berlin: International Institute of Management.

Spence, J. T. (1985). Achievement American style: The rewards and costs of individualism *American Psychologist, 40,* 1285-1295.

Spiro, M. E. (1982). *Oedipus in the Trobriands.* Chicago: University of Chicago Press.

Stake, J. E. (1983). Factors in reward distribution: Allocator motive, gender, and Protestant ethic endorsement. *Journal of Personality and Social Psychology, 44,* 410-418.

Stake, J. E. (1985). Exploring the basis of sex differences in third party allocations. *Journal of Personality and Social Psychology, 48,* 410-418.

Stephan, W. G. (1985). Intergroup relations. In G. Lindzey & E. Aronson (Eds.), *Handbook of social psychology* (3rd ed.) (pp. 599-658). New York: Random House.

Stephan, W. G., & Stephan, C. W. (1985). Intergroup anxiety. *Journal of Social Issues, 41,* 157-166.

Stephenson, G. (1981). Intergroup bargaining and negotiation. In J. Turner & H. Giles (Eds.), *Intergroup behavior* (pp. 168-198). Oxford: Basil Blackwell.

Stephenson, J. B. (1968). Is everyone going modern? A critique and a suggestion for measuring modernism. *American Journal of Sociology, 74,* 265-275.

Stogdill, R. M., & Coons, A. E. (1957). *Leader behavior* (Monograph 88). Columbus: Ohio State University, Bureau of Business Research.

Stone, L. (1977). *The family, sex and marriage in England, 1500-1800.* New York: Harper & Row.

Stoner, J. F. (1961). *A comparison of individuals and group decisions involving risk.* Unpublished master's thesis, Massachusetts Institute of Technology.

Strathern, A. (1975). Why is shame on the skin? *Ethnology, 14,* 347-356.

Strauss, A. S. (1973). Northern Cheyenne ethnosociology. *Ethos, 1,* 326-357.

Stryker, S. (1980). *Symbolic interactionism: A social structural version.* Menlo Park, CA: Benjamin/Cummings.

Stryker, S. (1985). Symbolic interaction and role theory. In G. Lindzey & E. Aronson (Eds.), *Handbook of social psychology* (3rd ed.) (Vol. 1, pp. 311-378). New York: Random House.

Super, C., Harkness, S., & Baldwin, L. (1977). Category behavior in natural ecologies and in cognitive tests. *Quarterly Newsletter of the Institute for Comparative Human Development, 1,* 4-7.

Suppe, F. (1974). *The structure of scientific theories.* Urbana: University of Illinois Press.

Suppe, F. (1977). *The structure of scientific theories* (2nd ed.). Urbana: University of Illinois Press.

Surber, C. F. (1981). Necessary versus sufficient causal schemata: Attributions for achievement in difficult and easy tasks. *Journal of Experimental Social Psychology, 17,* 586-596.

Sutton-Smith, B., & Roberts, J. M. (1981). Play, toys, games and sports. In H. C. Triandis & A. Heron (Eds.), *Handbook of cross-cultural psychology: Vol. 4. Developmental* (pp. 425-471). Boston: Allyn & Bacon.

Suzman, R. (1973). *The modernization of personality.* Unpublished doctoral dissertation, Harvard University.

Swann, W. B., & Read, S. J. (1981a). Acquiring self-knowledge: The search for feedback that fits. *Journal of Personality and Social Psychology, 41,* 1119-1128.

Swann, W. B., & Read, S. J. (1981b). Self verification processes: How we sustain our self-conceptions. *Journal of Experimental Social Psychology, 17,* 351-372.

Swartz, M. (1982). Cultural sharing and cultural theory: Some findings of a five-society study. *American Anthropologist, 84,* 314-338.

Tajfel, H. (1970). Experiments in intergroup discrimination. *Scientific American, 223,* 96-102.

Tajfel, H. (1972). Experiments in a vacuum. In J. Israel & H. Tajfel (Eds.), *The context of social psychology: A critical assessment* (pp. 69-119). London: Academic Press.

Tajfel, H. (Ed.). (1978). *Differentiation between social groups: Studies in intergroup behavior.* London: Academic Press.

Tajfel, H. (1978). Social categorization, social identity and social comparison. In H. Tajfel (Ed.), *Differentiation between social groups: Studies in intergroup behaviour* (pp. 61-76). London: Academic Press.

Tajfel, H. (1981). *Human groups and social categories.* Cambridge: Cambridge University Press.

Tajfel, H. (1982). Social psychology of intergroup relations. *Annual Review of Psychology, 33,* 1-39.

Tanford, S., & Penrod, S. (1984). Social influence model: A formal integration of research on majority and minority influence processes. *Psychology Bulletin, 95,* 189-225.

Tannenbaum, A. S. (1980). Organizational psychology. In H. C. Triandis & R. W. Brislin

(Eds.), *Handbook of cross-cultural psychology: Vol. 5. Social Psychology* (pp. 281-334). Boston, MA: Allyn & Bacon.

Tapp, J. L., Kelman, H. C., Triandis, H. C., Wrightsman, L. S., & Coelho, G. V. (1974). Continuing concerns in cross-cultural ethics: A report. *International Journal of Psychology, 9,* 231-249.

Tatje, T. A., & Naroll, R. (1970). Two measures of societal complexity: An empirical cross-cultural comparison. In R. Naroll & R. Cohen (Eds.), *A handbook of method in cultural anthropology* (pp. 766-833). New York: Columbia University Press.

Tayeb, M. H. (1979). *Cultural determinants of organisational response to environmental demands.* Unpublished master's thesis, University of Oxford.

Tayeb, M. H. (in press). *Nations and organizations.* London: Sage.

Taylor, D. M., Dube, L., & Bellerose, J. (1986). Intergroup contact in Quebec. In M. Hewstone & R. Brown (Eds.), *Contact and conflict in intergroup encounters* (pp. 107-118). Oxford: Basil Blackwell.

Taylor, D. M., & Jaggi, V. (1974). Ethnocentrism and causal attribution in a South Indian context. *Journal of Cross-Cultural Psychology, 5,* 162-171.

Tedeschi, J. T. (1983). Social influence theory and aggression. In R. Geen & E. Donnerstein (Eds.), *Aggression: Theoretical and empirical reviews* (pp. 135-162). New York: Academic Press.

Tedeschi, J. T. (1984). A social psychological interpretation of human aggression. In A. Mummendey (Ed.), *Social psychology of aggression: From individual behavior towards social interaction* (pp. 5-20). New York: Springer.

Tedeschi, J. T., Gaes, G. G., Riordan, C., & Quigley-Fernandez, B. (1981). Social psychology and cumulative knowledge. *Personality and Social Psychology Bulletin, 7,* 161-172.

Tedeschi, J. T., & Lindskold, S. (1976). *Social psychology: Interdependence, interaction, and influence.* New York: John Wiley.

Tedeschi, J. T., & Melburg, V. (1983). Aggression as the illegitimate use of coercive power. In H. H. Blumberg, A. P. Hare, V. Kent, & M. Davies (Eds.), *Small groups and social interaction* (pp. 255-266). New York: John Wiley.

Tedeschi, J. T., Melburg, V., & Rosenfeld, P. (1981). Is the concept of aggression useful? In P. Brain & D. Benton (Eds.), *A multi-disciplinary approach to aggression research.* Elsevier, North Holland: Biomedical Press.

Tedeschi, J. T., Smith, R. B. III, & Brown, R. C. Jr. (1974). A reinterpretation of research on aggression. *Psychological Bulletin, 81,* 540-562.

Thakerar, J. N., & Iwawaki, S. (1979). Cross-cultural comparisons in interpersonal attraction of females towards males. *Journal of Social Psychology, 108,* 121-122.

Thibaut, J. W., & Kelley, H. H. (1959). *The social psychology of groups.* New York: John Wiley.

Thibaut, J. W., & Walker, L. (1975). *Procedural justice: A psychological analysis.* New York: John Wiley.

Thibaut, J. W., & Walker, L. (1978). A theory of procedure. *California Law Review, 66,* 541-566.

Thomas, D. R. (1972). *Authoritarianism, child rearing, and ethnocentrism.* Unpublished doctoral dissertation, University of Queensland.

Thorngate, W. (1976). Possible limits on a science of social behavior. In L. H. Strickland, F. E. Aboud, & K. J. Gergen (Eds.), *Social psychology in transition* (pp. 121-141). New York: Plenum.

Timaeus, E. (1968). Untersuchungen zum sogenannten konformen Verhatten. *Zeitscrift für Experimentelle und Angewandte Psychologie, 15,* 176-194.

Tolman, E. C. (1951). *Behavior and psychological man.* Berkeley: University of California Press.

Toman, E. C. (1932). *Purposive behavior in animals and men.* New York: Century.

Trew, K. (1986). Catholic-Protestant contact in Northern Ireland. In M. Hewstone & R. Brown (Eds.), *Contact and conflict in intergroup encounters* (pp. 93-106). Oxford: Basil Blackwell.

Triandis, H. C. (1964). Cultural influences upon cognitive processes. In L. Berkowitz (Ed.), *Advances in experimental social psychology* (Vol. 1, pp. 1-48). New York: Academic Press.

Triandis, H. C. (1968). Some cross-cultural studies of cognitive consistency. In R. P. Abelson, E. Aronson, W. J. McGuire, T. M. Newcomb, M. J. Rosenberg, & P. H. Tannenbaum (1968). *Theories of cognitive consistency* (pp. 723-730). Chicago: Rand McNally.

Triandis, H. (1972). *The analysis of subjective culture.* New York: John Wiley.

Triandis, H. C. (1975). Social psychology and cultural analysis. *Journal of the Theory of Social Behavior, 5,* 81-106.

Triandis, H. C. (1977). *Interpersonal behavior.* Monterey, CA: Brooks/Cole.

Triandis, H. C. (1978). Some universals of social behavior. *Personality and Social Psychology Bulletin, 4,* 1-16.

Triandis, H. C. (1980). Introduction to handbook of cross-cultural psychology. In H. C. Triandis & W. W. Lambert (Eds.), *Handbook of cross-cultural psychology: Vol. 1. Perspectives* (pp. 1-14). Boston: Allyn & Bacon.

Triandis, H. C. (1980). Values, attitudes and interpersonal behavior. In H. Howe & M. Page (Eds.), *Nebraska symposium on motivation, 1979, 27* (196-260). Lincoln: University of Nebraska Press.

Triandis, H. C. (1984). Toward a psychological theory of economic growth. *International Journal of Psychology, 19,* 79-95.

Triandis, H. C. (1987). Personal communication, February 4.

Triandis, H. C. (in press). Collectivism vs. individualism: A reconceptualization of a basic concept in cross-cultural social psychology. In C. Bagley & G. K. Verma (Eds.), *Personality, cognition, and values: Cross-cultural perspectives on childhood and adolescence.* London: Macmillan.

Triandis, H. C. (in press). Cross-cultural industrial and organizational psychology. In M. D. Dunnette (Ed.), *Handbook of industrial and organizational psychology* (2nd ed.). New York: John Wiley.

Triandis, H. C., & Berry, J. W. (Eds.). (1980). *Handbook of cross-cultural psychology: Vol. 2. Methodology.* Boston: Allyn & Bacon.

Triandis, H. C., Bontempo, R., Betancourt, H., Bond, M. H., Leung, K., Brenes, A., Georgas, J., Hui, C.C.H., Marin, G., Setiadi, B., Sinha, J.B.P., Verma, J., Spangenberg, J., Touzard, H., & De Montmollin, G. (1986). The measurement of the etic aspects of individualism and collectivism across cultures. *Australian Journal of Psychology, 38,* 257-267.

Triandis, H. C., Bontempo, R., Villareal, M., Asai, M., Lucca, N., Betancourt, H., Bond, M. H., Leung, K., Brenes, A., Georgas, J., Hui, H., Marin, G., Setiadi, B., Sinha, J., Verma, J., Spangenberg, J., Touzard, H., & de Montmollin, G. (1986). *Individualism and collectivism: Cross-cultural perspectives on self-group relationships.* Unpublished manuscript, University of Illinois.

Triandis, H. C., & Brislin, R. W. (1980). *Handbook of cross-cultural psychology: Vol. 2. Methodology.* Boston: Allyn & Bacon.

Triandis, H. C., Hui, C. H., Albert, R. D., Leung, S. M., Lisansky, J., Diaz-Loving, R.,

Plascencia, L., Marin, G., Betancourt, H., & Loyola-Cintron, L. (1984). Individual models of social behavior. *Journal of Personality and Social Psychology, 46,* 1389-1404.

Triandis, H. C., & Lambert, W. W. (Eds.). (1980). *Handbook of cross-cultural psychology: Vol. 1. Perspectives.* Boston: Allyn & Bacon.

Triandis, H. C., Leung, K., Villareal, M., & Clack, F. L. (1985). Allocentric vs. idiocentric tendencies: Convergent and discriminant validation. *Journal of Research in Personality, 13,* 395-415.

Triandis, H. C., Marin, G., Hui, C. H. Lisansky, J., Ottati, V. (1984). Role perceptions of Hispanic young adults. *Journal of Cross-Cultural Psychology, 15,* 297-320.

Triandis, H. C., Marin, G., Lisansky, J., & Betancourt, H. (1984). *Simpatía* as a cultural script of Hispanics. *Journal of Personality and Social Psychology, 47,* 1363-1375.

Triandis, H., Vassiliou, V., & Nassiakou, M. (1968). Three cross-cultural studies of subjective culture. *Journal of Personality and Social Psychology, 8,* (Monograph Supplement No. 4), 1-42.

Trimble, J. E. (1981, August). *Folkloric methods in attributing differences to age and ethnicity.* Paper presented at the meeting of the American Psychological Association, Los Angeles, CA.

Trimble, J. E., & Richardson, S. (1982). Locus of control measures among American Indians: Cluster structure analytic characteristics. *Journal of Cross-Cultural Psychology, 13,* 228-238.

Trimble, J. E., Richardson, S., & Tatum, E. (1982). Minority elderly adaptation to life-threatening events: An overview with methodological considerations. *Journal of Minority Aging, 7,* 12-24.

Trommsdorff, G. (1983). Value change in Japan. *International Journal of Intercultural Relations, 7,* 337-360.

Trope, Y. (1986). Identification and inferential processes in dispositional attribution. *Psychological Review, 93,* 239-257.

Trzebinski, J., & Richards, K. (1986). The role of goal categories in person impression. *Journal of Experimental Social Psychology, 22,* 216-227.

Turner, J. C. (1981). Some considerations in generalizing experimental social psychology. In G. M. Stephenson & J. H. Davis (Eds.), *Progress in applied social psychology: Vol. 1* (pp. 3-34). New York: John Wiley.

Turner, J. C., Shaver, I., & Hogg, M. A. (1983). Social categorization, interpersonal attraction and group formation. *British Journal of Social Psychology, 22,* 227-239.

Tyler, S. (1978). *The said and the unsaid: Mind, meaning and culture.* New York: Academic Press.

Tyler, S. A. (1969). *Cognitive anthropology.* New York: Holt, Rinehart & Winston.

Valsiner, J. (1985). Common sense and psychological theories. *Scandinavian Journal of Psychology, 26,* 97-109.

Van de Vijver, F.J.R., & Poortinga, Y. H. (1982). Cross-cultural generalization and universality. *Journal of Cross-Cultural Psychology, 13,* 387-408.

Vaughan, G. M., Tajfel, H., & Williams, J. (1981). Bias in reward allocation in an intergroup and an interpersonal context. *Social Psychology Quarterly, 44,* 37-42.

Verma, J. (1985). The ingroup and its relevance to individual behavior: A study of collectivism and individualism. *Psychologia, 28,* 173-181.

Vidmar, N. (1970). Group composition and the risky shift. *Journal of Experimental Social Psychology, 6,* 153-166.

Wachtel, P. L. (1980). Investigation and its discontents: Some constraints on progress in psychological research. *American Psychologist, 35,* 399-408.

Walker, H. A., & Cohen, B. P. (1985). Scope statements: Imperatives for evaluating theories. *American Sociological Review, 50,* 288-301.

Wallace, A.F.C. (1970). *Culture and personality* (2nd ed.). New York: Random House.

Walsh, M., & Taylor, J. (1982). Understanding in Japanese marriages. *Journal of Social Psychology, 118,* 67-76.

Walster, E., Walster, G. W., & Berscheid, E. (1978). *Equity: Theory and research.* Boston: Allyn & Bacon.

Ward, C. (1987). Theory and method in cross-cultural psychology. In J. Greenwood (Ed.), *The idea of psychology: Conceptual methodological issues.* Singapore: Singapore University Press.

Ward, C., & Hewstone, M. (1985). Ethnicity, language and intergroup relations in Malaysia and Singapore. *Journal of Multilingual and Multicultural Development, 6,* 271-296.

Ward, R. E., & Rustow, D. A. (1964). *Political modernization in Japan and Turkey.* Princeton, NJ: Princeton University Press.

Warwick, D. P. (1980). The politics and ethics of cross-cultural research. In H. C. Triandis & W. W. Lambert (Eds.), *Handbook of cross-cultural psychology: Vol. 1. Perspectives* (pp. 319-371). Boston: Allyn & Bacon.

Warwick, D. P., & Osherson, S. (Eds.), *Comparative research methods.* Englewood Cliffs, NJ: Prentice-Hall.

Waterman, A. S. (1984). *The psychology of individualism.* New York: Praeger.

Watkins, D. (1982). Causal attributions for achievement of Filipino barrio children. *Journal of Social Psychology, 118,* 149-156.

Watkins, D., & Astilla, E. (1984). The dimensionality, antecedents, and study methods correlates of the causal attribution of Filipino children. *Journal of Social Psychology, 124,* 191-199.

Watson, D., Clark, L. A., & Tellegen, A. (1984). Cross-cultural convergence in the structure of mood: A Japanese replication and a comparison with U.S. findings. *Journal of Personality and Social Psychology, 47,* 127-144.

Watzlawick, P. (1984). Self-fulfilling prophecies. In P. Watzlawick (Ed.), *The invented reality* (pp. 95-116). New York: Norton.

Wax, R. H. (1960). Twelve years later: An analysis of field experience. In R. N. Adams & J. J. Preiss (Eds.), *Human organization research* (pp. 166-178). Homewood, IL: Dorsey.

Weary, G., & Mirels, H. (Eds.). (1982). *Integrations of clinical and social psychology.* New York: Oxford.

Weick, K. E., Bougon, M. C., & Maruyama, G. (1976). The equity context. *Organizational Behavior and Human Performance, 15,* 32-65.

Weinberg, I. (1969). The problem of the convergence of industrial societies: A critical look at the state of a theory. *Comparative Studies in Society and History, 11,* 1-15.

Weiner, B. (1979). A theory of motivation for some classroom experiences. *Journal of Educational Psychology, 71,* 3-25.

Weiner, B. (1980). A cognitive (attributional) emotion-action model of motivated behavior: An analysis of judgments of help-giving. *Journal of Personality and Social Psychology, 39,* 186-200.

Weiner, B. (1985). "Spontaneous" causal thinking. *Psychological Bulletin, 97,* 74-84.

Weiner, B., Frieze, I. H., Kukla, A., Reed, L., Rest, S., & Rosenbaum, R. M. (1971). *Perceiving the causes of success and failure.* Morristown, NJ: General Learning Press.

Weiner, B., Russel, P., & Lerman, P. (1978). Affective consequences of causal ascriptions. In J. H. Harvey, W. J. Ickes, & R. F. Kidd (Eds.), *New directions in attribution research* (Vol. 2, pp. 59-90). Hillsdale, NJ: Lawrence Erlbaum.

Wells, G. (1981). Lay analyses of causal forces on behavior. In J. H. Harvey (Ed.), *Cognition, social behavior and the environment* (pp. 309-324). Hillsdale, NJ: Lawrence Erlbaum.

Westermeyer, J. (Ed.). (1976). *Anthropology and mental health*. The Hague: Mouton.

Wetherell, M. (1982). Cross-cultural studies of minimal groups. In H. Tajfel (Ed.), *Social identity and intergroup relations* (pp. 207-238). Cambridge: Cambridge University Press.

Weyrauch, W. O. (1971). The "basic law" or "Constitution" of a small group. *Journal of Social Issues, 27,* 49-63.

Wheeler, L. (in press). My year in Hong Kong: Some observations about social behavior. *Personality and Social Psychology Bulletin.*

White, G. M., & Kirkpatrick, J. (Eds.). (1985). *Person, self, and experience: Exploring Pacific ethnopsychologies.* Berkeley: University of California Press.

White, L. A. (1959). *The evolution of culture.* New York: McGraw-Hill.

White, M., & LeVine, R. A. (1986). What is an *Ii ko* (good child)? In H. Stevenson, H. Azuma, & K. Hakuta (Eds.), *Child development and education in Japan* (pp. 55-62). New York: Freeman.

Whiting, B. B. (1965). Sex identity conflict and physical violence: A comparative study. *American Anthropologist, 67,* 123-140.

Whiting, B. B. (1980). Culture and social behavior: A model for the development of social behavior. *Ethos, 8,* 95-116.

Whiting, B. B., & Whiting, J.W.M. (1975). *Children of six cultures: A psychocultural analysis.* Cambridge, MA: Harvard University Press.

Whiting, J.W.M., & Child, I. L. (1953). *Child training and personality.* New Haven, CT: Yale University Press.

Whiting, J.W.M., Kluckhohn, R., & Anthony, A. (1958). The function of male initiation ceremonies at puberty. In E. E. Maccoby, T. Newcomb, & E. L. Hartley (Eds.), *Readings in social psychology* (3rd ed.) (pp. 359-370). New York: Holt.

Whittaker, J. O., & Meade, R. D. (1967). Social pressure in the modification and distortion of judgment: A cross-cultural study. *International Journal of Psychology, 2,* 109-113.

Wiggins, J. S. (1980). Circumplex models of interpersonal behavior. In L. Wheeler (Ed.), o*Review of personality and social psychology* (Vol. 1, pp. 265-294). Beverly Hills: Sage.

Wilder, D. A. (1986). Social categorization. In L. Berkowitz (Ed.), *Advances in experimental social psychology* (Vol. 19, pp. 291-355). New York: Academic Press.

Williams, R. M. (1947). *Reduction of intergroup tensions.* New York: Social Science Research Council.

Williams, T. P., & Sogon, S. (1984). Group composition and conforming behavior in Japanese students. *Japanese Psychological Research, 126,* 231-234.

Williamson, J. B. (1970). Subjective efficacy and ideal family size as predictors of favorability toward birth control. *Demography, 7,* 329-339.

Wintrob, R. M. (1969). An inward focus: A consideration of psychological stress in fieldwork. In F. Henry & S. Saberwal (Eds.), *Stress and response in fieldwork* (pp. 63-76). New York: Holt, Rinehart & Winston.

Wish, M., Deutsch, M., & Kaplan, S. J. (1976). Perceived dimensions of interpersonal relations. *Journal of Personality and Social Psychology, 33,* 409-420.

Witkin, H. A., & Berry, J. W. (1975). Psychological differentiation in cross-cultural perspective. *Journal of Cross-Cultural Psychology, 6,* 4-87.

Xu, L. C. (1984, November). *Economic reform and leadership study in China.* Paper given at 50th-anniversary conference, Faculty of Human Sciences, Osaka University, Japan.

Yang, K. S. (1981). Social orientation and individual modernity among Chinese students in Taiwan. *Journal of Social Psychology, 113,* 159-170.

Yang, K. S. (1981). The formatin of change of Chinese personality: A cultural-ecological perspective. *Acta Psychologica Taiwanica, 23,* 39-56. (In Chinese)

Yang, K. S. (1982). Causal attributions of academic success and failure and their affective consequences. *Chinese Journal of Psychology* (Taiwan), *24,* 65-83. (The abstract only is in English)

Yang, K. S. (1985). Value change and personality change among the Chinese in Taiwan: A literature review. In *Proceedings of the Fourth Social Sciences Conference* (pp. 75-100). Taipei, Taiwan: Institute of People's Three Principles. (In Chinese)

Yang, K. S. (1986a). Chinese personality and its change. In M. H. Bond (Ed.), *The psychology of the Chinese people* (pp. 106-170). Hong Kong: Oxford University Press.

Yang, K. S. (1986b). *Studies on Chinese individual traditionality and modernity: I. The construction of multidimensional scales.* Unpublished manuscript, National Taiwan University. (In Chinese)

Yang, K., & Bond, M. H. (1985). Dimensions of Chinese person perception: An emic approach. In C. Chiao (Ed.), *Proceedings of the Conference on Chinese Modernization and Chinese Culture* (pp. 309-325). Hong Kong: Chinese University Press.

Yang, K. S., & Ho, D.Y.F. (in press). The role of *yuan* in Chinese social life: A conceptual and empirical analysis. In A. C. Paranjpe, D.F.Y. Ho, & R. C. Rieber (Eds.), *Asian contributions to psychology.* New York: Praeger.

Young, F. (1965). *Initiation ceremonies: A cross-cultural study of status dramatization.* Indianapolis: Bobbs-Merrill.

Young, L., Pierson, H., & Giles, H. (in press). The effects of language and academic specialization on perceived group vitalities. *Linguistic Berichte.*

Young, R. L. (1980). *Social images and interpersonal interaction among Hong Kong and American students.* Unpublished master's thesis, University of Hawaii.

Zaidi, S.M.H. (1979). Applied cross-cultural psychology: Submission of a cross-cultural psychologist from the Third World. In L. Eckensberger, W. Lonner, & Y. H. Poortinga (Eds.), *Cross-cultural contributions to psychology* (pp. 236-243). Lisse: Swets & Zeitlinger.

Zander, A. (1985). *The purposes of groups and organizations.* San Francisco: Jossey-Bass.

Zern, D. S. (1983). The relationships of certain group-oriented and individualistically oriented child-rearing dimensions to cultural complexity in a cross-cultural sample. *Genetic Psychology Monographs, 108,* 3-20.

Index

Achievement motivation: 72, 73, 224, 234; individual-oriented, 70

Adjudication, 227, 228

Adversary procedure, 227

Affect (and culture), 277-280

Affiliation (see also Association), 199-201, 202

Affordance, 245, 246, 251, 255, 256, 263, 264

Aggression: 14, 207-217, 284; age, 211; biological contributions, 210, 211; crime, 211; frustration, 207, 209, 216; impression management, 216; power and status, 208; social learning theory, 209-210, 212-213

Alienation (and anomie), 70, 166

Allocation norms, 191

Allocentrics-idiocentrics, 166, 173, 180

Ancestor worship (see also Filial piety), 74

Animosity reduction, 228-229

Anticonformity, 185, 195

Arbitration, 228

Assertiveness, 73, 76, 78

Association-dissociation (see also Affiliation), 132, 196, 202, 206

Attribution(s): 128-129, 176, 230-244, 275-276; achievement, 233-236; intergroup, 33-35, 236-238, Kelley's model, 230, 231, 232-233, 242; theory, 128, 230; Weiner's model, 230, 231; yuan, 243

Attunements, 245, 246, 252, 253, 256, 260

Baby talk, 276-277

Behavioral intention, 130

Bio-cultural interactive model, 213-216

Carpentered environment, 26

Categories of person perception, 247-248, 252-254

Causal schemata, 239, 243

Centralization, 155, 156, 157, 158

Citation: frequency, 32-33; practices, 50

Cognitive idealism, 56

Collectivism (see also Individualism), 32, 35, 129, 131, 132, 133, 135, 136, 137, 160-161, 168, 169, 172, 188, 189, 191, 194, 208, 224-226, 228-229, 235, 239, 273-274

Commitment, 156, 157

Conformity: 182, 194; cultural differences, 183-186; eco-cultural factors, 186-187

Consensus, 232

Consistency, 129, 233

Constructionism, 19

Contact hypothesis, 177

Contents of person perception, 248-254, 263

Convergence: psychological, 64-81; societal, 65-66

Covariation principle, 232

Cultural complexity, 131, 132, 136

Cultural insularity, 45-49

Cultural materialism, 56-57, 60

Cultural relativism, 20, 122

Culture: 14-15; definition, 165; dimensions, 131-132, 165-167, 173, 179, 283; ecological approaches, 56-57, 269-271; nonrational approaches, 271; subjective, 120, 121, 192; symbolic approaches, 267-269

Culture broker(ing), 44, 49-54

Culture-free thesis, 154-156

Culture-specific thesis, 156-157

Decision rules, 190-192

Differentiation of social behavior, 199, 202, 203

Distinctiveness, 232, 254

Division of labor by sex, 213, 216

Dominance: 70, 78, 125, 201-202, 206, 256, 261; aggression, 212, 216

Double minorities, 188

Duhem-Quine thesis, 197

Dysadaptation syndrome, 111

Ecological theory (see also Culture—ecological approaches), 56-57, 245, 256, 259

Efficacy, 68, 69, 73, 76
Egalitarianism, 73, 76
Egocentric bias (self-serving bias), 234, 236, 242
Emic-etic distinction: 70, 101, 133, 152-154, 155, 157-158, 160, 162, 197-198; imposted etic, 160; insider-outsider contrast, 152; macro-micro issue, 152-154; methodological etic, 108, 112
Empathetic capacity, 73
Empiricism, 139-149
Equality norm (rule), 219, 223, 225
Equity norm (rule), 172, 173, 221, 223, 225
Equity theory, 128, 130, 138, 218-221, 288
Equivalence: 102, 152; conceptual, 92-93, 112-113; cultural, 112; functional, 92-93, 98, 112-113; metric, 92, 112
Ethics, 117
Ethnocentrism, 25, 90
Ethnolinguistic identity, 169-171
Ethnolinguistic vitality, 169-171
Ethnophenomenology, 146-149
Evolution of social behavior, 205-206

Familism, 78
Fatalism, 73, 78
Father absence, 213, 214, 215
Feudalism, 201
Filial piety, 73, 78, 81, 283
Formality (see Intimacy-formality)
Formalization, 155, 156, 157, 158
Fundamental attribution error, 240, 254
Future orientation, 67, 69, 73

Gender: aggression, 210-211; identity, 213-214; marking, 215; role, 213
Genotype vs. phenotype, 153
Group-serving bias, 236-238, 242

Habits, 123, 130
Hedonism, 76
Hierarchical, 152, 168
Historical diffusion, 204

Identity: cross-sex, 214, 216; social, 165, 167-171, 177, 178
Ideology, 21-22, 62
Illusions: 26; horizontal-vertical, 26; Muller-Lyer, 26
Implicit personality theories, 248-252, 255

Indigenous psychologies, 14, 243, 266, 283
Individualism (see also Collectivism), 46, 68, 71, 73-74, 122, 123, 129, 131, 132, 133, 134, 136, 156, 161, 165-166, 170, 171, 172, 174, 175, 176, 178, 179, 180, 186, 190, 192, 205, 219, 220, 234, 242, 248, 272-274, 279, 288
Individualistic orientation, 73
Individuocentric bias, 46, 47, 48, 83, 87
Induction, 143
Industrialization, 63
Ingroup (see also Outgroup): 126, 127, 132, 135, 138, 167-180, 181, 191, 208, 224-226; bias, 171-173; members, 130; stereotypes, 238
Ingroup, outgroup relationship, 165, 167-180, 238
Interaction goals, 223
Interaction rates, 120
Intergroup contact: 177-179; affect, 178; conflict, 178-179
Interpersonal outcomes: 223-224; harmony, 223, 224
Intimacy-formality, 132, 196, 199, 200, 202-203

James-Lange view of emotion, 278
Justice: 188, 218-229; distributive, 191, 218, 220, 221-223; procedural, 218, 227-229

Leadership: 159-162; contingency theory, 128; style, 159-162, 194
Level of analysis, 15, 165
Lexicon: color terms, 268; emotion terms, 278
Locus of control, 3-4, 70, 233, 239, 240-241, 244

Machoism: 211; compensatory, 215-216
Macro-micro fallacy, 77
Masculinity-femininity, 70, 71, 156, 167, 168, 170, 171, 178, 179
Mediation, 227, 228
Metaphor in person perception, 251-252, 255
Minimal group paradigm, 171, 182, 190, 191, 194
Minority group: claims, 190-191; influence, 182, 187-188, 194; rights, 188, 189

Modernity, 75, 76-78, 131
Modernization: 63-81, 90, 284; economic, 63; political, 63; societal, 64
Mother-child sleeping arrangements, 214

Need: autonomy, 70; exhibition, 70; heterosexuality, 70; information, 73; intraception, 70; self-actualization, 71; social, 71
Negotiation, 227
Norms, 43, 55, 120, 121, 137, 219

Openness to innovation, 67, 73
Optimism, 76-77, 78
Organizations: characteristics, 154-158; culture, 153; performance, 159; processes, 159-162; size, 156; structure, 153, 154-158, 162
Outgroup (see also Ingroup), 26, 199
Overgeneralization in person perception, 246, 259

Paradigms, 11, 16, 96, 141-149
Paternalism, 78
Person perception, 245-265
Physical attractiveness, 257-259
Power, 205, 206
Power distance, 32, 71, 125, 156, 157, 167, 168, 176, 178, 179, 208
Privacy (regulation), 132, 202, 253
Process control, 227
Proportionality rule, 219
Protest masculinity, 214, 216
Protestant Ethic Scale, 221-222
Psychological anthropology, 267-269
Psychological characteristics: functional, 79-81; general, 79-81; modern, 72-74; nonfunctional, 79-81; specific functional, 79-81; unique functional, 79-81
Psychological differentiation, 50, 72, 73
Psychological sociology, 55

Replications, 32, 37, 38-39, 48, 92-104, 128-130
Research: action, 105; laboratory, 9, 17-18, 19, 29, 90, 182, 283
Resource: 200, 201, 205, 285; abstract-concrete, 198; availability-scarcity, 226
Risky shift, 23, 182, 192-194, 288
Role theory, 55

Sapir-Whorf hypothesis, 19, 41
Self, 14, 127, 133, 266-281
Self-concept, 167-169, 224, 283
Self-disclosure, 174-175
Self-fulfilling prophecy, 4
Self-presentation, 195, 196, 279
Sex differences, 210-211
Sexual equality, 76-77, 78
Shamanism, 147-148
Simpatia script, 201
Social penetration, 174-175
Sojourner, 173, 175
Specialization, 155, 156, 157, 158
Standardization, 157
Structure of behavior, 196, 198, 199-203
Structure-process dilemma, 153
Superordination-subordination, 132, 196, 199, 200-201, 202, 205
Symbolic interactionism, 54-56

Technology, 154, 155, 157
Testosterone, 211-212, 216
Theory(ies): active, 121, 124, 132; affective, 121, 132; assertion, 124, 125, 135; attraction, 124, 126, 134; autonomy, 124, 128, 132, 135; becoming, 121, 124, 132; being, 121, 124, 132; categorization, 124, 125, 132; cognitive, 121, 132; congruity, 128; consistency, 124, 125; contagion, 123, 124, 135; control, 128; ego-defensive, 124, 127, 132, 135; emotion, 122; evolutionary, 205-206; expectancy-value, 221, 226, 229; expressive, 124, 125, 135; external, 121, 132; grand, 59; hermeneutic, 124, 127; identity, 124, 126, 134; impulse, 122; induction, 124, 127; internal, 121, 132; reaction, 121, 124, 132; repetition, 123, 124, 135; reward-cost balance, 128; social comparison, 128; social learning, 209-210; stimulation, 124, 125-126, 133; template, 124, 126, 133, 134; tension reduction, 123, 124, 135; utilitarian, 124, 125
Tight-loose societies, 128, 131, 133, 135, 137, 179, 198, 201
Trait perception: 259-263; behavioral determinants, 262-263; facial determinants, 259-261; vocal determinants, 261-262
Trust, 156, 157, 191

Uncertainty avoidance, 71, 156, 157, 167, 170, 171, 178, 179

Universalism, 83, 84, 89, 177

Universals: 20, 88, 108, 121-131, 167, 195, 197-199, 203-206, 207, 211, 231, 239-241, 243, 246, 252, 254, 259, 260, 268, 269, 277, 282, 283, 287; diacronic, 197-199; synchronic, 197-199

Values: 220-227, 284; Chinese, 35, 53; instrumental, 220; post-materialist, 71, 75; Rokeach, 220; system-maintaining, 62; system-transforming, 62; terminal, 220

Western folk models, 87

About the Authors

JOHN ADAMOPOULOS, although born on the warm and sunny shores of Greece, credits his encounter with Leonard Doob at Yale University as an undergraduate, and with Harry Triandis at the University of Illinois as a graduate student, for the beginning of his affair with cross-cultural psychology. His research interests have predictably focused on attitude theory, the structure of social behavior, and the perception of the social environment. Perhaps less predictably, in recent years he has become interested in exploring long-term changes in interpersonal behavior through the analysis of literary material from different historical periods. He is in the Psychology Department of Indiana University at South Bend.

YEHUDA AMIR is Professor of Psychology at Bar-Ilan University, Israel. Since receiving his Ph.D. from New York University he has served as head of the Israel Army Manpower Research Division and of the Department of Psychology at Bar-Ilan University. His present research interests pertain to intergroup conflict and cross-cultural psychology. He is coeditor of *School Desegregation: Cross-Cultural Perspectives*. At present he also serves at the university as Head of the Institute for the Advancement of Social Integration in the Schools and as Director of the Center for the Study of Prejudice. He is incumbent of the Bradley Chair for Ethnic Integration.

MICHAEL HARRIS BOND was born in Toronto, Canada, where he received a transplanted public school education from teachers with British accents. His cultural confusion was reinforced by trips to Québec, where he heard a euphonic language and saw people drinking wine at lunch. His fate was sealed when he was enchanted by another foreigner, Edwin Hollander, whose television programs on social psychology were beamed across the border from Buffalo. Subsequent travels took him to exotic cultures, like California, where he received his Ph.D. from Stanford University in 1970. His appetite for the extraordinary thus whetted, he continued going West as a young man until he arrived in the Far East, where he has now reached middle age teaching psychology at the Chinese University in Hong Kong. His most recent act of cultural hubris was editing *The Psychology of the Chinese People* in 1986.

GARTH J.O. FLETCHER received his doctorate from the University of Waikato (New Zealand) in 1981. He subsequently completed some postdoctoral research at UCLA and was Assistant Professor for two years at Illinois State University. His current position is in the Psychology Department at the University of Canterbury in New Zealand. His main areas of interest and research are social cognition (especially attribution processes), close relationships, and the philosophy of psychology.

WILLIAM K. GABRENYA, Jr. received his Ph.D. in social psychology at the University of Missouri in 1979 and is currently an Associate Professor in the School of Psychology at Florida Institute of Technology, Melbourne. He is coordinator of the Intercultural Program at FIT, and Chairman of the Undergraduate Program. His professional interests include research on cultural differences in social interaction, group processes and values, and development of computer simulations of sociocultural and historical processes.

WILLIAM B. GUDYKUNST is a Professor of Communication at Arizona State University. His research focuses on explaining uncertainty reduction processes across

334 THE CROSS-CULTURAL CHALLENGE TO SOCIAL PSYCHOLOGY

cultures and between members of different groups. His most recent books include *Intergroup Communication* (Edward Arnold) and *Intercultural Adaptation* (coedited with Y. Y. Kim; Sage). He recently completed *Culture and Interpersonal Communication* (with S. Ting-Toomey & E. Chua; Sage) and *Theoretical Perspectives in Intercultural Communication* (coedited with Y. Y. Kim; Sage), and is currently working on *Strangeness and Similarity: A Theory of Interpersonal and Intergroup Communication* (Multilingual Matters), as well as coediting the *Handbook of Intercultural and Development Communication* (with M. Asante; Sage).

GUSTAV JAHODA's education in Vienna, Paris, and London laid an early foundation for a cross-cultural outlook. As a Lecturer in Social and Developmental Psychology at the University of Manchester in 1950, he had the good fortune to encounter the New Zealand scholar Ernest Beaglehole, who suggested that any social psychologist worthy of that name ought to live and work for a period in an entirely different culture. Accordingly, he went to Ghana for five years, coming back first to a post at the University of Glasgow and then, in 1964, setting up a new Department of Psychology at the University of Strathclyde. Over a series of almost 30 years he regularly returned to Ghana and other parts of Africa (and occasionally elsewhere) to conduct fieldwork. Now Emeritus, he is currently editing (with Ioan Lewis, an anthropologist colleague) a book on the acquisition of culture.

ANDRÉ KUKLA is an Associate Professor in the Department of Psychology at the University of Toronto. He did his graduate work at UCLA, receiving a master's degree in philosophy and a doctorate in psychology. His major areas of research are the philosophy of psychology and the psychology of consciousness. His recent work has dealt with the status of introspective data, the role of aprioristic reasoning in cognitive science, and the nature of the linkage between thought and action. He is currently engaged in a field study of traditional Buddhist systems of mental science.

KWOK LEUNG is a Lecturer in Psychology at the Chinese University of Hong Kong. He received his Ph.D. from the University of Illinois in 1985. His research interests are wide-ranging and include distributive and procedural justice, conflict resolution, coalition formation, cultural collectivism, and organizational psychology. He is strongly committed to the search for pancultural theories and would like to promote more collaboration among colleagues from different parts of the world.

ROY S. MALPASS is Professor of Behavioral Science at the State University of New York College at Plattsburgh. His degrees in psychology are from Union College, the New School for Social Research, and Syracuse University. He is a past editor of the *Journal of Cross-Cultural Psychology*. His "mainstream" research is concerned with social memory: attitudinal effects on memory for sentitial material, facial memory, and research on eyewitness identification. He complains often about the continuing need for greater integration of theory and method in cross-cultural research.

LEON MANN was born in Broken Hill, Australia, a dusty, remote mining town located near the mythical Black Stump. He attended the University of Melbourne, where he received his bachelors and master's degrees (1961, 1962) and a very good education. He was attracted to Yale for his graduate studies, working under the supervision of Irving Janis. For the next seven years he commuted between the United States and Australia, holding teaching posts at the University of Melbourne (1965-1967), Harvard University (1968-1970), and the University of Sydney (1971-1972). In 1972 he took up appointment at

The Flinders University of South Australia, where he is a Professor of Psychology. His research interests include the study of decision making, cross-cultural psychology, social influence, and collective behavior. He is the author of *Social Psychology* (John Wiley, 1969) and coauthor with Irving Janis of *Decision Making* (Free Press, 1977).

DAVID M. MESSICK received his Ph.D. in social psychology from the University of North Carolina. From there he moved to the University of California, Santa Barbara, where he is currently Professor of Psychology. His qualifications for writing about cross-cultural issues include nearly four years living in Europe, the Netherlands, and Norway, and a passion for Italian food and French wine.

JOAN G. MILLER is an Assistant Professor teaching developmental psychology at Yale University. She received her B.A. from Barnard College, Columbia University, and her Ph.D. from the University of Chicago. Her previous positions include work as a predoctoral fellow at the East-West Center and as a Lecturer at the University of Chicago. Her research interests are in the area of social cognition, with a focus on culture and the development of social understandings. In a past cross-cultural study of American and Indian children and adults, she highlighted the impact of cultural meaning systems on everyday social explanation and person perception. She currently is undertaking a cross-cultural investigation examining the development of reasoning about role-related interpersonal obligations in the United States and India.

HARRY REIS is a born-and-bred native from the melting pot of the world, New York City. He attended CCNY and then received his Ph.D. from New York University. He is editor of the Interpersonal Relations and Group Processes section of the *Journal of Personality and Social Psychology*, and an editor of *Interpersonal Influence*. His interest in cross-cultural psychology began when he left New York City.

MARSHALL H. SEGALL—preferring sunny climes, a varied diet of food and drink, and the company of exotic women—long ago abandoned a promising career in the mainstream of social psychology (Skinnerian at Columbia, Hullian at Iowa) to become a cross-culturalist. By 1960, with Donald Campbell and Melville Herskovits, he was studying illusion susceptibility in noncarpentered worlds. As the 1990s approach, he is working with Swiss, Canadian, and Dutch colleagues (Dasen, Berry, and Poortinga) on a revision of his cross-cultural psychology textbook. Based at Syracuse University, where he directs undergraduate and graduate training in comparative studies, he lives only 10 minutes from the airport.

IRIT SHARON is a Lecturer in Psychology at Bar-Ilan University, Israel. This year she will receive her Ph.D. in social psychology from Bar-Ilan University. She is heading a research unit in ORT-ISRAEL, a large technologically oriented educational organization. Her present research interests are intergroup relations, mainly in schools; group dynamics in educational organizations; and evaluations of organizational functioning in educational settings (i.e., morale, scholastic achievement, dropouts).

PETER B. SMITH is Reader in Social Psychology at the University of Sussex. After completing his Ph.D. at Cambridge in 1962, he devoted much of his research energies to the study of social influence processes within groups and organizations. A particular interest was in the processes and outcomes of sensitivity training. More recently he has focused upon studies of Japanese management, as studied both within Japan and in

Japanese-owned plants elsewhere. He is author of *Groups Within Organisations* (1973), *Group Processes and Personal Change* (1980), and of a forthcoming volume (with Mark Peterson) that explores some of the issues in this chapter more fully, *Leadership In Context: A Cultural Analysis of Organisational Behaviour.*

MONIR TAYEB is Lecturer in Business Organisation at Heriot-Watt University. After working in industry in Iran, she took research degrees at the Universities of Oxford and Aston, leading to her monograph, *Nations and Organizations.* Her current interest is in the cross-cultural study of management.

JAMES T. TEDESCHI was a high school drop-out, but was intellectually resurrected by the Evening Division at the University of Miami (Florida). He was trained as a rat psychologist at the University of Michigan, and experienced his first culture shock in his first teaching job among the Mormons at Utah State University. As a result of his experience as a political activist in the 1960s, he became a social psychologist with a focus on questions of social power and influence. As a spectator, he enjoys all sports, opera, ballet, and classical and jazz music; as a participant, he likes to travel, jog, go bicycling, play tennis, read novels, and discuss political and philosophical issues.

HARRY C. TRIANDIS was born in Greece and learned Greek, German, French, Italian, and English, in that order, while he was a child. He became fascinated by differences in the "mentality" of people who speak different languages. After completing degrees in engineering and commerce and working in industry as an engineer, he decided that the old fascination was more important than making a living in engineering. He went to Cornell University, where he obtained a Ph.D. in social psychology (1959). He became a full professor of psychology at the University of Illinois (1966). He is the author of *Attitudes & Attitude Change* (John Wiley, 1971), *The Analysis of Subjective Culture* (John Wiley, 1972), *Variations in Black & White Perception of the Social Environment* (1976), *Interpersonal Behavior* (1977), and the general editor of the six-volume *Handbook of Cross-Cultural Psychology* (1980-1981). He was President of two divisions of APA, the International Association of Cross-Cultural Psychology, the Interamerican Society of Psychology, and is Vice-President of the International Association of Applied Psychology. In October 1987 the University of Athens, Greece, made him a *Doctor Honoris Causa.*

JOSEPH E. TRIMBLE (Ph.D., University of Oklahoma) is a Professor of Psychology at Western Washington University in Bellingham, Washington. His principal research efforts are concentrated in the mental health and substance abuse problems of native populations, particularly American Indian and Alaska native groups. He has also written extensively in the fields of cross-cultural counseling and the delivery of mental health services to American Indian communities. In addition, he has conducted research on the effects of life-threatening events on ethnic-minority elderly populations, and self-image and value orientations of American Indian youth. He is currently developing a cognitive-behavioral model for use in preventing drug abuse among American Indian youth.

COLLEEN WARD received her Ph.D. from the University of Durham, England (1977). With a primary interest in cross-cultural psychology, she held an Organization of American States postdoctoral fellowship at the University of the West Indies, Trinidad (1978-1979), and teaching appointments at the Science University of Malaysia (1979-1982) and the National University of Singapore (1982-1986). She is currently at the Department of Psychology, University of Canterbury, New Zealand.

LADD WHEELER is a native Texan who attended Stanford University and received his Ph.D. from the University of Minnesota. He is an author of *General Psychology* and *Interpersonal Influence*, and the editor of the first four volumes of the *Review of Personality and Social Psychology* (Div. 8 of APA). His interest in cross-cultural psychology began when he was on sabbatical at the Chinese University of Hong Kong; it is maintained by his mysterious and beautiful Chinese bride.

KUO-SHU YANG, who began his career as an experimental psychologist, has shifted his fields of research several times, just like Robert Lifton's protean man in the academic circle. Now he seems settled down as a social-personality psychologist, with a special interest in the analysis of Chinese behavior from a cross-cultural point of view. Orchestrating a group of Chinese social and behavioral scientists in Taiwan and Hong Kong, he has successfully promoted an academic movement for the Sinicization of social and behavioral research in Chinese societies. Having authored and edited 15 books and published more than 90 academic papers in Chinese and English, he is no longer anxious to lengthen his publication list. Instead, he is now working with his colleagues and graduate students in the Department of Psychology, National Taiwan University, to do some rather long-term, systematic studies on such Chinese psychological phenomena as traditionalism (and modernism), familism, filial piety, and achievement motivation from an indigenous as well as a cross-cultural perspective.

LESLIE ZEBROWITZ-McARTHUR is Professor of Social Psychology and Chair of the Psychology Department at Brandeis University, where she has taught since 1970, after receiving her Ph.D. from Yale University. Her scholarly work has been concerned with causal attributions, impression formation, and stereotyping. Departing from the mainstream in each of these domains, she has taken a perceptual approach that emphasizes the influence of external stimulus information as opposed to the constructive processes of the perceiver. Her current work has gone even further afield, comparing Korean and American perceptions of people's traits as a function of their faces, voices, and gaits.

Series Editors: Walter J. Lonner *and* John W. Berry

Volumes in the

CROSS-CULTURAL RESEARCH AND METHODOLOGY SERIES

LIFE'S CAREER-AGING
Cultural Variations on Growing Old
edited by **BARBARA G. MYERHOFF** and **ANDREI SIMIC**
Volume 4 / ISBN 0-8039-0867-9 cloth / ISBN 0-8039-6000-X paper

CULTURE'S CONSEQUENCES
International Differences in Work-Related Values
by **GEERT HOFSTEDE**
Volume 5 / ISBN 0-8039-1444-X cloth (Unabridged Edition) /
    ISBN 0-8039-1306-0 paper (Abridged Edition)

MENTAL HEALTH SERVICES
The Cross-Cultural Context
edited by **PAUL B. PEDERSEN, NORMAN SARTORIUS** and
    ANTHONY J. MARSELLA
Volume 7 / ISBN 0-8039-2259-0 cloth

FIELD METHODS IN CROSS-CULTURAL RESEARCH
edited by **WALTER J. LONNER** and **JOHN W. BERRY**
Volume 8 / ISBN 0-8039-2549-2 cloth

INTERCULTURAL INTERACTIONS
A Practical Guide
by **RICHARD W. BRISLIN, KENNETH CUSHNER,**
    CRAIG CHERRIE and **MAHEALANI YONG**
Volume 9 / ISBN 0-8039-2558-1 cloth / ISBN 0-8039-3441-6 paper

HEALTH AND CROSS-CULTURAL PSYCHOLOGY
Toward Applications
edited by **P. R. DASEN, J. W. BERRY** and **N. SARTORIUS**
Volume 10 / ISBN 0-8039-3039-9 cloth

THE CROSS-CULTURAL CHALLENGE TO SOCIAL PSYCHOLOGY
edited by **MICHAEL HARRIS BOND**
Volume 11 / ISBN 0-8039-3042-9 cloth